D1014657

EDUCATION AND THE NEW AMERICA

EDUCATION AND THE NEW AMERICA

BY

Solon T. Kimball

AND

James E. McClellan, Jr.

RANDOM HOUSE NEW YORK

SECOND PRINTING, AUGUST 1963

Library of Congress Catalog Card Number: 62-16207

Manufactured in the United States of America by
The Haddon Craftsmen, Inc., Scranton, Pa.

Design by Ruth Smerechniak

56,672

The dogmas of the quiet past are inadequate to the stormy present. The occasion is piled high with difficulty, and we must rise with the occasion. As our case is new, so we must think anew and act anew. We must disenthrall ourselves, and then we shall save our country.

—ABRAHAM LINCOLN

From the *Annual Message to Congress,* December 1, 1862

Preface

The present volume is the offspring of an academically unsanctioned union of anthropology and philosophy of education. In popular mythology, natural children are supposed to be marked by excessive vigor and ruthlessness in the pursuit of their goals. If these qualities are present in this book, we should count them assets. For the task of this book is a large one, and its accomplishment will require the sacrifice of the usual niceties of academic discourse.

The task? It is no less than that of bringing into contemporary focus the traditional message of the professional educationist, namely that the schools must change to meet the demands of a changing society. When Dewey, in 1899, delivered the three lectures which were issued as *The School and Society*, this message was already a standard one, and Dewey's contribution was to give it particular relevance to the impact of industrialism in America. Dewey recognized that the dynamic source of social change lay outside the school. He insisted, however, that the school's role was not merely a passive one of adjusting to changes already occurring but was also an active one of preserving the most precious values of an older culture that would otherwise be destroyed in the transition to a new society. (We explain this aspect of Dewey's thought more fully in Chapter 5.) Dewey's expression added a distinctive text to the educationist's message, a text to be reiterated by this book, but in a new form.

In the 1930's a new theme was added to the message. "This is a crisis! We must act now! Tomorrow may see the whole social fabric ripped apart and all values destroyed in the great maelstrom of class conflict!" The deep sense of urgency then became an overtone in all the discourse of educationists, among themselves and between them and the public. The reader will have no difficulty seeing this same sense of urgency in the present book.

But the *specific* social analysis made by Dewey is no more applicable to the present situation than is Hobbes' *Leviathan.* Even so, both Dewey and Hobbes would seem to have an enduring applicability that is sadly lacking in the crisis mentality we inherited from the thirties. However just *what* are the changes in the larger society to which the school must adjust? Just *why* is there an immediacy in the demands all about us? A changed role for the school? To be sure, but precisely changed from what to what? The literature available gave no answers, or at least gave no answers that seemed to us compatible with the actual world we saw every day about us.

And so we had to start afresh, hoping to bring forth new categories and schemes of thought adequate to the contemporary scene. We had to begin where Dewey began his own life, in agrarian America. We had to try to see just what sort of social system that time and place produced and what sort of school developed in it. Then, like Dewey still, we had to see the impact of the new industrial age, with all its power for producing good and evil for mankind. Then like the Social Frontiersmen of the thirties, we had to see the disastrous consequences of the new concentrations of power and the alienation of the proletariat from the forces of production in a capitalist economy. But unlike our predecessors, we know that neither social change nor social thought ended with Karl Marx and his world of exploitative capitalism. On the contrary, wholly new forms of human association have made their appearance since his time, forms that essentially make *all* previous social class analyses anachronisms. We had to discover the categories to account for these new forms, or where we couldn't discover them, try to forge them for ourselves.

For the message of the educationists has gone stale even in their own mouths, and nobody outside the "profession" bothers to listen at all. We can go on repeating what Dewey and others have said, but we cannot take their words with personal seriousness. The point is, however, that never was the educationists' message so clear and urgent as it is today. The educationists, charged by the public and their professional obligations with preparing a new generation to meet the problems of a new age, often feel themselves in the position of a lookout screaming, "Iceberg ahead!" to a strangely uncomprehending captain and crew. In this same illustration, the public and their leaders may be likened to a captain and crew who find it terribly strange that the lookout should be concerned about icebergs while the ship is sailing along the equator. What the lookout sees is a submerged reef, all the more dangerous because misnamed. If the educationists and the public they are supposed to serve cannot find a basically common social diagnosis, one that corresponds to the reality of the public's world, catastrophe is not unlikely.

Thus this book is addressed both to educationists and to the so-called lay public. In this day when so many of the fundamental decisions that affect our collective existence as a people have been taken as the exclusive prerogative of experts, it is indeed heartening that every man can and does feel himself an expert on education. The peculiar historical accident by which schooling was "reserved to the people" in the Constitution may be symbolic of the more profound fact that citizens *are* capable of both understanding the issues and problems of educational policy, and acting intelligently in cooperation with their neighbors to solve those problems. But to be intelligent, the citizen must fully comprehend what the professional is trying to tell him, and in turn, the professional must state his message in language that makes sense to the public at large. We have tried to provide the language and ideas that will make that discourse possible.

The book, then, is not modest in intent nor, perhaps unfortunately, in tone. In the text itself we have paid scant attention to the many profound scholars whose ideas are basic to much of our thinking. This may explain the very elaborate notes and references at the end of the book. In that section we not only refer the reader to other authors, we also take those authors seriously enough to criticize their ideas. In establishing the needed communication between a profession and its public, this book is, we hope, a good beginning, but it is not by any means the end.

Besides the authors from whom we have drawn, we must also pay tribute to another group otherwise not mentioned in these pages, namely those students who have listened to our ideas, have thought them through, torn them apart, and given them back to us much improved. Those men and women have left Teachers College to assume positions of authority and responsibility in every phase of educational work in all parts of the globe. To them our thanks and hope that we have helped them at least somewhat as much as they have helped us.

Acknowledgments should also be made to those who helped in typing the manuscript and in similar ways deserve all the thanks we can offer. In particular, we appreciate the faithful assistance of Miss Louise Stearns, without whose help our task would have been immeasurably more difficult. In addition, we also wish to thank Mrs. Helen Zolot, Mrs. Ruth Greenberg, and Miss Jinnie Hahn, all of whom at one time or another have worked with us. The completion of the manuscript was greatly facilitated by the freedom from academic duties made possible by our sabbatical year at Teachers College and, in addition, by the Faculty Fellowship of the Social Science Research Council held by Mr. Kimball. A final expression of gratitude has been reserved for our colleagues, both educationists and others, whose discussions helped us to clarify our thinking and who gave us, often unknowingly, much needed encouragement.

CONTENTS

PART ONE
THE REALITY AND THE PROMISE

PART TWO
EDUCATION AND COMMITMENT

PART ONE

THE REALITY *AND* THE PROMISE

1

INTRODUCTION: EDUCATION AND THE PROBLEM OF COMMITMENT IN CONTEMPORARY AMERICAN LIFE

A vague and persistent uneasiness about the future of America is a frequently encountered feeling today. One can find all sorts of beliefs to go with that feeling of uneasiness: that labor is getting too strong, or that it is getting too weak, i.e., that there is no effective left-wing political force in America today; that new technology is coming on at too fast a clip, or that it isn't coming fast enough to give us the absolutely essential rate of increase in productivity; that we are losing out to the Russians in the race for world leadership, or that our very success in "Americanizing" the rest of the world leaves us with a heavier burden of responsibilities than we can possibly bear; that the closeness and uniformity of present-day life destroys individuality and creates deadly conformity, or that the dissolution of close family and community ties leaves us a nation of isolated and alienated individuals, victims of anomie.

No matter how the diagnosis goes, there is one universal prescription for treatment: more and better education. This demand for a higher level of knowledge and morality in the American people hits many groups—politicians, publicists, parents, and preachers—but it falls most strongly on the educationists. The educationists, those who administer and teach in the schools of this country, have for very understandable reasons dodged and twisted in an attempt to escape the enormous responsibility that the American people have put on their schools. They have specialized their functions; they have taken refuge in technical progress without concern for the ends to be served by the techniques; they have worked themselves and their students harder and harder, often without considering whether the work has genuine significance or not.

In all honesty, we should have said "we" rather than "they," for we too are educationists, involved in the occasionally overwhelming task of giving graduate training to those who will go on to positions of leadership and authority in the schools of this country. At times we tried all of the dodges ourselves. But for the past five years, in giving a seminar for doctoral candidates from all fields, we have been forced to consider American society and education, not in our technical capacities as anthropologist and philosopher, but directly as educationists and citizens. We found ourselves compelled to examine the fundamental nature of American life today and the kind of education which that life requires.

In a very clear sense, we have been seeking the basis for a philosophy of education appropriate to our times. By a philosophy of education we mean a set of ideas that answer two basic questions: What part of our present culture is truly worth transmitting to the next generation? What methods of teaching, carried on in what institutional arrangements, will be effective in transmitting these most precious parts of our heritage?

Questions of this magnitude have engaged the attention of speculative philosophers ever since the days of Socrates. But at no time have such questions had the practical importance that they have today. The experience of this century has not only shattered the traditional wisdom of our culture but has also left a residue of corrosive skepticism that destroys all ideological and Utopian approaches to fundamental problems of education. Lacking a stable tradition, immune to ideology, our schools have to find their practical policies in rational, systematically formulated *ideas.* We have discovered in our teaching that truly workable, useful ideas, in turn, can come only from a fresh and wholly disillusioned view of the new culture emerging in America today.

In seeking such a view, we were immediately struck with two facts about American life that seem to us to be of utmost importance. The first is our enormous capacity to concentrate energy and maintain order; the second is the increasingly problematical nature of commitment in the men and women of our nation. These two gross facts are not of the same order, really. The first is an objective, demonstrable state of affairs; the second is more subjective and its truth must be felt rather than seen. But taken together these two facts go a long way to reveal the unique character of American life and education.

THE ORDER AND ENERGY OF AMERICAN LIFE

It is tempting to borrow a metaphor from physics in describing the phenomenon of the order and energy of American life, reminding ourselves that a system in a state of entropy exhibits purely random distribution of energy—complete disorder and incapacity for any useful work—and that an increase in negative entropy signifies pattern, organization, and capacity for doing work. The striking fact about America is that it *does work.* Max Lerner calls America a success, and in both senses of "does work," he is correct.[1]

The use of terms from physics, however, may have an unfortunate consequence of focusing attention exclusively on the mechanical or technological features of the order of American life, yet nothing would lead further from the truth of our situation. Our order is first and last a social order, even a *moral* order. Its physical manifestations are impressive, surely, but equally so are its less visible phenomena. Let us consider our new super-highways from both of these perspectives. First, these endless miles of constantly but gently banked curves flow together to form the finest, perhaps the only truly communal architecture in the country today. As sturdy as the roads of Rome, they are infinitely more complex; for the pace is not that of the man afoot but of two-to-twenty-ton masses constantly interweaving themselves in diverse lateral patterns while hurtling longitudinally at a mile a minute. The visual field of the driver must have diversity and interest within an undistracting unity. This necessity comes not from esthetic requirements but from the precarious dynamics of the driver's position and the need to keep him alive. A system for communicating to the driver has to be devised, a system that will enable him to receive complicated information and instruction from both the natural signs and the constructed symbols that constantly flow into his visual field. In contemporary highway construction, art and engineering face problems undreamt of by the builders of an earlier day. Despite the ugly, boring, and awkward sections to be found on our highways, the very concentration of energy required to put them there is a dramatic expression of the technological order in American life.

Keeping that image in mind, let us look from our other perspective to see the social and moral order of America. Two great tragic novels appearing in the 1950's were written by Russians, each a marginal man in the culture he portrayed in his work. In Boris Pasternak's *Dr. Zhivago* the railroad is the dominant symbol as well as a frequent setting of the story. Without the images of the hesitant locomotive, the long and frightening tracks, the tedious life of the switch house, the abandoned freight car, the crowded Moscow station, and the womblike sleeping car isolating and protecting its occupants from the Russian winter night—without these images, *Dr. Zhivago* loses its organic relation to the Russian countryside and to the unconscious motivations of the Russian people.

The American counterpart to all this is the highway system unfolded by Nabokov's *Lolita.* Both the brilliant comedy and the oppressive sense of depravity of this book depend upon the automobile and the social system that is inseparable from it. Though killing with an automobile may in itself be innocent, it is significantly that accident which sets the moral debauchery and ultimately tragic action into motion. But it is not the physical entity—the automobile itself—that provides the setting for Humbert's villainy; it is rather the highway as a social system: that marevlously far-flung, elaborate, and elastic network of roads, motels, service facilities, entertainments, and natural wonders. In this system, one can live as anonymously as the remotest hermit, and a great deal more comfortably. For the system is orderly, efficient, and above all, innocent. Nabokov's story requires the contrast of the innocence and orderliness of the highway system with the sordid and chaotic uses secured by it. (The author's genius with dialect makes the telling of this tale hilariously funny, and thus he achieves the sympathy and distance without which the reader could not live with the story.)

Innocence and order constitute no substitute for an adult, self-conscious morality. The system can protect a Humbert and Lolita from cold and hunger, from plagues and diseases, from thieves and bullies. But it cannot protect from anxiety and degradation. Even before Humbert's sexual peculiarities had ever touched her, Lolita was already prey to comic books and Coca-Cola. Judging from the minds of the adults around her, Lolita's precocious knowledge of good and evil could never have grown into a mature, self-conscious morality. Untouched by Humbert she would have become, like her mother and like the highway system itself, immensely decent and obliging but sinfully naive.

Literary expression only extends the statistical view of the American highway system. Millions upon millions of passenger miles are traveled upon it each year, with an accident rate that should be a source of amazement for being the world's lowest. By far the largest part of these miles are traveled in cars that are paid for with astounding regularity, month by month. (A month is a long time psychologically.) Without any visible exchange of money, automobiles are provided their requisite supply of specially prepared petroleum and their occupants with only less well-prepared room and board. A tenuous minimum of physical bolts and bars assures a degree of safety to person and property that enables the traveler to sleep without fear. The handsomely outfitted patrolman represents the very wide, the very formal, limits of the system within which the American traveler may pursue his own ends (even debauchery) with a rare combination of security and freedom.

We are all travelers, whether we use the highways or not. Our cities are being rebuilt as termini to the concrete and asphalt ribbons that connect them. Even our schools are coming to be designed as motels, not only in the obvious architectural sense, but more importantly in a scholastic sense. One must be able to find in any school one enters the same standard fare that one left at the last school down the road. With almost one-fifth of our youngsters changing schools each year, there must be a basically standard curriculum, a standard rating system, a standard set of rewards and punishments. It should be pointed out, however, that where there is a basic difference between the mobility culture of America as a whole and the aspirations of a locality, as in the racial ghettos of our large cities, the standard fare is a failure. We have yet to design anything appropriate for areas like these.

From the highway system, to the mutual funds of the stock market, to the courtship system in college—indeed, at whatever aspect of American life one looks—the dominant fact is the same: the big beat of constant movement and withal an immense orderliness and capacity for work. We are not efficient in detail; what concerns us is capacity. Our courtship system, for example, is extremely inefficient when our divorce rate is measured against the ideal of monogamy. But it possesses great capacity: very few unmarried men and women, and an extraordinarily low rate of illegitimate births.

Order, system, and capacity show the negative entropy. This is not to say, of course, that the order we have achieved is good in any final sense. We should probably be well advised technologically to spend more money on railroads and less on highways. We probably overextend credit; we very likely have an unrealistic courtship system; and unquestionably our school curriculum needs drastic modification away from the Howard Johnson-like set of uniform options. But before commending or condemning the system, one must understand it. And to understand it, one must experience the full heart-tugging sense that it does work.

But how are we to understand its working? The stale flatness of our ancient verities is not relieved by having them pronounced ever more ceremoniously from Pennsylvania and Madison Avenues. Nor can the innocent orderliness of *Lolita*'s highway substitute for an elaborate system of moral concepts that should both describe and extend the moral system in our society. We could, of course, *live* the commitment of contemporary America without ever formulating it; but we could not sift, evaluate, and deliberately teach this commitment of our strange and wonder-working culture without finding the words that express it. If we are to have a rationally grounded answer to our question, "What part of our existent culture is truly worth transmitting to the next generation?" then we must find adequate terms and concepts by which to understand ourselves.

COMMITMENT AND THE JOY OF LIVING

If we could avoid the word *commitment* altogether our task of explaining the nature of American culture would be easier, but unfortunately, our resulting comprehension would be much poorer. Let us begin with the simplest common sense notion of commitment: when we say that a person is committed to something, we mean that he has a rather clear goal or purpose in mind, that he is willing to work hard and sacrifice present enjoyments for the sake of that goal or purpose. We take commitments to be desirable things, and thus we mean it to be damning when we say of someone that he is lacking in commitment. Commitments are arguable: "Ought you to commit yourself to that end?" is a perfectly reasonable question, even though the only way one can justify any questioned commitment is by showing that it fits well with his other commitments. We take it to be a mark of a mature, healthy person that his commitments have a degree of stability and permanence such that, even as he adapts flexibly to the exigencies of his immediate situation, the pattern and order of his commitments remain unchanged.

Thus there is nothing mysterious in the meaning of the word *commitment*. Used in this common sense way it stands for something quite real, the presence (or absence) of which we can note easily in our own lives and in the lives of others around us. But there is something quite problematical about commitment in contemporary American society, specifically the relation of the individual's commitment to the larger social system of which he is a part. Let us look again to the American highway. Focus attention on a particular individual: the waitress in a diner, the operator of a giant crane on a construction crew, the musician hurrying to his evening's engagement. Each of these persons does his job well or poorly, attentively or thoughtlessly, with or without discrimination and taste, and in doing his job, contributes to the maintenance and enhancement of an enormous social system. Yet each is as unaware of the system he supports as is the kangaroo of the system of natural selection that made its evolution possible.

The deliberate economic activities of men and women will come most easily to mind, but in all spheres of life there is system. The mother who now rewards, now punishes, her child is forming personality in ways peculiarly suited to this social order. She is responding to a social definition of right and proper behavior that enters her consciousness at a far more profound level than does the reinforcing jargon she picks up through her women's magazines. The teacher whose conscious, explicit task is to teach the elements of arithmetical calculation is contributing to the ongoing of the system, not only by doing that but also, and perhaps more significantly, by representing a conception of authority essential to the kind of social order in the larger corporate world. The teen-age girl whose main concern is to be attractive to certain of the young males around her is playing her role in preserving the somewhat absurd system of courtship in America; that courtship system in turn makes possible the even stranger family system which we enjoy and without which the nation simply could not work at all.

We may presume that each of these persons has definite and personally accepted commitments. But would they, if asked, say that they are committed to the social system which, as a matter of fact, they serve? It is not likely that they would. For very few in contemporary America is it the case that their society—its welfare and enchancement—is the primary object of commitment.

Can a social system survive without being the object of its members' commitments? Obviously it can. There is nothing more mysterious about this than about the kangaroo's behavior contributing to the survival of its species without its being committed to anything at all.

Well, is it ever the case that individuals *are* committed to the social system of which they are a part? Apparently yes, although as Soviet educators have discovered, it is extremely difficult to teach a sense of commitment to a vast, technologically advanced, urban, industrial social order. It is somewhat doubtful that Soviet educators have even as much conception of the true nature of their social order (as opposed to an ideology about it) as do American educators about their own society. But in smaller, less radically mobile societies, where social myths have a living, organic relation to the everyday life of people, a full identity of individual commitment and social system is possible.

Is not the creation of integrated commitment like that of simpler societies a prime desideratum for contemporary America?

Not at all. Why should life be simple instead of complex? (The urge to lose oneself in a larger whole, whether this comes to be an urge for religious communion or social integration, is a death urge. We are not projecting that urge into a social analysis.) Freedom requires that we maintain our radical pluralism.

To us the disturbing feature about contemporary American society is something quite different: that in pursuing their own commitments, individual American men and women are not achieving a satisfying sense of each being a man or a woman related in a definite way to other men and women and to young people and old. The heterogeneity, the pluralism, the absence of national purposes to which individuals must sacrifice themselves—these can be, and for many are, sources of great personal freedom and satisfaction. But before an individual can make creative use of the freedom and energy available to Americans, he must himself become a free and powerful person. Despite the presence of a viable and resilient social structure, individuality is not flourishing. When we look for the causes of its absence, what we see is that something like a geological fault is developing between men and women and, at a ninety-degree angle to that, another fault between children and adults. All the talk about "improving communications" seems to have little effect on these ruptures. Their causes lie much deeper, ultimately in that very social system of orderliness and capacity compounded with incessant movement that is so manifest along our highways.

We have used the metaphor of the geological fault to point up a certain psychical isolation. In the current emphasis upon *selfhood* we may view a manifestation of that isolation. Unfortunately, the major spokesmen for the contemporary cult of self exacerbate the symptoms,[2] for they ignore the fact that true individuality can exist only in the context of identifiable roles within a social system. The definition of roles by generations should make explicit the responsibilities of the older to transmit the heritage, to share the obligations, and to state expectable costs and rewards in personal and social terms. And each sex must do the same for its members. The young must be *claimed* for both adulthood and their respective sex roles. Neither individual introspection nor peer group membership can perform this function. Our failure to carry out the requirements of our roles has left the young with a sense of abandonment, and our inability to transmit sexual identity reflects our own deficiencies. In purely spatial terms, the sexes and generations are very likely in as close contact now as they ever were. The much taunted "togetherness" of the American family is, among other things, a physical fact, both required and exploited by the larger social system through which the family moves.

Being lonely in a crowd has ever been a lure and a curse of urban living. What struck us so intensely are the desperate efforts all around us to escape this loneliness, efforts which seem to lack any sense of the source of the difficulty, any rational basis by which individuals can free themselves from the unseen pressures and strains that make them move like leaves in a windstorm. Such a condition can only be viewed as morbid.

What are the schools doing about all this? They are doing what needs to be done to keep the social system operating, but they are not teaching young men and women to understand and possibly control the society of which they are a part.

What the schools are doing has been demonstrated time and again since 1945 in their responsiveness to social demands. Both the increase in college and university enrollments and the expansion of noncollege post-secondary education have been extraordinary and, in each case, directly related to social needs for technically trained and properly, albeit undramatically, motivated manpower. American education, like the rest of American society, does work.

But what the schools are failing to do is not so easy to see and feel. Are they teaching young men and women the truth about this America we have created? Are they helping them to know why they find themselves so out of touch with their parents? Why do students find it so enormously difficult to foresee themselves surely and easily in their mature positions as men and women? Why do the old social myths and rituals seem so foreign to their sense and senses? Why are they being herded into church and bombarded with religious slogans? Why have their school marks taken on such an urgency, especially in the anxieties of their parents? Have our youngsters been taught relevant ways of answering these questions? The only accurate response, it seems to us, is a simple No. However well our schools have done what is necessary to keep the American society moving, they have not transmitted an accurate consciousness of that society to its younger members.

As we try to ask how the schools might help to relieve the morbidity of American life, we must rid ourselves of the common illusion that it arises in the personal deficiencies of individual citizens. Now that we know rather a good deal about how it is that attitudes are engendered and modified, we might be tempted to take a "human engineering" approach to the problem and try to change individual attitudes that we find unhealthy. But to do so would be only to attack symptoms and to leave the basic pathology untouched. There is no evidence that, individually or collectively, Americans are any less committed to high and noble goals now than they ever were, or that they are less committed to worthy purposes than are, say, the citizens of the RSFSR. As we have used the common sense notion of commitment, it does make perfect sense to speak of degrees of commitment; but in none of the pathological aspects of American life does it appear reasonable to think that merely increasing the degree of commitment among individuals is going to relieve the pathology. Indeed, insofar as "human engineering" techniques merely change individual attitudes without modifying the existential conditions in which these attitudes are expressed, the use of these techniques will undoubtedly do more harm than good.

Treating the problem of commitment in America as if it were a matter of increasing attitudinal devotion to more worthy objects is completely wrong. From this it does not follow that we are upholding the so-called "social reconstructionist" argument. That argument and ours would march together in rejecting the efficacy of individual therapy as the main goal of socially significant education. But the social reconstructionist would then go on to talk about the need for a school that will undertake not only to modify individual commitments but also to change the social order, to transform the social system into something that it now is not. There is this much to be said for the social reconstructionist: he does recognize, at least implicitly, the need for a concept of commitment that is more sophisticated and flexible than is the common sense notion we have employed to this point. He recognizes the dependency of individual attitudes on the external social conditions that sustain them. But he peculiarly fails to understand that whatever potential influence in social change the school may possess comes from its close, interdependent involvement with all the other institutions in the society. The school can no more stand apart and exert an independent leverage on society than can the tobacco industry, just to take a counter-case that is roughly comparable in size. But with its close and functional ties to other clusters of institutional power, the distinctive kind of school that has evolved in America is a powerful force in shaping our distinctive civilization.

This gives us the clue to a more precise definition of what we mean by the "problem" of commitment in contemporary America. In a stable, ordered, well-knit society, commitments of individuals are at the same time expressive of well-defined roles and heightened individuality. With us, this is seldom the case. Our individual commitments do organize themselves into a dynamically stable social order, one that reproduces itself at the same time that it changes in almost every detail, generation by generation. But do the commitments of individual men and women in this system sustain and enhance individuality? Does a man's commitment in this system add zest and dignity to the sense of being a man? A woman's to being a woman? Do a young man's commitments enable him to see his own strength and pride reflected in his father's past, his children's future? Does a woman's present commitment to her family make it possible for her to face the inevitable loss of her children and her own youth with grace and self-compassion? The fact that the social system works is no guarantee that these questions will be answered affirmatively. In fact, of course, these questions are not often answered affirmatively. In that lies the *problem* of commitment in contemporary America.

LEARNING ASSENT TO AMERICA: A PERSONAL NOTE

Despite our abhorrence of jeremiads, we must express just this once our sense of foreboding: unless we can find an educational solution to the problem of commitment (as suggested above), then the wonderfully dynamic, ordered, and free society of America will neither achieve nor merit long continuation. Perhaps we may be allowed a few personal words to explain our attitude. Like most Americans who have tried to make sense of the bewildering world around them, we went through a pronounced and (with the aid of hindsight) predictable cycle. As we sought a panoramic vision of American life, what caught our attention most strongly at first was evidence of the enormous psychical costs that our civilization demands of its citizens. Our strategic vantage point in the educational system of America, as well as considerable time abroad over the years, enabled us to see with shocking clarity what America was doing to people. The experience left us for a time curiously cynical and hostile. There were times when the direct question, "What distinctively American traits in contemporary culture are worth preserving?" would have drawn an equally direct "None!" for an answer. But we are suited neither by training nor temperament to be consistent nihilists. As we gradually learned to see and to describe the system of American life with at least partial success, we also came to know and value the goods which cost Americans so dearly in the currency of the soul. At the end of this cycle, there was an uncanny shock of recognition as we read these words by Raymond Williams:

> A very large part of our intellectual life, to say nothing of our social practice, is devoted to criticizing the long revolution. . . . But as the revolution itself extends, until nobody can escape it, this whole drift seems increasingly irrelevant. In naming the great process of change in the long revolution, I am tying to learn assent to it, an adequate assent of mind and spirit. I find increasingly that the values and meanings I need are all in this process of change. If it is pointed out in traditional terms, that democracy, industry, and extended communications are all means rather than ends, I reply that this, precisely, is their revolutionary character, and that to realize and accept this requires new ways of thinking and feeling, new conceptions of relationships, which we must try to explore.[3]

We did, in our own way, learn assent to this new society, a society that offers no fixed and eternal ends in life, but only powerful, dynamic means, as its major gifts to the individuals that make it up. Having learned this for ourselves, we felt the burden that Richard Pares assigned to

> *the historian in the modern world*—one thing at least he can do is to dispel the stupor and allay the anguish with which our older and feebler society views the rise of newer, and, for the purpose, more efficient social and political forms whose ideas of right and wrong so baffle us.[4]

In America, at least, the stupor needs to be dispelled and the anguish allayed more among the young than the old. It is those whom David Riesman called the "uncommitted generation" who most need to learn assent to the new and efficient social forms that surround them.[5]

Learning assent to the new society does not mean easy and passive acceptance of the status quo, a facile adjustment to life as it is encountered in the immediate vicinity. It does mean taking one's full part in the impersonal, complex (and therefore overwhelming) public, corporate world, as well as in the intensely personal, private (and therefore overwhelming) world of the mobile small family. In short, it means knowing the costs of modern life and being willing to pay them on demand. Believing that the world is worth the cost, we direct this book toward a conception of education through which our youth may learn assent to America.

2

EDUCATION AND THE TRANSFORMATION OF AMERICA

American education has come under intense and usually adversely critical examination over the past decade. Among professional educators, at least, there is a feeling that they have been unfairly charged with ills for which their responsibility is a minor one at best. It does seem more than a trifle absurd to credit Russian successes in space exploration to a failure of American schools or to attribute juvenile delinquency to school organization and curriculum. However ludicrous such charges may be, they are a clear, albeit backhanded, tribute to the belief that the educational process is a significant and perhaps even central aspect of contemporary society. (Educators have been making such claims for quite some time, although they hardly expected the acceptance of their assertions to return home in such force and number and under such unfavorable circumstances.)

American education presents, in fact, a spectacle of confusion that would be humorous to any observer who could take a detached view of it. Critics of the school abound, and each attacks his particular bête noire as if it were the whole of American education. The educationists smart under the attacks but suffer mostly in silence. Occasionally, however, one will speak out, chiefly to defend the main lines of educational doctrine that exercised the imagination and captured the loyalty of the preceding generation of school leaders.

This alternating current of reproach, sometimes labeled the Great Debate,[1] is pure smoke; the real fire is altogether somewhere else. Unaffected by the attackers and defenders of older educational doctrines, a genuine transformation of teaching is occurring, a transformation perhaps more rapid and profound than anything comparable in the history of deliberate education. But in a manner which we can only regard as tragic, their very success in freeing themselves from outmoded controversies has left those who are most effectively changing our schools oblivious and unconcerned about the basic questions of how an educational system ought to serve its society. And all this is going on just as some students of American society are giving us the only original analyses of our national life to appear since the intellectuals' response to depression and totalitarianism in the 1930's, but unfortunately, and in contrast to the earlier period, contemporary students of America often have the most naive views about education.

As we turn to the first group of players in this comedy of errors, the well-publicized critics of American schools, we shall not attempt to classify all the different charges that have been made against the schools nor to separate the spurious from the valid. The mere listing of accusations would be an interminable task, and no evaluation of their merits could escape the limitations imposed by personal prejudices. Let the obvious be recognized: any critic can spice his argument with a recital of the stupidities (if not worse) that occasionally issue forth from the mouths of educators; he can list the foolish activities to which children are sometimes subject in the name of education. Such occurrences are lamentable and, in their mere existence, are more frequent than they should be. Happily, the effect of these lapses on the fate of nations and the excellence of our educational system is insignificant.

Our concern with the controversy explicitly directed toward the conduct of schools is of a different sort. Its relevance to our thesis is in revealing a most peculiar difference between what is and what is not being said about education. We are faced here with an almost inexplicable conceptual opacity: within the great volume of literature on education that has appeared in the past few years, almost all of the issues or problems adduced for public discussion have little or nothing to do with the major urgencies that confront us as a nation. This is so regardless of whether one looks at critics or at defenders of current programs of public schooling.

SAMPLING THE CRITICAL LITERATURE ON EDUCATION

The most frequent accusation is that the schools are neglecting the teaching of subject matter in favor of a "life adjustment" approach, with the consequence that students receive a watered-down program which provides little challenge to their abilities, is repetitious, and results in boredom for too many, if not all, of them. Arthur E. Bestor, Jr., historian at the University of Illinois and among the first of the present-day academicians to raise a hue and cry about educational conditions, lays the blame squarely on the educationists and charges them with empire-building motives that are in effect, if not in intent, destructive of the fundamental intellectual purposes for which schools are founded. The power exercised by educational administrators increases as the school becomes all things to all men, a center for providing services ranging from hot lunches to psychiatric counseling. Under these conditions, says Bestor, education becomes merely one among many activities of the school, and its relative importance often declines to less than that of the football game.

Bestor's reasoning has changed somewhat during the ten years that he has stood as the chief spokesman for those members of the academic community who find intellect submerged in the multitudinous activities of mass public schooling, but on at least two points he has remained completely consistent: that it is the moral duty of a democratic society to give its best education to all its youth, and that the best education is one that promotes the ideal of disciplined intelligence.[2] It would be impossible for anyone of good will and intellect to deny either of these points were it not for the fact that Mr. Bestor more than occasionally identifies the ideal of disciplined intelligence with a mastery of a limited number of academic disciplines as taught professionally in graduate schools.[3] Now clearly one is not necessarily a knave or a fool to deny *that* identification, and over the years Mr. Bestor has shown, quite fortunately, a lessening tendency to treat all who disagree with him as if they were both.

Nevertheless, in his finer moments, Arthur Bestor may be called the moral conscience of American education; on the other hand, Jacques Barzun is its perpetual gadfly. Like Bestor, his views have changed over the twenty-odd years that he has been teacher, administrator, and critic of anti-intellectualism in American education. Unlike Bestor, Mr. Barzun has become more biting and less charitable over the years.[4] He has been placed, as Mr. Bestor has not, in positions of great political power in the academic world; and perhaps from that vantage point, the enemies of intellect seem more sharply defined than they would to a mere professor. Barzun's most important contribution to this debate is to reveal the shallow cant and hypocrisy in so much of our talk about education. The older symbols have lost their meaning, as Barzun shows with acid charm. But where may we find meaningful ways to analyze and guide our educational activities? Mr. Barzun does not tell us. Like his masters, Rabelais and Montaigne, he is content to reveal the follies of the world, leaving it to others to reform it.[5]

John Gardner tries to do what Mr. Barzun does not. Of all the contemporary commentators on American education, Mr. Gardner most deserves the title "classicist," for the model of argument of his recent book, *Excellence,* stems directly from Plato and, more specifically, Aristotle. According to Gardner there is an excellence—i.e., *arete* or *virtus*—in every human activity requiring that each individual have the education most appropriate to his own talents and capacities. In this way, not only can the whole complex range of activities in a modern society be performed excellently, but each individual can at the same time achieve his own maximum self-fulfillment.[6]

But Mr. Gardner's excellent prose tends to gloss over rather than genuinely reconcile the deep contradictions in American life and education: the contradictions between liberal education and vocational training; between the ideal of critical intelligence and the need for immediate and unquestioning obedience in the body politic; between the commitments inherent in the idea of a public world and our devotion to personal values in private life. A moment's reflection should convince that these conflicts are not going to be eliminated merely by pursuing excellence in all fields. In fact, there is something rather odd about the very expression "Pursuit of Excellence" which Mr. Gardner used as the title of a little tract he prepared for a Rockefeller study commission. One may pursue truth, beauty, property, or even, as the Declaration of Independence would have it, happiness. But excellence? Excellence, as Aristotle recognized, is a quality that inheres in activity when suitable means are employed for good ends. Mr. Gardner simply did not follow his Hellenic mentor far enough. For Aristotle makes it clear that schools do not, cannot, pursue excellence in general, but rather any school must serve a particular concept of excellence according to the nature of the society supporting that school. And despite his well-grounded, realistic portrayal of American life overall, Mr. Gardner fails to relate that portrayal to a clear conception of ends and means in education.[7]

In order to realize just how far we are from having clearly accepted worthy ends for our schools and well-designed means for their achievement, one has only to follow Martin Mayer's survey of *The Schools*.[8] Mr. Mayer's deliberately non-ideological journalism, his carefully controlled sense of outrage, and his obvious sympathy for the system, even with its defects, combine to make his work one of genuine revelation. We see through his eyes, as we could not perhaps from another perspective, the shocking degree to which our schools are a vast melange in which only an occasional teacher evokes a wonderful but fleeting climate of critical intelligence. We see also that in this social reality, a graceful eulogy to excellence is totally inadequate as a basis for reform to achieve the high ideals Mr. Bestor forces us to acknowledge as the rightful goals of American schools.

Nor are we likely to find an intelligible rationale for our rapidly changing school system in James Bryant Conant's many writings on American education. Mr. Conant, as a matter of fact, deliberately rejects the idea that our schools actually need any rationale other than their on-going, immediate objectives.[9] In view of Mr. Conant's distinguished service to his nation as scientist, university president, diplomat, and now senior statesman of education, one can understand both why he should take the perpetuation of the system as its own sufficient justification and also why, for others who lack his by now intuitive sense of just what the system is and why it works as it does, his writings are mischievously superficial. This is not to deny that there is great merit in taking the presently feasible and practical steps to improve the system as Mr. Conant suggests. But we are poorly served if we take those steps to be sufficient excuse for ignoring the task of appraising the worth of the present school system in relation to the larger educational needs of our changing society.[10]

Although school people have been acutely sensitive to the varied denunciations of their shortcomings, they have been notably unsuccessful in getting their case before the public. An effort in this direction is made by Raymond P. Harris, in a very pleasantly written volume entitled *American Education: Facts, Fancies, and Folklore.* Mr. Harris, who is director of secondary education in Mount Vernon, New York, shows clearly that most of the charges against the public schools are overdrawn, many to the point of being ridiculous; he implies, though he is too much a gentleman to assert, that a great deal of the anti-public school folklore is perpetuated in print by those whose economic, religious, and social class interests are not well served by expanding the public schools of this nation. His case in detail is very persuasive. But overall, the book fails to convince on its major thesis, namely, that there is nothing wrong with the present system of schooling that could not be cured by massive doses of dollars. Even those who are completely and totally devoted to the idea of public education find it hard to believe that under the present set-up only lack of money has stood between the schools and the really radical changes that would be required to meet the demands of the new kind of society we are living in.[11]

Among the defenders of public education who have recognized the fundamental nature of problems faced by the schools, the name of Myron Lieberman must be put in a position of preëminence. Mr. Lieberman recognizes the necessary role of leadership to be played by the professional educators in designing a really workable national system of schools, and he has the courage to make his case without the usual obeisance to the sacred cow of local and lay control of public schools. Unlike Mr. Harris, Mr. Lieberman sees the need for changed political structure within which adequate financial support for schools can be secured and adequate policies for spending these funds established and carried through. But Mr. Lieberman, for his own good reasons perhaps, has somehow refused to connect his excellent portrait of education to the larger social framework of the emerging American society. Seen in the light of the declining role of local community life in the country and the emerging dominance of great corporate superstructures in the public world,

Mr. Lieberman's proposals for increasing the power of the professional educator are eminently sensible;[12] without this background they sound somewhat like the empire-building tactics among the administrators that Mr. Bestor has fought for so long.

Whatever may be the reason in particular cases, the general conclusion stands that the shriller the voice of the critic the more widely, if perhaps fleetingly, his voice may be heard. And among those who propose reforms, the most likely to be given attention are those whose schemes are the farthest removed from the realities of the situation they seek to improve. This latter condition is not wholly to be deplored, of course; often those who have the detachment of the complete outsider can be more effective than those who are too intimately involved in on-going affairs. The efforts of the Ford Foundation in the improvement of education are a case in point. With great fanfare about innovation and an almost suffocating surfeit of money, the Fund for the Advancement of Education has spread its activities in many directions. Operating deliberately and consciously with no overall theory or ideology, the Fund has implicitly seemed to subscribe to the idea that in education, as in all other aspects of American life, improvement comes with advancing the level of technology and the consequent specialization of labor that advanced technology requires. This idea is eminently true and unobjectionable in itself, though in particular applications such as the use of airborne television in teaching in the Midwest and the accelerated training of liberal arts graduates for teaching positions, the final results have not always lived up to advance notices. If the Fund has been less than zealous in openly reporting the exact nature of its activities and their consequences, the reticence is understandable: its purpose was to serve as impetus to change, and no one can deny that, positively or negatively, the purpose has been served.[13]

If one asks what has been the total upshot of the critical concern with education in the past few years, the answer would be hard to give. One comes nearer to discovering lastingly worthwhile outcomes if he turns his eyes away from the magazine articles in which the great weight of the critical literature has appeared and attends instead to the quietly spectacular movement to reorganize teaching materials in mathematics and the sciences, in some of the humanities, and more recently in language instruction. This movement has been aided by grants from the National Science Foundation for retraining science teachers in new materials and methods, by the enterprise of certain able and dedicated individuals, such as Jerrold Zacharias of M.I.T., and by concerted efforts of scientific societies, such as the American Institute of Biological Sciences.[14] These stirrings are all to the good. The isolation of teacher training institutions and professional educators from the developmental streams of the sciences and humanities has been too great and has lasted too long. Renewed concern among academicians is to be welcomed. The consequences could be something genuinely novel in the world's educational history: a mass system of elementary and secondary schools staffed in toto by liberally trained college and university graduates.

But that inspiring thought is merely a desideratum for the future. At the moment we can look for a massive impact of current efforts to reform teaching only when new text and study materials get into the regular channels of distribution, when standard testing devices are reconstructed to take account of the new materials, and when new technological devices and teaching machines become normal features of ordinary schools. These changes are indeed occurring at a rate that would have seemed impossible only ten or fifteen years ago. They are bringing about a transformation in teaching, while the attackers and defenders of the schools are looking the other way.

But basic questions still remain unanswered. Let us suppose that the effect of the confluence of all these efforts brings new vitality to the schools, eliminates the boredom, provides challenges to student intellect, and according to ability, spurs each student on to excellence. Is the solution to this kind of educational mopping-up operation the only significant issue which bedevils

American education? Let us be clear that for the America of the past our educational system has functioned remarkably well. No detractor or critic could deny the orderly, massive, and effective job it has done to prepare, in a generation, the millions of young from native and alien agrarian backgrounds to participate in a democratic industrial society. The teachers in the little one-room country schools, in the tenement-like slum schools of the cities, in the middle-class urban districts and Main Street towns, and those who were their mentors deserve our praise for their accomplishment.

But yesterday is not today. And the America that was, is not. This fact does not seem to have penetrated the comprehension of those who are engaged in the controversy about American education. By implication they have assumed that the world surrounding the activity of education stands still. They complain and argue about what is and prescribe what should be, but they show only slight evidence that their concerns have relevance within any kind of a dynamic, on-going civilization in which they live. Neither do they seem to have become aware of, nor so much as engaged in conversation with, those thinkers and writers who are also concerned about our civilization although addressing themselves to aspects other than educational. We refer to those who are examining the basic assumptions and direction of our national life. In the process, these writers dissect the combinations of power in government and business; they analyze social philosophy, manners, and morals; they even search for or pronounce upon national purpose. Their writings are directed toward an educated American public; but in the subtle ways of a great conversation, each examines the ideas of the others against the background of his own perspective. There are five to whom we wish to pay special heed: John Kenneth Galbraith, David Riesman, C. Wright Mills, W. H. Whyte, Jr., and A. A. Berle. And while these five have been chosen for our special purposes, we nonetheless recognize that many, including Charles Frankel, Paul Tillich, Margaret Mead, Lewis Mumford, Peter Drucker, Arthur M. Schlesinger, Jr., Henry S. Commager, and W. Lloyd Warner, have made their contributions to the conversation.

THE GREAT CONVERSATION

The mood which pervades the conversation about America is a deeply serious one. But one also senses an underlying optimism which threatens to burst through the recitation of absurdities, of misplaced energies, and of false values, and to exclaim: "Look here, America, come to your senses! Can't you see the greatness that is really yours, if only you will comprehend and act? We aren't certain; if America fails, it may well be man's last chance. How sad the waste if we fail! But we have always made it in the past, surely we will do so again." Such sentiment can come only from an almost indescribably deep belief and faith in America's destiny. It arises in those who are impelled by a humanitarian dedication which links and extols the dignity of man and human freedom.

Each in his own way (and sometimes in opposition to the others) points to the dangers that confront us in the process of dissecting and anatomizing an America which has all but solved the problem of physical want, of brutalized personalities, and of demoralizing inequality. C. Wright Mills prepares us for the perils that he sees by submitting evidence to establish that there are three great centers of power: government, business, and the military. He argues that major decisions affecting foreign and domestic policy and the allocation of wealth and resources are vested in a handful of men who control these power centers and who, by virtue of their positions, inevitably find themselves in a network of official and personal relations, the net effect of which is to provide the basis for collaboration and mutual support. He claims that the power they wield is dangerous because it is held by the mindless and irresponsible, who are not representative men whom the public can respect. But he also condemns the American system which spawns such irresponsibility.[15] Mr. Mills sees little to fear in the power of labor unions, for he views their influence as partially corrective to the larger, more powerful concentration of the corporate world. What he fails to see, however, is that unions are in reality an integral part of the big-business complex, that the symbiotic relation between them and industrial corporations mutually reinforces and creates the power of both. Although difference of position is reaffirmed in recurrent contract negotiations these events may also be viewed as ritual performances which assert and strengthen the interdependence between labor and management. Hence, any enumeration of the power elite, we believe, must also list the Meanys, the Reuthers, and the Hoffas.

John Kenneth Galbraith exhibits little of the fearful trepidation about concentrated power which infects Mills. He believes that the force of countervailing power, sometimes exercised by consumer, sometimes by government, sometimes by unions, sometimes in fact by business itself, acts to maintain a balance and prevent monolithic centralization.[16] But he grants that hazards exist and warns us of the paradoxes in our affluent society. He believes that the conventional understandings of our economic system must be modified if we are to avoid heading for serious trouble. He insists that however well the emphasis on production for private consumption has served us in the past, we must now put much more of our capital into the public sphere of the economy, devote much greater wealth in the future to social goods: education, recreation, health, and all those communal services which are essential to building personal resources.[17]

A. A. Berle's longstanding interest in the modern corporation has led him along a route which began with anxieties about the concentration of power and at the moment leaves him with admiration.[18] He grants that those who manage these great oligarchies "hold the reins" but that their position is to be "essentially non-Statist civil servants—unless they abuse their power to make themselves something else." If this should happen, the obvious remedy, he contends, is to change the managers, not the system. The creation of a new class of professional managers and the separation of control from ownership neutralizes the power once inherent in wealth. In addition, not only is wealth more widely distributed through share ownership, but it is also increasingly concentrated in collectively owned fiduciary institutions which maintain a hands-off policy toward corporate management. The new position of the corporation has created a situation in which business and government can no longer really be separated, and through government the public has direct means of control over the misuse of power if the occasion should ever warrant this. Berle's faith lies in the efficacy of consensus.[19]

Where Mills, Galbraith, and Berle look at American life on the economic and political level, the field of vision of David Riesman and William H. Whyte, Jr., is on the personal-interpersonal level. Riesman probes for (and discovers a lack of) inner resources among those for whom the present system of superficial and fleeting relationships is rewarding. He is far from happy with his discovery, since the "other-directed," as he labels them, seek guidance for themselves from their contemporaries, and hence suffer from a self-imposed behavioral conformity and are driven by an insatiable need for approval. He attributes the predominance of this type among middle-class Americans to external forces associated with capitalism, industrialism, and urbanization. If his analysis is correct, then we must conclude that there is little hope to fill the inner emptiness, to dispel the superficiality which characterizes Americans. Even that slight ray of hope which he proffers, that other-directed people may become more "attentive to their own feelings and aspirations," can be only a mirage in the deterministic system he posits.[20]

The position which William H. Whyte, Jr., assumes in his analysis of the men of middle management differs little in its basic criticism and pessimism from that of Riesman. He has identified and dissected "organization man" for us, and in doing so has laid stress upon the almost compulsive emphasis which binds one to the group and, in turn, shapes and colors perception and behavior. What distresses Whyte is the lack of protest, on the one hand, at this destruction of individuality and, on the other hand, the acceptance of conformity as an openly articulated moral imperative. The source for the ideology which motivates the organization man he finds in the structure of industrial organizations, and his up-by-your-own-bootstraps-and-out-of-the-bloody-mess solution is as unrealistic as that proposed by Riesman.[21]

Those who have been engaged in this great conversation have been talking about the consequences of the transformation of America. They have been concerned with the changes in some of its institutions, with the obsolescence of some of the supporting conventional wisdom which rationalizes behavior in relation to these institutions, with the effect of these changes upon the person, and with the relation between ideal goals of an earlier America and the present. Some, such as Mills, are angry; others, including Riesman and Whyte perhaps, are pessimistic;[22] others, Berle among them, are imbued with a sense of great potentiality for future good. But without exception, these commentators on the American scene are deeply disturbed by what they perceive. Their disturbance is based on no mirage, no fanciful set of unrealized Utopian values. That they offer no panaceas is a remarkable testimony to the restraint they have imposed upon the natural American tendency to evangelize. They do not claim that the route to salvation may be discovered in known, or as yet unformulated, dogma. They offer neither Marxism, Christianity, Zen Buddhism, nor Science as the true glory trail. In their pragmatic faith in intelligence, decent human motivations, and democratic processes as the base for overcoming difficulties, they are in the best American tradition.

But what has all of this to do with education and with those controversialists who have directed their attention toward its deficiencies and its reform? In one camp, those who are part of the great conversation have either ignored the distinctive function of the American school or have treated it as a subsidiary topic. (Riesman's writings on education have not become part of the conversation.)[23] In the other camp, educators possessed of an intense preoccupation with the individual, have remained blind to the larger social system within which that individual must eventually live out his adult life. Their talk of developing skills and character to live successfully in and contribute to the community possesses an unusually hollow ring, as the community which they hypothesize disappears before their eyes. Their self-assurance that the school has taken over many functions of the family, functions lost either by default or by incompetence, bespeaks their lack of understanding of the place of the family in today's social world. They are committed to a private conception of the world, which is unlike anything that really exists.

For these reasons much of the recent discussion around education has been mostly beside the point. Of course the techniques of educational process, in all of their ramifications, must be improved. Of course the shallow platitudes, which some educators think stand for real life values, must go. But education also needs to be transformed in a much more profound sense if it is to serve and be served by the society in which it operates. In such a world, formal education moves from its peripheral position in an agrarian society to a central one. But the transformation of the educational process and organization is of the same magnitude as that which accompanied other institutional reformation in the change from an agrarian society to the present one. The problems of education and their relation to other aspects of the society need to be brought into the orbit of the great conversation. It is this to which we hope to contribute.

A certain amount of preliminary groundwork is necessary to establish the conceptual conditions which permit the incorporation of the discussions about education into the arena of the great conversation. For educators to be conversant with the issues—economic, political, ethical, or organizational—is in itself not enough. We may assume that most, if not all of them, are so informed, although their writings do not reflect this competence. Nor may we hope that those who are concerned with other facets of our civilization can elicit from the educational controversy those clues which illuminate the deep and fundamental connection between deliberate education and the fate of our way of life. The needed conceptual conditions assume a new perspective in which the deep dichotomy which separates the world of public activity, values, and organization, from that of the private and personal is fully understood. Only then are we in a position to assess the function of education in our type of society; to grasp the intermediate structural position of school organization between family and our public corporate system; and to recognize the contribution which the educative process makes to the individual in his transition from private to public worlds.

PRIVATE AND PUBLIC WORLDS

The physical expression of contemporary America is found in metropolis. Massive aggregations of population, with their internal differentiations in function and activity, now provide the setting within which life is shaped and its drama played. Metropolis is above all a milieu of contrasts: of central city and suburbs; of engulfed satellite towns and villages. Within it are contained the subtle differences in styles of life manifest in the graduated range from luxury apartments and town houses to the teeming slums in the core city, from elegant and sleek ranch-style and split-level dwellings of suburbia to the cramped, prefabricated box houses of the development. It is a diversity further exemplified in gleaming new multistoried buildings in which great varieties of workers plan, direct, and carry on governmental, financial, industrial, even religious and educational activities of a complex society; of the functional shopping and service center; and of the manicured industrial park. Ours is a richly textured society which offers a greater variety of interests and opportunities to a greater proportion of its people than any society the world has known before. The rewards availing those who do not shun struggle merit a dedicated insistence on making our institutions perform their jobs well.

Two clearly demarcated systems, differentiated by values, activity, and organization, bring into structural focus the nearly endless diversity. From these contrasting and sometimes competing ways of life, the American receives from and returns to all that he is. There is the *private world* of family and friends, of domestic life and sociability, of home and its environs. Its harmonies and tensions are rooted in values and expressed in emotions which are quite separate from the other, outer and sometimes even hostile, world of the great social superstructures. These latter—the corporately organized activities of industry, agriculture, finance, business, transportation, government, education, religion, and health—constitute the *public world* which stands counterpoised, structurally and spatially apart, in the great social and cultural dichotomy which characterizes our civilization.[24]

In an earlier America, and for that portion of the world which has not yet evolved into an industrial-metropolitan form of society, the functions of domesticity and community were joined. Hearth and place of work, whether field or workshop, were symbolically, if not physically, one. It is in their separation that the great transformation of American society is manifest. Today most of us are participants in each of these two great social systems: the nuclear family and its extensions, and the great superstructures. Our basic life rhythm reflects the sharp alternation in time related to space, activity, association, and even perspective and perception, which marks the separation between our public and private lives. From early adulthood, when we are first inducted into office, shop, market place, or laboratory, until the ultimate separation of retirement or death, we shuttle between abode and place of work. Inspiration and joy or drudgery and boredom may be found in both or in neither, and seldom does one or the other make a total demand on us.

There is as yet little in contemporary Western literature which directly portrays the conflict in the individual as he is torn between these two worlds in their demands of allegiance. It is all too new. Classical Greek tragedy, the story of the Biblical Job, and the Japanese Kabuki cycle have each dramatized for their time and place the tension and torment of individuals torn by conflicting commitment systems. It is true that some among our artists have sensed the inner travail which our civilization creates: the existentialists have acknowledged their alienation, the beatniks have rejected and withdrawn, the neo-Freudians urge love as panacea, and the message of the great Swedish film director, Ingmar Bergman, is despair. But nowhere has the stark simplicity of the conflict been shown with greater clarity and force than in the screenplay *High Noon.* Behind its allegorical symbolism of the struggle between good and evil lies another, deeper, and more relevant message. For when the ultimate choice is to be made between the tranquillity and safety of the private world and the needs of the public world, although he is abandoned by peers, threatened with rejection by the newly won bride, and faced with possible death, the committed man's only tenable moral decision is to defend the values of the public world.

But there is a danger in pushing this analogy of *High Noon* too far, for in the frontier western town the morality and the commitments of the public and private worlds still constituted one integrated system. In metropolitan civilization values central to the protection and preservation of the nuclear family may be antithetical to those of the corporate system, and the metronomic punctuality demanded by commuter train, factory whistle, or office clock does not reckon with the more subtle rhythm of crises within a family.

From the counterpoised position of the public and private systems, with their variant commitments, arise the tensions, the costs, and the rewards of our type of society. How well the whole meets successfully the stated goals of individual and group depends in a measure unknown in other societies (including our own agrarian past) upon the effectiveness of formal education, since preparation for participation in the public world has now become almost entirely a function of schooling. Hence the process of learning and the institutional aspects of education are crucial.

THE EDUCATIVE PROCESS

The educative process, if successful, transforms the individual through successive stages from infancy to adulthood. It instills in him knowledge and skills and the ability to perceive, evaluate, and organize the intellectual and feeling capacities. Family, school, peers, and often the church, all have separate although usually complementary roles in this activity. The child on his way to adulthood must, of necessity, be shaped by the experiences which his environment provides. As the conditions of existence remain constant or change, so also may we expect that people too will reflect the life and times of the world around them. In our response to the on-going events of the large or small social systems in which we orbit, each of us is molded by the events in which he is a participant. But we also make up part of the environment which shapes others. And thus, collectively, we form the great dynamic repository of mankind's past: the wisdom, skills, and conceits which are manifest in the present and, with their accumulations, are carried into the future.

However ignorant we may be of the subtle processes by which each individual learns to categorize and differentiate, to organize and use, to take part in and learn from the events of life, we know that there is growth and change in our environment and that we are its mirrors.[25] We accept the uniqueness of each individual as well as the unity of mankind as a species. However much we may urge pan-humanism, we also recognize that the variations of genetic inheritance lend distinctions to each person; and that into the infant's plastic reservoir of unrealized capacities come the sound and sense which will make him subtly but importantly different from all other human beings. But within the ego, within that satisfying knowledge that each of us represents a unique model, may lurk a serious danger, because the emphasis given to the individual and to the specific processes which gave him creation acts to inhibit our ability to see the great system which encompasses us all and from which there is no escape, not even perhaps through death.[26] We are much less well informed on the workings and characteristics of this system than we are upon the processes of learning. But we can and must assume that a relationship exists between the individual as a product of his cultural environment and the latter as the source of a systematic ordering of human activities and values. If this assumption is correct, and we are convinced that it is, then it is of even greater importance that we examine learning as a projection from the social and cultural world, rather than study it as something that is merely a result of responses by the individual to external stimuli.

The shift in focus which is proposed here is of tremendous importance, inasmuch as it holds that the individual can be understood only if we first comprehend the nature of the systems which make him a perceiving, believing, and participating member of society. The characteristics which distinguish man, as a solitary individual or within a group, and the activities in which he engages, whether alone or in cooperation with others, are both derivations of an external world, a world of relatively stable and persisting groups whose activities and beliefs are themselves manifestations of the conditions of time, space, and situation. The study of the educative process thus may be seen as the examination of the relation between the systems operating within a civilization and their effect upon the individual.[27]

The arrangements by which we consciously and intentionally educate our children constitute one of these systems. Its proper functioning in our civilization is crucial, for although our schools represent one of the great superstructures, their operational goal is not that of claiming their clients as future educators but of preparing them for the great range of institutionally organized activities which express our social and technical complexities. Thus, when we teach grammar, history, mathematics, or any other subject at the pregraduate level, we do not expect that all students will become grammarians, historians, mathematicians, and so on. It is for this reason, among others, that the unmodified downward extension of university subjects is such a questionable procedure. Few would accept any proposition asserting that the proper intellectual function of the schools is to prepare subject matter specialists, and there is an increasing tendency to argue that neither should this be the function of the four-year college curriculum. What, then, when we speak of the crucial function of the schools, do we mean?[28]

THE TRANSITIONAL FUNCTION OF EDUCATION

The perspective we hold is that of *the school as a transitional institution in which the process of education gradually separates the young from family and locality and prepares them to join the great corporate systems and to establish their own independent nuclear families.*

But an opponent to our view might pose this challenge: Even if educators have failed to conceptualize the schools as interpositional between the nuclear family and the superstructures, does not the process of education, in effect, fulfill the transitional role which you claim is essential? Or a critic of anti-intellectualism might have this reply to our thesis: Is not rigorous attention to scholarship, to subject matter, to the cultivation of excellence, just that aspect of education which will best prepare the student to participate in, and contribute to, the complex world which you describe? And those who adhere to life adjustment as the purpose of education might well ask: Does not the emphasis on "real" problems develop those inner strengths and values which are so much needed in this kind of stressful world?

These arguments are not easy to answer because they, too, can degenerate into the "I do—you don't" level of discourse, which solves no problems, however emotionally satisfying such argumentation may be for the cantankerous. We have already recognized and praised the really commendable contribution which American education has made. Nor have we any quarrel with insistence upon intellectual development as a central function of the schools. But we do not believe that the schools can teach moralistic attitudes, although the student's experiences in the school setting can reinforce or modify his perspective on the world. Let catechismal recitation of the good and bad remain where it is now taught. If all of this be so, then how do we differ from those we criticize?

The strategic position of the school rests on two factors. One is its interstitial position between the nuclear family and the corporate structures of the public world. It is from this position that it derives its function of separating and directing the individual in his pre-adult life away from his family and toward integration in the superstructures. The other factor is based on the peculiar and unique relation which the educational system has vis-à-vis the cultural heritage which comprises the technical, scientific, historical, esthetic, and literary traditions of our society. The universities with their scholars, scientists, libraries, and museums have become the ultimate repository for this heritage. But their function has also been that of extending this knowledge through research and study. Those who teach in secondary and elementary schools are directly exposed to this fountainhead in their training, and they must continue to draw upon these resources if their work is to stay abreast of new developments. That the strength of these connections has been far less than it should have is clearly, but unfortunately, exemplified in the contentious sparring between academic and professional educators. This separation is one which cannot be permitted to continue, although partially because of their different assumptions about learning, the reuniting may be difficult. How else can we explain why the educationists turned not to the university system but to the industrial corporation when they sought an organizational model for the public schools? (See Chapter 8.)

In the next several chapters we propose to describe first an impression of the promise and the portent of America, and to contrast the post–Civil War America of commercial agrarianism and Main Street towns with the contemporary scientific and industrial civilization of great metropolitan centers. This analysis serves the purpose of establishing the social context within which education functions and to demonstrate the differential educational needs as they are related to a social system. In this context, the progressive education movement may be viewed as a transition between the needs of an agrarian society and the contemporary one.

The last several chapters (Part Two) examine the relationship between education and the commitments our system requires of the individual and of groups. Here we make explicit the cost that the continued functioning of our system exacts from the individual.

3

AMERICA: THE PROMISED LAND

The development of American civilization has been felt and described as a great adventure. For well over a century its republican form of government and democratic participation in political decisions, its ideal of social equalitarianism, its renunciation of hereditary privileges and social constraints which shackled mankind to outworn traditionalisms, and its insistence on the right of the individual to develop and use his capacities have been guiding stars for Americans and a model of aspiration for much of the world, or at least so it was believed.

Those who participated in the development of America carried with them a sense of destiny, not unlike that of a Chosen People in a Promised Land.[1] But inseparable from this view was the belief that irrespective of the prodigal bounty provided by God, it was man's responsibility to determine how nature's benefits were to be used and that upon man himself rested the necessity for the decision and action that would lead to the realization of the Utopia.[2] Such basic modification of a static world view, contained within old-world agrarianism, was undoubtedly related to the beginnings of the great outward thrust of Western civilization, a movement that had origins in a rising commercialism, the secularization of institutions and thought, and the emergence of a world view based upon scientific empiricism. Whatever interpretations are offered for the course of American civilization, and they are many and complex, the facts are startlingly clear: today we are witness to the consequences of a process in cultural evolution that exceeds in magnitude and significance any previous event in human history, except perhaps the emergence of man himself as a culture-building and -transmitting creature.[3]

The new civilization that is forming around us is so recent that we do not as yet possess a conceptualization which would give adequate expression to it. We lack confidence both in our capacity to perceive the magnitude and scope of the changes which are brought in the wake of this new civilization and in our individual significance within its emerging social forms and values. If we could assume the vantage point of future social historians, their hindsight would prove of immense help in answering the many questions which confront us. But as we cannot transport ourselves to the future, our recourse is to examine the contemporary world in the context of its antecedents, and through contrast and analysis, inquire whether we remain upon the course which once we believed would take us to the realization of the promise.

PROGRESS: TECHNOLOGICAL AND SOCIAL COROLLARIES

The American solution to the problem of human misery arising from want has been to create an industrial economy capable of producing a superabundance of goods. In its realization new forms of human organization were invented and old ones transformed. The one called for the other, and together they now present a congruence of extraordinary power and potentiality. If our national genius expressed itself in manipulation and improvement of technological processes, it also appeared in the less frequently commented upon capacity for immediate and effective organization. In these qualities we were heirs to a British form of Western civilization, and we and they to an even older cultural tradition for the technology with which we began.

The basic elements of industrial process are as old as mankind itself. Simple bone and stone tools, uncovered in deposits dating back hundreds of thousands of years, attest to man's capabilities as a fabricator. But improvement upon methods which directly shaped materials provided by nature has been a slow process at best. The domestication of plants and animals, discovery or invention of metallurgical processes and the subsequent use of metal for tools, the invention of the wheel, improvements in the transportation of goods and people through various water- and land-borne devices, all marked advances in man's ability to more efficiently exploit the physical world.[4]

The roster of technological innovation, from the earliest beginnings of agrarian culture at about the sixth millenium B.C. to the time of the Roman Empire, includes most of the mechanical devices basic to modern industry. The principle of the substitution of animal and mechanical power for human muscle had been established. Animals were used to carry or pull loads, the wind was a supplemental source of energy to the ship's galley slaves, and water power turned the mill stones that converted grain into flour. There are severe limitations, however, on the amount of power that can be generated by teams of draft animals, water wheels, or wind. Man had merely started the process that could, in principle, provide him with abundance and with freedom from physical toil.

When, in the late eighteenth century, James Watt perfected a practical steam engine that could transfer energy to the purposes of manufacturing and commerce, a revolutionary process had been achieved. The way was open for the proliferation of mechanical and energy-producing devices that transferred the production and transportation of the world's goods from the backs of men and animals and led to the formation of an industrial-urban civilization. From these innovations came manifold consequences that were reflected in every aspect of life. Human population expanded enormously and was increasingly concentrated in cities. The misery of poverty gradually receded before an increased flow of goods. Specialization in production and distribution created great new occupational groups, and favored the division of labor and the necessity to rationalize the industrial process.

The rapidity with which innovation brought further innovation is a marvel that inspires wonder. The progression from animal-drawn freighting wagons to airborne cargo carriers, from candles to electricity, from horse-riding couriers to the telephone and radio, from single plow and scythe to tractor-pulled gang plows and combines, from an agrarian economy that had persisted basically unchanged for over five thousand years to an industrial technology—all these have been accomplished in little more than a century.[5]

The mastering and exploitation of the physical universe through science and instruments of technology constitute a major wonder of the world. And the evidence leads us to believe that we are probably on the threshold of even greater achievement, perhaps not so dramatic as spaceships and satellites, but of far-reaching significance in new sources of energy in new uses of material through metallurgy in biochemistry and in the continued extension of the processes of automation.

The end results of spectacular achievements in translating our advances in physical science to the launching platform of a satellite have provided a focus of world interest that supersedes even that of the release of nuclear energy. Thus the rhythmic chanting of satellite watchers on the sands of Cape Canaveral as they communally intone "Go! Go! Go!" should be interpreted as the inception of a new tribal ceremony providing vicarious participation in mechanical scientific marvels, which on ordinary occasions remain remote from the experience of the average person.

The complexities of industrial processes inhibit, if they do not prevent, their full grasp by any person or group. In fact, within modern industry, segmented specialization calls for varieties of experts, each group of which contributes its share to the total process. The commonalties which unite such diverse technologies as those connected with bridge building, sugar refining, textile manufacturing, or printing are found in the principles enunciated by physics and chemistry. But the social congruencies remain practically terra incognita.

The need for new forms of human organization to plan, direct, and coordinate was met by the proliferation of voluntary associations, by corporate and political bureaucracy. Other types of human groupings and activities either became peripheral or were lost or transformed. The autonomy of local community, represented by rural neighborhood, village, or town, became attenuated, as urban-centered financial, cultural, industrial, and political hegemonies extended their areas of control and limited the capacity for local initiation. The absolutes of history and religion crumbled before the new secularism and man's demonstration to himself that he could make and remake the world.

Transformation on such a grand scale is what our forebears learned to call progress. Within the burgeoning cities the bustle, clatter, and smoke were signs to them that the world was moving in the right direction. The interposed surcease of a Sunday gave emphasis to the purposefulness of weekday activity. Work became an end in itself. But change of such magnitude inevitably carries a measure of cost. Though the infrequent but regularly recurring depressions and panics may be viewed as temporary halts in the expansion, individual capacity to deal with such periods of stress has diminished with succeeding decades as increasing proportions of the population lost direct control over economic well-being through their incorporation into large-scale industrial organization. The popular saying, "Root, hog, or die," and the accepted belief that there are no problems that hard work cannot overcome, might fit an agrarian population that in hard times could tighten its belt and extend its self-providing efforts, but has little meaning to an urban worker whose connection with the soil has been severed.

The various remedies which have been devised were not intended to restore the conditions which permit individual or community self-sufficiency and autonomy. Quite to the contrary, they give emphasis to the dependence of the person upon the operation of the larger structure. Unemployment compensation, subsidized housing, food stamp plans, public welfare, and agricultural stabilization are examples of the myriad devices, each with its associated administering agencies, through which a welfare state overcomes some of the hazards of living in an urban-industrial society. Financial, commercial, and industrial groups utilize other devices—mostly regulations and subsidies—to set more stable conditions under which they can operate.

The requirements of industrialism have led to the proliferation of corporate structures—economic, political, educational, etc.—of varying sizes and complexities. Another way of saying this is that the present complex of social structures has arisen to meet the needs of a society containing new combinations of demographic, economic, and social forces. Yet the complexities of technological processes and of social groupings prevent a comprehension of the whole by the majority of that society. There is perhaps some parallel to this in the position of the agrarian husbandman whose superstitions, benign or otherwise, grew from his efforts to adjust to and accept the mysterious vagaries of such natural forces as drought, flood, wind, or insect infestation. At least his system prescribed supplication and sacrifice to the supernatural powers which controlled such visitations. Bureaucratic caprices must be endured without rituals of recompense and atonement.

THE SCIENTIFIC VERSUS THE AGRARIAN

We have said that we are now in a stage of development which is so new that we have not yet perfected the concepts necessary to understand it. If we single out technology as the focus for examining the distinction between the industrial-mechanical phase of culture and the present, we are struck by the immense amounts now being spent on scientific research.[6] Just a half century ago only a handful of physicists and scientists had established precarious footholds in government and industry. Today they number in the thousands. Whereas once industry depended upon the independent inventor, typified by Edison, Ford, and Bell, for its innovations, today astrophysics, nuclear physics, and electronics exemplify but a few of the fields which have been incorporated into the technological revolution. This newer revolution has been under way for only a couple of decades, having made its appearance with the utilization of pure and applied science in industrial problems. The word *automation* has been coined to express the process which joins mechanics and science—just one example of a new concept emerging to describe the new social reality.

Scientific research, however, has penetrated far beyond the purely physical. New horizons of understanding in social, cultural, and psychic behavior are being opened by those who are probing perception, values, linguistics, and interaction.[7] Organizational dynamics have become a concern of those who work in the new field of management. Never before have a culture and its population been so willing to subject themselves to scientific methods as participants in a consciously revealing self-examination of their habits, thoughts, and behavior.

Science, its philosophy and method, has rocketed from its almost exclusive habitat in the laboratories and classrooms of academia into the public arena of government, business, and private lives. Although in the past we have had fanciful tales by Jules Verne, popular treatment of science such as that of evolutionary theory by H. G. Wells in *The Outline of History*,[8] and a novel of scientific morality by Sinclair Lewis in *Arrowsmith*,[9] still the power of science to alter lives, to actually control life and death on this planet, has only recently been borne in upon the consciousness of mankind. Science, the once pedestrian explorer of the universe, suddenly finds itself in the uncertain role of savior and destroyer. And if only the exceptionally educated actually read the works of Darwin, Huxley, J. B. S. Haldane, Whitehead, Tylor, and Einstein, through popular magazines, newspapers, and paper backs millions receive at least a cursory introduction to the results of scientific exploration of the universe.

What has happened to the spirit of the great adventure in this transformation? Once upon a time the frontier was a tangible reality. There, each man according to his ability, determination, and luck could meet the hazards of adversity and hardship, could prove a homestead in the new West, and in the process could help to build the nation; or the adventure was contained within the competitive struggle of commerce and industry; or it was found in the search for God or for knowledge. Does the world today offer the same kind of challenge that was once open to the explorers, inventors, entrepreneurs, frontiersmen, and organizers of our past? What captures the imagination of contemporary man and gives him purpose to struggle and build, not alone for personal gain, but also because of deeply held ideals?

Perhaps, in retrospect, our adventure will be seen to have been the greatest. The conquest of space may symbolize, in ways so subtle that we do not yet understand them, the hopes of man. The unsolved problems in the scientific disciplines which undergird medicine, education, psychotherapy, and human organization and in the interrelationships between physical, psychic, and social systems are of no small significance. But although the present epoch may contain guiding purposes, there are marked differences between the present and the past. Where once the realization of the dream was theoretically open to all, today only a handful of the intellectual elite are actively engaged on science's frontiers. And when their activities are not closed to the outside world by reasons of secrecy and national security, they are conducted within the context of corporate exclusiveness or the isolation of the research laboratory.

It is important, therefore, to be clear about the disturbing difference between the frontier sense of the great adventure and the contemporary sense which locates it in the sciences.

Ability, determination, and luck still count, of course, but they count in a different way, for it has become ever more difficult to say exactly what constitutes success or failure. Power over others, access to the company of the intelligent and talented, personal wealth, escape from the mean and tawdry, were evidences of success in the older scheme. And other more moderate measures of success were open to all. A farmstead that survived drought and depression; a family that gave a good start in life to its children; a small business not quite so small as it had been at its beginning; a position in the lodge or on the board of deacons at the local church—success had many forms, all of them recognized by a system of values which bestowed upon each individual a measure of glory for his efforts. The artist and poet might find this system unresponsive to his own sense of achievement, but that this is so testifies to the existence of a recognized system of rating the outward signs of inner grace.

There seem no necessarily unfavorable consequences in the contemporary relations between the scientists and the remainder of the population as long as training in the methods and techniques of science remain available for those who seek careers in this area, and as long as there is continuous interpretation of the findings of science through the mass media.

But the scientific frontier does not reward its successful exploiters in the same way as those on the old frontier were accorded recognition. On the one hand, the uninitiated are excluded from grasping the achievements of the patient researcher or the brilliant theorist and from participating even vicariously in the subtle rewards which accrue. On the other hand, a genuine contribution to science outlasts the pyramids, but the scientist's ownership of it ceases with its publication. Within the highly abstract symbolic world of science itself, success has a clear meaning, one that admits no distinctions among the races, religions, sexes, or ages of man. Our social groupings outside science, however, do and must recognize at least some of these distinctions as important. In this period of transition, there is an imbalance between our social ways of grouping people and recognizing achievements on the one hand and the nature of the scientific collectivity and its criteria for success on the other. So long as the scientific laboratory was in no essential relation with society, this imbalance was of no concern. When this relation comes to be a central one, specifically when the scientific frontier becomes the primary locus of the continuation of the American sense of frontier, then this imbalance must be given serious attention.

The agrarian world view contrasted sharply with the rational, scientific one since it was based upon patterns emanating from family and community and because it was historically linked with supernatural explanations of man's origin and destiny. Most problems facing the individual could be met by him either as a member of the family or through communal arrangements in church, community, or government. The individual felt able to cope with the vicissitudes of life by the application of his intelligence and effort to the problems of livelihood and by cooperation with his fellows to meet needs beyond those of the family itself. The commonalty of a family system and its social adjuncts, combined with a community of interest in locality and nation, provided a universal base for rural village, open country, neighborhood, or plantation homogeneity.[10]

Deeply imbedded in the agrarian pattern was a view of the universe in which moral purposes, themselves extensions of family and community standards of behavior, structured ability to perceive and judge events in the external world. If all other explanations failed, there was ultimate recourse to the workings of divine will. Within this system of absolutes, of good and evil and of moral design, each person was presumed to possess for himself the discriminatory quality which gave purpose to the events of life and to its wholeness. Compassion did not rest upon the denial of standards, as contemporary relativism implies, but upon an acceptance that wrongdoing, however much warranted by the circumstances, must still be judged against a code of moral uprightness.

Although the standards by which one judged behavior were

widely accepted, their observance was far from universal. Public drunkenness, wife-beating, physical mistreatment of children, brutality to animals, and unnecessary violence were suffered to exist. Legal and customary practices gave wide discretionary powers to the male head of a family and to property owners. Adversities manifest in poverty and depravity were more likely to be accepted as evidences of divine retribution or individual deficiency rather than as brutalized manifestations of social disorder. We count the change in practice and belief as evidence of a more humane and enlightened civilization.

A deep sense of history, linked with the ideal of the great man, the hero, was also contained within the agrarian world view. It may seem surprising that a nation that from the days of its Revolutionary War has hailed the deeds of the young and has always associated itself with the spirit of youthfulness should also give such emphasis to the past. (Perhaps cultural continuities run deeper than suspected, and even in a new land the basic matrix of Germanic and Celtic interpretation remains fixed, even though we replace the demigods with men of flesh and blood.) The list of American heroes stretches from the rebels Patrick Henry and Samuel Adams through Washington, Jefferson, and Franklin. We revere the frontiersmen Daniel Boone and Davy Crockett, the good-bad men romanticized in Billy the Kid and Jesse James, the mythical characters Hiawatha, John Henry, and Paul Bunyan. The mechanical geniuses Eli Whitney, Thomas Edison, and Henry Ford may be joined with our empire builders and men of finance of uneasy fame, Astor, Hill, Morgan, Vanderbilt, and Rockefeller. Finally, we honor the great political leaders through Lincoln to Roosevelt. Only Lincoln, of all our heroes, is cast in the somber colors of deep tragedy. The others are expressive of that joyous company that were part of the great adventure, an adventure that endured the one great sacrifice of a fratricidal war, to set the course of common purpose.

The men whom we glorify epitomize action and success, but there also runs a deep stream of melancholy in our culture, a stream related to our sense of history. Although Negro spirituals express this as the tragedy of a whole people, tragedy has always been an intensely individual affair, in which inner emotional suffering assumes characteristics of a personal, sacred world. Yet in no sense were the experiences upon which these feelings were based held to be secret. Rather, there was the sense of hopelessness in attempting to transmit the depth of emotion. Our literature has sometimes caught the poignant loneliness which bereavement, as one form of personal tragedy, expresses. It was made explicit in the writings of Poe and Melville, Benét and Wolfe. But during the period when our culture still preserved the principle of generational continuity, it was incumbent upon the elders to transmit their experiences to those who were to follow. The sense of a specific tragedy might be extinguished, but the theme was kept alive in the cultural blood stream. Some tragedies, such as death, called for communal observance, but those associated with romantic disillusionment or personal failure had to be carried alone, awaiting time, the great healer.

Unlike the contemporary world, the agrarian provided absolutes imbedded in history and religion. Within this framework of conceptual certainties, both individual and group evaluated the events of life. The universe within which man operated was a moral one: it had purpose. And man possessed divine attributes which gave him a sense of destiny and the responsibility and capacities to exercise control over it. But man was also believed to be fallible and mortal—hence, the tragedies of life. Through the adversities of fate, through failure to realize one's capacities, even through conformance with the guideposts which led to success as measured in wealth or position, in fact through all aspects of living, one encountered the recurring manifestation of man's fallibility and mortality. Herein lay the contradiction; for although the world demanded struggle and striving, it also denied consummation. The burden could never be laid down. True tragedy, not just pain or frustration, was the price exacted from all who joined the contests of life. But true tragedy is possible only if there is a moral universe, one in which the acts of men have consequences, one in which commitment is concomitant with accepting the purposes of a social order.

The erosion of meaning in history has been accompanied by a corresponding decline in the understanding of the cosmic sense of tragedy. The separation of man from intimate participation in the great recurring drama of cyclical birth and death of nature has blunted his sensitivity to life's processes. Celebration of the Resurrection has become synonymous with a fashion parade. For a world busily engaged in directing the flow of bureaucratic memoranda or with manning its machines, the urgency of time and task does not permit frequent or sustained interruption. Thus the observance of death becomes a private memorial, while death itself as a significant process of nature has been for all practical purposes removed from the realm of human experience. American families no longer have a functional place for the sick, the old, and the senile. Hospitals and institutions become the last residence of the aged. The nature of institutional life and of the demands of the world inevitably separate the living from the dying. Under such circumstances death, which should call forth an expression from the living to unite and shoulder the responsibilities passed on to them, serves only to separate and isolate. The communal amelioration of personal tragedy has been lost.[11]

CULTURAL DISTINCTIONS

Inevitably, within the shift from an agrarian to a commercial-industrial and finally to a metropolitan-scientific civilization, there must be changes in the ways people behave and perceive others and in the values they hold. The basic standards of behavior, taste, and evaluation in American agrarianism were derived from distinctions organized around sex, age, race, and social status. Unlike a feudal order, however, where distinctions were solidified and transmitted in hereditary castes, the American revolution promised that the individual would find opportunities to demonstrate his capacities or, in current terms, to fulfill himself.

The ethos of scientific-metropolitan culture is one in which distinctions based upon many of the categories that once served as a basis for differential behavior are no longer universally applicable. Discriminations based upon race and religion, labeled prejudice and bigotry, are rapidly disappearing. Although in practice we may fall short of the ideal, the day when women can be denied the right of participation in all phases of public life is past. Logically, age distinctions should also diminish when they are in conflict with ability to perform. The operation of impersonal and equitable civil service policies must, of necessity, recognize only upper and lower age limitations as a criterion for employment.

No society has ever before successfully challenged the distinctions based upon age and sex as the fundamental division of a cultural system.[12] Although elimination of these distinctions is far from complete, we have already moved a long distance upon that road, and there is no evidence of a turning back. In gainful employment, for example, women now constitute one-third of the labor force and they continue to claim larger percentages of some prestige occupations formerly reserved for males. There are, however, changes of a more subtle kind which do not lend themselves to statistical treatment although observation substantiates their validity. In particular there seems to be a progressive blurring and merging of the behavior which distinguishes the two sexes. Within the home it is not unusual, in fact it may now be customary, for the husband to assume activities once considered wifely. On the other hand, participation in the community and economic world beyond the home is no longer purely a male prerogative. In manners and morals we may observe further diminution of the distinctions.

One might assume that the tendency toward homogeneity would favor greater ease in the relations between the sexes. But there seems in fact to have been a serious deterioration in the ability of the sexes, as male and female, to communicate with each other.[13] Superficial evidence will contradict the assertion. The happily married young couples and their children, who populate the suburbs and engage in activities together, do not present a picture of marital instability. However, divorce rates, the phenomenal rise of marriage counseling—a manifestation of connubial disturbances—and the emphasis of much popular literature substantiate the impression of deep instabilities at the individual and social levels. What a fantastic world that permits air castles to supercede reality! Advertisers exhort us to reduce the serious business of living to the level of the pleasurable. We should enjoy "fun" times, own "fun" cars, eat "fun" meals, and presumably select "fun" partners for "fun" marriages. But the play has a semblance of reality because it occurs in a real house, and girls possess warm, live babies unlike the synthetic kind whose vocabulary is limited to "Ma-Ma" and that can wet their diapers only with tap water. Perhaps the intensified dependence of children in the family has diminished the capacities of some to become differentiated sexualized adults, especially if the images of such roles are inadequate and if the elders fail to claim their own kind.[14]

In the generational pattern of the nuclear family change has manifested itself most strikingly. In industrial society conditions do not only permit but in fact enforce the abandonment of the three-generation family. The American nuclear family represents, during the period of childhood dependency, a two-generation system, but with the marriage of the children, or their departure for college, it becomes a one-generational type. However natural this kind of system may appear to those who know no other, nowhere has such a system ever before existed. What ultimate consequences may result from this radical shift in the fundamental structure of family are not now discernible. It is apparent, however, that the American type of nuclear family carries a greater responsibility for the emotional well-being of its members and for the induction of its young into the larger society than any other now known.[15]

Extensive modifications in the age structure of American culture are apparent in the continuously increasing length of child dependency and in the shortened period of full adult participation. The former is a function of the large number of persons who spend a greater segment of their lives in formal schooling. All but a tiny fraction of these live at home and are dependent upon their parents until completion of high school. The majority of those who attend college also remain dependent upon their families. The extension of the period of school attendance, by custom and by law, delays the entry of the child into economic, community, and familial adulthood. Only the most advanced of industrial societies can afford the luxury of keeping such a large segment of its population in economic idleness.

The enforced idleness of the aged at the other end of the spectrum is also a purely contemporary phenomenon. Retirement of most workers is mandatory at seventy, but this age limit is gradually being lowered and in some occupations years of service permit retirement at fifty or fifty-five. The pressures for further lowering of the mandatory age will increase as our productive capacity outruns our ability to consume, unless we change the direction of our society.

Commercial-industrial civilization requires mobility of a qualitative sort that has never been known before. Wherever we look we can see the signs of the contract-nomad in army, industry, or profession. Agricultural labor is transported by air from the Philippines and Japan to work in the harvests of California. Fifteen million Americans reside permanently in trailers but temporarily in the camps on the outskirts of towns or near construction projects. Millions of office and factory workers commute daily to their jobs. Peripatetic diplomats, experts, and businessmen scurry from one world meeting to another. Generational continuity linked with community is ever more rare in our culture. In its place we have substituted a rootlessness which has contributed to the aloneness of the individual.[16] Persons in transit have no need for local history in the sense of a rich storehouse of accumulated experience which has relevance for the present. On the contrary, to face reality—a cliché of psychotherapists—means to live in the present.

But movement is more than horizontal, it also carries one up in the world. Within the American tradition, the station in life to which one could aspire had little relation to the accident of birth. "From log cabin to White House" became expressive of this part of the American Dream. The millions of immigrants who populated the urban industrial centers from the Civil War onward believed the dream to be an achievable reality for themselves and their children. Other aspects of the American creed remained much more remote to the urban settlers, partly because they never experienced the agrarian environment in which they flourished and partly because they became caught up in the urban counterpart of agrarian egalitarianism. Al Smith, in his rise from sidewalks to governor of New York and in his stand for principles of social justice, epitomized the new urbanism that rose to challenge the hinterland as it expressed entrenched social position and agrarian puritanism. Events in the intervening years—depression, war, boom—have clinched the dominance of a (one hesitates to use the adjectival modifier "triumphant") metropolitan-oriented, corporate, and egalitarian society.[17]

It is still possible to find manifestations of social distinction in contemporary America. Distinctions based on those responsibilities and skills which an institutionally organized and technical society requires are to be expected, for the system explicitly grants rewards commensurate with position within an organized hierarchy. There is, for example, common acceptance that greater financial recognition and privileges should be given to a president than to a vice-president; to a foreman than to a laborer; to a skilled worker than to one who is unskilled. We continue to accept such distinctions as necessary and desirable, although there may be little agreement on how much difference in rewards the system should allow.

We recognize that some social distinctions are made without regard to individual capacity and service to society. Rear-guard actions are being fought by a few who, contrary to the evidence, believe that the accidents of race, sex, or property have some close relation to innate abilities and that distinctions based upon such factors ought to remain relevant. Exclusion, however, is not always a function of prejudice. Attention should also be directed toward those religious and ethnic minorities whose leadership endeavors to maintain or create special distinctions by isolating their members from the larger society.

No one should protest the elimination from our ethical system of no longer useful agrarian discriminations which were based upon sex, race, or social class; and all should welcome the access of a greater segment of the population to goods and facilities which increase the sum of human health and well-being. Nor can there be any justifiable objection to the relaxation or removal of restrictions which inhibit individual self-expression or accomplishments. Whatever purposes these cultural features served in an agrarian society, they are non-utilitarian in a scientific-metropolitan civilization. Furthermore, the elimination of these arbitrary restrictions on human aspiration and achievement is a sign of genuine ethical progress. But as is true of all change, the acceptance of individuals without regard to extraneous factors of birth has been achieved at a cost; the individual may suffer insecurity in the loss of a recognizable and stable rung on the social ladder. Yet we hold that the uncertainty is balanced by the right to strive and achieve, though in particular instances we recognize that a life of blasted hopes and blighted loves may be an excessive price.

Socially, too, there are costs in the freedom of each individual to pursue his own conceptions of success and happiness. The social costs which come from the disintegration of the need for universal and societally held values may be seen everywhere around us. When we concede to each individual that his opinion is as valid as all others, when we affirm that only the individual counts, or when we continuously defend the rights of the individual and place little or no emphasis upon concomitant responsibilities, we teeter on the abyss of anarchy.

Let us grant that the widest measure of individual freedom is a desirable goal, but let us not forget that the cooperative necessities of a society are contained within the differential distribution of functions as they are expressed in organization. Family, school, government, or factory are corporate groups composed of individuals who, as they discharge their separate responsibilities, contribute to the welfare of the whole. Within these activities exist standards of behavior and performance that cannot be abdicated to the whims of the child in the home, the student in the classroom, or the employee in the office or factory.

If you read these sentences as a defense of authoritarianism or conformity, you have missed the spirit and intent of the analysis. Authoritarianism, in reality, is a reactionary retreat from the exercise of leadership; it is an attempt to secure conformance through coercion. Although history is replete with accounts of the inevitable failure of such attempts, times of stress always evoke clamors for utilizing this avenue for the solution of problems. The utilization of externally imposed restraints to enforce obedience denies both the processes of education and educability, although it may teach fear of superior force.

Reward and punishment, to be effective, must operate within established and accepted standards of behavior and performance. The responsibility of parent, teacher, or employer is to make these known. Those who advocate or practice child-centered homes or schools, however commendable their intentions, are doing a great disservice to their children and students if they reject the fact that child development must take place within sets of conditions that provide a framework for evaluating the world and the child's place in it. These conditions include canons of discrimination through which items and events may be judged and evaluated. Otherwise, the learning process has been relegated to a vacuum. The attention that has been recently given to French novelist Françoise Sagan, actress Brigitte Bardot, and other youthful claimants to fame is not because of their protest against the values of their parental generation, but because that generation has given them no basis on which valuing can be achieved. Their emotional and intellectual development has failed to progress beyond adolescent egocentrism. In contrast, the plaint of a Camus is that since the canons of absolutism have been proved false, where can man in his agony turn?

PROBLEMS AND PURPOSE

It is a strange paradox that our intellectual elite should be engaged in an almost frantic search for purpose and meaning to life in a society which has been so successful in concentrating human energy and stimulating imaginative enterprise for the solution of problems, which has given us a superabundance of physical plenty, orderliness, and opportunity for the individual. It would seem that if we had lost our sense of destiny our society would be in process of disintegration, a conclusion hardly supported by the external evidence. It could be argued that we are living on the store of moral purpose which generated originally the impulses that created what we are and have, or possibly that the elite is in error. Neither of these explanations, however, will dissolve the paradox nor bring us to an intellectual understanding of the reality. We believe that an answer is contained in the commitments which arise from the relationships of individuals as these find expression in the private and public worlds of nuclear family and the corporate system. Our data include individuals themselves and their relations with others and the social and cultural conditions within which human activity occurs. These are the sources from which concepts of self, sex, age, group, values, and ordering of our commitments must be derived. It is here that evidences of strength or weakness, of erosion or regeneration, will provide us with those clues that illuminate the significant problems of our times.

Ever since George Herbert Mead alerted us to the significance of the self and the processes of its formation, there has been an increasing acceptance of the importance of this concept.[18] The contemporary emphasis upon the individual has provided a climate that has been favorable to analysis in this area. In particular, concern has been expressed for various pathological manifestations of incomplete or distorted self-perception, as revealed by psychoanalysis, and the general problem of individual alienation expressed in loneliness and separation. Durkheim's famous study of suicide turned up the same problem, which he labeled "anomie," the manifestation of which he attributed to the absence or diminution of participation by the individual in society.[19] Identification, which represents one aspect of the concept of self, cannot be separated from commitment. When the individual is uncertain in self-definition, he is also uncertain in the kinds of loyalties which bind him to the world external to his skin. When his experiences emphasize his separation from, or fragmentation in participation, the consequences must be either an imperfectly formed or skewed personality, or perhaps both.

But if personality is shaped by the environment so also is the capacity for the spontaneous ordering of relations among men. It has been amply proved that in man, as well as in many other animals, cooperative participation in groups is learned behavior.[20] Since this is the case then it is also possible that under differing conditions the capacity for cooperation will be more or less well developed. In fact, a situation can be envisioned in which the opportunities for such learning have been so limited that the individual shows extreme social pathology. Perhaps those who sense the isolation, separation, and estrangement of modern man are witness to manifestations related to this process.

The separation of the individual from his environment does not occur only on the psychic and social levels; it is equally pronounced in man's estrangement from the material universe. The obvious connections between food, shelter, and clothing and their relations to the organized activities of men utilizing skills that were common knowledge in simpler societies do not constitute a part of the experience of modern man. In the realm of everyday experience the individual is effectively, if not inevitably, separated from great segments of the natural processes of the material universe. Although the implications of such a separation have not yet been determined, we surely know that the denial or withdrawal of any type of experience is certain to have its repercussions. Remote intellectualization is no substitute for an attitude which seeks to understand the wonders and mysteries of life. Do we still possess the capacity for wonder?

Where should we look to discover the source and the effects

of social learning? The quest will take us into the family, the school, the community, and the corporate system. They are the groups in which one learns and expresses identity, cultural understandings, and social behavior. They provide the locale for the experiences from which values are formed and purpose and meaning made explicit.

However much we may regret the passing of the "good old days," there is not the remotest chance that we can return to them or that we may even stay the forces of change for long. The absolutes of history and religion cannot sustain us as they once did our forefathers. We must learn to live in the world we are in, not because it is the best of all possible worlds, or even because it is the only world we know, but because that is the only way open to us which permits the restoration of our sense of destiny. Perhaps we hardly appreciate the resources we have at hand to help us. These reside in the methods by which the world and its workings can be examined, understood, and eventually given direction. The great advances in physical science have enormously increased our understanding and control of nature and research about man is beginning to point the way toward solution of problems in psychical and social behavior.

The lesson the frontiersman taught us as he learned to adjust to new physical surroundings in order to survive should be remembered, even though the specific conditions of today are radically different. The pioneers did more than adjust; they also shaped the physical universe to express their values and social purposes.

4

THE IMMEDIATE PAST: MIDWEST AGRARIANISM AND MAIN STREET TOWNS

The coalition of northeastern commercial and nascent industrial urbanism, and midwestern commercial agrarianism, that eventually triumphed in the American Civil War gave to the American nation a direction and commitment that was to endure for more than half a century.[1]

The political power necessary to maintain this dominance was contained within the Republican party. The financial power resided in a banking system that was linked to London. The corporate system provided an organizational structure through which the dynamics of materialistic progress were expressed. The doctrine of Herbert Spencer, who espoused social evolution, gave intellectual interpretation to beliefs of inevitable and continuous progress. And salvation through work, a doctrine of Evangelical Protestantism, added spiritual substance and sanctions. Such a powerful confluence of forces working in relative agreement could scarcely be stemmed as they transformed the century-old traditions of subsistence agrarianism and brought into being a new civilization. The vitality generated by this unique coalition led, perhaps not inevitably but surely, to our contemporary form of civilization: metropolitan in external organization, corporate in structure, segmented and specialized in activity, empirical and pragmatic in outlook. Although it has evolved from older urban and agrarian forms, in shape and spirit contemporary civilization has no cultural parallels.

Our purpose now is to examine the antecedents of the present, to turn to that transitional period following the Civil War when a new kind of agrarianism, unique in world history, emerged to share power in determining the course of the nation. Calvinistic and puritan in temperament, commercial in economic orientation but democratic in spirit, post–Civil War agrarianism was the culmination of the great westward movement in American history.

Among the many interpretations of the genius of America, none has had greater popularity than that advanced by Frederick Jackson Turner. It was his thesis that the frontier, more than any other factor, put its stamp upon American social and political thought and its institutions.[2] Other interpreters of the American scene have followed his lead. James Truslow Adams adopted the same thesis in his book, *The American*.[3] H. Richard Niebuhr also turned to events on the frontier to explain the distinctive aspects of the Protestant ethic and its impact in shaping the American way.[4]

There is no question but that the frontier molded, refined, and emphasized certain aspects of the American ethic and that its influence extended into national life. Jacksonian democracy was, in part, an expression of equalitarianism bred by the conditions of pioneer life. In a situation where mere survival depended upon strength of character expressed in individual fortitude, determination, and hardihood, there should be little wonder that the concurrent values mirrored the realities. Thus, the cult of individual liberty and freedom, but not license, found expression in all aspects of life. The prevailing religious belief held that each man could and should establish a direct relationship with God and that, moreover, it was incumbent upon him to interpret God's will through his inner experiences or through His Word as found in the Bible. Despite the differences between Presbyterian, Methodist, Baptist, and their offshoots, differences that were of immense significance to the contemporary protagonists, the perspective of an elapsed century blunts the distinctions and highlights the basic uniformities of thought. Similarly, in economic and political thought and action the current belief and practice was one of individualism and pragmatism. The dominating social horizon was encompassed within the community: rural neighborhood, crossroads hamlet, or town. Although the residents could work in concert in the face of crisis or social necessity, the impelling motivation had been built upon a system of internalized values by which each man judged the actions of others and himself from a universally held perspective of individual responsibility.

COMMERCIAL AGRARIANISM OF THE MIDWEST

During the nineteenth century, American agrarian civilization rose to new peaks of influence and development as it expanded into and appropriated the lands west of the Appalachians. But it was in the half century following the Civil War that the great heartland of America, the Mississippi Valley, sought to dominate the political and moral life of the nation. It was here that the microcosm of commercial small towns or villages and of the dispersed farmsteads of the surrounding countryside became the prevailing cultural form in the territory which stretched from the Appalachians to the Great Plains and from the northern boreal forests to the delta. It was in this setting that the type of civilization which we denote "Main Street" grew and flourished.

Just as the middle colonies had produced the first American from their amalgam of settlers from diverse European origins in the eighteenth century, in the Midwest of the following century a new American evolved from a fresh fusion of settlers possessing varied backgrounds but joined in their common belief in the Promised Land. From the southern Piedmont and border states came those who carried a deep tradition of equalitarianism, political independence, and personal liberty. The Presbyterians were at home in both town and country. The New Englanders brought the spirit of commercialism, a preference for town life, and a reverence of things intellectual which they preserved in their beloved Congregational church with its educated ministry. From the Middle Atlantic states came those bearing all the characteristics contained within a tradition of an interdependent town and country. And from northern Europe came a stream of hardy peasants, whose disposition and aspirations favored their rapid assimilation. Whatever the cultural origin, the pattern of town and country predominated and proved to be a more complex and differentiated social system than that which had previously existed in agrarian life.

Midwestern vitality can be attributed to a number of factors. The diversity of its population, the fertility of its soil, opportunities for expansion, the new agricultural technology, the rapid spread of a railroad network after 1865, and the rise of railroad and river cities like Chicago, St. Louis, and Omaha all constituted contributing influences. But the growth of railroads and cities was as much a response to the settling of the land as it was a stimulant to further growth. If Chicago became the hog-butcher of the world, it was because the new commercialism motivated farmers to produce for the market rather than retain the age-old pattern of self-sufficiency which their ancestors had brought to the shores of the New World. Midwestern agrarianism became dominant because it had joined, rather than contested, the philosophy of the market place. It was a union for which it was to pay dearly in later years, however, for the alliance which gave it vitality in the beginning, also assured its transformation and eventual demise.[5]

But other factors also contributed to the emergent midwestern preëminence. The constrictions of rigid strata found in the older plantations of the South, the communal conservatism of the New England village, and the social segmentation of coastal cities were practically nonexistent. Although in reality social distinctions did exist within and between town and country, there was also the prevalent belief that America had no social classes and that each man could alter the circumstances of his life and build as he chose. There was not only the belief but at the same time the reality that each man according to his ingenuity, his virtues, and his individual effort could acquire for himself the symbols of success: land, wealth, and the esteem of his fellow men.

We might also consider the absence of a seriously competing system of agrarian values. The Civil War and the Reconstruction had dealt the plantation system of the South a mortal blow. The southern small farmers were increasingly depressed by soil exhaustion and a system of land tenure which gave each succeeding generation a smaller portion to farm, as the land was divided among the inheriting children. The thin soils of New England and upper New York State were already in process of abandonment by 1845, a process that was to continue as the promise of the West or of the mill towns of the Northeast drained off young and old. Moreover, the competition of cheaply produced and transported meat and grain from the new West doomed the marginal farmer, irrespective of his location.

Only on the high plains of the open grassland of the West did a competing agrarianism of equal vitality appear. There, for a few decades, the descendants of cattle-herding Scotch-Irish, who had swept westward ahead of settlements on the southern frontier, founded the colorful cattle empires which have contributed so much to the saga of the American West and to contemporary TV audiences. This open, violent, and relatively simple culture, which centered in the ranch headquarters with its boss-cowhand social distinctions, has all but disappeared with the coming of barbed wire, scientific and mechanical wheat and sorghum farming, and the latter-day descendants of homesteader and nester.

The image we preserve and cherish as exemplifying American agrarianism is not that of the New England village, the southern plantation, the Appalachian hill farmer, the western cattle spread, or the factory in the fields which was to appear later in California. It is the image of farm homesteads and Main Street which claimed America's heartland.

But for nineteenth century Americans it was more than an image, it was also a promise and a symbol. Individually and by groups settlers penetrated the thickly forested lands of the old Northwest Territory, felling the trees, erecting cabins, cultivating the land, and fighting Indians when necessary. Crossroad hamlets and later villages and towns appeared in the wake of this westward movement. By 1845 they had burst beyond the Mississippi on to the prairies of Iowa and Missouri. The world was witness to one of the greatest migrations in its history, one that demanded unusual qualities of physical and moral strength for survival. Of that migration Henry Nash Smith was moved to write:

> . . . and the Great Interior Valley was transformed into a garden: for the imagination, the Garden of the World. . . . The master symbol of the garden embraced a cluster of metaphors expressing fecundity, growth, increase, and blissful labor in the earth, all centering about the heroic figure of the idealized frontier farmer armed with that supreme agrarian weapon, the sacred plow.[6]

What was there in the beliefs and practices of individuals and groups to which we may turn for an explanation of the fortitude with which settlers bore hardship and adversity? What were the inner strengths which supported those who experienced grueling toil, privation, and monotony? What were their hopes and aspirations? And how in their system of social arrangements of family, church, school, and government were their values derived and expressed?

Most people had a deep commitment to America and a belief in its destiny as the Promised Land. The child learned his history either from those who had taken part in the stirring events of the past or from the remembrances of parents or grandparents who had it directly from those now dead. National history was also family history, for one's ancestors had fought against British tyranny, migrated westward in the face of hostile Indian and physical hardship, taught Johnny Reb a lesson, and preserved the Union. Decoration Day, with the inevitable parade of the Boys in Blue, the graveside ceremonies, and the recitation of Lincoln's Gettysburg Address, called forth the memories and rededicated the living. The Fourth of July, with its family picnics, patriotic oratory, and the inevitable contests of skill and strength, reaffirmed the cohesion based on unity of purpose and experience. But even though there were also bitter religious and partisan differences that separated the community into factions, life seemed to contain a grand design whereby each one in advancing himself contributed to the whole.

The destiny of God's plan was to be fulfilled through man's own efforts, and the evidences of progress toward Utopia were everywhere apparent. The settling of the land, the conversion of prairie or forest into plowed fields, the growth of towns, the extension and spread of the railroads, the new farm machinery, and other changes were manifestations of never ending progress that would ease the human burden and bring peace and prosperity to all. But in the meantime there was work to do and each man must carry his burden alone. Hamlin Garland extolled these people thus:

> The men and women of that far time loom large in my thinking for they possessed not only the spirit of adventurers but the courage of warriors. Aside from the natural distortion of a boy's imagination, I am quite sure that the pioneers of 1860 still retained something broad and fine in their action, something a boy might honorably imitate.[7]

The virtues of life were many. They included hard work, sobriety, prudence, thrift, prudery, and the care of one's family. They summed up the qualities that were likely to ensure survival in the struggle to meet the exacting demand of frontier life. But there was another side to this idealized piety. The exuberant roistering of Saturday night drinking, fighting, and whoring enticed hired hands and rural youth; there was brutality and sadism; and the sporting element gave glamour to the primrose path.[8] The church folk, led by the thundering condemnations of their ministers, avoided these pitfalls of the devil. They preached that the patrimony of family or nation must not be wasted through idleness or sensual excess. Prudence, sobriety, thrift, and hard work were the ways of God.

But the onward path of progress was not always an even one. There were bad times when prices were low, when crops failed from drought, flood, or insect pest, when the railroad monopoly and commodity speculators gouged the husbandmen. There was corruption in government, the selfish greed of Wall Street, the sin of the cities. These were the threats to the realization of the promise. In characteristic fashion farmers turned to self-protective associations like the Granges and the Farmers' Alliances; they sought relief through political action in the Populist movement, in the campaign for free silver, and in the Non-Partisan League; or they joined in temperance movements. The issues which called forth these efforts divided neighbors and kinsmen, but irrespective of their differences, all remained firm in their belief that it was man's destiny to find a solution. Day-to-day experience gave testimony to the belief that no problem was so difficult that it could not be solved through hard work. How else had the country grown to be so great and prosperous?

These were some of the conditions and this was the spirit of the times in which commercial agrarianism flourished. Their summarization provides the setting within which family and neighborhood is made more meaningful.

FARM AND FAMILY

The pattern of isolated farm homesteads, which comprised a cluster of buildings providing shelter for man and beast, was almost universal. Except for the meanest habitations, each house was divided into rooms which corresponded with specialized activities. Upstairs were the sleeping quarters. On the first floor were the parlor, kitchen, and perhaps another bedroom or storage annex. The parlor was reserved for the periodic visit of the minister to Sunday dinner, for family festivals, funerals, or other special occasions. It was in the kitchen, however, that family life really centered. Here the food was prepared and eaten; the day's events discussed and the next day's planned. Here children studied, games were played, and neighbors visited. In the winter months sick children and even animals shared the warmth of its big iron cookstove under the watchful and ministering eyes and hands of the woman of the house. The house was her domain and in its confines she brought to her family the never ending care and comfort which were deemed her duty.

The outdoors of barnyard and field, animal and crop, belonged to the man. Assisted by his sons and hired man, and on occasions by help obtained from neighboring farms, he plowed, planted, and harvested; fed and cared for his cattle, horses, and pigs; milked the cows; repaired and built; and performed the myriad tasks which custom prescribed and necessity demanded of the adult male who was husband and father. It was his task to provide and protect; the exigencies of life left little time for enjoyment of its pleasures and little room for softness in his manner if the whole were to survive and, if possible, prosper. It was each family's goal to be completely self-sufficient in foodstuffs and nearly so in the other requirements of life. Except for those occasions when harvesting or some other activity demanded cooperative endeavor, each man made do with what he had in his own and his family's labor. One did not interfere in his neighbor's business nor his practices, although occasional crisis would break this do-for-yourself austerity with the call to nurse a sick neighbor, to assist in childbirth, to lay out the dead, or to help those whose stress threatened survival.

The organization and beliefs of the times called for each man to stand on his own and thus to preserve the equality among men.

And on the shoulders of the male fell the heaviest responsibility. In neighborhood matters it was his voice which counseled with his peers on problems of taxes, schools, roads, religion, and politics or even concerning violations of the moral and legal code. On him fell the obligation to meet taxes and payments in interest and debt, to sell the harvest, and to buy supplies and machinery. Although the decisions might be shared with the wife, it was not the practice to do so.

The steady grind which those of the Middle Border demanded of themselves did not come from a tradition of endemic poverty. To be hungry was practically unknown, and other essentials of life requiring cash outlays could be kept to a minimum. There were those who lost their land through tax sale or foreclosure, but they had had little to start with and could start again. Bad times or poor management had been their downfall. The next attempt, it was believed, would bring success.

The outward symbols of success were expressed in new or enlarged houses, furnishings, new barns, farm machinery, purebred stock, and always more land. When good prices, hard work, and bountiful yields had cleared the land of debt, it was time to buy more land. Each man extended his holdings as he could, and with better machinery, hired hands, and the labor of his family he sought to produce more and acquire wealth. Farms grew larger. The successful bought out those who had failed or moved on. And even the best were not immune to "western fever," or the urge to seek the Promised Land.

Many documents provide us with descriptions of the life in those times, and one such informative account is found in *Grandmother Brown's Hundred Years, 1827-1927.*[9] She reports that only in matters concerning the education of her sons and of money did she ever disagree with her husband, and as she concludes, her differences of opinion were without effect. All other decisions of their life together were made by her husband, and she accepted these without question. The Ohio farm to which he first carried her as a bride, their new home in Iowa, their move to town, business enterprises were all matters which remained within his realm of male decision. Other accounts of frontier life confirm the patient, if not always willing, acquiescence of the woman in her husband's plans. Nor did children have any share in family decisions. They could express their wishes, but their duty was to obey the directions which their father set for them, whether these involved farm work or education. Only as they came of age were their rights respected although not necessarily approved. Hamlin Garland may have phrased the relationship for all when he spoke of his father as follows:

> I think he loved his children, and yet I never heard him speak an affectionate word to them. He was kind, he was just, but he was not tender.[10]

Those who had experienced midwest life and later came to portray it in fiction and description are not in full agreement on all details of farm life but the generalities are clear. Garland felt his mother followed a "daily routine of lonely and monotonous housework."[11] Grandmother Brown echoed the same sentiment when she said,

> I look back to those years on the farm as the hardest years of my life. But there are, of course, some happy memories of the life there. Always when there are growing things—plants and children—there is the beauty. Though I had not much companionship with the people of the neighborhood, we had visitors from time to time from Ohio.[12]

There was sweet with the bitter; when tragedy struck, as it sometimes did with the death of a child, or when the pains of childbirth were endured with only the help of a neighbor woman, there was always the comforting belief that one must endure and go on. That was God's way and although His will brought heartache and pain, it was the destiny of man to bear these crosses without complaint. For the work of the world must be done.[13]

And there was sweet without the bitter in the occasional gatherings of family and friends. Christmas and Thanksgiving were family holidays filled with special preparation for the great meal, with conversation, with songs and games. There were the summer picnics, the journey to town for the July Fourth celebration, the circus, or the county fair. These were occasions when the family traveled in buckboard or spring wagon, and later in carriage or buggy, dressed in their Sunday best and carrying bulging picnic baskets. Attendance at the neighborhood church during the summer and winter revivals gave excitement to the young and a chance for courting to the young adults. Always, however, there was the return to the evening chores and the workaday world.

Although social custom inhibited the display of affection between a man and his wife and children, and the nature of his responsibility reinforced the reserve which existed between a father and his children, the nature of the mother's role was quite different. She cared for her children when they were young and helpless, nursed them when sick, fed them when hungry, made and mended their clothes, and instilled in them a moral code of right behavior and belief in God. Until her sons became old enough to seek out the man's world of work and companionship, she was not barred from showing them affection. Afterward, they shrugged off such gestures with embarrassment. But the tie between mother and son, outwardly distant, seems to have been a powerful one if we accept the words and actions of those who have described their lives for us. In part motivated by the search for maternal approbation, nevertheless a deeper vein of feeling seems to have been a desire to release their mothers from the wearing toil of daily life. Hamlin Garland struggled to earn enough that he might free his mother of her burdens, and eventually he and his brother succeeded in bringing her back from her husband's Dakota farm to a cottage in a Wisconsin village where Garland had been born. But this did not fully sooth his anguish, for part of the price which commercial agrarianism demanded of its members was rootlessness and loneliness.[14]

The impact of women on the transformation of American society constitutes a chapter in American history that has never been fully explored. That part which is best known began with the great democratizing trend of the 1830's and led to the movement for the emancipation of women and the ensuing crusades for suffrage and temperance. Women fought for and won their rights, and in the process curtailed and reformed some prerogatives associated with the male world. James Truslow Adams believes that the growth of towns and the spirit of commercialism provided the entering wedge for the destruction of common enterprise between the sexes. The males being fully occupied with the accumulation of wealth freed their wives from household drudgery and gave them leisure, which the women devoted to cultural and community pursuits.[15] The divergent interests eventuated in a clash not yet resolved. The South, however, experienced no such movement, for a form of family prevailed there in which women were already romantically and realistically the center of the social system.[16]

The unpublicized though far more powerful and subtle influence arose from the woman's position in the family within the unique doctrinal climate of midwestern life. Anything which contributed to suffering was condemned, but suffering in women was particularly abhorrent. In other times and places women have been forced to endure hardship, but the prevailing life view for such cultures failed to evoke the compassion which the pioneer children, particularly the sons, held for their mothers. Some decades ago, when the urge to memorialize the pioneer tradition swept many midwestern communities, the symbol through which they chose to eternalize their sentiment was a heroic statue named, "The Pioneer Woman." This statue still stands where it was erected, alongside Civil War cannon or memorial shaft to the war dead, on courthouse lawns or in public squares. With rifle firmly grasped in one hand, babe clutched to breast with the other, and with a small child holding onto the folds of her skirt, this figure is shown in the posture of bravely pushing onward. No monument, however, could discharge the deep guilt felt by those sons who knew the privation, hardship, and cultural poverty which their mothers endured. Within the documents describing life on the Middle Border, we find this theme recurring time and again. The guilt was compounded when the sons departed to seek their fortunes, for they felt that they had abandoned their own.[17]

Rural schools were a responsibility and extension of the farm families in each locality. A locally elected board set the tax rate, hired the teacher, and built and maintained a building. Often the teacher was the daughter of some local farmer and lived at home, but if she was from another area, she "boarded round." Her background, values, and experience were akin to the families of the children she taught. School terms were adjusted to the needs for additional labor in periods of peak farm activity. The school house was also the natural setting for various communal gatherings. In all such details the peripheral position of education is demonstrated. There was little direct, observable contribution of the school to the immediate realities of farm life.[18]

The system was one which forced the continuous dispersal of most of the children as they came to adulthood. Sons of less affluent farmers hired themselves out as hands or moved to the towns in the search of uncertain employment. Others were apprenticed by their fathers to skilled artisans or given minimum assistance to continue their education for teaching or business skills. Still others started life on rented land or followed the pattern of their fathers a generation earlier in a push to unclaimed lands of the West. A few of the wealthier farmers could and did send their children to denominational or state colleges. But whatever course was followed, assistance from home was minimal, and where money was involved it was as likely to be a loan to be repaid as to be a gift or payment for work done on the land. The abrupt ending of family dependence when one reached manhood was expected. Within the climate of contemporary belief, the minimum assistance given to each child found sanction in the code that each must prove himself and that character and fortitude would lead to success.

Partings, however, were not without their stresses. Grandmother Brown recalls the deep heartache when her youngest left, although the event was forty years behind her.[19] Often the departures left bitterness behind them. The youth who ran away to seek adventure or to escape harsh parental tyranny was a common type. But it seems to have been the custom to recognize the right of children to leave when they reached their legal adulthood. There are stories of young men who appeared with bag packed on the morning of their twenty-first birthday, pausing only to bid farewell to their mothers before starting down the road toward town. Hamlin Garland's version of his own departure reveals to us the uncertainty, loneliness, and homesickness of the youth who has gone into the world. And, of course, as each in his turn did leave, it was to establish anew the process of family origin, growth, and dispersal.[20]

These were some of the affective aspects in the relations between parents and children. But there also existed a strong sense of equalitarian justice demanding that each child be treated exactly alike, a principle that was usually rigidly adhered to in the case of property and was reflected in the system of inheritance and land tenure.

The tenure system in the Midwest was in marked contrast to the practices found among many peasant peoples and in the American agrarian South, where it was the custom to divide the land equally among the residual heirs, a practice which after several generations of settlement led to a congested population of small holdings. In the Midwest the farm was transferred intact to the new occupier, who might or might not be a child of the previous owner. Each sibling, however, shared equally in the estate of his parents. If the land passed to a son, it was his responsibility to reimburse his brothers and sisters for their fair share of the value of the home place if the parents were deceased, or to pay his parents, who had presumably retired to some nearby village, for the full value of the property which they had relinquished. In the event of the latter procedure, brothers and sisters would not receive their portion until the death of the parents.

The independent family system of midwestern agrarianism was based upon a morality embodied in Evangelical Protestantism. The system also embraced the spirit of the market, encouraged change, was symbolized by the concept of progress, and was antithetical to traditionalism. The family demanded of its members a high order of individual responsibility. Achievement could be measured in the material realities of increased land holdings, greater production, and accumulated wealth, which although permitting ease, did not have this consequence as its goal. Its mobility rejected the necessity of correlating family stability with community continuity. There was a gradual but continuous replacement of farm families in each neighborhood. The movement led to the loss of friends and to the scattering of relatives.[21] But the nature of the relationships within the family was the most powerful factor in its own dispersal. Eventually, of course, the rationalization of agriculture through mechanization and scientific farming brought a decline to the system based upon the family farm and to the Protestant ethic associated with it. The system was one which carried the seeds of its own modification and eventual decline, a decline that was hastened by the growth of a competing social order that was urban based and industrially organized. In fact, the internal logic operating in the agrarian system prepared its members for eventual absorption into the new and powerful rationale.

These, then, were the generalizations. The agrarianism of Heartland, America, had aligned itself with the spirit of commercialism. Growth and change were evidence of a progress that promised an earthly Utopia for those who were willing to labor in the Promised Land. From each man's hand, and literally through the use of his hands, those who labored reaped the rewards which were intended for those who practiced the virtues and believed in the eternal verities. But the contradictions between the philosophical and the practical aspects were hardly perceived. The commitments to the absolutes of Evangelical Protestantism on the one hand and to a world in continuous flux in its march toward Utopia on the other were hardly compatible. Thus Garland, who had partially escaped the myths of his era, could praise Robert Ingersoll for his attacks on outworn tradition and empty creeds.[22] There were others, like Ed Howe, Sinclair Lewis, Edgar

Lee Masters, and Sherwood Anderson, who lifted the mask to reveal some of the unpleasant realities which had been obscured in the romanticism of an earlier era.[23]

TOWN AND COUNTRY

Both town and country were interlocking variants within a distinctive cultural form, and each was dependent on the other.[24] Farmers and merchants together prospered or suffered in the economic cycles of good and bad times. Lawyers and doctors provided services to town and country clients alike. Farmers who desired education beyond the primary level for their children, turned to the schools in town. And on those high days of commemoration or frolicking, townsman and countryman assembled together at circus, county fair, or patriotic observance to enjoy sights and sounds.

Although mutual needs tied each to the other, there were persistent tensions between the two. The realistic fear on the part of the farmer that he paid too much for what he bought and received too little for what he sold was continuously present. Townsmen were not always directly blamed for these grievances, since the commodity speculators, the Wall Street bankers, and the rich industrialists were viewed as primary sources of evil. But the townsman, in his roles of middleman in economic matters and of mediator in cultural or political affairs, was sometimes suspect in his behavior and allegiances. The frontal assault on town monopoly took the form of farmer-organized marketing associations and retail cooperatives. In these ventures, farmers established economic beachheads through which they hoped to retain the profits they believed rightfully theirs. Contests on the economic and political fronts were for positions of power in which the two might or might not find themselves in agreement against the "interests."

Other more subtle but equally powerful differences also separated and bound the two. These found expression in the style of life: mannerisms of speech and gesture, detail in costume, habits of thinking and reading, all those items which distinguish the cultivated from the rustic. It mattered little that small town elegance could be a matter of mirth in the regional city; in the eyes of the rural rustic the town represented a way of life that was to be both envied and condemned.

The transformation to town ways was hastened by many factors, but the school and friendships formed there were powerful influences. John Ise reported of his brothers and sisters,

> Away from home, at college and in their teaching, the children learned to dress and deport themselves like town folk; and when they came home, some of them were admitted to select social cliques in town—social circles that had once seemed almost as far away and as unattainable as the European orders of nobility.[25]

The town in its complexity was more than livery stable, general store, and bank, more than the source for professional services and advanced education; it was also an arbiter of prestige and of values through which the things and activities of the world were judged. In this role it reflected its own ties to an outside world, that of the urban East. Although townsman and countryman might join in condemnation of the wicked, corrupt, money-mad, effete inhabitant of the cities, they were of necessity recipients of that "higher culture" which seeped into the hinterland through literary magazine, fashion plate, or Chautauqua circuit.[26]

When American agrarianists broke from the centuries' old pattern of simple subsistence to produce for the market, they unwittingly yielded their yeoman status for one in which social status and advancement were significant elements. The mere accumulation of wealth, however, was not a sufficient earthly reward for engaging in this struggle. Farmers sought approbation from their peers, respect from the townsman, and a better start in life for one's children than had been their lot. Financial worth and respect were not absolutely linked but failure was equated with poverty. Hence the unending scramble for more. Values of town and countryside found rough congruence in this regard, but in the town social class distinctions reflected factors other than the purely economic. Agrarian equalitarianism might scoff at the values which supported these differences but ultimately the ambitious were forced to acknowledge them. Social advancement required the acquisition of urban refinements and the abandonment of rustic crudities. This might prove difficult for the farmer set in his ways, but his children under proper circumstances could make the transition. These conditions were met in the school and in the system of formal apprenticeship.

The town provided an environment much more favorable to education. The concentration of population, greater wealth, more varied cultural interests, aspirations of a middle class for their children, decrease in the economic importance of children, and other factors contributed to a more developed program. Educationally ambitious farm children were offered the opportunity for further schooling, and in turn became exposed to the more genteel manners of town life. Schools provided a setting in which social class differences were reflected and perpetuated.

For the many, high school was beyond the range of either aspirations or financial capability. For them the completion of the grades in a one-room country school gave one more formal schooling than Abe Lincoln had had. They could shed their country ways by imitating others, and the lure of the town was great. The bells that called Dick Whittington to London Town rang figuratively for many an American farm youth.

SOCIAL CLASS AND THE TOWN-COMMUNITY

The town pattern was a basically simple one, however much more complex it might be than the earlier New England village, the southern plantation county-town system, or the dispersed open-country settlement. The territorial unity included a central town and its rural hinterland. Between these two existed a symbiotic relationship which found immediate expression at the economic level in the division of labor for production and distribution of goods but which extended to and included other aspects of social grouping and cultural behavior. The social differences within the framework of educational, religious, political, economic, and associational institutions and activities formed the basis for social class discriminations.[27] Even those cities whose growth was stimulated by industrialization retained in those sections inhabited by old-Americans much of the flavor of town life. But the flood of European immigrants who jammed themselves into ethnic ghettos within the larger cities, or flocked to settle the mill and mining towns, within the zones of immigrant settlement preserved at first the cultural system which they brought with them. Their children were to find themselves in the main stream of American cultural evolution, not because they or their parents had become assimilated to town life, but because metropolitanism had triumphed as the prevailing cultural type.

The internal organizational structure of the town-community was such that no one institution, either of church, economic enterprise, or government, could exercise an autocratic control over other aspects of life. Instead, the institutional arrangements, irrespective of how interwoven and interdependent their activities might be, retained a theoretical freedom of action and initiative. It was through this type of system, in which controls were locally held, that the towns could maintain their semi-autonomy.[28] Later on, the intrusion of remotely owned and controlled retail store or industrial enterprise eroded the capacity of the town to meet its own problems. This effect is detailed in a subsequent chapter.

It is a curious anomaly that the prevailing beliefs of this period denied the existence of social classes although social differences were clearly perceived and accepted. The popular belief in a classless society can be partially explained because the system as a whole, the community in which social differentiation was a characteristic, worked so well. In the workaday world, the activities of commerce, politics, religion, recreation, and household duties brought diverse persons together in habituated relationships in which the situation, and not an abstraction of social class, determined the part each should play. These daily face-to-face relationships were given symbolic confirmation in the annually repetitive observances of Independence Day, Decoration Day, Thanksgiving Day, Christmas, elections, graduations, athletic events, county fairs, and religious revivals. In each type of event both differences and similarities were expressed. The differences were those of age, sex, status, and prestige: the commonalty was that of locality and adherence to similar values and symbols.

These seasonal occurrences provided the opportunity for each individual to comprehend the system as a whole and, on occasion, to participate with others as an equal. From participation one learned and reinforced the behavior that was expected of him and others. In this sense the community of group and activity was a reciprocal expression of the cultural differences which we label social class.

The differential allocation of prestige to types of activities, characteristics, and behavior provided a vast and inclusive background of distinctions against which it was possible to evaluate each person's place within the whole. Furthermore, there was a basic agreement between one's participation in the institutional structure and the possession of characteristics which placed one high or low in the scale of prestige reckoning. For example, those persons whose activities required special skills, as in the practice of medicine or law, or those who were associated with the control of economic life, as the bankers and merchants, or those who gave expression to community values in religion or politics were accorded and occupied positions of prominence in both daily and ceremonial life.

There is nothing particularly unique in the agreement between position in institutional hierarchy and status ranking. What is important, however, is the self-regulating autonomy, the localization, the realized face-to-face participation which virtually all members of the community, irrespective of their position, achieved in activities with one another. Thus, although each person viewed his place in the community from his own position, there was at least a rough correspondence between his perceptions and reality.

Indeed, the intensity of the internal participation by all social groups in the day-to-day activities of community life obscured from view the sweeping changes that were then altering American society.[29] Only rarely in the literature about small towns in this period does there appear recognition that the social class system was in process of dissolution and replacement by another type of cultural differentiation which had its sources in metropolitan civilization.

After the turn of the century the writings of the socially oriented novelists record the flavor, sweep, and crisis of American culture. Booth Tarkington in *Alice Adams, The Magnificent Ambersons,* and in some of his lesser-known works portrays some of the dislocations and tragedies which industrialism brought to midwestern towns.[30] Sinclair Lewis, in *Main Street* and *Babbitt,* is also concerned with the problem of change, and in *Babbitt* indicates the early effects of the impact of a standardized industrial civilization upon the town-community.[31] The cultural invasion of industrial values and behavior finds a favorable response in the spirit of Rotarianism, of "hustle," and of bigger and better things now and to come. Change is equated with progress.

Curiously, it is in *Point of No Return* by John P. Marquand, who writes of New York and New England, and in the deeper and more spiritual expression by Thomas Wolfe, from the Piedmont South, in his *You Can't Go Home Again,* that the irrevocable transformation of American culture is made explicit.[32] Marquand contrasts the town setting of an earlier period with institutional and suburban life in metropolis. He shows that the routines of day-to-day living in suburbia center around the family and children and the week-end communal gatherings at the country club. In general there is a massed uniformity in the style of life, but the minute differences in occupational prestige of the commuting male heads of families are accentuated in social behavior through groupings in semi-exclusive cliques. By comparison, town life was filled with a rich diversity of personalities and activities. Citizens from all social levels joined with one another in annual community observances. But they also separated to form those smaller groups whose activities gave expression to the cultural differences among them. The contrast also shows, however, that the decay was within the town and the vitality is within metropolis.

Independently and without intention, community studies and the novels about community found common ground in the examination of social differentiation. We can generalize this agreement by observing that social distinctions are based upon the reality of differential participation in the affairs of the community as well as upon the manifestations of values associated with one's activities. When changes appear in the setting within which social distinctions are given expression, we would also expect, and in fact we find, that the distinctions also change. Social differences do not disappear in the environment of metropolis, but the bases upon which these distinctions are made have been altered, and consequently their social and personal meaning has been changed.

Education also possessed its apostles of change who although nurtured within agrarian traditions heralded their metamorphosis. It is to these prophets that we now turn.[33]

5

PROGRESSIVE EDUCATION: THE TRANSITION FROM AGRARIAN TO INDUSTRIAL AMERICA

The end of the first half of the twentieth century found the United States at a peak in world prestige and power. The menace of Soviet expansion and scientific advance to the democratic systems of the American-led Western world had not yet been clearly perceived. Internally, the nation had made an almost miraculous conversion from war to peace. The honeymoon of postwar victory had not yet been dissipated by the McCarthy investigations and the contentions over civil rights. Still to come were the attacks on the objectives and methods of American public education, in particular the allegations that most, if not all, of the deficiencies of the educational enterprise could be traced to the deleterious doctrines of John Dewey and of progressive education as disseminated over the years through the teacher training institutions. In fact, the celebration in 1949 of John Dewey's ninetieth birthday had evoked world-wide recognition and acclaim for his contribution to education. Who then could have possessed the wisdom to foresee the reverse swing of the pendulum with its denigration, if not abandonment, of a philosophical position which had provided the basic ideology of the educational profession for so many decades?[1]

It is an often stated truism that if we are to understand the present, we must turn to the past. In this instance we turn back at least three-quarters of a century to the incipient formation of that great political, economic, and social movement which encompassed the era of progressivism. Within this movement, which culminated in the New Deal, may be discovered the origin and inspiration of the progressives in education. In essence, its compound was that mixture of ideas and ideals, of social aspirations and forms, of political and economic forces, sometimes in harmony and sometimes in conflict, that moved America through the difficult transition from an agrarian-commercial, town and country civilization to the metropolitan-dominated, secular, and scientifically oriented society of today.

Contrary to most scholarly and popularly accepted interpretations of the conflict of forces during this period, the viewpoint that the progressives constituted conservative and stabilizing forces within American society, during a period of accelerated change, seems to us more tenable and insightful than any other. The radical, and in fact probably revolutionary, position was expressed by industrial capitalism. Its proponents and practitioners, also marching under the banner of progress, were utilizing new types of social institutions and introducing new modes of thought that were bringing havoc to an older way of life. The conflict arose in the attempts to direct and control the direction of progress and, in particular, to contain and mitigate the destructive threats of rampant capitalism. Progressives were insisting that the power of the newly unleashed forces of social and technological change be utilized for the fulfillment of the American Dream and of the promise of America. In this insistence they appear, in retrospect, as faithful to a conservative tradition.[2]

Regarding the meaning of progressivism in education, we must recognize straightway that any definition is subject to controversy. The expression "progressive education" has been around for a very long time and has been used to refer to any number of very different programs and proposals for education. But we will restrict ourselves to a particular group of men and ideas in American education, that group which has recognized affiliation with the distinctively American philosophy of pragmatism. And about the very misunderstood term *pragmatism* perhaps the less said the better. Fortunately, one seldom encounters any more the vulgar notions that "pragmatism" stands for a repudiation of truth, justice, and beauty, nor that the meaning of the term can be accurately rendered by "Whatever works is right." The two dominant themes in pragmatism were a devotion to the methods of science and a firm adherence to the basic values of the American agrarian tradition (not, please note, the values of industrialism per se, as Bertrand Russell incorrectly asserted).[3]

That group of thinkers and educators who built educational doctrines on philosophical foundations of pragmatism, whom we shall call the progressives, thus faced a major task of intellectual synthesis and an equally difficult task of institutional reconstruction. For a synthesis of the methods of science and the values of American democracy required two prior and original analyses. Science had to be reinterpreted as something much broader than merely the activity of a remote specialist in a laboratory. And democracy itself had to be redefined so that it could have concrete meaning for a social world vastly different from the rural frontier in which it had taken form and substance.[4] Finally, the kind of school typical of the nineteenth century rural community had to be completely transformed if it were to serve to transmit the deeper values of the American tradition to the new generations in their urban, industrial environment. As we follow their attempts to solve these problems we shall see that in education, as elsewhere in American life, the progressives were, in the deepest and finest sense, conservatives.

THE MEANING OF SCHOOLING IN AGRARIAN AMERICA

One thing is certain about the agrarian tradition in America: it was versatile and hardy. In contrast with some of the exotic cultures of the Caribbean that faded almost immediately upon contact with the Spanish missionary and administrator, the American agrarian culture perdured through the conquest of a continent, through the violent resolution of its own internal contradictions, through the absorption and incorporation of a constantly changing stream of immigrants, and even through the initial stages of the transformation of its technological and ecological bases. It fell only as a victim of parricide, destroyed by its own legitimate offspring—contemporary industrialism. But like one of its most representative figures, Old Jules, the agrarian tradition resisted dying even when its time had come.[5]

For following the universal pattern of cultures in transition, the agrarian tradition in America did not change uniformly, but rather shifted markedly in some respects while remaining relatively fixed and stable in others. Technological change proceeded more rapidly than the transformation of political institutions. Symbolic codes took on new meanings in the context of daily life, while remaining unchanged in external form. Thus the immigrant groups who came to this country between the Civil War and World War I would seldom consider changing the words and rituals of their religious codes (though many individuals would simply abandon them altogether), but the actual meaning of these codes in the everyday lives of men and women underwent remarkable changes in this translation from one environment to another. Equally so the habits of thought of the native born: the idea of absolute national sovereignty, for example, remained (and too frequently still remains) unquestioned, even after the world had reached the stage that this principle led inevitably to periodic mass murder. Likewise, for reasons that we shall try to understand, the *content* of school instruction tended to change far more slowly than did the actual life situations of those who taught and attended school.

It is clear that for anyone who was going to remain stationary in his agrarian community,[6] all that he would need to know, in terms of knowledge, skills, and attitudes, he could learn *without* schooling. What he could not learn without formal instruction was how to move and change. And as the conditions of life changed around him, not to move and change was to fall behind. Hence, the fact of *being* schooled became of great importance, while the content of that schooling remained a secondary matter.

This is plainly seen from the content of instruction in the agrarian school. The cognitive aspect, that is the knowledge transmitted, was largely of a kind of language usage far removed from the actual spoken language of the community. One is not at all surprised that at the level of the little attended secondary school, language instruction should not be that of the local community. In this country, as indeed throughout Western nations generally in the nineteenth century, the secondary schools taught Latin, possibly some Greek, and modern foreign languages, while instruction in English was primarily in the literature of England and New England. But even in the common school, the elementary school, the language taught bore scant resemblance to the speech the youngsters heard in everyday life. The persistent attempt to eliminate "ain't" from the vocabulary of children was an inescapable part of the elementary school program. "We used to see the calf go down the path to take a bath, but now we see the cahlf go down the pahth to take a bahth." Thus chanted rural children in unison, explicitly recognizing that a different language system was being offered them, the language of city folks, of the East, of big business, of opportunity and success. It didn't matter that this perception was by and large false, that the classroom voice of the midwestern school teacher would have seemed just as quaint in a Boston drawing room as would the more natural speech of her pupils. In the parlors of Algona, Iowa, this marginal differentiation was noted and respected. It marked the attempt to make a civilized, and hence delineated, social order out of the crude egalitarianism of the frontier. It didn't matter particularly *what* knowledge was taught by the schools; it did matter terribly that schooling provide *some* basis of differentiation that had at least an ostensible relation to life outside the agrarian community.

In the teaching of attitudes, especially moral attitudes, we see the same basic phenomenon. The agrarian community was rich in a variety of attitudes it could encompass with relative harmony if not logical consistency. The saloon and the W.C.T.U. were mutually dependent: without the demon rum, the good ladies would have had nothing to attack; without the good ladies, the customers of the saloon would not have been driven to drink. There was prudery in the parlor and license in the hayloft; fear of the stern, all-seeing God in the church and not-quite-honest horse trading in the wagonyard; tunes that carried the repentant to the altar of the revival preacher and bawdy parodies of them afterward on the river banks. These apparently conflicting attitudes were reconciled in the day-to-day life of the farm-town complex. Everyone growing up in the system knew that they existed and moreover knew where in the system to find his own resolution. For boys, at any rate, the morality of the community was taught more effectively by the town loafers than by McGuffey's *Readers.* How to distinguish between "good girls" and "bad girls" and what was the appropriate treatment of each, what were the acceptable causes for fighting and the rules that accompanied it, just how much money one ought to spend for specific articles, and the style of life for which one should aim—all these elements of the morality of daily living were learned largely outside the school. But within the school the distinctive contribution was made only in relation to life outside the community. McGuffey taught what his readers believed to be the moral attitudes necessary to success in the city. Again, it didn't matter that this perception was at least partly false. The city was the locus in iniquity, and the agrarian boy or girl who was to succeed there must be protected by a double dose of all the Protestant virtues. The function of teaching these attitudes was to enable the youngsters to move effectively toward a new life outside the immediate environment.

The skills taught in the agrarian schools, insofar as these skills differed from the technical and social habits that were learned just by living in the community, were essentially literary skills. Were these skills also more related to life outside the agrarian community than to life inside? Here a distinction has to be made. Whereas in the agrarian village of other parts of the world a style of life had been developed before printing became a dominant role of communication,[7] it has been estimated that the practicing farmer, storekeeper, and artisan of the frontier actually required the reading and computational skills associated with about a sixth-grade education in order to function effectively in those roles. And whereas the frontier settlement of America never extended far beyond the newspaper, the mail-order catalog, the record books of the legal and business offices, and the ladies' poetry circles, commercial farming and spreading industry put a demand for literary and computational skill on agrarian America that distinguishes it rather sharply from agrarian life elsewhere.

But these skills were not taught in their functional relation to life as found in the local community. If the youngster learned to read so that he could understand his local paper, that was happy accident; for he was taught to read what might literally be called escape literature. Exotic history, geography, biography, and moralistic fiction constituted the bulk of his prescribed reading diet. And it was the literary skills necessary to master this literature, literature that meant escape from the existing conditions of life, that were demanded by many southern Negroes after the Civil War.[8] Thus it may be said that the skill training in the schools of agrarian America, like the knowledge and attitudes they taught, was related only tangentially to the existential conditions of life. This would explain in part why the content of instruction could change ever so slowly while the world around was changing ever more rapidly. There was essentially no relation between the two.

The enormous importance of local control of schools was also responsible for this relatively slow change in the content of instruction. When American educators visited Europe in the nineteenth century, they were most impressed by the way in which the schools on the Continent, especially in Germany, had been redesigned to meet the demands of expanding industrialism. Of course, they did not always perceive it in this fashion. They thought they were witnessing the application of newer and better ideas to the practices of schooling.[9] And they returned to extend the application of these ideas to American schools. But one overwhelming fact soon struck all of them: in Europe, new ideas—theories, philosophies, or concepts of education—could be applied and changes instituted as soon as a central agency was convinced of their desirability. In America, the situation was quite different. The local school boards in many states of the Union had almost unlimited authority over the entire operation of the schools.

Even more important than the legal autonomy of the school boards was the system by which American teachers were recruited and trained. At the elementary level this system drew almost altogether upon itself and recruited those who had been taught the things the existing system taught. The teacher institutes and training classes for elementary school teaching frequently were operated under the jurisdiction of local boards of education in the rural areas of the nation. Examinations for positions were constructed around the actual skills to be taught in the elementary schools. All this means that there was literally no place where outside influences could be brought directly, consistently, and deliberately to bear in changing the attitudes and perceptions between generations of teachers. Thus, one of the dominant means for changing education—the centralized control for the training of teachers—existed in Europe but was unavailable in this country.

A second feature of this system is that those who had been most effectively educated in the total system of community education did not want to return to local school teaching. We have seen how the school itself was educating people to leave, not to live in, the agrarian community. Those who had been taught the posture of escape were not ready to forget their teaching and remain put in the local community. The stories of successful careers in the nineteenth century are full of the use of a rural teaching job as a stepping stone to further education and ultimately to employment in the city. Now this bears on our problem in two ways. It means that the change-minded young people in the schools were not primarily oriented toward changing the schools but in changing their own relation to it, that is, in getting out. It also means that those who stayed in the rural schools—and who in any case did not stay in one community very long—were not likely to be the kind of people who would take it upon themselves to revolutionize the content of their teaching.

These interrelated conditions were almost ideal for keeping the educational program of the regular school systems intact and unmodified by reflex actions from the changes going on in the rest of the society. Perhaps the most striking illustration of this is to be found in the history of agricultural education itself. With the passage of the Morrill Act in 1862 and its constant subsequent extension through other legislation in support of agricultural education, the nation built a magnificently effective system by which research into farming methods could be carried out and the results transmitted to farmers. Almost by accident, this system of agricultural research and training was attached at several levels to the regular school system and carried independently from that system at other points. Now the initial expectation might be that the connection between the agricultural program and the rest of the school program would lead to some noticeable interpenetration of the two. But with certain dramatic exceptions, nothing of the sort occurred.[10] The academic curriculum of the regular school system expanded slowly in both the city and country to embrace the sciences and more advanced mathematics and to include more elective offerings that might have some vocational significance. These changes, however, came much more decidedly from the sheer expansion of the curriculum itself and from the longer time youngsters remained in school than from any significant effect of the academic curriculum's being organically related to the program of agricultural education.

(The whole history of agricultural education is one paradox

after another. The Morrill Act was passed as part of the grand alliance in which eastern businessmen and abolitionists combined with midwestern grain farmers to crush the Confederacy. Its passage was supposed to protect the interests of the agricultural elements of the nation. In effect, of course, it so increased the productivity of farmers that they now constitute an insignificant fraction of the population and will inevitably lose their unjustly favored economic and political position. *Sic semper tyrannis.*)

We have emphasized the lack of relation between the program of the local school and other features of agrarian community life. This fact made the school an almost irrelevant institution for those who were to remain in the local community. But from the point of view of the nation as a whole, the agrarian school was doing a very significant job and doing that job effectively. For in preparing people to literally and figuratively escape from the agrarian way of life, it performed its vital function in the larger context of the changing American society.

THE PROGRESSIVES IN EDUCATION

As is true of the progressives generally in American life, the progressives in education are too close upon us to permit anything like a full evaluation of their efforts for social betterment.[11] They recognized that a new society was a-borning, and they knew that education had to become very different from what it had been if it were to be of any assistance in relieving the birth pangs. But this meant also that an old society was dying. Now a succession of generations does not necessarily mean progress. It signifies progress only if the new generation carries the finer things of the old on to new heights. Were the progressives really willing to give up enough of the old to make progress possible?

Notice that regionalism is exclusively an agrarian phenomenon. It is symbolic that the three major figures associated with the philosophy of progressive education came from the three major regions of agrarian America. John Dewey from New England, William Heard Kilpatrick from the South, and Boyd Bode from the Old Northwest—each was rural and Protestant in family origin. Each reflected in his personal life and associations a deep commitment to the public morality, that scarcely definable sense of the fitness of things in relation to the general welfare, that in the rural community distinguishes those who come to be regarded as its best people.

Still, despite Dewey's Vermont twang, Kilpatrick's courtly southern manner, and Bode's close resemblance to Lincoln, not one of this trio could rightly be regarded as merely a regional figure. Certainly after the Civil War, and probably even before, it was no more possible to be a really effective spokesman for education than to be a major force in national politics, while retaining a primarily regional identification.[12] Even in the Senate, where Clay, Calhoun, and Webster had earlier spoken to the nation in regional terms, Johnson, Watson, Borah, La Follette, and Norris made their national impact as representatives of economic or social forces of trans-regional character. And even less than their counterparts in politics could Dewey, Bode, and Kilpatrick speak in purely regional terms to the emerging profession of education. But neither were these men to be identified as representatives of a particular class or economic group in the society when they spoke in their capacity as philosophers of education. It was only when they spoke, as they sometimes did in the depression of the 1930's, as representing specifically the farmer or labor interest, that they tended to lose contact with the day-to-day life of the school and its problems. Finally, Dewey, Bode, and Kilpatrick made their impact, when speaking in their professional voice, as representative of the values of the agrarian tradition that were being threatened by the omnipresent cultural changes around them.

Because the schools had been least affected by the changes occurring in the culture generally, they constituted the last hope of the agrarian way of life to preserve what was best in its system by incorporating the changes into its way of life.[13] Progressive education attempted to provide a basic outlook on the world that would enable the coming generations to use the new technological power to achieve the older values The three major doctrines of progressivism could be labeled its metaphysics, epistemology, and axiology. But as for very good reasons the progressives distrusted the traditional philosophical labels by which ideas are categorized, it is more fitting to speak of the world view, the theory of intelligence, and the conception of values in progressivism. Let us begin with the theory of intelligence.

1. It has become generally accepted that the progressives' theory of intelligence was erroneously labeled the "scientific method." The actual procedures by which scientific discoveries are made and tested bear resemblance to Dewey's theory of how we think only in that both methods represent ways, albeit quite different ways, of using human intelligence.[14] Dewey's model for *How We Think* is neither Newton, Darwin, nor least of all Einstein. His nearest model is Tom Sawyer. Life for Tom is a series of existential involvements with a rather obdurate environment including people and things that seem constantly to get in the way of his on-going activity. More than once Tom is shocked out of a delightfully precognitive state of existence and forced to deal with the recalcitrant objects and events that surround him. He draws upon his culture for resources to deal with recurring emergencies. And if that culture is not rich with all the scientific and literary lore of Western civilization, it is at least intimately known by Tom. It has become Tom's culture, not because he read it in a book, but because he has used it in as full a sense as any human being can use the experiences of other people in meeting his own problems.

But Tom is not a complete progressive hero. He lacks the element of reflection, of backward looking. Like boyhood culture everywhere, Tom's culture is composed of unchallengeable and perennial truths, no matter how often experience shows them to be false. If only Tom had the intellectual curiosity of the boy Edison, he would complete the picture. But the young Edison himself would not do either, for he lacked Tom's feeling for the immediate, the tangible, the esthetic experience. For Edison, the world was only what it would do; for Tom it was what it was, a living *Ding an sich.* But why not construct an educational system that will provide a synthesis of Tom and Thomas Alva? Why not teach Tom true beliefs about his world and teach him to know these in a reflective, critical way? But do this without destroying the sense of being *engagé* that characterizes Tom's present way of knowing the world? Notice that Tom's education came from the entire community, his family being an already truncated version of the producing-consuming unit of American life. An education given by the entire community digs deep into the habits of behavior of the individual, but it may educate falsely as well as deeply. The dominant motive of the progressive was to combine in one educational experience the maximum depth of personal incorporation with the breadth and sureness of the scientific traditions of Western civilization.

For if the two are disjoined, the coldly scientific way of knowing will destroy the kind of world in which Tom's richly personal way of knowing can flourish. It will treat the world as a place of lifeless material, to be manipulated for the sake of symbolic success, not as a realm of human consummations. And if science is separated from the context of human consummations, it will be used apart from, and ultimately in opposition to, human experience. When Tom Sawyer becomes a grown man, the cultural resources he knows so well will be of scant help to him against the combination of money and science. But if Tom had learned science in the same way he learned the lore of boyhood, in cooperative ways with his fellows, he would be a match for any competitor. What boys know together can be the basis on which boys cooperate against their myriad natural enemies. Just so, if the members of the Grange had known economics and agronomy as intimately and directly as they had known their boyhood culture, they would not have been the victims of eastern bankers and railroads. Tom's way of knowing (but not young Edison's way) was as much a method of social cohesion as it was a step toward the individual consummatory experience.

2. In history there are no beginnings. Every phenomenon has its analogues in some earlier phenomenon. The progressive con-

ception of what it means to promote intelligence, as described here, is no exception. One could easily show that in their attempt to rescue schooling from dry formalism by bringing the life and purpose of childhood into active play in classroom activities the progressives were one with a tradition of educational reformers going back at least as far as Augustine. But the progressives' conception of intelligence was combined with (or, if you prefer, derived from) a world view that could have appeared only after the achievements of physics and biology in the nineteenth century.

From man's basic nature as a cultural animal arises the need for an overall view of the world, for a psychologically satisfying (if not logically consistent) set of ideas that can be given ritual expression and enables the individual to relate himself symbolically to his environment. The world view of the progressives involved the substitution of an organic scientific conception of the universe for the Protestant Christian view that had been standard in the agrarian tradition of America. Nevertheless, the world view offered by the progressives shared many features in common with that which it attempted to replace.

When it is said that the world view of the progressives was an organic scientific one, the intent is to avoid the frequently heard charge that Dewey and others held a mechanistic conception of the universe. The billiard ball metaphor of Hume and Laplace had no role to play in progressive thought. In "The Influence of Darwin on Philosophy," Dewey makes it quite clear that his Hegelian mode of thought could never have been channeled into a sympathy with modern science until science itself had acquired a dialectical, rather than a mechanical, frame for the interpretation of its objects.[15] Change, growth, and emergence are as real as the apparently eternal laws of motion.

The *Weltanschauung* of the progressives is expressed most simply and movingly in the first few pages of Kilpatrick's "Reconstructed Theory of the Educative Process."[16] Here we see the great polarities of philosophic thought—organicism and mechanism, chance and fatality, good and evil—related as mutually inescapable aspects of the world people must live in. But even more important, we see men and women as continuous with the rest of nature, adaptive organisms striving to maintain their equilibrium in the face of constant disturbing stimuli. Judged by its dramatic qualities, this is a signal achievement; it sets man in his own habitat and gives him dignity and purpose without the deceitful device of a (literal) *deus ex machina.* Taken just this far, the progressive view of the world emerges as one appropriate for heroes who neither ask nor expect any favors from the world around them. The hero can find his moral purposes within himself, requiring neither cosmic nor biological sanctions.

But the progressives realized that most teachers are not heroes. And so Kilpatrick explicitly propounds the moral obligations of all those who are engaged in the teaching of children. As the world offers no guarantee that good shall triumph over evil, it thus becomes the duty of each individual to engage himself actively in the overt, objective reconstruction of the world. By a very obvious sort of connection, this duty translates itself into that of promoting the adaptive intelligence, as described above, of each individual boy and girl.

As in man the biological animal is continuous with nature. Likewise, man is a cultural and historical animal. One does not have to posit any external cause for cultural change, for culture, like the cosmos itself, is inherently dynamic. And history, as the record of cultural evolution, offers no guarantee that progress is assured. Men working cooperatively, and using their highly evolved adaptive intelligence, may be successful in shaping their historical destiny, or they may not. The existential dynamic forces are supremely indifferent as to the outcome. In the practice of politics, this view of culture and history required of the progressives a sustained high courage that the Marxists, for example, did not need to possess since the latter could occasionally relax in the certainty that history was working for them.

3. Notice that as the world view of the progressives does not guarantee that good will be achieved, neither does it provide a definition of the ultimate human good. Reticence on this point is not accidental; it reflects the deep abhorrence of idolatry that

characterizes both the Protestant and Judaic traditions. Proximate goods can be pursued openly and cooperatively; final goods—e.g., salvation—can be known only in the sanctity of the individual soul. Now education is necessarily an open, public affair; it develops the kind of intelligence that enables men to pursue, both individually and cooperatively, their proximate goods. And science is the mode of human knowing that enables man to understand the world around him and to control that world so that it yields the stability and security necessary to the achievement of all human purposes, whether proximate or final. Hence, education must be concerned with promoting the kind of intelligence that can use science in controlling the world. And the line of reasoning has thus proceeded back to the original conception of intelligence without more than casually touching the question of final or eternal values.[17]

Yet we do find such expressions as "consummatory experience," "restoration of equilibrium," and "sense of shared achievement" in the educational writings of the progressives. Perhaps these expressions, like the name of Yahweh, are but circumlocutions to suggest the unspeakable. But in a more frequent phrase, we encounter the word *democracy*. This word came to symbolize two of the most important aspirations of agrarian America. The first was the struggle for economic, political, and social equality by the agrarian regions vis-à-vis the industrial and commercial complexes of the East. The progressives in education were one with the general progressive movements of the fifty-year period commencing with 1875, and their peculiar contribution lay in teaching people how to use knowledge in effective and cooperative fashions for the achievement of their objectives. But there was a second, a deeper, almost mystical sense of democracy on the Protestant frontier. If eternal salvation was an unknowable, inexpressible experience of the individual soul, the nearest earthly, temporal equivalent was the communion of *equality among the elect*. Here was a contradiction that could never be resolved. The drive toward social equality with the East required the kind of civilization that cannot be achieved without strongly marked delineations in the system of social relations. The local poet, or musician, or intellectual, or shrewd banker could be as good as anyone in the East, but only if he were a damned sight better than anyone else in his local community. Yet he could not be better in such a way as to threaten that underlying, that deeply sensed, feeling of equality. This feeling has its European root extending beyond the limits of our vision, yet the frontier experience gave it a distinctive American tone, a tone that permeates the American concept of democracy.

There is no way to describe this sense of equality to those who have not experienced it. The poet may evoke the sentiment, as in Carl Sandburg's "The People, Yes!" The reverential attitude it engenders may be seen in Dewey's *Common Faith.*[18] Its power for evil as well as for good may be understood by looking at the Deep South, where a whole race is denied full humanity, since it cannot be admitted to the sacred round table of white man's equality.[19] But however difficult it may be to achieve, a rather thorough sense of this feeling of equality is essential to anyone who would understand the dilemmas of the public school educator in contemporary industrial America. This mystique of equality is called up whenever one raises such questions as education for the gifted child, anti-intellectualism, local control, and above all, religion and the public schools.

If there is any truth in the analysis given so far, it allows us to understand both the radical and the conservative elements in the progressive.

Consider now just how radically different from the agrarian school would be the institution designed to preserve and extend this conception of democracy in the new industrial civilization. While the expression "the whole child" came to be associated in the public mind with the progressives' conception of the school, a much more descriptive expression would be "the whole community." For in the new environment, the school must provide the whole range of educational experiences that had earlier been given by an organic complex of community living. (Notice that the expression "educational experiences," now dreadfully hackneyed, is unavoidable if one is to make clear the progressives' radically changed conception of the role of the school.) The nuclear family, now a fact but even by 1910 the emerging pattern for urban life, did not have the capacity to provide the deep sense of continuity that the extended family system in an agrarian setting gave to its young. The productive system of the urban world was incapable of teaching its habits and customs to those who would be the next generation of producers. The church, by putting itself in opposition to science, by its deliberate obscurantism and fundamentalism, had lost its capacity to give a unified world view that would enable youth to establish an intellectually satisfying picture of their relation to actual conditions around them. And entertainment, now commercial rather than communal, could no longer establish the joyous rituals that related man to man.

Progressive education now undertook a revolutionary transformation of the school into the agency by which a total, unified education could be given to the youth of the nation! The very conditions that made the school a marginal institution in the agrarian community—its separation from the constantly accelerating changes occurring around it—enabled it to appear as a stable base on which a new comprehensive education could be built.

The conservative aspect of this philosophy was the program to preserve the core values of the agrarian society in the new industrial age. Yet the progressives were hard put to it when it came to defining what these values actually were. For the final values of the agrarian society were internal, personal, inexpressible. The words *freedom, democracy,* and *equality* were but pale reflections for the inner feelings they were supposed to represent; after a time, even these words tended to lose their magical qualities as evocative of the agrarian sense of values. In an age that lives by symbols, changing fashions are inevitable. When the living basis for the symbols is destroyed, change in fashions soon takes away the quality of the words.

Just because the progressives steadfastly refused to erect a symbolic system which they feared (and rightly) would become an object of worship in itself, they were particularly vulnerable to changes in fashions. Their value words arose out of the existential conditions of life in agrarian society; when those conditions changed a dreadful gap appeared between the words they used and anything those words might stand for. The case of religious freedom and education shows this gap quite clearly. Religious freedom in the agrarian community did not mean religious indifference. Rural children could debate the various sides of the doctrine of predestination with more than a little sophistication. There was a choice among churches and there was the perfectly respectable choice of being unchurched. Joining a church was a kind of puberty rite implying, albeit not always achieving, the exercise of uncoerced personal choice and commitment. An entire system of relations with associated strong feelings were involved in this complex, among them being the sense that there was an inner grace which was the business of the individual to manifest outwardly however he saw fit. The marginal status of the agrarian school was nowhere more evident than in matters of religion. Many activities in the agrarian school had vaguely pious overtones; it was thoroughly permeated with the Protestant ethic. These facts bothered no one particularly. Religious freedom concerned two matters only: whether to join a church or not, and if to join, of what Protestant denomination. The school fit into this system quite well so long as it remained non-denominational. The school did not have to be indifferent to religion per se, it simply had to keep its hands off the open competition as each of the denominations tried to capture its equitable proportion of the community's youth. The system was certain to keep denominational churches small and poor, religious interest high, and school interference at a minimum.

Now remove the concept of religious freedom from that social system, and its meaning becomes extremely confused. By its very nature, it cannot be explained in other symbols; it is an undefinable, primitive concept. Hence, when the separation of church and state in education became problematical and the progressives spoke of religious freedom, it was hard to see exactly what they were trying to conserve. They could not point to the agrarian community and say: "See the way those people behave and feel? Well, we want to preserve that behavior and feeling." They could not say this, because they were perfectly aware that the conditions that made that sort of behavior and sentiment possible simply did not exist any longer. And when they talked about the equivalent in an industrial society for this system in the agrarian community, they were forced back on legalistic, external arguments that necessarily lost the real import of what they meant by "religious freedom."[20]

If we tried to follow the progressives in their defense of education for personal fulfillment, for productive citizenship, or for any of the other aspects of "education for democracy," we should encounter the same basic gap. It is not that they said nothing on these value questions; quite to the contrary, they filled libraries with their arguments. But arguments are with words, and eventually the words have to be connected in some recognizable way with a non-verbal reality if they are to have meaning. In 1899 Dewey could talk about "the other side of life," i.e., the living alternative to the growing industrialism of Chicago at the time, and his hearers would know well enough what he meant; they would have had the direct experience with the world to give meaning to the idea of an alternative. Forty years later this background of experience could no longer be assumed. Then the question of final end arose when the possibility of an answer had been lost. It is not essential that every system of thought have a built-in answer to the question: "What is the ultimate human good?" It has to provide an answer only if the question is genuine, that is to say, only if an answer is actually necessary to distinguish what is truly good from what may falsely appear so in the realm of proximate goods. So long as a basic common understanding prevailed, the progressives could say "democracy" and "growth leading to more growth" and this was a sufficient answer to guide proximate choices. When the common background that gave birth to those words had disappeared, no amount of reiteration could bring them to life again. The progressives had recognized the dangers of delighting in words at the expense of what the words mean, but the time came when their own symbols of value lost connection with the living reality of the world around them.

PROGRESSIVISM AND THE MORAL COMMITMENT OF TEACHERS

It is not at all difficult to see how the system of thought we call progressivism appeared out of the confluence of American agrarian democracy with the rising industrialism and the intoxicating new developments in science. What is more difficult to explain is how it came about that this system of thought captured the imagination and loyalties of so large a number of teachers not only in the rural areas of this country, but most strikingly in urban centers here and abroad. Perhaps as far as the United States is concerned it is of significance that the period of the rise of progressivism corresponded more or less exactly with the period in which Americanization became the dominant job of the urban schools.[21] We do not mean that there was a greater population of immigrant children than native-born of native parents in the schools. But, nevertheless, this job had an urgency and an immediacy that was overriding in the perceptions of those personally engaged in the teaching process. And at this moment the progressives entered the educational scene with a charge to teachers that matched in urgency and in moral determination that same imperative sense the teachers themselves faced in their day-to-day work.

To understand why the ideas of the progressives were couched in terms of moral imperatives, we must remember the conditions under which change could be instituted in American education. Not being dictated from the national level nor, except in externals, from the state or county levels, the actual control of the teaching procedure depended to a large degree upon the individual teacher's perception of his task and function. In order to change the practices in the schools, one had to change the heart as well as the mind of the teacher. Scientific evidence from psychology, careful surveys of the existing state of human knowledge, and precise predictions of social trends were valuable tools, but the progressives had to translate these into the kind of language that would resound in the inner consciousness of the teacher. Thus, prior to Dewey, the language of progressive educators was almost that of an apocalyptic vision. And even Dewey, who in his logical works developed a style so dry as to be acutely painful, pronounced his educational beliefs in the language of inspiration.

The release of ethical energy by the language of progressivism may best be illustrated by looking outside the continental United States. There is no better evidence of the propitious setting for progressive ideals than in that spirit of urgency and determination with which American teachers assumed the responsibility of teaching in the newly acquired colonies of Puerto Rico and the Philippines following the end of the Spanish-American War. The official definition of the task for which they had volunteered differed little from its requirements in an American school. But the role which these teachers defined for themselves was quite different. They attempted to transmit the entirety of a cultural system to children whom they believed to have been denied the blessings of American life. Their schoolroom became the citadel of American virtues, and its symbols were the flag and the portraits of Washington and Lincoln. These were the lineal descendants of the Yankee schoolmarms who went south with the Freedmen's Bureau after the Civil War; they were the ancestors of today's Peace Corps. But for a glorious moment as their nation stood for progress in the world and they for progressive education, the progressive movement provided an ideology which they spread around the world.

Despite exaggerated claims by ignorant writers,[22] it is very difficult to judge exactly how much and in what particulars the conduct of American schools was changed by the progressive movement. A possible candidate for being genuinely influential was Kilpatrick's "project method," especially after it had come to be taught as the only acceptable basis for lesson-planning in teacher training schools and incorporated as the form of chapter organization in many elementary school textbooks (and thus, of course, lost all organic connection with the fundamental premises of progressivism). It is, on the other hand, eminently clear that the "New Movement" in educational administration and the testing movement associated with it really affected the content and climate of a great many schools.[23] This claim is made on the assumption that when the materials of instruction have been changed and also the procedures for testing and evaluating student performance, then a significant effect on the school has been achieved. By this criterion, the spread of clearly progressive practices from a relatively small number of pilot schools was neither nonexistent nor yet a major social movement. The lesson is clear: the success and acceptance attained by the progressives was in the realm of moral purpose, not in the translation to educational procedures. In setting forth a noble conception of the social role of education, they served America well and perhaps more lastingly than the psychologists, for their contribution was straight to the self-esteem of those who maintained the system during times of unparalleled expansion, change, and travail.

If the prologue to the progressive movement occurred within the rising tensions between an agrarian-commercial and an industrial-urban civilization, its epilogue appeared with the demise of agrarian civilization and the triumphant emergence of metropolitanism in the period between the two great wars. The spirit of militant reform of the 1930's produced an environment favorable to the conversion of progressive ideals into plans for action. These proponents were the reconstructionists, the activists who believed that the burden of building a new America lay within the realm and responsibility of education. Two of them, George Counts and John Childs, had received their own early schooling at a time when the schools had yet been marginal to the society. Their championship of the cause of education and their insistence that the issues be debated at the loftiest level reflected a zeal worthy of the puritan and pragmatic backgrounds from which they came. But progressivism proposed more than a new definition of function. It insisted on the moral purpose of education.[24] It asked a commitment which, in its extreme form, assigned to the schools the moral responsibility for the entire society. Seldom has any group been charged with embracing a commitment of such breadth and depth. If there were those who faltered it should be remembered that the burden was heavy and that others in American society failed to understand the necessity or the purpose. The impetus for their cause was lost in a complex of forces and factors; the most important of all, probably, was that America had moved on. In any event, with the reluctant retirement of the giants from the academic stage, there were few disciples to perpetuate their arguments. *Sic transit gloria mundi.*

But we cannot leave the progressives without expressing some of our own feelings toward the movement. Our admiration and respect are, we hope, evident throughout the chapter. Their abiding legacy is this: neither in this country nor elsewhere in the world may one mention schooling without raising visions of social welfare and individual intelligence. That is deliberately putting it negatively. It seems to imply that in their positive contributions they must be regarded as having failed.

Did the progressives actually fail? One would know just from the *size* of the question that its answer must be both Yes and No. The case against them is quite damning. From Dewey's lectures of 1899 to the going-out-of-fashion of both pragmatism and progressivism, the program they set for themselves was to design an educational system adequate to the transformation of America, and to put that system into operation. By now it is quite clear that even now American educators know neither what constitutes an adequate education for the new society we live in nor how to quickly and precisely change the conduct of our schools. We know a good deal more than we used to know on both these matters, enough in fact to make us rather humble in our ignorance. Since 1899 we have solved certain problems—how, for example, to build, finance, and police a national highway system; but we have failed to solve certain others—how, for example, to equitably finance medical care. Education falls clearly in the second category. Insofar as the progressives were charged with (or assumed) the responsibility of leadership and did not produce lasting results, they were failures.

But there is another side. Because they took the broadest possible view of the school's responsibility in cultural change, they could not, therefore, accept the purely technical context as the most significant one in education. But it is only in the purely technical context that problems are ever solved. Hence the criterion for success or failure that we have been applying—Did they solve the problems?—is not the only applicable test.

In some ways education and highways are alike, and in those ways educational theorists and highway engineers are judged alike. Did a new way of designing an interchange reduce traffic tie-ups? Did the use of a new programmed text result in more rapid and retentive learning than did the old? In each case there are fairly straightforward goals and fairly clear-cut connections between technique and goal.

But the progressives restored an old (and purely academic) interest into the living context of American education: the question, What is education for? And they made the answer problematical in a way it had never been before. By refusing to accept a priori or tautological answers, they *forced* educational attention onto the social and cultural conditions of the times, onto the plight of democratic values in the emerging industrial culture. They thus set going an argument to which an ever increasing proportion of the world's population (including the Communist world) will be forced to attend.

Must we, then, grant a posthumous garland of success to the efforts of the progressives? Yes, perhaps in a curiously dialectical fashion they were all *too* successful. The indictments on this bill are many and grievous. First, as they turned the attention of educational theorists away from mere technique, so they turned the attention of the most capable theorists away from pedagogical technique altogether. The consequence was exactly what anyone would have foretold. Only in the past few years have we seen a reunion of fundamental consideration of the technical problems involved in teaching with equally fundamental consideration of what the enterprise is supposed to be for.[25]

Second, the inspiring language of moral exhortation with which the progressive movement began has degenerated into jargon and cliché.[26] This would be objectionable enough on purely esthetic grounds, but there are more serious consequences still. So long as the effort to change education was focused on driving new beliefs and attitudes into the heads of teachers, the political and economic conditions affecting the schools could be ignored. The final upshot of this tendency may be seen in the 1961 publication of the Educational Policies Commission of the National Education Association of the United States and the American Association of School Administrators, a publication grandiosely entitled *The Central Purpose of American Education.*[27] In twenty-one beautifully printed pages the Commission presents a collective and confused summary of the Socratic argument on the primacy of knowledge among the virtues. Needless to say, the wit, irony, and drama of the *Protagoras* are notably missing. Also missing is any recognition whatsoever of the institutional arrangements within which operating decisions on educational policy actually occur, where "purpose" comes to mean what we genuinely purpose doing. This regrettable tract cannot be blamed solely on the tendency of the progressives to speak of education in the language of moral imperative. But neither can they be held blameless.

The obverse needs attention also. There are times in a civilization when moral imperatives, at the highest level, and directed squarely toward the exigencies of the moment, need to be brought forward to enlist the basic commitments of all the individuals who are truly members of that civilization. The record of the great public statements by political and religious leaders of this nation, more than any other one thing, is the collective conscience of America. But nothing is so easily debased as is the language of moral imperative. When every statement, even though it be of the slightest moment, is couched as, "We must . . ."; "The future of our nation requires us to . . ."; etc., then one soon learns to ignore the voice of the collective conscience. Even if the Educational Policies Commission had happened to have something to say, they would have been ignored. For this debasement also, the progressives cannot be completely absolved.

Third, and finally, the accusing finger must be pointed squarely at John Dewey for a fundamental inconsistency in social theory that has plagued those liberal, democratic educators who have tried to take seriously the social function of schooling. On the one hand, Dewey accepted the premise that political form is not itself a primary matter but rather something that follows upon the more basic and dynamic social forces. This premise is Marxian, without question, but it also has deep roots in American social thought, in Thomas Paine, James Madison, and Thorstein Veblen, just to mention a few Americans who have explicitly accepted the premise. Dewey recognized, of course, that the basic social dynamism of *our* day is found in expanding technology. On the other hand, Dewey developed a steadfast adherence to one single political solution for the ills of contemporary life, namely, the establishment of democratic socialism.[28] Dewey saw his own age as one of crises, as a transitional period between a static equilibrium of the past and a dynamic equilibruim of the future.[29] His vision of the future included communal control, through public agencies, of mass industries whose workers would be not mere appendages to machines but rather cooperating citizens in the control of their own destinies. His sense of political organization, like his sense of education itself, derived from his theory of intelligence: What are the required social arrangements to develop habits of collective, cooperative problem-solving in the public?

The inconsistency? Simply this: changing technology would no more spare the cooperative community of industrial workers than it had spared the New England village life from which Dewey's social vision had sprung. As technology becomes allied with science, and as the laboratory (whether industrial or academic) comes to command a sizable proportion of our national income and an even larger proportion of our most talented young men and women, then social changes of so radical a nature that Dewey's vision could not comprehend them become commonplace. Under those conditions it becomes senseless to hold on to one single *idée fixe* concerning the right form of political organization; it contradicts the first premise with which this discussion, and Dewey himself, began.

There is a lesson to be learned from Dewey's mistake here. In the final analysis his conservatism overcame his devotion to change, growth, and process. Deeply convinced that ultimate human values were to be found only in a particular form of face-to-face community,[30] Dewey was so concerned to see that community survive and grow that he forgot to notice one peculiar fact: the world no longer has a place for it. The full acceptance of change does not admit of the reservations which Dewey never overcame. It is fruitless to berate Dewey for not being an omniscient prophet, for not recognizing in the embryo before him the full structure that has since emerged.[31] But we have to acknowledge and accept that structure. We cannot regard Tom Sawyer as an acceptable model for intelligence in the modern world. Neither can we take the Vermont village of Dewey's childhood as representative of the needed social commitment in our time.

6

METROPOLIS IN TIME AND SPACE

During the past quarter century the pace of social and cultural transformation in the United States has quickened. We can now view the boom and depression of the late twenties and early thirties as the agonized death throes of an earlier form of society. From this period of low tide in the national spirit and well-being, a dominant culture-type—previously emergent in the industrial railroad cities—has appeared, a new civilization which is as different from the town-community which it supplanted as the latter was different from the small farmer frontier agrarian community of Jefferson and Jackson that was its predecessor. By "different" we mean modification or decline in older types of groupings and the rise to dominance of others, new symbols and new meanings for old symbols, altered values and spirit expressing those values; in short, we mean a reconstituted form of culture.

The demographic expression of this new civilization is metropolis. Today almost all America lives either within the physical limits or under the shadow of the influences of the great urban concentrations. Their social structure is epitomized in the great superstructures of government, industry, education, health, and commerce, in the isolated conjugal family of parents and children, the family of "togetherness," and in the ephemeral but repetitive gatherings of the "lonely crowd." These groupings include the extremes of cohesion and atomization.

This new society demands of the individual an enormous capacity for mobility in the frequent changes of residence from one locality to another, in the shifts from one job or position to another, and even in changes in occupation or profession. It values in the individual his capacity for "adjustment," which is stressed in the new psychology, and his ability to work with others in a "team," which may be learned in "group process." It is a civilization which through organization and technology provides a theoretical and potential freedom and autonomy to the individual that in past epochs were the privilege of a minority only. It is a civilization which views change as inevitable and desirable and, as a consequence, understands the past less as the source of the present than as a concern of academicians. It is a civilization which, if it does not founder on the rocks of material prosperity and destructive leisure or of the senseless exhaustion of resources through competitive armaments, can achieve the stars. The literal search for the star is a quest demanding our best energy, resources, and intelligence. But the figurative stars are far more important, not as a Utopia, but as the restoration of the sense of wonder in the harmony of the universe.

Institutions and human activity, no less than the stars, can be shown to express orderliness in their dynamics. The external form of hamlet, town, or city reveals, in part, the lives of those who are their occupants. Although the reconstruction of the central city and surrounding suburbs has not been a product of overall conscious planning, their transformation reflects the new social arrangements and correlative values of our modern world.

In the description of metropolis we shall seek for that orderliness of which we spoke.[1]

THE DEMOGRAPHY OF METROPOLIS

The triumph of an urban-industrial way of life is unquestionably the most important social fact of recent decades. When we remember that only one hundred years ago 75 percent of our population consisted of farm families and that today they number under 10 percent, we can appreciate the magnitude and rapidity of the change. Although statistics of population distribution and occupation can tell only a portion of the story, they provide a picture of the transformation that has taken place.

The present population is estimated at slightly over 180 million. Of this number approximately 113 million are concentrated in 212 metropolitan regions.[2] The greatest concentration of population is found within thirty-two metropolitan areas stretching along a 600-mile belt from New Hampshire to Virginia and counting 31.5 million inhabitants. Over the past decade the suburban areas within this "super-city" increased 44.2 percent while city population declined 2.8 percent. This is the pattern of change found everywhere in the nation.[3]

Thus within the demographic pattern of ever greater urban concentration the larger cities are in slow decline while suburbia booms. Urban population rose to 70 percent of the total in 1960, an increase of six percent over 1950, but the 28-million gain in numbers during this decade took place in urban centers and 97 percent in metropolitan areas. Yet eleven of the twelve largest cities (Los Angeles was the exception) declined in size. The difference is explained entirely in terms of suburban growth, which counted two-thirds of the total increase. Suburban population increased almost three times faster than the rate for the nation as a whole and accounted for half of the total gain.

Population density also exhibits great variability. There are sections of New York City where density approximates 100,000 per square mile. In contrast, the horizontal suburb of single-family dwellings ranges between three and five thousand per square mile, and in those localities where zoning laws demand two or three acres per dwelling, the density may drop to one thousand or less. Density, however, may be a widely fluctuating factor. As an example, the City of London proper is one square mile in size. It has a permanent resident population of only 5,180 but a working population of 375,000 who daily pour into and out of its heart. Comparable figures for American cities also show a similar ebb and flow of workers in their downtown districts.

But daily mobility is only one aspect of the problem; available statistics establish that residential mobility is of major importance. It is estimated that one family in five changes its residence each year. This includes those who move from one locality to another within the city, to and from the suburbs, and from rural areas. The extension of industrialized-scientific agriculture to the rural South and to Puerto Rico has resulted in displacement of an agrarian population which is directing itself cityward. In the decade from 1950-60, Negroes in the North increased from 4.2 to 6.5 million and in the West from less than 600,000 to over a million. They have also moved into southern cities but not in such proportions. The growth of the urban South has come from a small southward trickle of whites but more particularly from southern rural whites. The migration of over half a million Puerto Ricans, primarily to New York City, has been an added factor of population growth.

Concurrent with the migration of a displaced and depressed agrarian population to the cities has been the outward movement of city folk to the suburbs. This migration has also been selective in that it is composed primarily of persons with incomes and occupational skills traditionally associated with a middle class. The consequence of this population adjustment has been to increase the proportions of the working class and to decrease those of the middle class for the central city. Although the outward movement to the suburbs may have been accelerated by the influx of new population to the cities, it is much too simple to attempt to explain the movement by this factor alone. England has had no sizeable rural population nor a sizeable alien accretion to its cities for many decades, but it is experiencing a comparable type of suburban growth. To a greater or lesser extent the forces of urban change and suburban spread are manifesting themselves in all the cities of the world. The outskirts of Paris, Rome, Beirut, Teheran, and São Paulo all exhibit rapidly growing suburban populations. Actually, the movement in America goes back several decades. Originally, semi-country living was pioneered by the upper middle class. But with the advent of the automobile, a means of inexpensive and flexible transportation, this style of life (or some variant form of it) was made available to a vastly increased number of people over a vastly expanded area.

The metropolitan-urban concentration of today presents a continually altering pattern that is different from the railroad metropolis of an earlier epoch.[4] With the exception of Los Angeles and a few newer cities, it is characterized by a central city, the heart of which contains the major business, financial, civic, and amusement activities, and by satellite towns and suburbs. Its real hinterland, the territory into which its influence reaches and from which it derives sustenance and recruits population, as in the case of New York, may be world-wide. But such centers as Atlanta, Kansas City, and Salt Lake City constitute regional counterparts.

The concentration of population and expanded territorial habitat is partially a response to the growth of the city's organizational function accompanied by a parallel concentration of economic and social functions and power. There has not been, however, a comparable centering of industrial activity. On the contrary, the outward dispersion of population, which the automobile hastened, has also aided decentralization of industry. Improved facilities in the transportation of workers, raw materials, and finished products have helped establish both heavy and light industry ever farther from the immediate concentrations of populations. The industrial park and the isolated open country industrial plant have become commonplace.

The decline of the central city as a producing center is only one of several changes that may be observed. No longer are the extremes of skid row and Gold Coast so apparent. These sections are being replaced by new housing developments, and by civic, educational, health, and commercial centers. And concurrent with these changes has been a gradual transmutation of the belts and districts which once gave expression to ethnic and racial distinctions and divisions and to differences of social class and occupation, the exceptions being those cities which have received large increments of rural migrants. Although remnants of these spatially segregated cultural divisions may still be observed, they are as vestigial as the pockets of subsistence farming which may still be found in the backwaters of our agricultural states. The process of reformation has not resulted, however, in a homogeneous population devoid of internal distinctions. Quite to the contrary. The separation and variety of differences have been intensified and have appeared in new spatial distributions, which, unless they are carefully observed, give the illusion of conformity and unity.[5]

Inevitably and increasingly the city is creating an intricate mosaic pattern expressed in settlement and activity. Societal functions of health, education, commerce, finance, transportation, entertainment, and government are illustrative of a few of the specialized activities which are continuing to concentrate in special areas. Physically the separations remain interconnected through communication, while sociologically they are interrelated through organization.

The emerging pattern of the central city will be clearer if we give brief attention to the form which preceded it and which is being recast to give expression to the new social and cultural realities. Burgess was the first to conceptualize the form of the American city for us as a giant circle concentrically zoned around a hub.[6] The commercial district claimed the heart of the city which was surrounded by a zone of deterioration, an area of light industry and family dwellings which had been converted into residences for a migratory population of unmarried young people and newly arrived ethnic or racial groups. The instability of its population was combined with a high incidence of crime, suicide, disease, and other pathological characteristics.

Surrounding this area was the zone of working class residences, a location permitting easy accessibility to the light industries which stretched in a ribbon pattern along the spoke-like railroads which fanned outward from their termini in the hub. Middle and upper income districts constituted outer zones of largely single-family residences, and beyond lay the open country and autonomous towns and villages. Suburban developments, closely linked to the railroad network which provided rapid transit into the city's hub, had also begun to appear. The growing system of freeways has now supplemented and in some instances displaced the railroads which once provided the major arterial connections with the outlying portions of urban settlement.

Districts with specialized function remain a characteristic of the urban pattern, but they are no longer so tightly grouped, and the residential pattern has undergone considerable alteration. The great masses of newly arrived immigrants are no longer relegated to a zone of deterioration as their first point of entry and settlement. The massive resistance of ethnic concentration and residential district has been broken so that in addition to the belts of concentration, like those of the Black Belt of Chicago and Harlem of New York, there are few sections which do not have their cell-like clusters of the newly arrived adjoining or nestled within the residual pockets of the middle class, those survivors of the exodus to the suburbs.

The bulk of the city's population is now composed of the working class: the white-collar workers of bank, office, store, and government bureau and the highly paid blue-collar workers in communication, construction, repair, and light industry, both of these groups seemingly held by the canons of lower middle class propriety; and the semi-skilled and the unskilled, many of whom are the newer migrants from an agrarian environment. Theirs is an anomalous economic position.

The life-style of this latter group constitutes a genuine alternative to the dominant cultural pattern found elsewhere in the country. Unskilled labor, because it is cheap and available in the largest cities, can economically survive there long after it has lost its market value elsewhere. The technically necessary tasks, the lifting and hauling, washing and cleaning, scraping and painting, digging and pounding that are rapidly being turned over to machines in newer and more accessible areas, remain as jobs in our largest and oldest cities. The fantastically high costs of construction and reconstruction in the cities mean that only corporations seeking favorable tax write-offs can construct new, automated, and efficient buildings. The vastly larger proportion of the city's work is done under technological conditions that make unskilled labor a readily saleable commodity; the availability of that labor makes it cheap. Welfare services of many kinds subsidize both employers and employees. And inevitably a cultural pattern appears offering a peculiarly secure and stable life to replace that to which the migrant knows neither he nor his children can return. Opening of the suburbs and raising the technological level of social services in our cities are inevitable, but the consequences for the city's working force have yet to be calculated.

The middle-class remnant is composed of professionals, young unmarried college graduates, the aged, the new bohemians described by Lynes,[7] and the successful executive who, when his children have left the home, has returned from the suburbs to take up residence in the elegant and highly protected newer apartments.

The urban pattern we have described applies to American cities which came to prominence with the development of railroads, industrialization, and heavy European immigration. Urban concentrations in the South and West developed later and in response to different conditions. They do not exhibit an identical type of internal differentiation; their population accretions have come primarily from old American stock; and new forms of transportation have permitted and enforced greater dispersion of population and industrial activities.[8]

LOS ANGELES: AN ALTERNATIVE METROPOLITAN TYPE

Los Angeles may be counted as representing a newer form of metropolitan organization. Whatever its distinctive qualities, it should not be as cavalierly dismissed as in an article in *The New York Times* which described it as "a horizontal monster crawling almost endlessly from the sea to the desert and mountains." Monster or not, the Los Angeles pattern is one toward which other metropolitan areas are moving. For that reason alone it is worthy of careful examination.[9]

Today its metropolitan region contains over six million persons living in the central city and 49 separately incorporated surrounding communities. These latter are dependent upon Los Angeles proper for those public services and governmental functions usually associated with separate municipalities. In fact management of the public schools remains about the only public function for which control is almost wholly localized. It may indeed be highly significant that the dominating feature of the downtown area is a huge and growing civic center, as is the case for several other western cities.

In contrast with other cities, there has been no comparable centralization of merchandising, entertainment, light industry, or professional services in a central hub. These activities are localized in the endless miles of strip development, the shops, offices, and service stations which line the major streets and the newer, compact, and inclusive shopping centers built to accommodate a population on wheels. Incoming industries have not competed for centrally located costly space along railroads and near sources of labor supply but have scattered themselves in open countryside which was soon filled with the split-level and ranch houses of tract developers.

Los Angeles has proved that it is no longer necessary to concentrate the traditionally downtown activities in a central hub. Although areas of specialized activity persist, they are widely separated one from another within the urban spread and at the same time united by complex systems of communication, technology, and organization.

Informality as a style of living has reached its greatest emphasis in the cities and suburban portions of California and the Southwest. It may be seen in dress and mannerism, in entertaining and leisure, in relations between male and female and old and young. Ease in establishing and terminating relationships is a necessary trait in a culture which demands mobility of its members. And in the spatial arrangements of the Southwest and Pacific Coast the physical mobility which permits assembly and dispersal is highly developed.

Although California climate contributes to the pleasures of outdoor living, this factor alone cannot explain the manner in which land surrounding one's house is utilized for a new style of life. The ideal is for each householder to possess all of the requirements for leisurely and relaxed living. There is the garden, patio, barbecue grill, and swimming pool. The troublesome mixing at public facilities is, thereby, avoided and the range of social contacts reduced. The physical arrangements limit gatherings to family and friends but produce a spatial isolation from the immediate environs.

Elsewhere in America the same pattern of exclusiveness for the nuclear family within relatively homogeneous surroundings has made its appearance. But those who inhabit the Greenwiches, Dariens, Beverly Hills, Forest Parks, or Levittowns are carefully screened in the great winnowing process which unites and separates those who are similar and dissimilar. The suburb has become the residential spatial expression of the complex hierarchies of government, business, industry, or profession which organize and direct the American system.[10]

THE FACE OF THE CITY

The face of the city which most of its inhabitants would recognize is found neither in the upper echelons of *Executive Suite*[11] nor among the dispossessed depicted by Nelson Algren.[12]

These are the extremes of privilege and privation. Chayefsky has caught some of its pivotal flavor and action in his drama *Marty*.[13] He portrays an environment deeply segmented into circumscribed locales composed of adjacent streets containing dwellings, shops, and tiny service establishments. Companionship among youth and men, and sometimes women, is sought on the street or within the corner bar. These groups may have originated in childhood days, as described by Whyte in *Street Corner Society*,[14] or they may be the fleeting association of sidewalk or bar stool.

There is no necessary relationship, however, between the life and needs of the family and the street or bar-gathered group and those who sell the goods and provide the services. No human requirement demands or encourages that resident and merchandiser join together for communal goals. Police and fire protection, sanitation, education, entertainment, and in most instances even religion are determined and controlled from afar. The decisions which determine their quality and availability are not matters about which there is direct control. Protest, complaint, or perhaps influence is the available device through which one may be heard. During the decades of boss rule, the ward heeler and precinct captain provided a living link between the little man and the remote powers of government. Today the connection between citizen and civic activities is tenuous at best.

The same discontinuity also exists in other areas of life. Although the resident may be employed within his own circumscribed neighborhood, there is no necessary or functional relation between the two nor between those with whom he works or serves and the other aspects of his social or political life. The greater likelihood is that his place of employment is at some distance, and except for those personal aspects of status, material reward, or individual satisfaction, his source of livelihood and occupation is quite irrelevant to familial, social, political, or community behavior. The exceptions, however, are of major importance, for they control one's ability to satisfy many needs of life, and they are doubly important in a situation in which their effects are limited primarily to family and peers. Kin and friends, and possibly some associates from the place of employment, are the only ones with whom there can be a sharing of the minor victories and defeats which one experiences in the world of work. These are the ones whose judgment counts; others neither know nor care. It is not that the world of work does not have meaning. It does. But its meaning is perceived in terms of the individual's relation to his intimates. The contribution which the worker may make to the social whole is incidental and remote, for the organization in which the work is performed is elusive. It is abstractly referred to as the office, shop, bank, or company. The separation between the circle of intimates and one's work is nearly complete.

The urban neighborhood is not necessarily mean or hopeless, but its orbit is narrow and remains unenriched by the larger environment. Its tendencies are to encapsulate its inhabitants ever more tightly until there remain only the gossiping old cronies who, in good weather, habitually sit upon the tenement stoop in the older city and exchange passing comment upon the moving scene of the street. Among the more affluent there is the isolation of the widowed person or married pair who inhabit the apartment hotels and whose social relations are limited to the doorman, the nearby tradesmen, and occasional dutiful visits of grown-up children. Middle-class neighborhoods differ only in degree from those of the working class. The street has ceased to be the focal center of life, although adolescents may gather in the vicinity of neighborhood drugstore or café. Daytime brings forth clusters of young mothers to assemble with infants in an available protected spot. In the morning and evening there are the inevitable strollers with dogs attached to leashes, protective devices which, startlingly, are also used to limit the ranging of small children. In these areas of middle- and upper-range housing one may observe those human and physical barriers—doormen, watchmen, and walls—which serve the double purpose of protection and enforcement of privacy but which also imprison those whom they secure. These barriers give symbolic expression to the isolation of family and self, a separatism that is intended to exclude the uninvited but is also a measure of the extent to which the centripetality of life has progressed.

The middle class resembles the lower in the lack of opportunity to take part in problems which could unite them with their peers. Their isolation from one another may actually be greater than that of the working class, for within this latter group the extended family of old-world ethnicity and imported customs of coffee house or bodega give some unity which moderates the isolation. And though all groups may share in the communion of church or synagogue, and occasionally of the school, these are activities that at best bring the like-minded and the culturally similar together and reinforce that which is already customary and perceived.

The final notch along the scale of pecuniary and prestige standing belongs to the Social Register. Their identification may be a confusing experience, for in New York and in other American cities there is no one elite which stands squarely astride the social pyramid. Instead, there are a number of elites, each of which is related to the diversity and variety of population which composes the city. The day when a Ward McAllister could preside as an arbiter of social acceptability has passed. Today the divisions are drawn along religious, occupational, and status lines, although among the "upper bohemians" and at the very top the lines may cross. Old family, Protestant city families still constitute the remnant of a once solidly entrenched "high society." In New York, unlike Boston or Philadelphia, their ranks are continuously augmented by successful outlander parvenus. The Catholic elite remains strongly identified with its church and circulates in the orbit of its hierarchy. The top echelon of the Jews is measured by the magnitude of its philanthropic activities and its contributions to Jewish culture. An additional elite is Café Society formed by the International Set and stars of the entertainment world. Urban Negro elites have long existed and add their uniqueness to the variety.

But metropolis is much more than its variegated human population, its circumscribed neighborhoods, and homogeneous suburbs—more than contrasting styles of life expressed in class differences. These cultural aspects do not in themselves call forth the endless movement of people and goods nor explain the vitality which casual observation verifies. Nor should the characteristics we have described be thought of as causes. They should more properly be viewed as manifestations of individuals engaged in activities whose sum total appears as a neatly balanced system of interlocking cooperative endeavors. Material goods are produced and distributed; services are maintained; young men and women marry and beget; and all ages die. Man learns, works, and plays. But whatever the activity or event, it occurs within the context of customary practices and established groups. The flow of life itself sets the limits of our inquiry. Our problem now becomes one of looking beyond the manifest characteristics of metropolis and seeking the nature of the systems and subsystems within which event and activity occur. Our ultimate goal remains that of tracing the existing or absent interconnection and correspondence between the characteristic and cultural perception of the individual and the structure of the groupings in which he participates. Only then may we begin to speak with some assurance of the images which different sorts of human beings hold of themselves and their world and of the commitments by which they are bound.

One may expect that the great metropolitan masses will never perfectly resemble each other. Those of the East Coast will retain both by design and by the limiting restrictions of the past an appearance which links them to old-world urbanism and to the newer American industrialism. Midwestern cities will not completely lose their touch of Main Street. Those of the West will continue relatively unfettered by past rigidities which inhibit further change. But East or West, the great similarity will be found in the correspondence between the type of social groupings, functions, and activities and their representation within the great social superstructures of industry, business, and government.

SOCIAL DIFFERENTIATION AND METROPOLITAN CULTURE

On the surface the new American of metropolitan background seems equalitarian and conformist, a perception which paradoxically is both true and illusory. The insistence upon democracy in public is supported by a mythology which denies fundamental differences among men and is often accompanied by the fiction that each man's opinion counts as much as that of any other. The insistence upon equality is being written into legislation which prohibits discrimination based upon race, color, religion, or national origin and with a strong tendency to include sex and age as additional elements. In contradiction to those who in the 1930's feared that social classes were crystallizing with a diminution of social mobility, there exists today a wider range of opportunity and an approximation to the condition that each man can advance as far as his abilities and the wheels of fortune permit. The illusion of conformity receives additional support from the general upward leveling in the access to consumption goods and the consequent democratization of the "pursuit of happiness." In its extreme form there is the insistence that all persons are equal to all others and especially equal if there is a suspicion of social superiority.

The conditions of life reinforce the illusion. Within the city the pattern of interaction reduces contact with others. And the majority of existing relationships are casual; that is, they have no essential meaning in terms of the problems of the locality or of the larger community. Social separatism is accentuated through the limitation of movement and activity to those who are similar. The situation in the suburb is only slightly different, and although there may be opportunity for greater spatial movement, it occurs within social boundaries which enclose a more rigorously homogeneous and restricted environment than is the case in the city.

In the once prevalent town-community type of organization the basis for defining social class depended upon a configuration of cultural elements which represented organic subcultural systems. One face of the system was the spatially compact residential area for each class. Its other face was the type of community assemblage which brought all or a representative part of the citizenry together for communal purposes. Under these conditions the child, as he moved toward maturity, could have direct experience through participation and observation with those of his own and other social groups. Each individual from time to time expressed and reaffirmed his position and that of others in group life and class structure and thus acquired a sense of community as a whole. By contrast, the cultural limitations within the homogeneous one-level suburbs or the culturally isolated fragments within the city mass inhibit the opportunity to experience or conceptualize the community as a whole. Where the effective experiences of the child represent only a fragment of the whole, he must by necessity interpret and conceptualize behavior and values different than his own in the only frame of reference which he possesses—that of his own isolated experience. Thus, the conditions of metropolitan life encourage the progressive individualization of culture and the fragmentation of the larger social classes into more explicitly defined and narrow social layers.[15]

It may well be that this narrow limitation of individual experience has contributed to ideas of conformity and mass society. When one encounters only those who are like himself in his daily activities, when movements in time and space are channeled in comparable environmental grooves, it is easy to understand why concepts of equality or conformity become accepted. There are few experiences which deny or threaten alikeness. And the cult of "togetherness" throws one further inward and away from even the minute variation of the immediately external world. The intentionally isolated family resembles those religious and ethnic groups which have attempted to resist the centrifugal pull of the larger society by encysting themselves as nearly autonomous cult-communities. The Amish and other pietistic sects attempted to preserve the purity of an earlier agrarian culture by dropping an isolating cultural curtain around their settlements. Such atavistic survivals have little importance except as anthropological curiosities. But the hard fact remains that the contemporary American society encourages, if it does not enforce, isolation of the individual in ever smaller cultural groups. How, one may ask, can such a conclusion be accepted in the face of the extensive mobility of the American people and of their daily comings and goings and of the extensive development of the mass media? Let us seek the answer in the great corporate superstructures of commerce, industry, and government.

It is not our purpose to describe the intricacies of these systems but to emphasize that within and between them may be found graded hierarchies of positions carrying greater or lesser prestige and responsibility. Parallel with these structures are the professions with their own systems of prestige and internal divisions which simulate in structure, although not in size, those of industry and government.

The significant point for us is this: each corporation, each branch of government, each educational institution, each hospital is not only an organization performing some specialized function in the complicated workings of an industrial society but is also organized on the basis of a system of graded positions which carry differential responsibilities, rewards, and prestige. The system of positions usually preserves considerable stability, but movement within organization is never ceasing as individuals are hired, promoted, retired, or resign. The strivings, intrigues, maneuvers, and struggles which determine one's position within the hierarchy of the organization also become a significant factor in the social position which one occupies in the place of residence. These factors are not mutually exclusive, although position within the institutional structure reflects mobility achievement more precisely than does social climbing within the locality.

The type of training which middle-class parents insist their children receive in preparation for adult life provides clear evidence that the goals are institutional rather than community oriented. The least of the expectations is that the new generation will remain in the same locality as their parents. But in order to compete successfully, it is an almost essential requirement that one receive a college education. Hence the compulsive pressure of the parents upon the children for success in college preparation and in the subsequent choice of a college whose name carries prestige.

To a considerable extent industrial workers have been outside the middle-class system of individual competitiveness. Labor's improved status has come from cooperative action through labor organization. But the new industrialism requires fewer and fewer laborers, a fact expressed in the statistics which showed that in 1957 the proportion of industrial workers declined below fifty percent of the whole and continues to decline slowly. Increasingly, their children must seek advanced educational training if they are to find a place for themselves. This conversion to middle-class behavior has already begun through the growth of suburbs for workers.

The careful research that is needed to establish the degree of conformity and the internal dynamics which explain the relationship between the homogeneous suburbs or urban enclaves, on one hand, and institutional position, on the other, is still lacking. But empirical observation combined with census data on income and occupation clearly establishes the correlation. Human society has not yet become an ant hill, but those of comparable occupation and status seek out residential localities composed of others like themselves. Religion, ethnic background, and place of origin are factors which sometimes influence behavior, but these seem less important than institutional status.

Thus, the regrouping of the internal population of the city and its outward spread (with the correlative growth of suburbs) constitutes a cultural reformation based chiefly upon the growth of institutional complexity. This settlement pattern is much more an expression of institutional hierarchy than it is of the basis upon which social class in town-community was formed. The concomitants of family lineage, hereditary occupation and wealth, and participation in community ceremonialism no longer have significant cultural meaning; and the institutional linkages which once tied class to class have no spatial base upon which to operate. The differences within metropolis are not the sum of spatially discrete residential localities but the projection of the remote superstructures.

Community, in its sense of face-to-face interaction, is no longer the containment within one locality of the cultural divisions of social class or of the variety of local groupings—religious, economic, educational—which meet the manifold needs of human life. In fact community disappears before the linkage of status based on corporate position and one's participation in the affairs of place of residence. Under such circumstances there can no longer be the autonomy nor the wholeness of the town-community. Metropolis may contain within its boundaries all that constitutes the concept of community, but the parts have become separated and isolated. The demand for mobility constricts the sense of time in depth, and the fragmentation of functions alters the relation between contained space and the environment. Since the system does not encourage, nor does it perhaps even permit, continuity in the generational sense, history in its functional sense disappears. Instead, the institutional needs of the present take precedence over those of the individual, who must remain constantly poised for social or spatial mobility. Under such circumstances deep ties to community can only prove to be restrictive. To remain settled is to be left behind in the race of life.[16]

What within metropolis replaces the sense of time in continuity that is found in the generational linkage of flesh and blood, in the tradition of locality and event, and in the communication from generations of the past to those of the present? In reality, the great superstructures bridge both time and space, but in this function they cannot remain community bound. Historical pageantry may continue to entertain, but the organic linkages from which the symbols derived their meaning have disappeared. The new organic linkages are those of the superstructures and these must operate within the fluidity of the present. With the loss of history and continuity does there also disappear the sense of tragedy and sacrifice?

These qualities—the sense of history, the meaning of tragedy, generational continuity, and community—have been characteristic of every civilization thus far known. In one sense metropolis is a type of community. Its institutional structure provides continuity beyond that of family lineage. And there may be no real reason why tragedy or history are essential elements of personal or group life. But there does seem to be a real danger in the individualization of culture, since the communal categories of evaluation arise from comparable experiences which have their basis in direct and personal relations with others.[17]

7

VALUING IN CONTEMPORARY AMERICA: A FAMILY CENTERED PERSPECTIVE

As one tries to understand the nuclear family in its relation to the corporate superstructure in American life, one cannot escape the analogy of organism and environment. To a certain point, that analogy is useful; while looking at the details of life within a family situation one senses a background in movement, a subtly but constantly shifting pattern of social organization in the larger public world without which the nuclear family could not exist. But beyond that point the analogy may be more confusing than helpful. In the biological world, gross changes in the physical environment may be considered as primary causes while structural or behavioral changes in organisms are secondary effects. But this mechanistic way of thinking will not do when thinking about the human family as a social institution. The right way to say it is this: the nuclear family is the microcosmic aspect of the same world of which the corporate superstructure is the macrocosmic aspect. Neither is cause, neither effect; each is as it is only because of its systemic involvement with the other.[1]

If we focus attention directly on the contemporary family, we recognize straightway that we have encountered a vital center of American values. But how are we to understand the notoriously tricky word *values*? The word can be used to make fixed and irrevocable moral judgments, as one might say, "The purpose of marriage is to preserve the value of monogamy." Our use of the term, however, is different; we are not concerned with what forms of action and desire ought to be preserved and what forms proscribed, but rather with what desires Americans do, in fact, act upon in the family setting.[2] Hence the gerundive *valuing* is used to indicate that our object is to describe a form of behavior.

Ordinarily, of course, the term *valuing* is used less frequently than *choosing, preferring, selecting, electing,* or even *opting,* when describing the sorts of things one does while shopping, getting married, or professing a religion. But the very generality of the term is its major advantage here.[3] We are seeking to discover what general pattern underlies some of the most important aspects of life in which this form of behavior occurs. It is this pattern, if we can discover it, that we shall call the values of contemporary America.

We are, then, in one sense seeking to discover what American people want from life. But we must, in the process, be very cautious not to substitute tautological verbal formulas for the careful examination of the actual social scene. It is, for example, true that Americans want to be happy. But there is nothing very profound in Aristotle's proposition that happiness is the good for Man; the word *happiness* is simply the most general term in the language for what people in the general tradition of Western culture want from life.[4] And thus the statement that the American people want happiness is true but tautological and not at all illuminating.[5]

The same conclusion must be drawn when it is said that Americans want justice, truth, and beauty in their lives, or in the popular equivalent of W. I. Thomas' four wishes, that they want love, fame, fortune, and adventure.[6] And it is true but of little consequence to say that the American people want what people want. What is instructive we must seek for in the details of *particular* kinds of behavior within a *particular* social setting.

Concerning the social setting in which valuing occurs, one great fact is of overriding importance: the range of choices for satisfying wants has increased exorbitantly and is still increasing in an accelerating fashion in America today. It is, indeed, impossible to exaggerate and difficult to apprehend the significance of this cultural phenomenon. In most times and places the details of human life have been regulated within narrow limits by the twin forces of custom and necessity. When, for example, rice is the available food, people eat rice, and the way of life associated with a rice-growing and rice-eating culture perseveres.[7] But the series of technological revolutions of the past two centuries have attenuated the force of economic necessity, and in so doing have splintered the customs.

Today when the American housewife enters a supermarket, she is literally forced to choose among a bewildering variety of articles of which almost any combination will satisfy the physical needs of her family and the accepted standards of her social group. Nor is she driven by any hidden necessity whose recognition would free her from the illusion of choice. For choice *is* the ultimate reality of the situation; the illusion is in the standards by which choices must be made. She must choose between a half-dozen brands of bottled milk whose contents would be indistinguishable to the most precise chemical analysis. Or she must select from among the powdered and canned milk products which provide equivalent calcium and protein at lower cost but also (for most) less pleasant taste. And she must decide whether it is better to save a few cents here and apply it to other goods or to elect the convenience and flavor of the homogenized, pasteurized, vitamin-enriched bottled product.

The example is trivial, but the point is profound. The economic theories of choice behavior based on the concepts of marginal differentiation and utility simply do not apply here. When the range of choice has been increased beyond a certain critical point, the choosing itself cannot be other than arbitrary at the conscious level, manipulable at the unconscious level.

A vast qualitative gulf lies between the kind of choosing nearly all contemporary Americans are forced to do and the kind of choosing a few fortunate members of an agrarian society were privileged to do. For the latter, special training in moral standards and esthetic taste became the central matter in all deliberate education. Both classical economic theory and the liberal democratic state assumed the beautifully effective education-for-choosing that was characteristic of English and colonial gentlemen. The downward extension of schooling was always ideally viewed as a necessary corollary to the downward extension of the ballot and economic freedom.

The difference between privileged and mass choosing is not merely in the opportunity for choice. This difference between the earlier condition in which a few well-instructed men had opportunities for choice and the present condition in which virtually everyone, instructed or not, can and must select from a variety of physical and spiritual goods as he wishes certainly exists, and it certainly poses some obligations to educators. But the difference is really minor when compared to a second one: the range of choices has increased to the point where no one can be said to choose rationally on any significant portion of his life style.

Both John Dewey and William James took the forked-road example as the basic image of intelligence operating in choices.[8] A stroller is passing through a pleasant wood, casually aware of and attentive to the various details of his surroundings. He encounters a fork in the road. The casual interest disappears; he begins to regard clouds, the clock, distances, and temperature not just for what they are in themselves but for their meaning, that is, as signs indicative of the consequences of the alternatives presented. Having appraised the situation, the traveler then chooses one or the other in accordance with his purposes, which include not only the enjoyment of the present moment but also the duties and obligations inseparable from his deepest conception of self.

There is more than a touch of anachronism in this quaint picture. Suppose there are a large number of alternatives rather than only two; suppose these come every few steps rather than only once in the course of a stroll. Suppose one's purposes, as both Dewey and James would hold, are themselves reconstructed in part by each decision made. What then would it mean to be intelligent in choosing? The immediate, common sense response is probably the most accurate. It would mean simply to continue moving without trying to do more than keep a general direction so that at least one does not double back onto the same trail. The man who tries to apply the techniques of problem-solving at each decision point is, in effect, electing to stand still, and that, in contemporary America, is to die.

Despite its nightmarish quality, the latter picture is probably closer to the actual quality of choice-making in this day than is that of Dewey and James. To deny the inner-directed, pragmatic model of intelligent choosing leaves us with the picture of men and women more conscious of the need to continue in motion than of the direction in which they are going or of the reason for moving at all. Let us turn now to some of the different kinds of choices that are made in this movement through life, testing, as it were, this conception of valuing as behavior. Keeping in mind the centrality of the housewife in the supermarket as the basic image for conveying what we mean by valuing, let us turn to the family itself and then outward to religion, art, and politics.

FAMILY LIFE: ISOLATION—BELONGING VERSUS PRIVACY

In our discussion of settlement patterns we obtained an insight into the values associated with family life. The new metropolitan pattern represents a peculiar form of compromise between the ultimate isolation of the small family unit and the sense of belonging which makes that isolation tolerable. This same kind of compromise also operates within the small family itself in respect to the relations of the individuals and generations that comprise it. What specifically does this mean?

Everyone is well aware of the ideal of a good neighborhood in suburban communities. It is one in which this compromise has been worked out to the satisfaction of all concerned and is maintained by a system of subtle but significant symbols. It is typically expressed in language like this: "We have a good neighborhood. The people here are very friendly. We visit back and forth occasionally; we even get together every so often for cocktails. But we don't intrude on each other's privacy."

This is quite obviously a very delicate sort of adjustment to make, and all the more difficult because of the absence of commonly recognized symbols to indicate desire for companionship or privacy. In some English colleges, so we are told, there are double doors to the dons' rooms. If only one is shut, it implies that the person inside is willing to receive visitors. But if the occupant has "sported the oak," that is, closed the outer door, he has signed himself off from disturbance. This device, in all probability, did not come into being simultaneously with the college system but rather developed slowly in response to that same problem of reconciling social intercourse with privacy that the small family in contemporary society faces.

In the absence of such obvious devices, the individual American family simply must be extra-sensitive to the social cues that determine the particular symbols of his own neighborhood. We are flooded with examples, showing more pathos than tragedy, of neighborhoods and families that failed to make the compromise work. In the time when Park Forest was a brand new Chicago suburb, many young couples found their privacy lost in the morning *Kaffeeklatsch*, the afternoon invasion by neighbor's children, and the evening community project. When in desperation a wife closed her front door and opened her Plato, she may have unwittingly overstepped that narrow line of "unneighborliness" and found herself ostracized by her environing residents.[9] While this situation was often quite uncomfortable for a time, in the long run Park Forest, along with other American neighborhoods large and small, old and new, did manage to evolve compromises that worked with fair success. Given enough time and the continuation of present rates of geographical mobility, a nation-wide system of standardized symbols will probably evolve, and this will certainly ease the burden of day-to-day adjustments by those who move in and out of new neighborhoods.

The first level of observation, then, would show the American seeking a synthesis between the values of friendship and privacy. But we wish to probe a bit deeper and ask, Privacy for what? Interaction for what? Is it not true that neighborhood interaction in America has fundamentally no object outside itself? We recognize, of course, that there are many illustrations of neighborhood projects that are very purposeful in nature: working out plans for harmony in home decoration, preparing petitions, improving neighborhood facilities, or joining to protect local tranquillity against invasions by the corporate world. But these examples do not vitiate the main thought of our hypothesis. For even when purposes are quite real, neighborhood projects tend to be more concerned with process than product, more likely to be thought about and discussed in terms of the interaction that occurred than what results were achieved. More importantly, neighborhood projects seldom touch upon those aspects of life that reach most deeply into the human spirit. The great ceremonial occasions of the human cycle—birth, puberty, marriage, and death—are recognized in neighborhood interaction but only in the most attenuated and symbolic fashion. The actual agencies which participate with the family in these ceremonies are not neighborhood groups but professional functionaries. Neighborhood friends may prepare a dish or send a wreath, but the hospital delivers the child and the undertaker buries the body.

To say that neighborhood interaction has no object outside itself is not to say that it is unimportant. The very absence of obvious utilitarian purpose makes possible the wealth of phatic communication that is apparently as necessary to human beings as singing is to mockingbirds. Yet the infinite variety of this form of human behavior should not blind us to its underlying uniformity. Around whatever common symbols are available—whether baseball, the weather, the Russians, Sartre's latest play, the house or yard, children and school, an outbreak of illness, violations of mores, or any other—discourse rambles, while identity of person and structure of group become established. Jane who simply has to have her way about things . . . George who has infinite patience in explaining how to do-it-yourself . . . Dorothy who is too good for her own good . . . Alice who shirks her neighborhood responsibilities while trying to get ahead in the next higher social group . . . and so on. The neighborhood system permits almost infinite variety of personal idiosyncrasy because it has few utilitarian functions to which individuality must be subordinated.

These few utilitarian functions are well known, for certain forms of behavior threaten the welfare of the neighborhood group, and these must be made known to newcomers early. They include failure to maintain the external appearance of one's property in accordance with the neighborhood's standard of decency, failure to repress vandalism in children, entertaining in kind and amount that disturbs neighbors, and the like. A newcomer to a neighborhood needs no explicit warnings when he hears the history of the Smiths "who were really never happy here. She would insist upon sunbathing in the front yard, he let that house go unpainted, and those kids, well . . ."

There appear to be some differences between Jewish and Protestant neighborhood behavior. The pattern we described above is typical of the Protestant suburban way, which depends in the main upon the individual conscience to apprehend the true light and follow it. In economically comparable Jewish neighborhoods, there seems to be somewhat more explicitness about the Law of the Neighborhood, which helps considerably on the points that it covers, as for example, just how often you should repaint your house. But when a contingency that has not been taken into account arises, the difficulties become greater. For instance, in a not-too-wealthy neighborhood, just how much affluence does one have to achieve before he is entitled to build a private swimming pool? Should he move out of the neighborhood if he is determined to have one although none is to be found on surrounding properties? It requires considerable ingenuity and even more good will to keep the Law up-to-date.

The functions and values of neighborhood interaction are open to observation, and thus their description is relatively simple. Interaction expresses personality and in so doing establishes a group that supports the personalities of its members. It regulates certain relatively superficial aspects of personal behavior. But when we attempt to look inside the small family itself, we are suddenly met by an opaque screen. Privacy is well-nigh inviolable, and when we ask, Privacy for what? we find the question difficult to answer. Clues are available as to what goes *into* the home. We notice from the fluctuations in the do-it-yourself industry that this form of family action has moved from hobbies to essentials, from luxuries to currently defined necessities. Television fare seems to follow certain predictable fashions. Vogues in home furnishings and decorations as well as in the mythology of child rearing can easily be traced.

But what values are being sought and what values have been achieved behind the façade of the home? Because we do not know, we are likely to say that privacy is sought purely for the sake of privacy, and that while the wall between the neighborhood and the small family is erected to secure privacy for the family, the continual struggle within the family is to secure privacy for the individual person. There is certain evidence to support this hypothesis, as in the ideal of one bedroom, and more strikingly one bathroom, per person. A best seller by Robert Paul Smith, *Where Did You Go? Out. What Did You Do? Nothing.* made a convincing as well as amusing case for the thesis that the major problem of the relation of generations is to be found in their lack of privacy from each other. Tom Sawyer and Penrod had a defensible privacy from adults that Mr. Smith sees as regrettably disappearing.

On the other hand, it may well be that the companionate family, as defined by Burgess and Locke, is in search of a deeper and richer form of human association than can be found in neighborhood or peer group relations.[10] The thesis of this chapter is that a blind necessity to keep moving is the most obvious fact about all contemporary valuing behavior. The pattern described for neighborhood interaction is admirably designed to facilitate rapid and unfettered movement. It is a pattern of relations that comes to dominate friendships that are not distinctly neighborhood in location. But all this leaves out that form of human association which penetrates to the roots of personality and overcomes the loneliness which so often occurs in a crowd. This deeper kind of relation we must call by its right name: love. For persons on the move and moving in small family units, other relations necessarily remain tenuous and easily broken; love must be found, if at all, within the small family. And we know, both intuitively and on sound psychological evidence, that without love the human spirit simply cannot survive.[11]

But what sort of love? Not the brotherly love of the Greeks, the charity of Christianity, nor the romantic passion of every generation's youth. The apotheosis of brotherly love is in the sacrifice of self for the other, of Christian charity in Christ's sacrifice for *all* humanity, of romantic love—as in Romeo and Juliet, Dante and Beatrice, Rudolfo and Mimi—in the parting (whether by death or social convention) of the lovers, which is the only suitable denouement of the problem set by the attachment itself.

But in the modern nuclear family none of these models is appropriate. Love is not considered a relation in which one loses or even transforms self; rather it is a support to the search for self-fulfillment. There is no parting save the anticlimactic separation by the long-delayed death of one (usually the male) partner. It is the relation most peculiarly tied to the profound wells of human selfhood in contemporary America. But it is unsung, indeed unsingable, in our literature. The nuclear family has no universal symbols; rather each family must painfully establish its own identity by and with *things*, a practice fostered by misleadingly named community property laws.

The things a family accumulates, as one very astute set of observers has pointed out, become a part of its identity more deeply than the house which the family so tenuously owns. "It is really the movables which create the air of homeliness, and which are psychologically immovable, rather than the physically rooted house which is there to be moved into, grown into, moved out of and left behind—an outmoded shell to be reoccupied by another mobile family."[12]

The small family, then, is required to support the deepest sort of human relation, to accomplish within itself what the agrarian society was able to spread out over an entire community. An extended family system and peer relations that persevered for a lifetime allowed love to be extended and received in various amounts and in various modes, all of which are now concentrated in the small family. Togetherness, recently and significantly banned from the cover of *McCall's Magazine,* becomes a potentially explosive force. In fact the truly amazing thing in historical and anthropological perspective is that the system works at all. But work it does, even the divorce rate having hit some relatively stable plateau, meaning in effect that it simply takes a certain amount of trial and error to get the particular people together who can manage this potently destructive system of relations.

Changes in dating and courtship patterns indicate a growing seriousness on the part of adolescents as they face the prospects of marriage. The constantly improving art of marriage counseling helps to minimize the number of initial mistakes in undertaking family living and to relieve the tragedy of failures when they occur. These counselors have come to recognize the marvelously functional value in our apparently chaotic system of dating and courtship. The response of the heart may be the best evidence a young man or woman can find for deciding whether to lock a lifetime into one orbit or another. For the old saying about "marrying and settling down" no longer applies. One's lifetime is still in motion, only now its motion is linked with that of another, a condition that must produce strains and stresses.

For in the final analysis the culture requires that the man and the woman and the children constituting a family shut the doors of their house or apartment, to face each other day after day, either to love or to perish.

Measured against the traditions of the human race, the small family pattern of contemporary suburban America represents a genuine transvaluation of values. For although the relations between concrete individuals were always less than completely predictable and culturally determined, they were nevertheless supported within a larger system of relations that provided stability and predictability not directly found in the personal interaction itself. The larger system provided support for the exigencies of interpersonal intercourse in the very concrete sense that individuals who found difficulty in one relationship were able to find reinforcing expectations, social control, and personal solace through a wide range of other relationships. Studies ranging from Chinese village life to American peer culture reveal the universality of this social phenomenon.[13] But given the psychological necessity for movement, both geographically and socially, and for the acceptance of the outward movement of others, the contemporary American man, woman, and child must find within the small family itself the social control and personal solace necessary for human existence. The values formerly given with membership in a larger group now become the values sought for in the small family itself. This is the transvaluation. It is illustrated in the attention of employers to personal relations among employees, and more dramatically, in the changing systems of interaction during courtship. Only a few years ago, young men and women relied upon the stability of their peer group status and participation in its broader sense in the affairs of the community to relieve the strain of interpersonal relations with potential marriage partners. Today just the opposite seems to obtain: within the stability of the relation of the "steady date," young people find a basis for adjusting to a rapidly and unpredictably changing larger social system.[14]

CHURCH ACTIVITY: AN EMOTIONAL ADJUNCT

Very many explanations have been offered for the current resurgence of interest in religion and the growth in church membership in the United States, which for lack of time and space cannot be considered here. But in the points made above concerning the problem of small family life in America, there may be a definite clue for the so-called revival of religion. For like the small family, the church has no essential relation to the community in which it is found. It does not collect the taxes, nor dispose of the sewage and garbage, nor protect property and person, nor provide light and heat, nor even take care of the community's obligations for benevolent, philanthropic care. These tasks have become, as they had to become, the domain of professional functionaries. Well, then, what does the church do? Madison Avenue has given us a clue in the doggerel cliché: "The family that prays together stays together!"

The behavior required in the actual church service seems to bear an isomorphic resemblance to behavior in the small family. One can move from community to community and still find in the church or synagogue of his (euphemistically labeled) choice the same rituals, the familiar, self-enhancing, and supporting activities. And church behavior can and does go on out of *any* relation, either to the details of the particular community in which it is found, or more importantly, to the intellectual content of the religious beliefs. Sophisticated morals and taste are shocked by the overtones of primitive cannibalism in the symbolic act of the Sacrament of Communion and by the ethically repulsive doctrines of the Covenant and the Atonement. None of this matters essentially, however, for no one attends to the doctrines. The visual and auditory sensations of the service itself, the élan of the shared activity, are taken by the communicant of whatever faith essentially at their surface value, without attention to the content of the symbols.

As we might expect, the "message" of the contemporary church in the United States—Catholic, Protestant, or Jewish—says this:

"The relation of love which you seek so desperately in your personal life is supported by the basic structure of the world. Do justice, walk humbly with thy God, seek with a contrite heart, and you will find that the relation you *must* establish can be established." It is a message that can be apprehended in the privacy of the individual and shared within the small family circle, without giving any hostages to the local community that would complicate the ever present necessity to be on the move. But the words of this credo have to be specifically set within the context of the rituals, perhaps better, within the behavior of the church itself; hence the emphasis on specificity in church dogma that is characteristic of contemporary society. The movement toward union of community churches devoid of specific doctrine has been arrested if not definitely turned back. For the message mentioned above simply cannot be personally incorporated within the abstract language of rational science or philosophy. Technically it is an attitude rather than a belief, and we are well aware that attitudes are formed by participation, not by argument. But cast in language that pervades the behavior and emotional participation of the church itself, the message becomes personally significant. That he can find in his church support for the love he must establish in his mobile family is at least (or perhaps, at most) the hope of the church communicant. How effective churches are in the support of love in families is difficult to determine. Though there is some evidence that community of religious persuasion is correlated significantly with family stability, interpretation of this evidence allows a great deal of latitude. There may well be some more obscure third factor. But the obvious signs of church membership, the official adoption of religious motifs in national symbols, the increasing attractiveness of theology in nonreligious studies, and the apparent rise in the quality of church functionaries all point to a kind of faith that the church communion is essential to the system of values in American life. And the analysis above, if correct, would center this faith in the dominant locus of valuing behavior, namely the mobile small family.

It is necessary to try to comprehend the significance of non-ritualistic forms of association that often center around church activities. These follow without any serious modification the pattern and function of neighborhood interaction we have described. The church merely serves as a convenient locus and occasion for interaction which could occur just as well, and perhaps a bit more convivially, elsewhere. And yet is this the entire picture? Isn't one's church membership possibly a surrogate for feelings of blood, for extended kinship, for traditions that transcend generations, for a sense of belonging to the saved and of separateness from the damned—in short a surrogate for all those exclusive feelings which are rightly regarded as inappropriate in the great corporate world of metropolis? One hesitates to answer affirmatively, for surely American churches have finally learned to oppose the destructive particularisms of race and nationality. But have they learned to oppose *all* destructive particularisms? Is any binding and constructive particularism between nuclear family and corporate outer world really possible? The churches of America have not yet found an answer.

Will Herberg says that Americans understand the question, "What are you?" as asking for one's religious affiliation. Certainly it *can* carry that meaning.[15] And if, as we have been arguing, the burden of Americans is to keep forever asking "Who am I and what shall I become?" then the association within the church is at least a starting point; here one is for the moment sure of what he *now* is.

Despite the inevitable tendency of church groups to separate along socio-economic lines and, in turn, to transform the mosaic of metropolitan settlement into a religious design, still the church is not a distinctively community agency. In ever more formalized corporate structures, the churches represent associations that divide the nation but could in principle unite the world. The search for privacy and relatedness in the church is subtly different from what it is elsewhere. And thus the family strives to assure identity to its children by giving them their names while enrolling them in a church.

THE ESTHETIC VALUES: MASS ART AND PRIVATE SYMBOLS

When we turn to the question of the values sought for and achieved through activities related to one or more of the art forms in contemporary society, our thesis that the necessity to be on the move is the key fact for understanding typical modes of valuing seems to break down completely. Now it would be easy, and superficially correct, to point out that some particular level of taste is associated with a particular life-style, that as families change life-style—and this involves changing neighborhood, forms of inter-family association, and often church affiliation—they are also expected to change taste in the arts, to acquire new symbols for the public communication of their neighborhood-type association. Thus in one social group it is quite proper in the course of conversation to mention an article in the *Reader's Digest*. In other groups this would mark one immediately as outside the pale. Selection of television shows, choice in music, pictures on the walls, furniture, and the various objects possessed by a family can all be rated on some scale of taste; and a family that is moving may find itself faced with the necessity to spend money and to part with comfortable possessions in order to meet the demands of a new life-style, whether the move is geographical or social. The valuing of objects, like the valuing of other human beings in neighborhood interaction, has to be at that psychic distance which enables the dissolution of the relation to take place without serious stress on personality. Hence the superficiality of taste in America, the hypocrisy of expressed judgments, and the other indictments of Americans' relations to their arts.[16]

Still, when we look at the situation in the arts we must ask whether those values traditionally conceived as being distinctive to esthetic activities are changing their significance in the contemporary social scene.

It used to be good fun to identify Communists and fellow

travelers by their judgments of the arts. Experts at the game would refrain from the obvious questions, such as asking for a relative ranking of Hemingway and Howard Fast. Rather, depending upon the interest and sophistication of the respondent, they might mention the architectural merits of the Brooklyn Bridge and the Eiffel Tower (the first is beautiful, the second stinks), Tintoretto versus Raphael as painters, respectively powerful and effete, and so on through media and periods. No single answer determined the issue; pattern and consistency were the telltale symptoms. Genuine cognoscenti were seldom surprised by the judgments that they made and verified by turning to such topics as an interpretation of the Spanish Civil War.

But all that was long ago. It was a reflection of an anachronistic—and as you wish, amusing, pathetic, or infuriating—wholeness in value judgments. The separation of esthetic values from moral and political values in a total society is a recent, perhaps unique phenomenon. If we may judge from Plato's violence in rejecting it, *ars gratia artis* was an ancient doctrine before Latin was a civilized tongue. But its ancient, or medieval, or even nineteenth century adherents were always a small minority sitting atop a folk society in which the arts were integral with the rest of life, in which the standards of esthetic taste and moral worth were indistinguishable to those who used them. The pre-Korean left-winger was, as he would have wished to be, much closer to the "natural" tendency of human beings in all times and places than were his tormentors.[17]

The dominating fact of contemporary society, however, is that these judgments are now quite distinct for the masses as well as for the literati. Most of those who deplore, applaud, or apologize for the mass arts seem to miss the crucial significance of the fact that when the masses revolted they seized, among other things, the right to make esthetic judgments on bases that are quite separate from utilitarian effectiveness, political expediency (Plato), moral worth, or any other basis whatsoever. Far from being cynical, it was a remarkably accurate stroke to make *ars gratia artis* the motto of Metro-Goldwyn-Mayer. Whatever may have been Sam Goldwyn's personal motivation in producing his films, the general public accepted or rejected his offerings on one, purely esthetic, criterion: whether or not they enjoyed them.

This is not to say that enjoyment is the only esthetic criterion that could or should be applied to motion pictures. It is only to say that, save in a truly insignificant proportion of cases, people do not attend movies to make money, save their souls, gain political advantage, appease the gods, or reinforce a sense of community. For these purposes one might go to work, to church, or to lodge meeting. But one goes to the movies in order to give attention to a work of art for the purpose of enjoying it. At least in this residual sense the criterion applied to movies is a purely esthetic one. (One genuine exception to this will be found in those who attend the movies in order to engage in the non-consummatory love making that is central to the American courtship system. But even so, the number of passive observers is still overwhelmingly greater than the number of active participants.)

What has been said of the movies applies a fortiori to the other forms of mass art. And on the next point, we have to accept the verdict of the viewers-with-alarm: in contemporary American society, there can be no permanent separation of mass art from high art. The efforts of the *avant-garde* to get ahead are matched by the efforts of the masses to catch up. Dance sequences in musicals, whether on Broadway, the movies, or television, owe more to Diaghilev and Isadora Duncan than they do to the significantly named "production numbers" of Florenz Ziegfeld and George M. Cohan. Poems used as fillers in the *Saturday Evening Post* have more than traces of Edgar A. Guest, but the patterns of *Poetry* are penetrating, and Ogden Nash is already there, waiting. The distortedly long legs found in calendar art may not owe their direct inspiration to Picasso, but somehow people learned not to expect photographic accuracy in paintings, even in those done with an airbrush. The picture window in every split-level home owes a debt to the Bauhaus. In however degenerate form, Detroit each year pays tribute to Moholy-Nagy. And so on through all the popular arts and art objects. Whether one judges it as advance in mass art or loss of creativity in high art, the fact remains that the gap between is very difficult to maintain.[18]

There is, admittedly, a possibly alarming aspect to the marching together of mass art and high art. If we define mass art as all those objects or activities produced specifically to provide enjoyment for large numbers of people, high art becomes that which is produced to satisfy canons that transcend but do not exclude enjoyment. For high art must be enjoyable, at least to some, before it can be art at all.

It is, moreover, difficult for the serious artist to avoid such hazards as isolation from his audience, involvement in the cultism of a select circle, and over-attention to uneducated taste. The standards that enable high art continually to enliven mass art are undoubtedly difficult to maintain in the face of the pressure and the all-encompassing demand of mass art for the immediately enjoyable. There are those who claim that we are still reaping the benefits in mass art of developments that occurred several decades previously in high art, benefits that will cease as soon as the wells dry up. But one is led to doubt the immediacy of the threat as one observes the vitality and dedication of college and university departments devoted to the various arts. If some posturing is to be found there occasionally, there is also the protection necessary to create new forms. And if what is true of college and university finds its echoes in other enclaves within the total society, it is not fatal that all high art is under constant pressure to become mass art and give up all criteria other than pleasing mass taste. The pressure will overcome some (Erskine Caldwell), it will drive others to self-stultifying extremes of eccentricity, but a sufficient number will survive to provide the nucleus for the constant reënrichment of mass art.

(The analogy between the basic and applied sciences and the high and mass arts is obvious. The best reply to those who claim that industries are using up basic scientific knowledge without replenishing the store is to point to the well-known fact that more basic research is now being carried on in industrial laboratories than in all colleges and universities a generation ago. Insofar as they are not doing so now, distributors of the mass arts might do well to take a leaf from the same book. Colleges and universities are perhaps not the only places in which to nourish the rare spirits who will add new techniques and stimulate jaded appetites for the mass arts.)

The problem of the high arts is, however, not our concern. The major fact we have to contend with is that the esthetic goods of life are now for all Americans what they once were for only a small elite; that is, available without let or hindrance, to be chosen in supermarket-fashion as one finds enjoyment in the choosing and appropriating. This seems much more fundamental than the relatively obvious relation of taste to social class. The cobbler who likes opera, the professor of English who reads comic books—these are much more the current symbols of the status of the arts in America than is the pathetically affected discourse of the Literary Society in *Main Street*.[19] For a minority, designated the Upper Bohemians by Russell Lynes, participation in the high arts is definitive of a life-style; but for most Americans, for those who spend more money on concerts than on baseball and more on recordings of serious music than on either, the arts—high or low—stand outside the major determinants of social position.[20]

It is in this context that our original thesis concerning the necessity for mobility has to be tested. And put to the test, it offers little explanation for the phenomena mentioned here. Perhaps the tremendous range of available choices and the wide limits of social acceptability for choosing make it possible for individual families to develop some bases for love and companionship that center around participation in the arts. But this is pure speculation for which no evidence is offered. Is it really the case that watching television, listening to the hi-fi, or reading the same books form a basis for establishing love within the small family?

What is the typical mode of interaction while engaging in these activities jointly? Is entertainment as found in whatever art form an effective means for shielding the different ages and sexes within the small family from irritating contact with each other? These are questions for research that are suggested by the overall analysis, but they cannot be answered by abstract speculation.

This much, however, is clear. The individual family need not relinquish its privacy while securing the richness and fullness of the arts; they come to the family through the good offices of the corporate system. Today when one asks about the meaning of the arts in American life, he is asking about one of two things: What do the great corporate superstructures of American society do to, and for, the arts (and vice versa)? And what do the arts do in the lives of individuals? In the struggle of families to find a bearable balance between privacy and belonging in local communities, the arts, seem to make no contribution. We must later inquire whether they have actually no contribution to make.

THE POLITICAL VALUES OF THE AMERICAN PEOPLE AS SYMBOLIC SYSTEMS RICHLY, WIDELY, DEEPLY EXTENDED

American culture is blessed with a magnificent range of symbolic values extending back in time, outwardly wide in application, inwardly deep in conscience. The distinctively American documents expressive of our values are built upon literally millennia of progress in refining values—the Hellenic conceptions of virtue in man and polis, the Roman conception of impartial justice under law, the Judaic feeling for the brotherhood of man under the fatherhood of God, the Christian ideals of charity and love, the medieval search for peace and order—all of these are preserved and caught up in the definitely political progenitors of our Declaration of Independence, Preamble to the Constitution, Gettysburg Address, Fourteen Points, Fair Deal, and now a New Frontier. In history there are no absolute beginnings, but there can be disastrous endings. Fortunately, the American system of symbolic values is tied neither to a beginning nor to an end but is as cumulative as the steady progress in mathematics.

The importance of this can be grasped only by seeing it in contrast to the system of values of western Europe. Since the eighteenth century a transvaluation of European political values has been taking place; that is to say, those values that stood uppermost in the symbolic systems prior to that time have been deliberately devalued and other values substituted in their place. In actuality this is probably a continuous process, but certain cataclysmic events can be pointed to by way of illustration. The first was the French Revolution. Whatever values came to be associated with the *ancien régime* were regarded by the revolutionists in France as the antitheses of real ones. Local and religious loyalties were attacked deliberately and as nearly as possible wiped out. In other European nations the revolutionary movements of the first half of the nineteenth century were also, almost without exception, carried forward under banners that repudiated the traditional symbols of value of the previous eras. But the nihilistic aspects of the French Revolution gained a strong foothold neither in this country nor in England. A second event, however, did have repercussions in England, namely the appearance of revolutionary socialism or Marxist communism. The main tenet of Marxism, so far as symbolic value systems are concerned, is that all the symbolic values of a bourgeois society are merely tools for the psychic manipulation of the proletariat. A person who comes to feel that his respect for patriotism, honesty, and compromise is in actuality a tool in the hands of his enemies can experience this transvaluation of values in an intensely personal sense. And if, when the lines are drawn, he still marches with his nation rather than with his class, he no longer does so out of motives that he can defend to his own intellect but rather out of deep, irrational urges. This is what took place in the third event, with the appearance of fascism. Symbolic value systems sprang up that were not only contrary to the traditional values of western Europe, but out of all historical or continuous relation to them. The symbols of church, science, humanism, democracy, and progress were distorted out of all recognition in the Fascist ideology. The major problem of reconstruction facing western Europe even today is essentially that of revivifying its traditional political symbols.

But the United States by and large felt only the most remote tremors from these European cataclysms. On the contrary, the dominant value symbols were strengthened by the challenges they faced in this country, specifically the challenge of being ingested by a continuing press of new immigrants. For although there seems to be a limited life span to symbolic values, however long the extrinsic form of the symbol survives, those of the United States escaped extinction by being continuously renewed in the process of becoming the symbolic values of new Americans. Hyman Kaplan was made a bigger and better man by the Gettysburg Address, but the Gettysburg Address was given a new meaning and a fresh significance through the mind and spirit of Hyman Kaplan.[21] Thus the American political symbols were not only extended but also rejuvenated.

If a long enough time span is considered, the outward extension in application is also seen as a linear curve. We have yet to accord to the once heathen, now Communist, Chinese truly full equality to life, liberty, and the pursuit of happiness in whatever form they wish to pursue it; but we have also moved a long way from those ambiguous words in the Constitution that speak of "other persons" as being only partly entitled to the full protection of the law. Women, children, aliens, Indians, Negroes, and now the mentally ill have gradually been incorporated into the body of all men to whom are due certain goods that society has to offer. And as with time the available goods have increased in scope, so too has the meaning of the rights. Society can no longer offer the right to suffer, starve, and perhaps succeed on the geographical frontier, but it can and does offer freedom from starvation to those no longer able to work productively. The application of the value system has thus been expanded to more people and extended to a more inclusive conception of our society's goods.

The extension inward into private conscience is indicated by the public statements of political leaders who seem compelled by inward motives to couch the most obvious matters of expediency in the ceremonial language of our symbolic values. This behavior, particularly noticeable in President Eisenhower, was frequently criticized as being hypocritical; but a more reasonable interpretation would be that Eisenhower, like other Americans, has so deeply internalized these symbols that they have become the natural vehicle for expressing anything whatsoever. More revealing indications of this phenomenon may be found in the advertising and public relations industries. It seems impossible for many of these highly literate and articulate men and women to take their job at face value, as simply a kind of activity that is rather highly rewarded in the economic system. In private conversation and in public utterance they display the most curious ambivalence. Privately they pay the most reverent homage to the symbolic values by the direct flouting of them, for there seems to be a compulsion on their part to assert (1) "We do not, we cannot contribute anything to the general welfare, to the promotion of happiness in its best sense among men," and (2) "We are therefore the most abominable of creatures." At the same time in public utterances, spokesmen for these industries attach their activities as directly as possible to the dominant value symbols. Such behavior could not reasonably be interpreted as a purely cold and calculating pursuit of power and fortune. It seems rather to be a kind of ambivalence that we should expect from a group directly concerned with symbolic action having no obvious congruence with dominant value symbols of the culture. Production men, who are concerned with things other than symbols, do not seem to require so desperately to be identified with the political symbols of our nation.

The situation of the profession of education, another occupation that is predominantly symbolic, is in a way precisely the opposite of the advertising profession. Educators have already identified their function with the dominant political symbols. Schools are readily associated with the preservation of democracy, with maximizing the potentialities of each individual, with the establishment of socially useful habits and skills, etc., all of which obviously and directly connect with the symbols of the great historical documents expressive of national ideals. And in turn educators become afflicted with uneasy consciences because their work *is* so closely tied to the dominant value system. The language of moral imperative becomes the natural speech of educators, and every discrepancy between the ideals of this language and the often grubby facts of educational practice becomes a personal affront to the conscience of educators.[22] Here again, we find that among those who deal directly in symbols, the inward extension of symbolic values to private conscience is an observable phenomenon.

It is quite easy to see that in America an ever larger proportion of men and women work not with material things but with symbols. And whether as workers in the so-called media industries or as jealously individual poets, those who have succeeded in escaping traditional clichés of language and thought display a frighteningly articulate objectivity toward every aspect of their world. Cynicism, nihilism, withdrawal, and despair are not unknown among those who have most clearly succeeded in the largely verbal education they have received. But when we examine the meaning of this disaffection among those who live by words, we must recognize the complete absence of any formulated alternatives to the long tradition of symbolic values that represent America. Disaffection is a personal, not a social or political phenomenon, and this is in many ways unfortunate, for our tradition of symbolic values has been kept vital and growing because of the constant enrichment of criticism. But this same phenomenon also is evidence that the symbolic values of America have extended so deeply into the American consciousness that even the disillusioned intellectual cannot seriously conceive of an alternative, however personally alienated he may find himself from the social system that is supposed to express those values.

Let us now look, superficially though it must be, at the substance of American value symbols. The fact that they cluster largely around the state as an institution is no mere accident. This is to be expected in the light of American history, especially that portion of our history in which primary commitments to the nation, its establishment and its preservation, gave the dramatic tone and the emotive meaning to our national symbols. Our national heroes are almost without exception men of state. Americans have had no authentic geniuses in the field of religion; the nearest candidates—Mary Baker Eddy and Brigham Young—were primarily geniuses of organization, not prophets of deep spiritual insight. They were religious statesmen.

But there is a curious balance in the United States between loyalty to the state as such and loyalty to symbols that are non-state in origin and meaning. While the symbols cluster around the state, they are not symbols-of-state. Thus the vaunted freedoms from state coercion center, by definition, on a relation of the individual to his state but not on a subordination of the individual to his nation-state, much less on a subordination of the individual to any existing government. This balance (it might be called more accurately an extremely dangerous tension) is seriously threatened in the transition to industrial society. The facts and our interpretation of them carry us to two opposing hypotheses. The question is whether American civilization can retain the flexibility which has carried us through many immediate crises as well as a long-term revolution from agrarian to industrial-scientific culture; or whether the process of rigidifying is not so far advanced that we will attempt to retain all we now hold (for fear of losing any part of it) and by so doing, lose all. Let there be no illusion that conquest of space and unraveling the mystery of the universe can substitute for a value system firmly grounded in the living, hence changing, reality of American life. Such events, when they come and however marvelous they may be, will constitute only spectaculars, not the realization of man or of the promise of America.

Which of the two hypotheses will be actualized depends upon

future events about which we can now do no better than offer speculations. The answer to this question lies within the relation between the individual and the state and, by extension, to the other great superstructures. If this relationship is not direct and vital and close to actual valuing, then the dream remains unfulfilled. It is for this reason that the clues offered us by religion and esthetics are of such prime importance, since a church serves as a place of common assembly for families from the neighborhoods, and art symbols, whether experienced publicly or privately, ultimately remain completely individual in their impact.

How then may we interpret the current urge to blend religious with secular symbols, particularly political symbols? Should we view this as an attempt to restore faith and appeal in the political symbols? Or should we accept such intermingling as evidence of religious weakness and an effort to make secure the only local institution (except for the school and hospital, which are special cases) that gives support to the family in its isolation and privacy? On this interpretation, religion has found a place for itself within industrial society and has withdrawn its challenge to nation and rational science. It makes no pretense to resolve the tension between individual and superstructure and may actually counsel withdrawal and thus repeat the solution offered before Christ by separatist Jews, by primitive Christianity, and by pietistic Protestant sects. Such a procedure might shatter Western civilization by erosion from within; it cannot solve the human problems produced by it.

The situation for esthetic valuing seems a little clearer, although the answer we derive should heighten our apprehensions. If the individual no longer possesses the capacity to respond to art forms with a wholeness of value judgments, an inability partly produced by the separation of esthetic from moral and political values, the artist now also lacks the capacity to evoke symbols which either express the whole or represent a congruent part thereof. Thomas Wolfe agonizingly sought to comprehend the whole but was ultimately shattered by his own compulsions and fell back upon reporting endless minutiae, hoping the immensity of the volume might somehow compensate for his failure. The contemporary artist no longer even struggles toward such conceptions. He has taken his stand firmly inside his own psyche and whatever emerges he takes for the expression he has sought. Unfortunately, high art both rejects and distorts the linkage of the individual with his total society by insisting in its symbolism that only the personal is real. It may well be that we shall have no more Faulkners, Lewises, or Marquands, not alone because the world they reported upon is gone, but because the fragmented vignettes of Mailer and Salinger represent the only visible reality. In such literary works we find Pilgrims but no Progress, only aimless wandering.[23]

Political values are paradigms for behavior in the public world. But whether they are achieved or not is determined not only by events in the public world but also by the subtle nuances of interpersonal relations in the millions of families that comprise this nation. As the political scene shifts into foreground, the family becomes an all-pervading background. We have yet to produce a literary vision portraying the American and his constant interplay between these two worlds.

8

SCIENCE AND SELF-FULFILLMENT

Many factors have contributed to the formation of contemporary America. Its abundant resources, energetic people, democratic institutions, and pragmatic beliefs have all been mixed in the crucible of history to produce a unique civilization.

No other nation can match this country's high level of material prosperity, and only a few equal the orderliness with which its citizens meet the daily tasks of keeping fed, clothed, and housed, while at the same time, applying an immense amount of energy to its social, political, and economic machinery. No nation and no civilization has ever granted to so many freedom from the demands of the labor market, so they could spend their youth in preparation for life's tasks and their old age with assurance of security. No other nation has ever shared its knowledge and means so generously with others and asked so little in return.

But if security, power, and glory have been the reward, they have not been achieved without a cost.

The cost with which we are concerned cannot be measured in the statistics of trade balances or production units, nor counted in the heavy requirements of civic duty, family responsibility, or job performance. No, the cost must be related to intangible human values intricately interwoven in the concept of self, and through self to the purpose and meaning of life and the universe. The price is paid in the currency of self-consciousness.

AMERICAN CIVILIZATION AND SELF-CONSCIOUSNESS

The consciousness of the contemporary American is sharply marked off from other historically significant concepts of selfhood,[1] as the Hindu's effort to lose himself in contemplation, the medieval Christian's renunciation of self-will in order to achieve a higher selfhood through grace, and the Chinese Communist's identification of selfhood with the commune and its idealized concept of material production. Like these others, the American's consciousness is determined by a world view acquired in total innocence during the process of growing up, but unlike these others it gives him neither afterlife nor collectivity in which to overcome his finitude, sin, and anxiety. It puts upon him the onus of self-fulfillment within a world that can offer only change itself as the touchstone of enduring reality. To grasp the full impact of such a consciousness of self is to understand the extraordinary burden our civilization puts on each individual.

In his compelling (and surprisingly successful) play *J. B.*, Archibald MacLeish chose the Biblical character Job as the prototype of modern man.[2] In some ways the choice was fortunate, for Job clearly exemplifies the American's sense of individual responsibility for the public weal. J. B. prospers in the objective public sense as he carries out his duties to his fellow men.

But at least until the penultimate scene of the play, J. B. is not an adequate exemplar of the American's consciousness. For

J. B. is a terribly dull person and seems to feel no obligation to become anything else, whereas for the contemporary American things are otherwise. His responsibilities to the external world do not preëmpt his whole life; in fact they are ordinarily subordinate to his obligation to fulfill himself: to ever grow, develop, and utilize his potentialities. Yet though this obligation is a challenge and a promise, it is also a burden, for there may be rest from labor, but retirement from the field of self-development is never permitted. When McLeish's J. B. departs from the course taken by his Biblical predecessor, it may be to assume this peculiarly modern burden. (It *may* be, for the tortuous ending of the play does not permit an unqualified interpretation.)

But let us be clear that an identification of self with an ever unaccomplished mission is not peculiarly modern. To seek the infinite, the perfect, and the unattainable runs deep in the cultural blood stream. The search for the Holy Grail, Utopia, the Fountain of Youth, El Dorado, and the New Jerusalem have, in their respective epochs of history, filled the imaginations of men trudging the *via vitae*. The specific nature of the search, however, is defined differently for each era. Whereas once the search for a sacred chalice stirred men's imaginations and concentrated their energies, the quest has now centered on the inner self. Those who ask "Who am I?", those who are concerned with the problem of personal identity, certainly reflect current confusion and malaise, but in so doing they say, in effect: If we are to fulfill ourselves, we must understand what is meant by the "I."

In the period of American agrarian culture the external form of the search was derived from the Biblical concept of the Promised Land and became specific in the American Dream. As with all such goals, its attainment was not expected to be easy. Struggle and work were necessities. But there was no thought of failure, for the capacity of mortal man was deemed adequate for every earthly task. Success could and would be realized. The folk language gave voice to the purpose, the means, and the optimism, as in Franklin's catchy aphorisms for all the homey virtues: prudence ("A stitch in time saves nine"), thrift ("A penny saved is a penny earned"), fortitude ("God helps those who help themselves"). In substance they proclaimed that man's destiny was his own choice and doing, with success or failure observable in the public market and forum.

The American Dream could be realized only if the material conditions of sin were removed. And to accomplish this end it was necessary for the American to become a materialist.[3] Only when man had been released from his enslavement to poverty, disease, and toil could soul and intellect flower. Franklin's life presents the American ideal of personal, psychological Utopianism just as his aphorisms represent the other side of American life, that of unalloyed materialism. Franklin sought wealth that he might have leisure to pursue the study of nature, uncontaminated by any mercenary intent. The honors he received from his countrymen for his public services he lightly deprecated; for one thing, these services fell in the category of duties that *had* to be performed, and for another, neither honors nor riches could recompense for time and youth that might have been spent in purely intellectual pursuits.

Like Franklin, we too have earned enough wealth so that we are free from the drives of hunger and cold, free to pursue the spiritual and intellectual ends of life. And too we find that our expectations do not come to pass as we (and Franklin) had rather naively believed they would.

But our case is different in that our goals are no longer predominantly external (to understand nature and the material world) but internal. Freed from the crushing burdens of material existence, we proclaim that man must now confront the obligation to fulfill himself as an individual personality. And yet we still hang back. Nor is it the demands of public duty that keep us from directly pursuing the ideal of self-fulfillment. It is rather a strange failure of nerve. We advertise ourselves into a hankering for yet more material objects. We propagandize ourselves into seeing the Russians or the Chinese as the prime threats to our corporate security. And thus we artfully try to escape paying the price of being who we are and what we are at this historical moment.

THE BASIC IDEAS OF AMERICAN SOCIETY

Beliefs may be considered from either of two viewpoints. On the objective side, certain dominant ideas in a society are functionally related to other aspects of that society; thus, for example, it is a prime objective of many social scientists to explain how the religious beliefs of a people are related to their economic and political behavior, or how cosmological beliefs derive from a society's level of technological achievement.

But beliefs may also be considered on the subjective side: from this angle of regard an observer attempts to understand how an individual's sense of self exists in and is expressed through the ideas of his society. The subjective side is our concern here; specifically, we want to see how the individual American comes to have a distinctive self-concept, derived from those unquestioned ideas he learned along with his native tongue.

American Society and the Nature of the Universe

Americans departed from the authentic Christian interpretation of history and nature long ago. The Christian account of man and his world presented human society, the *civitas terrae,* as a vale of tears and shadows, a temporary stage on which was played the drama of God's purposes—divine creation, human sinfulness and finitude, the redemption of man in the passion of Christ, and salvation availing to man in his suffering on this earth. Rather early in the nineteenth century the American mentality split salvation into two parts: divine and earthly, not to say earthy.[4] The resulting schism did not receive theological reconciliation until much later (the Social Gospel movement), for theology is necessarily a parasitical and *post hoc* intellectual activity.

In practice Americans worked hard, even feverishly, to free themselves from the curse of Adam by inventions, by opening up more fertile lands, and by establishing social systems to protect men from overwork, poverty, disease, famine, and exploitation. Though they may have hesitated to utter the sacrilegious statement, "This land with its bounty is our salvation," they nevertheless acted it out in health, in strength, and in pride. Yet when they were afraid, or old or sick, or struck with the death of loved ones, they did not forget that other salvation. They confessed their sin and pondered their personal and collective guilt. They ate the bitter fruit of tragedy in loneliness, or they sought collective forms of repentance in evangelistic movements, in bizarre and incongruous cults, in sectarian shifts over hairsplitting points in a theology that was, in effect, all anti-intellectual fundamentalism. The nineteenth century American was, and knew he was, a Christian heretic in the most profound sense. He could never forgive himself for it, and he knew the God of Vengeance would never forgive him. Having accepted his alienation from God, the best he could hope for was peace with the moral demands of this world.[5]

The mid-twentieth century American has evolved beyond this cosmic sense of guilt, though not beyond all sense of guilt. He now believes that there exists a method for understanding the forces of the universe and that American society was once, though it may be no longer, the society most fully in possession of that method. The method, of course, is that of science, and its outward manifestation is technology. The idea of the scientific method, as represented in the philosophy of logical positivism, is a theological masterpiece. It provides, at least in principle, an answer to any question about the nature of the universe, dismissing those questions for which no answer is forthcoming as meaningless. "Meaningless" or "heretical": both mean that which cannot be said while maintaining conformity to the accepted system.[6]

In addition to answering fundamental questions, the scientific method also enables us to bring into the daily practices of life—into the production, promotion, and distribution of goods, into military defense, even into the morality of dealing with people—the revelations vouchsafed us in research.

To understand the operative religion of a society, one must look at the *prescribed* rituals surrounding the great events of life, particularly birth, marriage, and death. In America today the rituals performed by the medical profession and sanctioned by scientific method have truly sacred status. Babies are born in hospitals and their coming is preceded by elaborate purification ceremonies that drive away or wash away unseen threats to their health. (The ceremonial ablutions of surgeons make particularly effective film sequences.) Men and women who wish to be married *must* present themselves to a functionary of the science and there give their blood for his examination. If signs in the microscope augur ill, neither priest nor politician is powerful enough to perform a fully legal marriage for the couple. At death, a man *may* have his priest to absolve him, and his family or friends to mourn him, but he *must* have a doctor to pronounce him dead and to explain in the language of science why this man had to die.

To describe our communal regulations of birth, marriage, and death as ceremonies and rituals is not to deny that we do these things for good scientific reasons. Of course we do; that is just the point. Our unquestioning belief in the scientific method is such that we are unlikely to recognize that we organize and carry out the great ceremonial occasions of life in the language and accouterments of science. We do not ordinarily see anything to remark about these actions; they are natural, normal, and expected. The language and accouterments of science enable us to bring into one more or less harmonious whole our beliefs about the origin of the universe and of life within it, about human beings and their special (but not too special) place in the scheme of things, and about birth, death, and sex in their particular appearances. So it is with any smoothly working system of religious beliefs.

This great scheme of things is invoked not only in the great rhythmic occasions of life but also in both the more routine and the more spectacular decisions we are forced to make. The appeal to science in advertising and public relations is so well recognized that it needs no comment here. The use of pseudo-scientific criteria in both legal and literary judgments has also received considerable attention. The interstices of daily life—those pauses when we ponder, judge, and decide—are filled with the sound if not the spirit of the scientific method. We wouldn't know how *to decide* anything (as opposed to choosing in a purely arbitrary manner) if we did not have the scientific method ultimately to rely on.[7]

What is true of daily life is also true of the truly epochal decisions that confront us as a people. When Harry Truman was forced to decide whether to use the atomic bomb over Hiroshima and Nagasaki, he turned to military men and scientists as his advisers. Their presence and the nature of their counsel remind one willy-nilly of the augurs of ancient Rome examining chicken entrails. Mr. Truman noted his own prayers to Providence but said nothing about answers to them. He consulted neither a cleric, nor a moral philosopher, nor even a respected political savant, but he asked the scientists whether the (to him) inscrutable Fates would favor alternative plans. They told him that only the dropping of the Bomb had favorable omens. Who among us would have, could have, dared defy the voice of science?[8]

In our unquestioning devotion to science lies the solution to why the appearance of Sputnik I struck us so forcibly. We are no longer sure, as we once were, that we are the chosen people of science. The fact that European theorists had made major contributions to scientific knowledge could not shake our faith in our chosenness, for we believed in salvation by works, not by theory. And we had proved in numberless ways our unique capability to put scientific revelations to *work*.

Our faith has been shaken by Sputnik; it has not been lost. In typical American fashion we are putting pressure on the schools to regain for us the leadership we feel is morally ours. We have not only to teach more science and teach it more effectively, we have also to liberate young minds so that they may add creatively to the total store of scientific knowledge.

Because science is our most fundamental system of beliefs, because science requires a mental discipline different from any that we learn in the informal training of home and neighborhood, and because science is itself an ever changing system of beliefs—because of all these things and more, our schools have, or ought to have, a distinctive character and spirit. Let us note one feature of a school dominated by the scientific habit of thought which in turn becomes part of the unquestioned system of beliefs of the individual, that is, that in a very special way among us, the future *always* belongs to youth. For as scientific study depends less than any other study on a wide range of concrete experience and more on abstract symbolic formulations, scientific thought can be learned and known by very young men and women. This is special. In all other systems of thought, the highest forms of knowledge are those acquired through a lifetime of experience, discourse, and contemplation. As opposed to any other form of knowledge, science is altogether communicable. The mature and experienced scientist cannot say to his student: "I know certain mysteries of nature that you must discover for yourself." This makes sense in any other system of thought, but not in science. If the scientist knows what he claims to know, then he can *say* it, and moreover he can express it with such precision that his students can learn it exactly as it is taught. What he cannot say, he does not know.[9]

This fact of the relative advantage of youth carries on to the interpersonal relations between teacher and pupil. Teachers know and pupils sense that immaturity is no longer the barrier that it once was to full knowledge of the world. Immaturity actually means greater potentiality. The reasonably intelligent boy of twelve will inevitably have a better understanding of his world at age sixty than does his teacher of that age now, and the mutual recognition of that fact colors the relation between them. Respect, authority, and discipline in the classroom are altered in character when the scientific mode of thought dominates the intellectual scene.

This is not to say, of course, that Americans really know science and practice scientific method in their thinking nor that American schools are altogether like scientific *technicums.* The influence is more subtle. For no one can seriously doubt that the honorific sense of the "scientific" dominates all classroom instruction: "What *really* happened?" "How can you explain that?" "What will happen if we do this?" "How do you know?" "What's the importance of that?" These are the standard classes of questions in ordinary pedagogy, rightfully asked in the teaching process.[10] Now imagine two answers given to any one of them, one answer beginning, "Scientifically speaking . . . ," and the second, "Of course it's unscientific to say so, but. . . ." Which of these carries more weight, inspires more respect and attention? Please note that the answer would be the same whether we are speaking of the first grade or the fourteenth, of physical education, physics, civics, Russian history, English literature, or driver training. How far the canons of truly scientific thought have penetrated school practices is a question to be answered only after extensive empirical investigation guided by rigorously formed definitions of what is scientific, but it is easily seen that the honorific sense of the scientific has come to dominate schooling as well as the rest of the culture. Its identification with youth, change, and anti-authoritarianism adds one element to the distinctive character of American schools.

It goes without saying that these features are also elements in the distinctive American sense of self.

American Society and the Drama of History

If the fundamental idea of the scientific method provides a remarkably successful way of giving reasoned consistency to a wide range of beliefs about the nature of the cosmos and man's place in it, this theology has more difficulty in providing an interpretation of history and man's place in the drama of his own species. The first step in a historical interpretation is fairly simple: the United States has achieved its status as chief among all the nations by virtue of its devotion to the free application of the scientific method. Our efficiency, our orderliness, our ability to organize things in a scientifically acceptable fashion are taken as the touchstone of the rightness of our social conventions, of our right to regard ourselves as the chosen people of all history.

This importance we have attached to "getting things done" is seen most clearly, if paradoxically, in the discontents with existing social relations that are found in the ordinary American. His gripe about the way things are run is always most emphatically expressed in the name of getting things done. This tendency has given an odd cast to the history of reform movements in the United States. The moral horror aroused in Grant's Army of the Tennessee on contact with slavery was not so much because of the injustice of the system as because of its inefficiency. Thus in the last quarter of the nineteenth century the country could applaud the use of federal troops against strikers because strikes interfered with production of steel or delivery of mail. Similarly our sense of outrage which follows revelations of irregularities by unions, the military, and civic officials stems less from the inherent immorality of individual actions than from the fact that irregular practices interfere with the effective, scientifically acceptable ways of organizing people to get the job done, whether the job be the production and distribution of goods, national defense, or public schooling.

But all this is essentially static. It doesn't satisfy the deep-seated need to see our own nation in the dynamic flow of human history. Does the average American today regard his country as standing in the vanguard of social changes that are heading in the direction foretold by our older American ideology? It is doubtful. Our professed aim in 1917 was to make the world safe for democracy, in 1941 to achieve the Four Freedoms, in 1950 to prevent successful Communist aggression. These represent a steady retreat from a unitary and simple-minded view of our place in the history of mankind. The idea of automatic progress has fled the American's consciousness. We are no longer sure that we lead the world nor even that the world is heading in the direction indicated by the ideals of liberty and equality, which we appropriated and made peculiarly our own in the nineteenth century.

But if none of these older notions of America's role in history still have compelling force in the beliefs of our citizens (in the name of science we rewrote our history to debunk our traditional heroes and to get rid of these outmoded notions in our historical consciousness) and if the scientific method, our most fundamental religious notion in the cosmic sense, does not provide us with a viable myth concerning our historical destiny, there is one sense in which we still have an ideal by which to interpret history and our role in it. That ideal is personal, individual self-development.

Kenneth Galbraith complains that we have a completely unbalanced ratio between the production of goods for private consumption and goods for our public, communal life.[11] Though justified from an economic viewpoint and even from the standpoint of capacity of satisfying personal needs as these are influenced by the public conditions of life, Galbraith nonetheless overlooks the fact that our level of private consumption is all that still distinguishes us historically from the rest of the world. Here is where we take our stand; this is what we have to offer as our contribution to the historical destiny of the human race. And so we are sometimes taken aback when others seem to be less than overwhelmed by our standard of living, when we are accused of being idle materialists in our views on human welfare. For we regard our high standard of living as the necessary condition for individual self-fulfillment, and we find it impossible to believe that other societies would not like to move toward this ideal if they were not prevented by poverty or by selfish leaders who hold the people in subjection and forbid their expression of true desires and aspirations. The ordinary man in the street believes that everyone in the world would like to be an American, not just in order to have an automobile, but because the possession of an automobile is a step toward that ideal of individual self-fulfillment which we have created and offered to share with others.

Insofar as our policies toward other nations reflect our unconscious belief that they all would like to join the Union, we may find ourselves badly misunderstood on the international scene. Likewise, if we do not grasp what the historical ideal of self-fulfillment offers besides automobiles and refrigerators, we will badly misunderstand ourselves.

1. For it does not mean, as some have thought, that the American is free from the pressure of work. We are not fulfilled by being freed from work; on the contrary, our work is a part of our fulfillment. Indeed, a distinctive feature of the new American way of life that we wish to share with the rest of the world is the ideal of a job's being a part of man's movement toward his own personal potentialities. Although, as we shall see in a moment, this belief becomes part of a fundamental ambivalence in the individual, at the social level there is no contradiction. The evidence of science supports our belief that the worker who finds his job a contributing increment toward his own personal growth is also the most productive worker, and we can thus easily reconcile this part of our historical contribution to mankind wtih our belief in a scientific theology.[12]

2. As leisure time becomes available to all classes of people and as more and more activities become priced within the reach of everyone, then everyone can pursue whatever kinds of play-pursuits he finds helpful in achieving his own maximum growth. In the nineteenth century, play in the urban environment was one of three very different things: the vulgar, ostentatious, esthetically ridiculous pursuits of the idle rich; the limited, restrained, and sometimes uncomfortable Sunday family picnic of the bourgeoisie; or the brutal drinking, whoring, and wife-beating Saturday night among the working classes. All these, fortunately, are obsolescent today. In play and in work, we hold up our high consumption of material goods as the condition that enables us to make these an aspect of personal self-fulfillment for every person.[13]

3. Our patterns of sexual relations and family life admit of

precisely the same analysis. When Marx said that the capitalists made of the family an economic relation stultifying love and creativity, he was describing quite accurately the conditions in Europe at the time.[14] Our high level of material wealth makes it possible for us to remove most of the purely economic functions from the family. Young people can marry for love, not dowries; girls can regard their virginity in terms of its intrinsic relation to their personal growth rather than in terms of its market value; and young people are no longer forced either to have children or prevent them for purely economic reasons but can plan families in relation to the self-fulfilling aspects of child rearing.

The point should be clear enough by now. We see our place in the historical scheme of things, in the great drama of the human species, in the cosmically brief interlude between the appearance of the human race and its extinction in the inevitable course of astronomical heat cycles, as offering to mankind the ideal of self-fulfillment through (though not exclusively by) the production of a sufficiently high level of material wealth to free the individual from economic determinism in his work, play, sexual relations, family life, and indeed all the manifold realms of human activity. These are the terms in which we now interpret the lines inscribed on the Statue of Liberty, except for the fact that we no longer require that the people come to us. We will go wherever we are asked, to help others achieve the requirements of self-fulfillment for themselves.

We have discussed the ideal of self-fulfillment as if it had no intrinsic or necessary connection with the metaphysics of science-technology. From one point of view, this is quite obviously justified. We can point to other civilizations, particularly the USSR, where a scientific, technological, world outlook is deliberately cultivated, but the American ideal of self-fulfillment is regarded as bourgeois-decadent nonsense. (As the ideal of self-fulfillment comes operatively to dominate individual lives, the USSR will most likely have to change its official line. Mass production must either find this outlet or be used for war.) On the other hand, the Catholic Church is committed to a particular version of the ideal of self-fulfillment, though strongly rejecting the total scientific world view.

But at a deeper level, the ideal of self-fulfillment and the scientific world view are related by more than historical accident. The very progress in scientific inquiry that dispelled the illusion of man's centrality in the universe also revealed his hitherto unsuspected powers as the animal that knows. In the history of philosophy, epistemology—or the investigation of how man can know—marched together with his increasing knowledge. Then came an exaltation of man as a creature of feeling and will, because these aspects of the human animal were so markedly different from the blind mechanical conception of nature that science was elaborating. Today, as the study of man is developing its appropriate scientific techniques and theories, one cannot but see the results as revealing "human potentialities," the possibilities for men and women "becoming" more of what they could be.[15]

A thorough study of the historical relation between these two ideas (self-fulfillment as the supreme human good and a scientific world outlook) is far beyond the scope of our present purposes. It may be the relation is purely accidental. Even so, when the American wants to explain the world or his place in it, his appeal is to science, and when he wants to interpret American history and to give a moral justification for our enormous wealth, he appeals, more or less articulately, to the ideal of self-fulfillment and our willingness to share it with the rest of the world. These two fundamental ideas make up the distinctive American character.

INDIVIDUAL EXPRESSION AND COMMITMENT

How does the individual American see himself in relation to these cosmic ideas and ideals? By and large he has followed an American tradition and made his peace with the universe. He has built for his scientist-shaman the world's largest radio telescope, magnificent research centers and nuclear accelerators, fine hospitals and medical research facilities, even a "think-tank" for the social sciences. The universe, Dr. Einstein and his successors, and the average American get along quite well together, the last being convinced that the first two know each other rather well and that the second will promptly pass along any secrets he has about the first. (If the relation between the first two is not as good as we should like, why we'll jack up the schools and remedy the situation as quickly as that sort of thing can be remedied.)

What are the beliefs of the American about himself in relation to American society? What are the beliefs that are expressed in the everyday lives of millions of Americans who work conscientiously at their tasks—on the job, in the home, at school, and in their community—who thus maintain the most fantastically complex social, political, and economic system that the world has ever known? We must try to see this set of beliefs at two levels: the overt, explicit, manifest level and the covert, implicit, latent level.

Aboveboard, things are rather smooth, at least for the vast majority who are integrated into the main stream of what Lerner calls the American success. The necessary social services are performed within institutional arrangements that do protect men and women from the worst features of human exploitation. There is a fluidity of social structure, giving objective validation to the American's belief that he can move, physically and socially, just about wherever he would like to move. And withal, there is a permanence and stability about the system, assuring that his achievements will amount to something and give him a place and role that will endure through the rapid changes going on all around.

In this country there are many different status systems. Business, science, military, the arts, community service, academic life, old-family, and sports—these are not all occupational groupings, but they are all status systems with (more or less well-recognized) ways of deciding what spot in any one system corresponds to a spot in another. To us it is most significant that each of these varied status systems provides a minutely graded series of steps from the lowest rung to the highest. Because the individual person knows truly that he can move fairly easily to the next, objectively scarcely distinguishable, rung above him, he can believe that he can move anywhere on the ladder—whether on his job, in his play, his activities as a consumer, or his family life. In this fact is found the functional reason behind the clever and much-maligned Parkinson's Law in administration.[16] There is some evidence that if the measure of social mobility is in big jumps, as is found in Europe, then our belief in an open social status system is a myth.[17] But this is not the way of our system. The easy movement from rung to rung is the meaningful movement, and it is for this reason that most Americans are not seriously disturbed when N. S. Khrushchev and C. Wright Mills tell us that there is a ruling clique in America with very severe restrictions for admission.[18] We do not ask to be admitted to *that* level in the status system; at any given moment we want to be able to move only to the next higher level. We feel this step easily possible if we are willing to behave in the manner demanded by the particular system we happen to belong to.

In this belief the mind of the American seems adequately attuned to reality and withal peaceful enough, but at the implicit level there is a rub. For the American finds that he has committed himself to the cult of self-fulfillment, and its requirements are more exacting than the demands from Cotton Mather's pulpit ever were. At least the demands of Cotton Mather's God were clear enough so a man might know precisely wherein he had transgressed. If they were beyond human power to accomplish and if God were utterly implacable in his justice, a man might stand in deadly fear of his Lord, but he need not have the constant, nagging anxiety that besets the modern soul. The Organization Man is the inevitable outcome when one must look upon his job not merely as a way of making a living but as an avenue toward personal growth. "I want to work with people" is a recurring comment heard by those who prepare teachers, and the reason given is always the same: "Because working with people comes closer than any other work to giving me an apportunity to continue my own growth as a person." Because work is thus tied in with the historical ideal of our civilization, its demands are limitless. The vaunted growth in leisure time as offering the ideal of self-fulfillment is a will-o'-the-wisp in actuality, for the demands of the job also become the demands of self-fulfillment, and these can know no limits.

And, in effect, work and its demands also still involve, and must involve, many activities that could never be called opportunities for personal growth. In any job, the individual finds himself torn between the (at least occasionally) dreary actualities of his existence and the moral demand that he must continue always to grow as a person. Even to the extent that the job does contribute to this ideal, its demands become greater upon all aspects of a person's life and thus prevent him access to other forms of activity which he knows must also be included in the well-developed personality.

The same is true of play and family life. How is a man to choose among the plethora of play activities available in every sphere of life? The popular magazine asks us to ponder this question: "Does *your* marriage help you grow into the kind of person you could be?" But just consider the range of things you might know, but do not. The sights, tastes, and sounds you could enjoy, but have not. The depths of feeling you might plumb, but have not? Marriage is no longer a contract, nor even a companionship. It is a union, temporary or permanent, of two persons seeking the infinite, vaguely aware that the search must be futile, guilty in that awareness, and constantly upbraided by their culture for their failure.

The resulting anxieties, being too great to be borne by the human psyche, are projected into the external condition. "If we only could afford a larger apartment. . . ." "If only there was one more week of vacation in the year. . . " "If we could just be sure that Johnny could get into college. . . ." These and all the other "if only's" are pure fantasies. Self-fulfillment is not like an asymptotic curve with a limit; it is like the infinite progression of natural numbers. At least so it seems to those who live with this ideal, who must exhibit it to the world as the central core of the American way of life whose origin and meaning elude the understanding of the rest of the world.

Perhaps the tension is seen most clearly in the behavior of American tourists abroad. Unfortunately no longer innocent, Americans abroad discover that the cult of self-fulfillment has left them guilt-ridden in the extreme. Relieved of the discipline of daily work, they find themselves driven to see, to experience, to climb to the heights and plumb to the depths as far as their talents and education permit. The more and the less sophisticated separate themselves according to the objects pursued, but both exhibit the same drives. And when the inexhaustible demands become too great, they escape into drink and debauchery, again dividing themselves by capacity. The overwhelming impression of the observer is the humorlessness of the whole thing.

For this reason, we must also deny the fact of death and deal with the existence of pain and tragedy as symptoms of an illness to be treated by practitioners of the scientific method. No matter who you are or what you are, you can, ought, and must be more and better than you are![19] Thus proclaims our new American creed, thus sermonizes scientific psychology. There is no room here for the coward or the sluggard. It is impossible to overestimate the importance of this doctrine, if we are to understand the contemporary American mind. Our scientific world view has removed all purpose, meaning, and finality from the universe as a whole. The disillusioning experiences of this century have taken the idea of automatic progress out of our conception of history; they have left us incapable of fully accepting any social or collective goals as the ultimately valuable ends of existence. The logical last step has to be taken: each person must create within his own brief life his own reason for being; there is nothing beyond, before, or behind from which he may draw ultimate justification. He cannot even accede to C. I. Lewis' appealing doctrine that the final value is "a life found good on the whole," for this life might be one of passive accommodation to circumstances.[20] No, he must take upon himself the full burden of self-fulfillment because, in the final analysis, that is life's only justification. That he may share that burden in the nuclear family does not lessen its weight, but each of the partners may shift the load so that the combined burden may be borne.

It is quite clear that this attitude toward life can and does have pathological consequences,[21] and yet the creed of self-fulfillment is accepted and internalized and successfully lived with by the overwhelming majority of Americans. There are several phenomena that help to explain how this is possible. First, the culture provides a very wide range of acceptable avenues for temporary regression, ways in which one can be idle (for at least a short time) without excessive guilt.[22] Second, a marriage and family pattern has evolved that allows (in principle) the fullest expression of all ranges of selfhood and thus permits a sharing of the burden imposed by the creed. And third, the corporate system, with its own potentialities for unlimited growth, provides a public analogue, if not an object of identification, for the individual's own socially imposed drives.

But all these are no more than palliatives, unless the man or woman who is caught up in this system can at once *feel* its pull for change, for the exercise of initiative, and for personal growth and at the same time *know* the system with sufficient objectivity and detachment to escape being victimized by it.

9

THE CORPORATE SOCIETY AND EDUCATION

The private world of family and individual must be considered as one extreme of a great continuum which joins in bipolar contrast the public world of the great social superstructures. The one cannot be understood without the other, and the tensions which unite and separate them create difficult problems in the relations between individual and group. With neither design nor planning education has found itself heir to a distinctive function in the intermediate position which it occupies between family and corporate system. For the crucial structural position which the schools occupy is that of a bridge across which the child must move preparatory to his participation in the adult and public world, and as he does so there is a simultaneous weakening of his ties to his specific nuclear family and his bondage to its narrow social orbit.

Given this fact of social and cultural transformation, there are two principal questions which we must examine in our quest for an understanding of the relation of education and commitment. What are the significant forces creating the transformation, and how have they been manifested? And secondly, what are the consequences for the process of education and the organization of the schools? If we begin with a brief treatment of the second question, our subsequent analysis of the first one will be better understood. The ever sharper separation between the private world of family and locality and the public corporate world has placed a responsibility upon the schools which does not yet seem to be understood. A part of our effort will be to examine the extent to which the transitional responsibility is now being met and to propose modifications in the educative process which the situation demands.

Teaching is no longer, if it ever was, the simple interchange between a symbolic Mark Hopkins on one end of the log and a student on the other. Like other institutions, education now reflects the massive complexity of our society. An almost endless list of details surround, affect, and interpose themselves in the educational process: problems of school finance, budget, construction, and maintenance; of administration, public relations, reporting, and law; of curriculum, testing, subject matter, and placement; of training, mechanical devices, and auxiliary personnel; of guidance, mental and physical health, recreation, and professionalization. The coordination and supervision of increased administrative and specialized personnel to meet the demands of much larger school systems and their complex operations have led to a bureaucratization which in outline resembles that of a government agency or of an industrial corporation.

Although, in theory, the opposite effect has been intended from the modern tendency to devote ever greater attention in energy, time, and budget to operational and organizational problems in the schools, the result has been a corresponding diminution of emphasis upon what transpires in the classroom. For although the bureaucracy has been created to facilitate and improve the teaching process, inevitably the coordinating and supervising function becomes paramount, as can be witnessed in the sad state of the New York City school system. Inherent in the managerial ethos, at the point where authority touches the supervised, is distrust of freedom, initiative, and nonconformity. In schools the point of contact is found not only in the relation between the teacher and student but also in the relation of administrator to teacher. College presidents, deans, superintendents, and principals suffer persistently from anxiety that their teachers may do or say things that will attract unfavorable attention to their institutions, and parental concern of possible ill effects of teacher behavior upon their children also finds expression from time to time. Infrequently, parents or school administrators bestow their approbation upon dedicated service, but teachers know that the full measure of appreciation can come from only one source—those whom they teach.

Censure and reward in teaching illustrate the distinctive structural position of the educative process. Parents send immature human beings possessing the capacities for growth and hurt, for whom they retain responsibility, give love, and have aspirations, into a situation in which they no longer have full control. As they relinquish, they must also entrust. If the child is subject to an incompetent teacher or, in the more extreme case, ends up in a blackboard jungle, the courses of action open to the ordinary parent are relatively few. The teacher, on the other hand, must operate within the conditions imposed by the bureaucracy. These may aid or hinder the educational task, but in either event there is an implicit conflict of interest between the managerial and educative functions, posing a threat to the kind of educational institution which a society that prizes individual development and personal liberty must have.

The dilemma arises because of the necessary juxtaposition of both managerial and educative functions: if the former takes precedence, then the latter must suffer, yet the complexity of the educative process requires both specialization and coordination. The resolution of the impasse, we believe, rests in necessary modification of both aspects. Reform of the educative process in accord with the principles of scientific discovery is mandatory, but a necessary corollary is organizational reform. The present school organization, with its traditional chain of command and bureaucratic patterns, destroys initiative and inhibits the creativity of the teaching-learning process; it cannot accomplish the task ahead. In its place must come a type of human association which releases the student from his debilitating supervised role and places the organizational structure at his disposal for purposes of learning. Such an arrangement is so utterly strange to present practice and to the direction in which elementary and secondary education has been moving that we doubt many can work out procedures for achieving it, let alone grasp what the objectives or results may be. To those who have some sense of the urgency and the worth of the solution let us give assurance that the scientists, engineers, and technicians at the Red Stone Arsenal have unwittingly evolved just this type of organization as a necessity for projecting man into space. Later on we shall sketch a form of human association different from the lock-step bureaucracy that has come to dominate school organization.

Our first step, however, is to understand the social habitat in which the educational enterprise operates. To that end, we propose to trace briefly the organizational changes in American society and to describe some aspects of the corporate system. In the process we shall indicate what structural similarities and differences the schools exhibit in comparison with corporate organization.

THE ORGANIZATIONAL REVOLUTION

When Henry Adams traveled west in 1904 to attend the St. Louis Exposition, he was aghast at the changes which had transformed the people and the countryside in a ten-year span. He found tall chimneys reeking smoke, "dirty suburbs filled with scrap iron, scrap paper and cinders," but more distressing to him was the new American, "the child of steam and the brother of the dynamo . . . a product of so much mechanical power, and bearing no distinctive marks but that of its pressure."[1] However much the comments of this wry observer may be overdrawn, they dramatize the change which the diffusion of industrialism brought to America's heartland.

But his perturbation extended beyond the surface effects of this new force let loose upon the land. He looked back to the period beginning in the 1840's and saw there the initial emergence of that new power vested in the corporations which through the years had fathered those great trusts with which Teddy Roosevelt battled just after the turn of the century. Adams called them "obnoxious because of their vigorous and unscrupulous energy. They were revolutionary, troubling all the old conventions and values, as the screws of ocean steamers must trouble a school of herring. They tore society to pieces and trampled it under foot."[2] Although his detachment took him to the sidelines as a curious onlooker, he gauged that the problem before the public was not merely to control the "trusts" by law but to create a society that could manage them.

If Adams could visit the America of the early 1960's, he would discover that he had observed only the incipient stages of the phenomenon of bigness. He would marvel and perhaps despair at the new industrial giants, some of them not yet born in 1904, that now eclipse the meat-packing, railroad, and oil monopolies of his day. He would encounter mammoth and powerful labor unions whose leaders negotiate contracts with the managers of the great business leviathans, contracts that insure union members ever expanding chunks from profits and added protection for the status quo. He would be astounded at a central government grown huge with new functions for the general welfare but also forced into the role of arbiter in the conflicting tensions that arise in the struggles among corporations, labor unions, and the best interests of the general public. He would find a military establishment whose massiveness and capacity to draw upon the national wealth menacingly overshadows all civilian functions.

Adams would nostalgically recall an older America that also had been transformed, if not utterly burnt away, in the crucible of change. But above the noise of the dynamo he would hear the voices of concern: the hysteria of those seeking a return to the American virtues of the turn of the century, an America which Adams could tell them had itself doomed the one he loved in his boyhood; the strident arguments of economists, planners, and financial manipulators peddling their nostrums to insure prosperity; the dilemma of a public caught in a sequence of alternating alarums and excursions over international crises or defects in the national economic system; the pondering of kindred souls over questions of legitimacy and control of big business, of the protection of the individual against the mammoths of power, and of the meaning and nature of the forces that produced this new world.

It might surprise Adams to find that Americans continue to call their country a democracy, for he would know that the term now refers to something quite different from what his generation had meant by it. He would discover that a few, however, had begun to refer to the new industrial metropolitan complex as a corporate society, although what they had in mind was something quite different from the totalitarian corporate state. Like Adams, those who speak so today are concerned to create the devices to constrain the new powers.[3] Only the future will tell if a nation founded on democratic political processes and dedicated to individual freedom and personal dignity can maintain those principles and objectives in the face of a vast reconstructing of American life. For the corporate form which troubled "the old conventions and values" now dominates the national life. Ours has become a corporate society.

Through a strange twist in the meaning of words, the corporate descendants of the entrepreneurs, who unwittingly led the initial assault upon traditional American social forms from the early 1800's on, consider themselves and are labeled—conservatives. In truth the entrepreneurs who fashioned the social forms joining wealth, skill, resources, and human organization to the new technologies in textiles, transportation, machinery, steel, food processing, and oil were the real social revolutionaries. They concentrated in single enterprises the energies drawn from numerous sources and in the process created new combinations of power heretofore unknown.

The legitimacy and protection of the corporation were bestowed originally by state-granted charters. Its bureaucratic organization was borrowed from government and the army, but principles of flexibility and initiative were derived from entrepreneurial industrialism. The centralization of authority in a small managerial elite guaranteed the control necessary for coordination and supervision, and the gradually evolving principle of unlimited objectives permitted a catholicity of interest and activity that could encompass any aspect of the environment which impinged upon or could be utilized to enhance the organization. Eventually these groups came less and less to depend upon outside capital for their growth and proliferation, and drew increasingly upon their self-generated profits for these purposes.

There remained but one source of power not wholly or continuously within their orbit of control, the federal and state governments. They feared the extension of state power, either through direct competition or through restrictive regulation. Legislatures could not always be intimidated or controlled, and over the years a body of statutory law evolved which was designed to curb the extreme excesses of corporate power. Examples of such legislation include the Sherman Anti-Trust Act, the designation of certain industries as public utilities with regulatory commissions for their control, the creation of the Tennessee Valley Authority as a yardstick against which privately owned utilities could be measured, and the establishment of the Securities and Exchange Commission to bring some order into the abuses of corporation financing. These are all examples of governmental intervention, and their justification was twofold: the necessity to protect the public against unscrupulous exploitation and the hope that the power of the private corporation could be used to promote the general welfare.

The progressive movement, which made the fight for the control of corporate power in the first quarter of the century, culminating in the social legislation of the New Deal era, was led by men who wanted to make the system work through reform, not to destroy or to modify it radically.[4] Even the Socialists had no quarrel with the basic system. They believed simply that the public purpose would be better served with a transfer of control from private to governmental hands.

In this view, then, the business entrepreneurs could be counted as conservative in one aspect only: they wanted no change in governmental structure or function that would inhibit their freedom of action. Thus aligning themselves on the side of freedom, they ardently echoed Thomas Jefferson's belief that that government governs best which governs least. A democratic government, according to the business point of view, was one which protected the rights of the individual and of his property. And, by extension, the rights of the individual *de jure* were bestowed upon the corporation. The legal sanction of the courts had been won through the application of the "due process" clause of the Fourteenth Amendment to their activities,[5] and they sought protection from the demands of labor unions as an unconstitutional infringement upon these rights.[6] In fact, the activity of any group which threatened their power and the free exercise thereof could be castigated as un-American and undemocratic.

But it was in the very exercise of its freedom to act that the business corporation "tore society to pieces," and although the effects of their activities may have "trampled" the traditional American system underfoot, they also brought into being a new social order as different from the one it displaced as the mercantile era was from the preceding feudalism. In this sense the leaders of American business have not only been the architects of a new society but also its social revolutionaries, for the culprit responsible for the demise of American agrarianism and its way of life was the American corporate system. Under the banner of progress and with the concomitant commitment to perpetual change the battle was won.

Ironically, in one of those apparently strange reversals of position which history plays upon us, the initiative for extending access to incorporation was centered in the liberals. In the New York State constitutional convention of 1846 the Democrats overpowered the conservative Whigs in writing a liberal constitution which increased the ease with which charters for incorporation could be granted by the State. Opposition to all the liberalizing provisions was centered among representatives of big property interests. In contrast the liberals of that day viewed the corporation as merely a joint-stock company, entitled to economic freedom.[7]

From 1840 on there was a gradual increase in the number of business enterprises which utilized the corporate form for their organization. (Charters for new business corporations have been granted at a rate of over 200,000 per year in recent years.) It was particularly useful in providing the structure within which new types of enterprises, such as the railroads and mechanized production, could be organized. The corporation with its greater internal complexity, its capacity for concentrating increased resources and energies in the utilization of new technology in the productive processes, and its range of influence extending beyond the local community proved superior to the individually operated and small-town or village-centered workshop. Gradually the craftsmen in leather, wood, iron, food, and fibers gave way before the influx of machine-made products.

The shift in the social form of the productive unit was only one of the changes which came in the wake of the proliferating corporate system. Some socio-economic historians have decided that the first casualty was the plantation system depending upon slave labor.[8] Granted that its destruction was forced from without as a result of war, nonetheless one must not discount the power concentrated in the alliance between the nascent corporate industrialism of the 1860's and the commercial agrarianism in America's heartland and their mutual antipathy to a competing system. However intended, the effect of civil war was to give a boost to industrial urbanism.

There were other casualties, most of these manifested by the slow erosion of the traditional and its replacement by the new. Not the least important of these is the now nearly complete obsolescence of the family farm and rural neighborhood. It will be remembered that Jefferson pinned his hopes of American democracy upon a country of land-owning yeomen, and even Hamilton admitted the primacy of agriculture over manufacturing. Although farmers have been generally reluctant or hesitant to utilize the corporate form in agricultural production, they are deeply and intricately woven into the pattern of the corporate society. Verbally, they espouse the classical laissez faire theory of production—price determined by supply and demand in an open market with perfect competition—but in fact they have enlisted the most potent of our power centers, the federal government, in support of their social and economic aims. The conversion of agricultural production into a form ready for consumption, however, is big business. Food processing concerns, such as Armours, General Mills, General Foods, Borden, and others now number among the giants of our great enterprises, but it may be that for some time to come the individual entrepreneur will still remain the primary agricultural producer. Probably the big distributing corporations—A & P, Safeway, etc.—will soon dominate both basic production and process packaging. But in any event, the groupings of a rural way of life, including country school, rural church, neighborhood festivities, and mutual help, have either disappeared or are functionally residual.

The significance of the social changes in rural life has been overshadowed by the startling effect of technology upon production and manpower. For four decades a major political and economic concern has been the almost unmanageable surpluses of agricultural products resulting from an accelerated increase in output. During the same period, the proportion of the population engaged in farming declined from 35 percent in 1910 to less than 10 percent in 1960. In contrast, during the same period Russia's attempt to rationalize agriculture has been only partially successful and, by its own admission, still requires 45 percent of the nation's manpower.[9] For reasons which are difficult to comprehend, the blessings which flow from this cornucopia of plenty have not been adequately appreciated, but the lesson is clear. A metropolitan-industrial civilization can come into being only when its accompanying agricultural system supplies massive surpluses of food and fiber. This entails the creation of new social forms to utilize scientific and mechanical resources, and thus the full transition to the corporate form is in process. The "factories in the field" predominate along the East and West coasts where the emphasis is upon production of fruits and vegetables.[10] A chicken ranch in Georgia that markets a million broilers a year belongs to a different world than that of the small town produce merchant who annually bought the two or three dozen surplus fryers from the farmer's wife. Agriculture has changed from an activity that provided subsistence for a family to big business; it has joined with those other segments of American life which together constitute the great superstructures. And with its transition, another bastion of traditional America has crumbled.

Inevitably the transformation of rural life wrecked the neat symbiotic relation between market, town, and countryside. In the Midwest and South hundreds of these once flourishing centers of commerce and social life are experiencing slow death from stagnation, and unless rescued by industry or tourism, they are as certainly doomed as were the lumbering and mining boom towns of the West. But these casualties are of much lesser significance than the effect of the outward reach of the corporately organized merchandisers—the mail-order houses and the chain stores—upon the local system of owner-operated retail establishments.[11] The consequences of their spread extend in directions beyond the purely economic throughout the community. We may observe changes in family organization, in social class system, in the functioning of voluntary organizations, and in the essential capacity of the community to meet its internal problems. Of course, not all of these changes can be directly attributed to modification in the system of retailing, but it was nevertheless one aspect among many.

In the Main Street towns, the business district was the center for much of the life of the community. In addition to its ordinary commercial pursuits, this was where professional men received clients in their upstairs offices, fraternal associations maintained their club rooms, luncheon clubs gathered at restaurant or hotel, city hall or courthouse received the taxpayer and law violator, and upper stories housed the faceless nobodies and sometimes ladies of easy virtue. With the exception of the private clubs, the doors of these establishments were open to all, the high and mighty and the lowly. Worker, tradesman, farmer, merchant, and housewife moved freely in pursuit of their various ends. Business and professional men were accorded the rank of substantial citizens, and their decisions, singly or collectively, gave direction to the public destiny of the community.

The first important change began with the appearance of machine industry, as the Lynds showed in *Middletown.* Population increased, wages stimulated business, and ties to the outside world were deepened. Before the era of consolidation and remote control by absentee management, these small industries gave new economic vitality and reduced the dependence upon agriculture. Their owners assumed a significant, if not dominating, position in the affairs of the town, and in turn the relative influence of the retailer-businessman declined.[12]

But the real assault upon the dominating position of the business district began with the spread of the chain stores. First came the variety store, the five-and-ten. Soon others followed in the fields of dry goods, drugs, hardware, and groceries. Their names are those of the great merchandising giants: J. C. Penney, Montgomery Ward, Sears, W. T. Grant, the Great Atlantic and Pacific Tea Company, and on and on. Initially the role the managers of these branch stores played in community life was quite different than that of the independent retail merchant, whose personal life was bound up with the problems of the community. Here today and gone tomorrow, these retailing birds of passage were primarily concerned with the success of their operation, as was the manager of the branch plant.

The ultimate in the evolution of merchandising is, of course, the shopping center. Its relation is not to a community but to customers; and it is quite irrelevant who owns or manages the individual stores, where the employees come from or where they go. The locality in which these workers live has no importance to the function they perform. This, then, has been the course of change, which in its ultimate development has divorced business from any community function, except a purely commercial one.

The ultimate, of course, is not yet universal. Hundreds of thousands of small retail and service establishments still remain scattered across the land performing essential services, and through the persons of their owners contributing to the well-being of their locale. In their operation these shops remain outside direct control of the corporate system. But their position is at best interstitial, at worst marginal. Just as in all highly mechanized industries there are still some operations which can be more cheaply or more easily performed by hand than by automation, such as window washing or floor scrubbing, so, also, there persist interstices within the business structure, where the small entrepreneur finds room to survive. But the pattern is not one in which he is dominant, for like the subsistence family farmer, he has become obsolescent. What then has happened to the value we place upon free enterprise and how must we redefine the "ladder of success" for those young men who once aspired to strike out on their own after some brief apprenticeship in a business? Should we conclude with Galbraith that the opportunity for individual initiative in much of American business is an illusion?[13] Or should we rather say with Riesman that given the right personal and social conditions, initiative and opportunity can be exercised within the corporate system?

VOLUNTARY ASSOCIATIONS WITHIN A CORPORATE SOCIETY

There is a temptation to assert that the real test of the extent to which our institutions have been transformed into a system of superstructures depends upon what has happened to the voluntary association. It is a type of socal organization that is deep in our social fabric and more than a century ago de Tocqueville marveled at the rapidity and effectiveness with which Americans could come together voluntarily to solve any problem which called for group action. In fact one of the first and most famous agreements was born off the coast of Massachusetts; it is known as the Mayflower Compact.

If there is any one trait which sets Americans apart from other peoples it is their proclivity and genius for organization. A standing jest among academic colleagues is that if three or more of them should fortuitously meet and discover a common concern, one could be assured of a new *ad hoc* committee at the very least, and not improbably an association possessing constitution, officers, and a resounding title. The jest is probably just as appropriate in business, government, or sports circles; it illustrates both the spontaneity with which we utilize the organizational form and our efficiency in handling it.

Examination of the changes in the system of voluntary associations must be made within the context of the other transformations in American life: the shift from the town-community to metropolis, the growth of big business and big government, the elaborated complexity of technological processes, the proliferation of occupations and spread of specialization, and the modification of our values around sex, age, and status. In particular it is necessary to concentrate on understanding the function of voluntary associations in the larger social structure, that is their tangential position between institutions, persons, and activities. To draw upon an analogy from biology, voluntary associations constitute the connective tissues between the major institutional arrangements of the society. They provide organizational links through which the diversities of a social system are brought into some kind of an integrated whole. If we contrast the type and function of voluntary associations in the community setting with their counterparts in the metropolitan setting, perhaps the principle will be clarified.

The associational pattern of the American community at the

turn of the century was relatively simple.[14] One found fraternal lodges and mutual aid societies, patriotic organizations, women's clubs, and other groups dedicated to athletic, social, political, and occupational activities. Today their names are less familiar and their activities have diminished in importance. One recalls the Grand Army of the Republic, the Women's Relief Corps, Odd Fellows, Masons, Modern Woodmen, the Grange, and the W.C.T.U. Later, these were joined by the businessmen's groups, the chambers of commerce, and luncheon clubs, Rotary and Kiwanis, and, among youth, the Boy Scouts and the Girl Scouts. The ones we have named were national in scope, but there were also local associations, organized for cultural, recreational, or civic purposes. These groups enriched community life in the range of interests they served and elicited. They gave expression to, and joined, differences of age, sex, status, and activity. They organized the communal observances of national holidays, and in times of national crisis, they were the groups that sold bonds, solicited funds, collected scrap, and rolled bandages.[15] They were, and still are, a vital part of the traditional American community, but neither suburbia nor the core city provided a congenial environment for their spread.[16]

The associational pattern of the community reflected its internal social and cultural divisions. The significant associations that express the complexities of contemporary society are those related to the great superstructures and to their internal specializations. They join together the thinkers, managers, and doers in scientific, professional, technical, commercial, and trade associations. The practitioner of each minute specialty can freely unite with those others who share his activity or position, indeed his freedom not to unite is severely restricted. Doctor, lawyer, merchant, banker, teacher, engineer, clerk, physicist, barber, chef, manufacturer, postman, machinist, conductor, or airline steward, all have an association which beckons them to membership.[17] Some of them are widely known and their pronouncements publicized, and those with large memberships or great financial backing maintain national headquarters with paid professional staffs. The American Medical Association, the National Association of Manufacturers, the American Psychological Association, the United States Chamber of Commerce, and the American Association of University Professors are but a sampling to illustrate the range.

The professional associations, in particular, promulgate codes of ethics and may censor or expel members for their violation. All types maintain lobbies, through which attempts are made to influence legislation. They support, condemn, or attempt to modify what is taught in the schools. They make statements about foreign and economic policies, civil rights, and a host of other topics. They provide a mouthpiece for otherwise mute or ineffective segments of the population. The more affluent among them buy the services of public relations experts, whose skill is directed toward swaying the public or some special segment within it.

There is little need to further elaborate upon their activities: they are sufficiently well known. However, their social significance in the scheme of the great superstructures can be made explicit by contrasting differences between voluntary association related to community life and those related to the superstructures. Whereas membership in a family or factors of sex, age, status, or residence are of prime consideration in the community-type association, they are irrelevant or of no importance in the professional or trade group. A doctor, physicist, professor, manager, beautician, or cab driver may be of either sex, and the limitations of age are those related to laws governing employment and the necessities of acquiring skills. (Some of the larger professional societies may have local groupings, but geography is not restrictive.) Nor is eligibility a function of wealth or status. In other words, an entirely different set of qualifications, governed by the characteristics of the special population to which each type of organization appeals, operates to determine who does or does not take part.

These great encompassing networks of membership and communication penetrate into every locality and honeycomb corporations, government agencies, universities, and other organized entities. Through these groupings the individual is brought into relation with his corporate peers, professional colleagues, and occupational counterparts throughout the nation. In each locality the retailer, beautician, real estate broker, contractor, city employee, or professional is touched by one or more of these associations. The engineer in government agency, industrial laboratory, university classroom, or as private consultant, reaches beyond the confines of his organizational structure into a professional and technical brotherhood which is supra-local and supra-organizational. Salesmen, personnel directors, buyers, brokers, and laborers do likewise.

To a very considerable extent the ethics, regulations, and techniques which govern the practice of a trade or profession as well as the values and attitudes which govern the relation with complementary groups are derivative from and given formal expression within the association. Some, such as the American Medical Association, possess quite formal machinery for determining eligibility or imposing sanctions on members, but administrative, legislative, and judicial devices exist in greater or lesser degree in all, validated through their use at general membership conventions and in the on-going administrative process of meeting day-to-day problems. Trade and professional journals advance the interests of their members by presenting issues, ideas, new developments and products, and through advertising, bring to their attention notice of new books, services, machinery, or drugs.

Through multitudinous voluntary associations we possess a vast non-governmental, non-community mechanism which adds that needed cohesiveness to a metropolitan civilization, a set of linkages that are not found in the specific entities of corporations, universities, municipalities, and neighborhoods. Their essential relation is to the components of the superstructures rather than to locality. The devices for internal communication assure the rapid dissemination of new developments. The specification of standards of conduct and performance provides some minimum level definition of responsibilities to co-workers and to the public. These provide at least a modest check upon the unscrupulous and rapacious corporation and upon unethical practice in general. In this function, they supplement the concern for the public welfare given expression, for example, in the pure food laws, but they may also go counter to public opinion in such matters as medical care of the aged. The agreements reached among the separate enterprises of a given industry may also be suspected of contributing to violation of anti-trust laws.

For good or evil, the voluntary association provides the meeting ground on which divergent and even competitive elements may seek to reconcile their differences and to define their common interests. The effect is to give stability to the corporate system otherwise theoretically possible only through monolithic state control, but the latter course lends itself to the inflexibility which has appeared, among other places, in the regulation of the railroads and is, we believe, a common feature of totalitarian systems.

CORPORATE ORGANIZATION

The corporation as a form of human organization had its origin in the medieval period. In England it was used by the kings as a device to buttress the royal power against that of the feudal lords and the Church and to meet the new needs of an emerging nation-state. The flexibility of its social form permitted its successful application to a great variety of enterprises. Hence, it is not surprising that exploitation and settlement of the New World was advanced through the issuance of royal charters. In the First and Second Virginia Charters of 1606 and 1609 and the Massachusetts Charter of 1628 the Crown bestowed political and economic authority upon the grantees. In fact public government in America was based upon an ordinance of the Virginia Company of 1621, which became the model for later English colonies. In this sense the commercial corporation was the progenitor of the American form of government.[18]

After the establishment of the Republic, and in keeping with the doctrine of individual freedom, the laws governing corporations were liberalized to extend to individuals the right to utilize the advantages of corporate organization for private ends and purposes. In effect government provided the instrument and laid down the conditions through which individual initiative was extended to the group. This principle was validated and strengthened during the last half of the nineteenth century by a sequence of decisions of the Supreme Court, which called the corporation a person before the law, hence possessive of the rights, privileges, and protection accorded to the individual under the various provisions of the Constitution. Although these decisions have been interpreted as a defense of property and the power of great corporations, they may be viewed in another sense as a radical, perhaps revolutionary addition to the American doctrine of freedom. The frequent use of corporate power against the public interest was an almost inevitable consequence of the freedom corporations acquired by court decision. It enabled them to move in a variety of directions to meet changing conditions, allowed them unparalleled growth toward monopoly, and consequently threatened destruction of the very principles of American democracy that made corporate freedom possible. Hence arose the necessity for legislative restraints and governmental encouragement of what Galbraith calls countervailing power.[19]

The reason for our emphasis upon the business corporation should be fairly obvious, for the successive stages in the transformation of American society have thus far been mostly in the direction of extending the commercial spirit and keeping our energies and attention fixed upon the production and distribution of goods. The designation of our way of life as a business civilization has not been unjustified, and corporate organization has been the social form through which this has been achieved.[20]

Few persons would question the central position which business corporations occupy in American life nor the near imperialistic economic power which a few great mammoths possess.

Numerous studies have presented in detail the overwhelming proportion of wealth and production concentrated in the handful of giants.[21] Such analyses have frequently served the purpose of illuminating a variety of problems deriving from the concentration of economic power and its effects on competition, price, and market; on ownership, financing, and control; on legal restraints, social responsibility, and legitimacy; on ethics and democratic values; and on the position of the individual in a corporate society. Conclusions about these problems of jurisprudence, economics, history, and ethics are achieved through public debate and reflected in policy and legislation. Although none of these problems may be ignored, and several have more than a peripheral interest for us, we have concentrated our attention upon two aspects only: the effect of the corporate system upon community, and its internal organization and operations. Both of these are of immediate relevance to the structure and functioning of the schools which will be examined in the final section of this chapter.

The Corporation's Impact on Community

Intrusion of corporate business enterprise into Main Street America has weakened the system of local leadership, increased the proportion of population which is civicly non-participative, introduced areas of strife between workers and management for which the mechanisms of solving community problems are inadequate, and accelerated the erosion of the capacity of local community to maintain its autonomy. Those who hold a nostalgic longing for the past may well count these consequences as the basis for a serious indictment of corporate society. At the least they should engender the thoughtful consideration of all of us who are deeply concerned about the future direction of American civilization and the on-going transformation of our society.

The unintentional attrition of local community vitality may be attributed to several factors. Since the declared objective of the industrial enterprise is the production of goods for profit, concern with community welfare must remain incidental and the expansion of community services entailing higher taxes is a burden to be avoided. The plant is ordinarily not dependent on the locality for its raw materials nor as a market for its product. Except in the increasingly rare instances of home owned industry, financial and managerial ties are to the outside. Thus, in its organizational pattern and in its mode of operation, the corporation transcends the locality. In its supra-community functions its problems are not at all, or only incidentally, those of the community. Since its success or failure is partially dependent upon the favorable combination of raw materials, available labor, and market, no single enterprise can permit loyalty to community welfare to override that of decisions based upon business expediency. The New England owned and operated textile industry readily abandoned the towns of that region when necessity or advantage dictated. The owners felt little if any responsibility for an unemployed population left behind. One vivid account of the natural history of the transference of control of local industry into remote hands and its ultimate fate is given in J. P. Marquand's *Sincerely, Willis Wayde.*[22] A generation earlier, Booth Tarkington dramatized in *The Magnificent Ambersons*[23] the decline of a town's first family under the onrushing sweep of industrialization.

But the bodily transfer of an industrial enterprise from one locality to another is far less common than the comings and goings of those who staff the managerial posts in branch plants. By all rights, these capable and energetic newcomers should provide a desirable increment to the reservoir of community leadership, for their outlook and education and the prestige and power which their positions carry are factors conducive to civic contribution. Yet the facts are otherwise, and their inability to exercise leadership creates a lacuna which is not filled from other sources.[24] To account for this strange state of affairs, it is necessary to look at the organizational structure of the corporation.

The group comprising top management, from which leadership might be expected, looks to a remote central headquarters, not the local community, for its rewards. In the competitive race of "up or out" they cannot afford to become embroiled in controversies that might reflect adversely on their companies. And community problems inevitably entail controversy. The battleground on which they are at home in their infighting is the corporation itself; as Cameron Hawley's *Executive Suite* so convincingly details, it is here that one is tested and proved.[25] Why should the ambitious executive engage in causes, especially those involving politics, the outcome of which adds little to his position and which may seriously jeopardize it? Is not the much safer course, as Norton Long points out, to ally oneself with the thoroughly respectable Community Chest, Chamber of Commerce, or Red Cross, where the ritualistic performance that is required offers no threat?[26] He interprets the position of the corporate manager as being primarily proconsular, the representative of a foreign power, and our own analysis would support this conclusion.

The system which rewards those who are continuously alert for advancement through transfer does not encourage the sinking of deep roots in community life. Just as one must earn his right to leadership in community life, so also must position be won in corporate organization; neither one can be bestowed. Inevitably the situation is one of conflicting loyalties in which the community is most often the loser. The career pattern of the successful aspirant is geared to successive steps upward through the corporation hierarchy and does not allow sufficiently lengthy residence in any locality, at least not until the head office is reached, for full community participation.

Residence in metropolis poses no such problems. One can accept or reject active participation in child-centered suburban affairs, or one may sink into anonymity in the urban apartment. The way of life and pattern of settlement are congenial to those who dedicate themselves to profession or career. Ancestry and past performance are reckoned less than present position and future potentialities. There are no tribal elders to whom homage must be paid nor from whom reward for merit is received.

Although we have focused upon the business corporation and its top personnel, our description applies with equal force to transient members of the military, labor unions, government employees, and some of the professions. The crag-jumping school administrator, the itinerant teacher seeking greener pastures, the career oriented college professor, the aspiring clergyman—together they constitute a vast army of mobile Americans, making their contributions through the institutions of community but never really a stable part of it. The vans that shuttle household effects from locality to locality are familiar sights on the American landscape and inescapable parts of the corporate society.

Those who defend the local community as the bastion of democracy do not reckon with the relentless extension of metropolis. That which binds all segments of public life, all regions, and all localities into a vast new American system is only in part the diffusion of cultural standards and norms of behavior through the mass media; it is much more the interpenetration of organizational forms that has done so. Even the belief that education remains a local function proves on careful inspection to be merely a comforting illusion. State legislatures have long since placed educational control in state boards and departments of education, the teaching profession establishes the ethics governing activities within the classroom, and textbook publishers (in conjunction with makers of standardized tests) determine the content of instruction. The interrelations of many different kinds of corporate organizations—public, private (profit and nonprofit), and voluntary professional—are seen clearly in their impact on the community's education. This is typical of community life in general.

Internal Organization and Operation

The internal arrangements of the corporation provide an ingenious mechanism for concentrating human and mechanical resources, for directing energies toward long-range objectives, and for eliciting cooperation from a technically and culturally heterogeneous group. From without, its organization and operation look neat and orderly, almost a thing of beauty in the symmetrical arrangement of positions on a personnel chart and in the precision with which job requirements of each little box are succinctly described. Its internal departmental and subsectional divisions give expression to the variety of functions and their relationships. The neatly angled lines that connect each echelon of descending rows of positions symbolize lines of communication and authority and of prestige and power. This is the hierarchical pyramid of supervision and coordination—startlingly similar to the chain of command of the traditional army—which Chester Barnard so brilliantly and abstractly dissected in *The Function of the Executive,* and other scholars have taken great pains to define and some to note that it fails to operate in exactly the way it is conceived.[27]

One can but marvel at the demonstrated capacity of the corporate form to organize the technical processes for efficient productive purposes. Its success, however, may in part be attributed to the great flexibility accorded the corporation to meet changes in varied types of conditions, whether these arise from the surrounding habitat or from internal tensions, and to exercise some control over its environment through elimination of competitors or by influencing courts and legislation. This flexibility of action extended to the regulation of its employees—hiring and firing, hours of work, wages, and promotion—except as this autonomy was circumscribed by law or the countervailing power of the unions.[28] And when people, things, and processes are instruments of production humanitarian considerations are either incidental or fortuitous.

F. W. Taylor was one of the first to advocate the utilization of technical processes to lighten the burden of industrial drudgery.[29] His proposals were subverted by management to increase production through time-and-motion studies and rate setting, and hence "Taylorism" became a term of opprobrium among workers, particularly in Europe. Then, in the 1920's and '30's, Elton Mayo and his associates at the Harvard School of Business attempted a new tack. Their research led them to a socio-psychological view of human behavior that challenged as folklore prevalent notions of motivation based upon concepts of the economic man, and opened up insights into human organization which unfortunately have continued to be almost completely ignored in practice.[30] Organizational research during the past two decades in industry, hospitals, mental institutions, and at least one school has established that all is not well behind the orderly façade of corporate groups. Certain aspects of organization produce stultifying effects: they exact an immeasurable human cost.[31]

We may gain some understanding of the tensions in organizational operation by examining two sets of relationships: those of client and supervisor. The term "client" designates that individual (or collectivity) which receives goods or services from an organization or possibly, as in the case of professional advice, from an individual. The specific label will vary somewhat from one kind of arrangement to another. For example, retailers and manufacturers deal with customers, railroads serve passengers and shippers, hospitals treat patients, governments aid citizens, churches possess communicants, and schools educate pupils. There may be a client relationship between any two organizations. When the government, a hospital, a school, or a business buys goods or services, it is in the client position. The only exception is the Constitutional provision that prevents organized religion and government from entering a client relationship, although the Catholic Church is now attempting to modify this arrangement by seeking federal aid for its parochial schools under the guise of labeling the issue a political one. The relationship in education is also a special one because of legal and social custom, which grants to an educational institution the role *in loco parentis*—a fact that is crucial in understanding the transitional position of the school between private and public worlds. Viewed from a different angle, we observe that there are a series of publics, each one of which is served by different institutions. We call this the client relationship.

The other major relationship may be labeled "supervisory" and is entirely internal to the organization. In its simplest form it represents the relation between the managers and the managed. In industry it includes the management and the workers; in the army, officers and enlisted men; in a hospital, the technical and professional staffs and the patients; in the Indian Bureau, the administrative staff and the Indians; in the Bureau of Internal Revenue, the tax collector and the taxpayer; in the schools, the school staff—including administrators, specialists, and teachers—and the child.

The significant aspect of the supervisory relationship is that one individual or group initiates action for another individual or group and that the latter is rewarded or punished according to the response. The person in charge is responsible for making decisions and giving direction to the enterprise; and in the fulfillment of his duties he must impose limitations of action through regulations, coordinate individuals and functions, and issue direct orders. Intermediate personnel receive and transmit these instructions and inevitably in the process interpret and modify the action in relation to the immediate situation. Ultimately, the flow of action reaches the outer limit of the organization, its lowest echelon. The army private is told to pack his gear; the hospital patient receives an injection; the typist copies a manuscript; the worker changes his operation; the student writes an examination. In very few instances does this lowest man have any opportunity to participate in the decision of what, how, or when he is to act. Nor is it his prerogative to question why.

In certain types of institutions, the restrictions placed upon the individual are intensified through the exercise of custodial functions. These are exhibited in their most extreme form in prisons and insane asylums, collectivities which show least evidence in our society of modification in the direction of the corporate form. In these, the absorption of the inmate within the supervisory system is nearly absolute. Even "free time" is rigidly controlled. Much less apparent are the custodial functions of a government agency, except in the rare instances of a Los Alamos or Oak Ridge under wartime conditions, or on an Indian reservation. In industry, except in the instance of a company town, the custodial function is minimal and restricted to the point of operation, the factory. In the nuclear family parents exercise custodial responsibility for children and pets.

The custodial function is not a necessary attribute of organization, and in certain types of institutions the client and supervisory relationships are merged. If we plotted types of organizations along a continuum expressing the degree of custodial responsibility extended to either inmates or the supervised, we would find business corporations and certain government agencies (e.g., the Weather Bureau, the SEC, and the U.S. Office of Education) at one end, and schools, prisons, hospitals, orphanages, and insane asylums at the other. When we ask what reason may be advanced to account for the difference, our attention is directed to the extent to which there is a coalescence of the client and the supervisory relationships, as in the roles of pupil, patient, orphan, and prisoner. The special public served by each special type of institution becomes the managed, with consequent severe limitations upon freedom of action. (Business monopoly would achieve the same effect.) But in the case of the schools the adverse effects of institutionalization are ameliorated by the countervailing influence of the parental relation to the child and by the effect of the educative process, the goal of which is the development of the child's capacities.

Now to what extent are the supervisory and the educative functions of the school contradictory? Until about 1890 rigid discipline and learning were linked in agrarian classrooms, but the educative process was always paramount as the ideal objective. In contrast, in the urban blackboard jungle the pretense for learning is subordinate to the need for order. Admittedly, the ritual of teaching and learning is still observed in most schools, but adverse consequences lie ahead if the process of bureaucratization continues. Evidence from research in other organizations may help us to formulate the problem and determine the direction and the danger.

That all is not well behind the organizational façade finds expression in such popular sayings as "the rat race" or "I'm just serving time," in the apparently irrational but applauded behavior of the bus driver who can't take it any more and heads for Florida with his bus, or in the more serious instance of the person who walks out on job and family, and disappears, and in the deep concern among those intellectuals who speculate on the meaning and purpose of modern life.

It is time that all of us should be concerned because the manner in which we operate our organizational system subverts the principles of individual freedom and human dignity. The chain of command, inert bureaucracy, and excessive supervision belong to the horse and buggy days; they are the antediluvian relics of a period preceding the contemporary complexity of interdependent functions. Please note we are not condemning the corporate form. It permitted a flexibility and freedom of action absolutely essential for our national development. What we protest is the failure to extend the same principles of action to the internal operation. As a consequence, a heavy burden of responsibility has been placed upon a small managerial and professional elite, and the great mass of the population has been denied the full contribution of their talents to the public welfare.

Some measure of the magnitude of this debilitating effect upon the individual, and indirectly upon the organization, has been revealed by research in industry. These have been collated by Argyris, who comes to the conclusion that the needs of the individual and organization are incongruent.[32] In the adjustment between the two, the worker is the one who has been forced into an adaptive posture, often becoming apathetic or hostile and feeling a wide gulf between himself and those in control. Self-protective activity takes the form of restriction of output, informal and extraorganizational controls, and in extreme cases, sabotage. The response of management is to intensify the procedures which created the original situation, and hence to exacerbate the dependent, submissive, and passive feelings. Other research, however, reveals a situation in which the plant is viewed by the workers as a point of vitally significant activity and a refuge from a barren and meaningless community life.[33] It is not mere coincidence that one of the bitterest and most prolonged strikes in labor history was against a company, i.e., Kohler of Kohler, whose management was also one of the most paternally beneficent.

The evidence is clear. Ill effects flow from the concentration of freedom of action in the hands of a few and its denial to the many. The problem which now confronts us is to examine the relevance of school organization to the corporate form and to the function of education in our type of civilization.

SCHOOL ORGANIZATION AND THE EDUCATIVE PROCESS

We have reserved until now full consideration of the second of the two questions we posed at the beginning of this chapter. We explained there that only after some understanding of the organizational revolution that has transformed America has been achieved would it then be possible to assess the consequences for the process of education and the organization of the schools.

The organizational correspondence between the schools in metropolis and the other superstructures should by now have become increasingly apparent to those who know school operation. Bureaucratization, internal specialization, elaboration of a hierarchy of coordination, centralization of authority in a managerial elite, and expansion of activities are all characteristics resembling other corporate systems. Even some of the language and imagery of industrial organization has been taken up by educators who talk of packaged programs and view end results as products.

Despite the protestations of the professional educator (usually a non-teaching specialist) that each child be hand-crafted in terms of his individual needs, the process more nearly resembles an assembly line operation in which a conveyor belt receives the roughly stamped bodies at one end, and after modifications and additions delivers them as finished products at the other.[34] (The temptation to draw further comparisons by allusions to chrome plating, body trim, and tail fins must be resisted.) The conscious or unconscious aping of the industrial process in education, based upon coordination of men, machines, and materials in technical procedures, can only subvert the educative process. Unfortunately the malady from which the schools of metropolis seem to suffer results from just this kind of affliction. Yet the causes are easy to diagnose.

In an earlier America the one-room country school was an extension of the family, and in the towns schools were an expression of community. But to what social segments may we say the public schools of metropolis are related? To parents? Professional experts and bureaucratic organization have effectively blocked most avenues of participation. To business corporations? They have long since declared their position by opposition to federal appropriations for education and by their implied resistance to increased taxes at the local level. To churches? They are barred by law from direction or control, although some Protestant groups have vigorously defended public education. To universities, or even to teachers colleges? They have proclaimed an academic and professional aloofness. To voluntary associations? Groups composed of public-spirited citizens and professional educators have attempted to bring educational advances and prevent the worst abuses, but whatever their influence, their role does not include responsibility.

The obvious relation is to an elected or appointed school board, presumably representative of the public. But, in fact, is not the board's position comparable to that of the directors of a corporation, who at times act in the interests of the government from which the corporation received its charter, of the clients who buy the firm's products, of the stockholders, of the employees, or of the management to which they have delegated operational responsibility? But the significant relation is between the directors and the management.[35] This is also true with our schools. Under such an arrangement the ties to parents, community, and other groups are tenuous. In actuality school operation is a projection of an educational bureaucracy composed of administrators, specialists, and clerical workers. Theoretically and ideally these personnel serve the teaching functions; in practice they may actually hinder it.

In American schools the educative process is being increasingly subordinated to the necessities of administration and coordination. Particularly flagrant in the large cities, but nowhere absent, the growth of educational bureaucracy is justified under the rationale of providing the auxiliary services necessary for the classroom teacher to do his job. It is seriously questionable, however, whether the intended effect is being realized. It seems more likely that teachers are under increasing pressures from above, which in turn they transmit to the students. A good deal of indirect evidence and at least some research support the conclusion that the teacher-student relationship has been transformed into one resembling that of the foreman-worker in industry.[36]

Teachers no longer possess the autonomy with which they once conducted their classes. Discipline problems which were once settled between teacher and student, or in exceptional cases taken to the principal or parents, have now been institutionalized in guidance officers; and they may eventually reach the school psychologist. The numerous specialists in techniques and subject matter maintain close surveillance of classroom activity. Their professional expertise gives them a decided advantage in recommending or installing modifications in the curriculum. Auxiliary personnel in health, social problems, or recreation intrude in the learning process and fragment teacher-student relationships. School-wide examinations are prepared at the central office in the remote state capital or in Princeton, New Jersey; they force the teacher to adhere closely to prepared lesson plans, and they create a tension in learning as students are crammed with facts to insure a good showing. Parents, with high hopes for admission of their children to prestige colleges, add directly or indirectly to the burden of pressure as they point to the barrier of College Entrance Board examinations. These being the facts of life, the tendency is to accept them as normal. Only the socially impoverished apparently remain ignorant of, or indifferent to, the necessity of formal education for those seeking to secure any decent kind of status in our society. At least that is one explanation educators offer to explain the failure of a large proportion of their school population to give serious attention to learning. (In New York City one-third of the students become truancy cases each year.) Is it possible that other factors are also contributory?

Research in industry has revealed that apathy, rejection, and sabotage derive from the operation of a system that denies men freedom. When there is no investment, there can be no commitment. Our type of society requires an educational system in which the schools function as a transitional structure for children as they move from the private and personal world of the nuclear family into positions in the public world of the superstructures. This requirement is impossible to achieve within an organizational form in which the supervisory relationship is dominant.[37] Learning of the sort we require can occur only where there is freedom and autonomy.

Earlier we advocated that in order for students (and teachers) to engage fully in the educative process the solution is to place the organizational structure at their service and thus release them from custodial and supervisory restrictions. If the principles implicit in the corporate system of organization are applied, this objective can be achieved.

The possibilities for freedom and initiative which the corporate form permits have never been realized, much less adequately understood. Neither the supervisory relationship, bureaucracy, nor the custodial function are essential ingredients of corporate organization. But the principle of freedom of action to adjust and to modify the environment for corporate purposes is. The utilization of this principle in groups requires the exercise of coordination and leadership. These qualities are needed to assure a situation in which each individual and subgroup knows its relation to the others in pursuit of a common objective. Such a system does not assure any necessary reduction in tension, but it does provide the channels and procedures by which these can be resolved. Ultimately it extends to each unit a measure of freedom equivalent to that which is enjoyed by the corporate whole. The alternative is the purely mechanical arrangement which now prevails.

Only in an environment of freedom and autonomy can the educative process function.

With this chapter we conclude the description of America and its transformation. Our goal has been to convey an understanding of the present and of its relation to the past and to insist that those solutions which once served us well can no longer cope with the problems that lie ahead. The perpetual tension which arises from the conflicting demands of public and private worlds exacts its toll from all. All those who join that company for whom belief in the great adventure persists must be prepared to bear the costs which dedication to the promise requires. But this time we cannot permit ourselves the luxury of illusions about our system or about ourselves. For us, the only course open depends almost completely upon what can and must be accomplished through education. But a philosophy of education which takes no account of the commitments which our society requires seems particularly useless. For that reason in the next several chapters we propose to determine first what is meant when we speak of commitment and then to apply this understanding to several aspects of American life. Finally, we shall propose what we believe our educational system must be and do.

PART TWO

EDUCATION *AND* COMMITMENT

10

THE NATURE OF COMMITMENT: A COMPARATIVE APPROACH

In an age that has made anthropology one of its more fashionable academic disciplines, it is not very difficult to gain verbal assent to the proposition that commitment is more a matter of social structure than of internal feeling tones of individuals. But the full acceptance of that proposition, along with the consequences for education that follow from it, is quite another matter; for there are many influences that subtly push our conceptions in the other direction. Our legal system operates on the assumption that the basic causes of individual behavior are within the person, else he could not be held responsible for his actions. According to the myth that underlies the constitutions of our various state governments and federal government, political decisions are made ultimately by individual citizens, each an isolated figure protected from all outside influences by the walls of the voting booth. When our economic system outgrew its chrysalis of individual entrepreneurship, we did not surrender the idea of individualism in business enterprise; instead we established the fiction that a corporation was a full-fledged individual person, with all the legal rights a person possesses under the Constitution. We even individualized our mental image of General Motors, for example, and treated the growth of such a corporation as though it represented a triumph of one individual's initiative in competition with other individuals.

The unasserted metaphors within our language itself conspire to perpetuate these myths; thus educationists can scarcely escape speaking (and what's really disastrous, *acting*) as though the abstract noun *intelligence* referred to some quality or property present in varying amounts inside the cranium of each child—equally with the word *commitment*. We can believe that commitment comes from the outside, as it were, but when asked about the "nature" as opposed to the "cause" of commitment, our language almost forces us to think of it as we do of intelligence; that is, commitment is some sort of "stuff," a possession that everyone ought to have inside of him in as large a quantity as possible.

Recognizing all of these forces that tend to make us visualize commitment as an internal property of individuals, we ask our readers to allow us to describe two social systems other than our own—other systems in which the relation of commitment and social structure may be seen more clearly than it can be in the detailed complexity of the contemporary scene. In these societies, as in our own, we may well say of an individual that he is committed to some goal or value, but when we say this of an Irish farmer or a Navaho shepherd, we recognize immediately that what we are talking about is not an internal property of that individual, but rather a feature of a social system.[1]

IRISH FAMILISM

The agrarian system of the small farmers of Ireland can be understood only within the context of familism. The routine activities of daily life, the progression of the individual from birth to death, and generational succession are all firmly embedded in a set of values and represented by symbols which provide goals and give meaning to the course of life. Briefly, it is a system which organizes the relations between male and female and between the generations and assures the continuity of the family and its name on the land. The central event in the perpetuation of the family is matchmaking, consisting of a number of steps which eventually lead to the establishment of a new family, and to the transference of farm ownership into its custody.[2]

The bride joins her husband's household and the newly married pair now embark on a career which carries them through a succession of events resembling those of the generations which preceded them. Initially, *de facto* control of household and farm operation might still reside in the old couple who continue their residence in the dwelling into which the new woman enters as daughter-in-law, and hopefully, as mother of heirs not yet born. Often the process of establishment of the new family is accompanied by tension between the generations, as when fear of displacement by the old may make them reluctant to give up their position of ascendancy. For although the customs governing the procedures and obligations of all persons involved in this process are widely known and ordinarily observed, there are occasions when parents fail in their responsibilities or circumstances that prevent the realization of clearly accepted objectives.

An explanation of the degree of commitment to family by the small farmer leads us in two directions. One is the system as it works contemporaneously. There we discover that full manhood and womanhood, the goal of individuals within the system, cannot be achieved except as those who carry these qualities join together as procreating members of a society in a specifically allotted space—the farm—to form a community. Second is the nature of the relationships between members of the family. There we discover that within the daily, seasonal, and yearly activities is a division of function (based upon age and sex) which expresses the corporate whole. The activities and sentiments of each member are congruent with the structure of family relationships and thus, from analysis of the dynamic present, we may infer the social source of the commitments which are manifested in individual lives as routine duties are carried out or as the exigencies of life are met. One of us was actually witness to the following instance, which may serve as an example.

One dreary January day the old woman from a nearby farm burst into the neighboring cottage to complain that her children wanted to turn her out "upon the road," as she put it. There was little need for her to elaborate upon the details of the story, not alone because her neighbors already knew her life story, but also because the context from which she spoke was a familiar one. Hers was the difficult and sometimes tragic situation which the old of Ireland face when the time has come for them to clear the house of the remaining adult sons and daughters and to bring a new woman into the house to be the wife of their son. In this instance the old had delayed too long. The remaining son and daughter were already well into their thirties. The old woman as well as her neighbors knew that the time was overdue when provision of a dowry for the girl and land and wife for the boy should have been accorded to them, and that the day could not be put off, for both the old woman and her husband were under increasing pressures to arrange a match. The facts themselves, however, are not sufficient to explain the particular phraseology she used to express her anxiety. Yet another aspect of Irish familism needs to be described before we can understand her fear.

In the contract which is executed at the time of marriage there is a clause which reserves certain rights for the old couple for the period of their natural lives. These include the use of a specific bedroom, the right to sit by the hearth, the provision of a quantity of fuel and food, and often the payment of an annual token sum of money. It would seem that in a family system as tight as that which characterizes the Irish such precautions are unnecessary. Certainly, the ties based upon blood, as well as upon respect for the aged and the preservation of one's good name in the community, would seem to preclude the danger of familial disruption. But in reality these provisions are inserted to protect against the very factors which hold the family together and insure its perpetuation. If for any reason any person, even one within the family, threatens the generational progression, then that person must go, and even the protection of the contract is sometimes insufficient to insure against this. In times of stress old couples have been turned out of their homes, with only the county poorhouses as a haven in which to die. The old couple has the power to resist the entreaties, pressures, and threats to give up the land, but the children may use devices to force the issue.

One of these devices is for a girl to have her "character" destroyed. If this happens, her entire family feels shame, and its reputation is lowered in the community. Some of the moral condemnation also extends to the boy and to his family. The family attempts to prevent, at all costs, any such circumstance. The Catholic Church regards such action with horror, and condemns it as a mortal sin. Thus, on all sides, one finds the strongest possible sanctions against those who transgress the puritanical sexual code. (It should be noted that the same restrictions do not operate among landless agricultural laborers.) Yet there are situations in which young couples will threaten to violate all of the prohibitions and to make their action public. They will do so in order to force the girl's parents to provide a dowry and those of the boy to relinquish the land. The young people know that the fear of family shame may be enough to win their goal. But if the families are adamant, the alternative the young couple faces is to accept defeat and to wait for such time as the parents decide to arrange a marriage or, on the other hand, to make good their threat and accept the consequences. These are severe. They are disinherited and in their sinful state the Church denies them communion. They must seek refuge in the poor laborers' section of the town or in a foreign country. The rules governing the establishment of new procreative landholding families *must* be observed. Cohabitation outside the rules is rejected by church, state, and community.

Another aspect of familism—that of the linkage between family and land—further illuminates the nature of the commitment. One of the continuously occurring acts of violence which the Irish countryside experiences is called the "agrarian outrage." Many of these are in the pattern of the vendetta, or feud, and have their origins in disputes over land, cattle, or family status. The outrage is usually perpetuated by stealth at night. It takes many forms, the most common of which is the maiming or killing of animals, particularly cattle, the burning of hay, destruction of fences, or firing of a gun through a window into a house. If personal harm is intended, an ambush is used. Although each victim promptly reports the offense to the police, he remains curiously ignorant of the offenders' identities, and prosecutions are rare. Previous or subsequent activities establish pretty clearly to police and outsiders who is involved and, of course, the local residents are completely informed, if uninformative, as to the participants and their motives.

Many of the quarrels are based on conflicting claims over fence lines. According to reports the area involved may be only a few square feet, but feelings are deep and tempers are short. Hostility between families may be generated by some real or imagined injustice connected with the fulfillment of obligations in connection with the marriage contract, or where inheritance or succession to the land is involved. In one such instance two old bachelors had been cared for by their niece, and when it became apparent that they either had no intention of, or were lax in, passing the land to her, their house was fired into by the girl's brothers. In a slightly different case the son of a widow who had sold the land to a town shopkeeper fired into the latter's house. By this threat he hoped to force the relinquishment of the land so that he might possess it.

Land hunger has for generations been a dominant cause of many of the disturbances in Ireland. Although in psychological terms it might be explained as greed or compulsion, the full meaning of its emotional expression must be sought in the identification between the "name on the land" and the family which that name represents. To preserve or destroy one is to preserve or destroy the other. Both family and land must be defended with equal intensity, for they are identical.

The glimpse into the earliest period of Celtic history reveals a family system exhibiting many similarities with the present. There were extensive obligations binding kindred together under the leadership of a clan chieftain. The clan had territorial identity which necessitated frequent skirmishes to protect clan lands. Little, if any, of this ancient past remains as folk history, although a modern school system disseminates some of it through textbook learning. But a great deal of recent history constitutes a living memory connecting past and present. Much of this is in the context of the struggle against British overlordship and the land wars which eventually destroyed the plantation system and left a rural population of small holders.

In little more than a century the rural Irish have experienced the great famine of 1845 and subsequent dispersal and decline of the population and the land wars beginning in 1870 with boycott, eviction, violence, and eventual land purchase acts. Finally, the rise of Irish political and cultural nationalism culminated in the "troubles" at the end of the First World War and the establishment of a virtually independent nation. These were events in which small farmer, clergy, and political leader found common cause against the enemy, be he landlord, Protestant, or Sassenach. Out of these disturbances there emerged triumphant the right of the occupier to his acres and security to the Irish family thereon. If stress is a prerequisite to commitment, the struggle and sacrifice of this period may help explain the impress which the pattern of small farmer life laid upon Ireland to this day.

Whether we turn to culture history or draw upon the dynamics of family life in the present, we are impressed with the degree to which both supported and defined the nature of commitment. Family activities were founded in community tradition and supported by both supernatural and secular sanctions of Church and State. In most instances the powerful alignment of custom and supporting institutions were sufficient to assure the smooth functioning of the family and its generational transition. But when conditions which could not be corrected intervened, there was recourse to actions contrary to prescriptions and injunctions of both Church and State, as well as to customary procedure. Individuals sometimes engaged in activities that were labeled immoral, illegal, or sacrilegious to attain their ends. Normal constraints became inoperative in the face of the necessity felt by the individual to fulfill the commitments inherent in particular ways of life. *With the Irish countryman these included the realization of full productive, directing, and procreating adulthood within the context of family and land.* Our point is that since commitment is socially derived, its power overrides all other considerations, even those which themselves appear to be socially based. Although this condition may appear to be a paradox, in fact it is not. Each social arrangement requires its own commitments and these must be congruent with the symbols which express them.

Confusion may arise out of the failure to separate the instruments for commitment—institutions and things—from the ends themselves. Church and State, even family and land, should be viewed as instrumental arrangements, or objects, which facilitate the realization of goals. When absoluteness is claimed for the symbols and coercive sanctions are applied for their maintenance, the harmonious concordance within the relations among persons and with things and their symbolic representation has been destroyed. The use of the instruments to force conformance inevitably leads to serious disturbances in personal behavior and also in the relations among men.

The commitments which support Irish rural familism are beginning to weaken only because of the conditions within which it operates. For neither poverty nor the repressive measures of English overlordship have been able to destroy it. But the influences of the new urban industrialism are gradually modifying and replacing the older way.

NAVAHO REALITY AND SYMBOLISM

The Navaho Indians were aboriginal occupants of northern New Mexico and Arizona, a region possessing a plateau desert environment. When first encountered by Spanish explorers, they depended upon hunting, gathering, and a simple garden agriculture for their subsistence. A small cluster of families, probably an extended kinship group, lived together. The major European contribution to their way of life was the introduction of domesticated animals. This innovation brought a number of marked cultural changes, in particular, permitting and enforcing expansion over a much wider territory as their flocks and herds grew and the population increased. Livestock also increased the economic security and strengthened the position of women, who came to hold the major proprietary interest in the flocks, for upon them fell the responsibility for their care.[3]

Within the present-day reservation, clusters of related families occupy, and graze their sheep in, traditionally established areas. Since descent is through the female side and residence is matrilocal, there exists a powerful connection between a family lineage and its territory, in most instances extending backward over several generations. Ties of blood link a woman with her sisters, their mother and her sisters, their common grandmother, and their own children. Since husbands come from other family lineages, and brothers and sons marry out, the continuity of land, property, livestock, and name is assured through the female line. Together the families constitute a corporate whole which cooperates in endeavors requiring communal effort. In such enterprises the sons-in-law must respond to the direction of their wife's father. In fact he maintains a close and critical scrutiny of their behavior, and if a son-in-law proves unsatisfactory in any one of several respects, he will be sent packing. Tension between mother-in-law and son-in-law is reduced somewhat by the mother-in-law taboo which proscribes direct contact between the two. Dissatisfaction on her part can lead to indirect intervention and a breaking of the marriage. In this type of family arrangement it is the male who experiences continued insecurity. He must constantly respond to the demands of others, be always ready to prove his own qualities in whatever kind of task or mission is required of him, and even if he is responsible and industrious, he remains subject to what he may consider capricious behavior. Eventually he will succeed to the position of having married daughters and will exercise the same scrutiny and direction of their husbands to which he was formerly subject.

The education which the Navaho youth receives instructs him in the hazards of life and what he must do to overcome them. From his father, grandfather, and uncles he obtains advice and training, and from the medicine men who recite the mythological tales of heroes of the past he learns of the acquisition and use of supernatural power. His education is only partially, and perhaps incidentally, related to his role as husband and father; rather it prepares him to prove his male adulthood through the acquisition and use of power in the service of others. For him it is a never-ending quest requiring obedience, responsibility, and endurance to withstand hardship.

The young Navaho is taught that the true path of life is a straight one, filled with beauty and harmony, and that prosperity comes to him who has acquired certain supernatural gifts which provide protection and power. He is taught that several courses are open to him in his efforts to prove his capabilities to others. He might set his life in the direction of becoming a farmer, or concentrate on livestock, or apprentice himself to a medicine man to learn the chants and ceremonies, and in a former day he might have aspired toward becoming a tribal leader. Whichever course he chooses, others will stand ready to assist him in acquiring the necessary knowledge and skill, but the effort must be primarily his own, under the guidance and leadership of the one who has accepted responsibility for his training. There is no insistence that a boy is limited to one career, nor having made a choice, is there assurance of success. Girls are not barred from such decisions, although the number who set such goals for themselves is extremely limited.

There is an additional area of cultural behavior which is relevant to our analysis and which we should examine. Many societies ritually observe the transition from childhood to adulthood by ceremonies which have been labeled puberty rites.[4] Such ceremonies may or may not coincide with physical evidences of maturity, although the easily accepted explanation is that they do mark a change in the physical condition. Among the neighboring Zuñi Indians, a town-dwelling agricultural people, as well as among the Navaho, ceremonies prepare the young to participate in ceremonials without danger of spiritual harm. The real initiation for the Zuñi, however, comes during puberty, at which time he is inducted into a tribal society of all adult males, who jointly are responsible for the dances of the masked gods, that is, the performance of the ceremonies that control life. Male adulthood is thus equated with the acceptance of the mysteries—to reveal them is to die—of the supernatural in a ceremony in which the dancing gods claim the initiated to be one with them. The induction of the youth is required and becomes public knowledge. There is no escape from its consequences, which are primarily those of continued participation in sacred ritual with all the accompanying sacrifices and obligations which this entails.[5]

Navaho culture presents a pattern of some contrast. As each girl reaches physiological maturity, as evidenced by her first menses, she undergoes a four-day ceremony in which the qualities of womanhood are given emphasis. Upon its conclusion she joins the ranks of female adulthood as a junior member, with consequent changes in her behavior. For the boy there is no comparable observance. Even marriage does not release him from a subordinate status nor confer full manhood upon him. The relative ease with which Navaho traditionally dissolve their marriage ties, a decision most often resting with the young man's mother-in-law or father-in-law, is testimony to the insecurity of the younger male, even in his domestic life. It is also indicative of the relatively minimized significance of the male role within the purely domestic aspects of the household. The male wins status not within the family, but through his capacities as a representative of the family in the larger world. As agriculturist, medicine man, or leader he can and must excel. Recognition has to be won from, and bestowed by, others. The way to female commitment is precise and automatic and Navaho culture contains within it the devices for its perpetuation through female culture, almost irrespective of male activity. It is not fortuitous that Navaho men sometimes jokingly refer to themselves as studs.

Earlier we made the point that one of the prerequisites for commitment is a system of symbols through which an individual can identify himself and interpret the behavior of others and the conditions which surround him. It was not feasible to attempt an analysis of the function of symbolism for the Irish small farmers. Christianity is not indigenous to Ireland, and the generalized interpretation of Christian symbolism is not completely applicable to a culture which still retains such deep cultural ties with an ancient pagan past. The situation with the Navaho is otherwise. Here is no seriously disturbing cultural intrusion, so that such congruency as exists between human relationships and cultural practice and mythological belief is readily determined. Fortunately, an excellent thematic analysis of the explanatory myths of the Chantway ceremonies, the set of major rituals, has been made by Katherine Spencer.[6] Her findings demonstrate a startling correspondence between the social reality and the mythological belief.

The myths which she examines explain how certain ceremonies were obtained from supernatural beings. They detail how an earthling hero overcomes great obstacles to obtain ritual control over supernatural forces and how the hero then utilizes his achievement in the service of the people.

Her accounts show considerable uniformity of plot construction from myth to myth. Repeatedly the hero finds himself in a tense situation involving relations with his father, some other member of his family, or with his father-in-law. Or he may have violated some taboo, entered forbidden territory, or got himself into trouble with the supernaturals. A combination of mishaps may have made him restless, dissatisfied, or forced him to desert his surroundings. The separation from his original condition is then followed by a series of misadventures in which he is constantly threatened by powerful forces from the outside. He is attacked, rendered helpless, or captured; he suffers disease or is ridiculed and abandoned. Supernatural beings rescue him from these predicaments, and through their good will and help he learns how to protect himself, and most important, how to reach those supernatural beings who hold great power. After further hardships and rebuffs he obtains supernatural power for future use, in most cases the ceremony used by the gods to restore him to health. Thus he returns to his family where he is joyously received, and he brings as gift the supernatural powers which he acquired and which he now teaches to others. The significant point in his welcome and his behavior is that he has proved his adulthood. His full adult status is evident in his active self-assertion, his independence, his responsibility, in his having learned discipline and responsible participation, in his ability to establish himself successfully in marriage, and in his changeover from exclusive concern with his own problems to the use of his power in the service of others.

The richness of Miss Spencer's detail is excluded from this brief summary, but the degree of correspondence between myth and reality is precise. The course of life for the Navaho male is one of difficulty and hardship, but it is one he must follow in order to achieve adulthood. Unlike the Irish, this is not a condition to be found within the family but in the context of continuous struggle. Wealth and power are instrumentalities, not ends; they prove achievement for the individual only to the degree that their use redounds to the betterment of all.

CONFLICT AND COMMITMENT: CLAIMANT, SPONSOR, SYMBOL

Let us now return to our original claim that commitment must be sought, not in the inmost heart of individuals, but in the details of social relations, particularly in those relations that create stress and friction among individuals. But commitment can be inferred, and only from a particular type of event in which there is a conscious effort to achieve some goal. We saw, for example, that the familism of the small farmers of Ireland is the source for the significant commitments of this group, for the entry to full adulthood, in either a male or female sense, is achieved only through marriage and acquisition of title to the family farm. Historically, the Irish peasantry won rights to permanent tenure through the sacrifices made during the period of land wars when control was wrested from the landlords. Currently, possession is ensured through resistance to any encroachment, and the occasional appearance of "agrarian outrages" are manifestations of response to such threats. The orderly transfer of the land from generation to generation is accomplished through "matchmaking" and the establishment of the new couple within the household. But the older generation of parents is often reluctant to initiate the process which leads to their loss of control and inclusion of a new younger woman as daughter-in-law. If the parents fail to initiate the process of transferring the land, there is little that others can do to force them. The grown children may, directly or indirectly, through relatives or the parish priest or, supernaturally, through prayers for intercession to some saint or the Virgin Mary attempt to force the old ones into action. All of these measures failing, the recourse of the desperate is to shame the family through open defiance of the wishes of their parents, the mores of the community, and the supernatural sanctions of the church by open cohabitation. Through such action they become adults in the procreating sense alone, and they face the dire threat of disinheritance and excommunication. Thus commitment can be seen to originate in conflict, in the behavior of a claimant who is at once forced to strive for a goal and, at the same time, frustrated in his efforts to achieve it. Although the specifics for the Navaho are vastly different, this generalization which emerged from the Irish is equally applicable. The pattern of action is clearly expressed in a number of mythological tales which recount the experiences of a tribal hero. A young man (only rarely a woman) is discontented, restless, or experiences stress in his family relations. He departs from the household, and in a series of episodes is subject to frustrations, threats, and dangers. The correspondence between the mythological tales and symbolic representation of commitment and the actual cultural condition which Navaho male youths face in their traditional culture is remarkable. Both in myth and reality the youth must prove himself in the course of life through deeds. The acquisition of sacred ritual or of wealth and respect are evidences of the success. In both there are difficulties to be overcome and sacrifices to be made. As in myth, so in actuality: the same set of circumstances that force the youth to strive for certain goals and rewards also seem almost perversely to prevent his achieving them.

To be a claimant, then, is not enough to effect full commitment. For the Irish couple who take the dramatic course of unsanctioned cohabitation, and fortunately they are few, the sacrifice is in vain if there is no sponsor and symbolic sanctioning. From this we learn that commitment cannot be realized alone, nor does it arise from within one's self. That course leads to tragedy. There is, of course, tragedy of another sort awaiting those who never become claimants for full adulthood. The cottages of rural Ireland are filled with aged spinsters and bachelors, brothers and sisters whose parents made no provision for their marriage. Their passivity, or if they were demanding, the strength of the parents' refusal to act, has condemned them to a social existence less than complete, for they are not and can never become husbands or wives, join the community of elders, and through parenthood ensure the passage of the land through generations. If commitment is to be brought to full fruition, Irish parents must also sacrifice their own position and serve as sponsor to the claims of the next generation.

Likewise for the achievement of commitment through conflict in the Navaho youth, by his own unaided efforts he is helpless against the forces that beset him. In mythology he eventually acquires a supernatural protector who advises where and how he may acquire power from remote supernatural beings. His first approaches are rejected, but with the help of his sponsor he is finally admitted to the presence of these beings and learns from them the rituals which assure his success. He then returns to the earth people, is honored for his achievements, and uses his power in the service of others. In time he teaches the ceremonies to another, usually a younger brother, and finally departs to take up permanent residence among the supernaturals.

In actual life, as in the mythological, there is a debt to be discharged to the sponsor. Those who are lazy or irresponsible, or who find no one to help them along the way, do not acquire wealth and power and cannot serve their people. This service expresses more than the personal obligation owed by the youthful claimant to his sponsor; through its complex representation in symbolic myths this service transcends its backward look toward one's sponsor's past favors and turns toward the future, and toward the welfare of the entire social group. Thus for the Navahos commitment, through symbolic extension, becomes something more than a mere relation of debt and debtor. Does this same symbolic extension of concrete social obligations occur in commitment as a feature of Irish familism? Exactly; among the Irish the ultimate commitment is found in the mythological ideal, the Holy Family, composed of Joseph, the Virgin Mary, and her Son, Jesus. A Mother's sacrifice of her Son and the Son's self-sacrifice for all mankind mitigate and transform the conflicts of claimants and resisting forces in the bleak Irish countryside.

Although the supernatural, mythological, symbolic world may portray commitment as an absolute that can be grasped, possessed, and incorporated, in the world of men this is never so; the absolute remains ever an illusion. It is for this reason that commitment can be strengthened or lost, that some who strive are broken and defeated, and others fall by the wayside where they remain as passive onlookers. Alienation and estrangement for some may be inescapable in a social framework that makes the price of commitment very high. Personal withdrawal, disavowal of one's claims on the system, may be the response of those within the younger generation who cannot find (or perhaps fail to recognize when they encounter) a sponsor willing and able to set them on the road to full adulthood. Those deny the world whom the world denies.

THE AMERICAN SCENE

When one attempts to draw conclusions from this analysis of commitment elsewhere for the American scene, he must be quite clear as to just what America he has in mind, for the specifics of the American commitment cannot be transferred from its agrarian past to the present. In an America of Main Street towns and rural hinterland the young men came to adulthood through the claims they asserted and the corresponding sponsorship by their fathers and other men within the community. The claiming was validated by the inclusion of youth within the activities and associations of the adult male world, but the proof of the right to such inclusion rested upon and within the individual himself. No simple test, deed of valor, or affirmation constituted adequate demonstration. Instead, the whole range of cultural diversity of town and country provided the proving ground. Equal levels of attainment might not be demanded in all of them, but in one or more the youth claiming manhood must establish his primary competence in the never ceasing struggle in the economic world of farm or business or in educational, political, religious, or professional lines of endeavor. The measure of a man was established within, and conferred by, the community of which he was a member. It is not surprising that for some the means through which they worked should become confused with, and a substitute for, the ends sought. Money, status, power became ends in themselves, and the desperate were willing to sacrifice much for their attainment. (Any commitment that fails to extend itself to the larger system, even if only symbolically, is stunted and ultimately corrupting.) Nor is it surprising that the rigors of the course led some to abandon the effort early and others to fall short or to suffer defeat. But the unceasing energy displayed by so many reflected the deeply imbedded necessity to push on.

(If thus far we have emphasized the processes of commitment in the male world, it is because the connection between activity and community was more obvious and direct among men than among women. In contrast with the Navaho's deep differentiation between male and female, in agrarian America the requirements of girls seeking womanhood were no less rigorous than those of boys, although simpler. From childhood they were taught the arts of the household in preparation for their role of domesticity. But the basis for its full realization demanded husband, home, and children and in their strivings they were often forced to act as aggressively as the male. They, too, had to prove themselves, but in most instances being denied direct access to the battleground of male striving, they were forced to contest in the narrower sphere of the wife-husband relationship. Although the route to their ends appeared more direct and immediate, their goals were as deeply imbedded within the larger community as those of the males.)

The change that came to America with the rise of metropolitanism altered all of the elements necessary for commitment and hence modified the processes of its realization. Metropolis presents no total community for which the fathers can claim their sons in the same sense that youth had been previously inducted to the institutional arrangements and cultural practices of the town-community. In fact the connection between the family and the locale has been seriously weakened, since the community is no longer either the geographical or social ground upon which the proof of manhood is established. Maleness and femaleness in the bio-cultural sense have been relegated to the nuclear family and romanticized in its narrow sexual sense by radio, television, movies, popular fiction, and advertising. In the process, domesticity, per se, is no longer idealized as a goal of womanhood. The family has not lost its significance, but it has become disconnected from other institutions and from any general symbolism in which all of life may be interpreted.

Other institutional forms of great significance are only indirectly related to either family or community. These are the corporate structures of business and government and the professionally centered and directed activities of health, education, and religion. It is within these institutions that youth, now either male or female, and increasingly without regard to or consideration of sex, act out their adult roles. The commitments which are asked of them here have no essential relation either to locale or to family, and conflict between the two is frequent.

Given such structural noncongruency, such discontinuity within the life process, such confusion arising from the irrelevance of symbols to the experienced relations with others and things, it is no wonder that those who advocate a turning in toward the self in the search for purpose should have been so well received. A list of such persons constitutes an illustrious roster and stretches from Freud through Fromm, Tennessee Williams, and Norman Mailer to the members of the Commission on National Goals, which proclaimed the search for individual self-fulfillment as the supreme goal of American society.

Granted that the development and growth of the individual is a worthy ideal of any society, it is our contention that its realization depends upon the nature of the conditions, social and cultural, within which one must live and work. This being so, self-realization is to be seen not as a goal but as an unearned dividend arising from certain kinds of structural connections in the public world. Our real concern, consequently, is that the structural discontinuity between family and locale on the one hand and the great superstructures on the other is creating an environment in which commitment, in its public, objective sense, is becoming obscure. We are fearful that technological superiority, material prosperity, the institutions which ensure their achievement, and the cult of the individual have become ersatz goals in American civilization. Originally these were to be the instruments through which the dream was to be made real, not the end-all of the struggle.

11

THE SYMBOLS OF COMMITMENT AND INSTITUTIONAL LIFE

John Childs once asserted that education is inescapably a moral enterprise.[1] By that he meant that any deliberate system of schooling involves choices among alternatives, choices that are not merely matters of a technical procedure to achieve a desired end but are much more significantly choices among ends themselves. The design of a school program (in however loose a sense the word "design" is used) represents some conception of the goals that ought to be pursued by individuals and by society as a whole. Without going into detail at this point, we must recognize one simple truth in Childs' assertion. There is *some* difference between the activities of teachers and those of, say, garage mechanics. The latter can find ample justification for their occupation right within the technical competence of the job. The educator must seek for the justification of his skills in something other than the exercise of them. This is not only a simple truth; it will be seen as a key to understanding the moralistic attitude of educators to their work, and ultimately, to themselves.

A corollary of Childs' proposition is that all deliberate education is concerned with developing moral commitments in the coming generation. As a society holds that certain ends are worthy of pursuit, it holds also that the young must be taught to pursue them, or better, become committed to their pursuit. Education for commitment is more an affair of developing dispositions than of training in particular skills, for it is impossible to teach in schools the precise behavior that persons are supposed to exhibit for the rest of their lives. The assumption is, however, that if certain dispositions to behavior are promoted in the young, these same dispositions will persist in the face of new circumstances and that the person so educated will demonstrate his commitment as he responds to the continually changing situations he faces over a lifetime.

Perhaps because educational thought has been dominated by psychology, contemporary educators have interpreted this dispositional sense of commitment as a matter of establishing certain feeling states in the young. As we have argued earlier, the equation of commitment with personal feelings is fallacious. It remains for us to show what else besides personal feelings is involved in commitment and to suggest what kind of education would be required to teach it.

Let us begin with a rather abstract picture of the condition we would refer to as one of commitment. (Later we shall add the concrete details of contemporary life to illuminate this abstract picture.) There are essentially four elements that must be accounted for. First is the person, the concrete man or woman, possessing particularities that distinguish him or her from the rest of the universe, particularities which include spatio-temporal existence as well as private psychic phenomena. Second is the world of things and people, again considered as concrete and existential. Third are the relations among the various aspects of the external world, particularly the relations between the person and the rest of the world around him. (The ancient metaphysical dispute over the reality of relations need not detain us; we are speaking only of the common sense way of looking at the world, such that we can say (1) A is a woman, (2) A lives in a world that includes B, a man, and (3) A and B are related as wife and husband.) Finally the set of symbols through which the person identifies and understands himself and the rest of the world around him, for however two persons might be related to each other, we could not say that they are wife and husband unless this relation occurred within a symbolic system where the expression "wife and husband" has a determinate cultural reference.

Now a situation that we would call one of commitment requires a particular ordering, or configuration, of these elements. But what sort of ordering? We might be inclined to say that the simplest model of moral commitment would be one in which these four elements are indistinguishable from each other. Thus we could conceive of a society in which individuals do not consider their own existence apart from the relations they bear to others, in which the world as it actually is and the world as described in the symbolic system of the culture is exactly the same world, in which the symbolic system and the existential relations of individuals to each other are in such perfect correspondence that the person does not see them as separate entities. In such a society there would be no problem of commitment; the woman who should say, "I am the wife of A," would in that one statement at once describe herself as a person, posit a world of other people, assert the relation she bears to that world, and accept the symbolic system that makes the world intelligible. We can at least imagine a condition in which our analysis of the elements involved would be incomprehensible to the person involved, for she would see only one unified whole (which doesn't mean that the student of society might not find the analysis meaningful).

We call up the image of that simple condition of moral commitment neither to praise nor to blame it, neither as a goal to strive for nor as an evil to avoid. Our purpose is to reveal what makes commitment a complicated problem for contemporary educators.

For in understanding these four elements as distinct from each other, commitment becomes a matter of ordering these elements and not of eliminating their separateness. Furthermore, we must try to see the particular ordering of these elements of commitment that characterizes the style of life of certain typical representatives of metropolitan culture. We must look at this ordering not just as a curiosity of cultural life but as response to a set of social conditions that may be the emerging pattern for American society as a whole.

The psychically isolated person, pursuing his search for selfhood, is an inescapable feature of our moral climate, as indeed he probably has always been among the highly educated groups in advanced civilizations. With our decision to have everyone highly educated, we have made this isolation the birthright of all. We have irrevocably lost our innocence with respect to symbolic systems; having become conscious of the power of propaganda and ideology, we can never again dwell comfortably with the illusion that the world and our symbolic construction of it are really the same thing. If we are disillusioned concerning symbols, we are also apparently deliberately oblivious to the world itself. We are so seldom confronted with sheer obduracy in natural objects that we decline to recognize the monumental recalcitrance of our social world, its seemingly uncontrolled and uncontrollable movement. And concerning the relations that people bear to each other, we need only recall that these relations (as we have seen) must be kept at the lowest degree of psychical intensity in order that we may move, physically or socially, whenever movement is demanded. (Given the ephemeral, transitory character of the symbols and relations in the contemporary world, it is not surprising that educators have turned by and large to personal feelings as the foundations for moral commitment. At least personal feelings seem more real, more solid as it were, than the other elements involved.)

There is no reason to suppose that the social tendencies which have brought about this condition of isolation among the various elements of commitment will suddenly reverse themselves. We would rather be well advised to consider that education for moral commitment will be effective only to the extent that it recognizes and attempts to deal with the actual, existential situation instead of seeking some panacea in the mythical past. A modern person, deprived forever of primitive innocence, is committed to something when he has achieved a cognitive comprehension of his personal and social situation, is conscious of the elements involved, and has accepted some aspects of the situation as part of self and rejected others as foreign to self. Thus, education for commitment involves both learning the process of acceptance and rejection and learning to judge among the objectives for those that are worthy of acceptance, meaning that it is primarily an intellectual affair though with emotional overtones that cannot be ignored.

COMMITMENT IN THE CONCRETE AFFAIRS OF LIFE—MOBILITY

Still, only instances of actual behavior can give meaning to our analysis. Let us see what conditions call out the behavior that best illustrates what we mean by commitment. It is perfectly just to say that all behavior is a reflection of commitment, that the day-to-day performance of tasks, the simple adjustments of people to the world around them all give some clue to the commitments that supposedly underlie them. But it is very difficult to judge exactly what commitments are thus exhibited. The fact that the American people, by and large, pay their debts without coercion is certainly a fact of great significance, but the social analyst who would attempt to read directly from that fact to what it signifies is foolhardy, to say the least. So also with the fact that the American people will tolerate outrageously libidinal symbols in their mass media. Does this mean that we are committed to the excitation of the libido per se, or committed to the freedom of advertisement, or that we are simply unconcerned one way or another? It is well-nigh impossible to determine the moral significance of these facts in themselves.

Let us turn, then, from ordinary behavior and consider the periodic rituals of life. In many primitive societies it is easy to see the basis of commitment in the rituals that accompany the major acts in the great drama of life: in the individual acts of birth, puberty, marriage, and death and in the social acts that mark the cycles of the group's activities, the planting and harvest. But in contemporary urban culture these rituals are very difficult to interpret. The symbols of the rituals tend to be those which in ordinary circumstances we would regard as purely ideological. The rites of the church may be comforting to the bereaved, even though the symbolic content of these rites never penetrates consciousness. Or consider the holidays of the winter solstice in America: we celebrate the season, sometimes with rewarding gusto, but the symbols of our celebration might seriously confuse the scholar who should try to examine their content as a means of determining the basis of our moral commitment. He might well say that this seasonal celebration illustrates the profoundly Christian basis of our culture, and he might as easily say that the celebrations prove that Mammon is our god and Henry Ford his prophet. Neither interpretation would contribute very much to our understanding of the nature of commitment in contemporary culture.[2]

If we find it impossible to derive significance either from the uncomplicated daily life or from the periodic rituals of our society, we may have more success if we examine a slightly different facet of contemporary life: namely, the kind of behavior that is exhibited when interpersonal conflicts threaten to appear and disrupt the normal day-to-day adjustments of people. There are two reasons for believing that this aspect of life may yield more insight than the others we have mentioned. The first reason points to a cultural universal: interpersonal conflict arises in all societies and must be resolved within certain prescribed limits if the society is to maintain itself. And since the resolution of conflict requires the acquiescence of persons to the demands of the group, it must reveal something of that group's definition of commitment. The second reason points to the depth of American preoccupation with smooth personal relations. We expend great efforts to minimize conflict among persons and groups, and we have created many instruments specifically for this purpose. These include interracial and religious councils, formalized training in human-relation skills in industry and government, and professional counseling. We deplore and avoid open eruptions. We show anxious concern over any hazards that might prevent our working easily with others, and we go to great lengths to assure painless interpersonal contacts.

It is unnecessary to inquire into the sources of interpersonal tensions. To draw an analogy from mechanics, we might say that friction is an inevitable consequence of people rubbing together in human association, and the way in which a society provides a lubricant to limit the effects of friction is the interesting part of the story. For each person in the society will have contacts with others, some of whom are like him in age, sex, and social status and some of whom are different in these respects, and thus the same lubricant will not work equally well for all points of contact. It is in the different ways that we resolve our interpersonal tensions that we may get some insight into the nature of commitment in the contemporary scene.

The only sure way to avoid friction, of course, is to prevent contact altogether. The obvious anonymity of impersonality of contemporary urban life is, by definition, the maintenance of the social distance that prevents interpersonal conflict. People whose bodies are separated only by the thickness of two sets of garments are still effectively isolated from each other in the subways or in the passing crowd upon the street. This anonymity is a social mechanism, one that must be learned and one that must be paid for at some point in the total system.

The opposite extreme from the subway is the nuclear family; here, albeit intermittent, interpersonal contact is total among persons who are different in age and sex. Between the contacts of persons on the subway and in the family are arranged all the other institutional forms of association of the urban society. Within this middle range of association—the church, the business, the neighborhood, the civic groups—interpersonal conflict is usually resolved by withdrawal from contact. A moment's thought will show that this is a key consideration in trying to understand the nature of commitment in contemporary society. But one must be cautious in his interpretation of what this phenomenon signifies.

THE "OLD ARMY"

It would be easy to say that a person who is psychically prepared to leave a system because of interpersonal conflict has no real commitment to it. But we can see why this easy generalization is false by contrasting the nature of moral commitment in the teaching profession with that of the United States Army and Navy prior to World War II. In the Army and Navy there was an almost deliberate attempt to intensify interpersonal conflict and to force the persons so involved to remain in, and live with, the situation. The context was one of effective separation of "the service" from civilian community life by spatially isolated military units on reservations, posts, and stations. Ritual and regulations enforced strict codes of behavior upon and between officers and enlisted personnel in official roles. But within this context, club life, especially among the officers but also for enlisted men, enforced an intimacy of association that could be made bearable only when interpersonal relations were the most cordial. At the same time the enormous importance given to minute gradations in rank constituted a constant source of interpersonal friction. And as these gradations were felt as strongly by the wives and family as by the men themselves, there was no escape from them in the home. Yet there was always one escape: a man could request a transfer. But to do so was to run risk of disgrace; it was to demonstrate a lack of personal courage and an absence of firm commitment to the service. The system, in short, forced the persons in it to find some means by which they could transcend interpersonal conflict and learn to live with unpleasant tensions without being personally destroyed by them. At the same time the calculated practice of assigned individual rotation and mass transfer of units required a constant posture for movement and physical readjustment in the new situation. The functional value of such training for the purposes of the military services is immediately evident.[3]

THE TEACHING PROFESSION

Now the structural relations within the teaching profession are quite different. Teachers and administrators are an extremely mobile group. Anyone in the least bit acquainted with the school as a social system will intuitively recognize that an immediately valid reason for leaving one situation for another is that the first contained a considerable degree of interpersonal conflict. The idea that one has a commitment to live with a situation of unpleasant personal relations is indeed found among teachers and administrators, but when a member of the teaching profession behaves in this way, it is ordinarily a matter of personal courage and integrity.[4] Rather than providing external support for "sticking it out," the school will ease withdrawal for all parties in actual or potential conflict. The high rate of mobility among teachers and administrators reflects the fact that this occupation has defined roles in such fashion that persons can move freely within a very wide range of situations without loss of personal integrity.[5]

Yet there is a similarity between the military services and the teaching profession that is instructive. In both cases loyalty and commitment are defined by reference to the system as a whole, not to the particular persons with whom one is associated. More accurately we may say that the commitment is to the job or task of the system rather than to the actual relations among persons who are associated at any particular time or place. We need more systematic evidence on this point, but empirical observation establishes that personal justification of movement, either horizontal or vertical, from a situation of tension is usually given in terms of inability to perform the task that is associated with that situation. This is especially evident when interpersonal conflict has become overt. In this case, we are likely to hear that the supervising principal was not a bad person really, but he would not give the support needed to get the job done.

This attitude makes sense only if there is a set of symbols that give point and plausibility to the task the system is supposed to perform. For the teaching profession this set of symbols has the additional burden that it must be sufficiently general to apply to any situation whatever, without being concretely exemplified in any one situation. For example, the teacher must be committed to developing the maximum potentiality of every individual learner, but this commitment cannot impede the movement of the teacher if movement is demanded of him. This accounts at least in part for the highly moralistic tone of the symbols by which educators communicate with each other, and more significantly perhaps, for the fact that these symbols are extremely abstract. The teaching profession holds its moral commitment to the preservation and extension of democracy, to the promotion of personal growth of students, and to maximizing the contribution of each young person to the welfare of the society. But in concrete situations these symbols are not intended to provide a basis on which the teacher or administrator can intellectualize and adjust to a condition of interpersonal conflict; on the contrary, they serve as a rationale for movement. *The potentiality and rationale for movement in the final analysis serve as the lubricant for friction within the teaching profession.* One does not have to accept the actual system of relations that surround him in any ultimate sense. Any person within this system can move. Since all know this, interpersonal conflict is kept at a minimum. One does not have to conflict with others when association is viewed as transitory. Or to return to the mechanical analogy, friction is reduced when the pressure between objects is lessened.

The point of this contrast between the military and teaching professions should be clear by now. Commitment can serve either to force the person to remain within a situation of interpersonal conflict or to provide the rationale for leaving such a situation, thus reducing the conflict within it. Other occupational pursuits would fall somewhere on the continuum between these two. But the trend in the long run will inevitably be toward the pattern of the teaching profession. The reasons for this are partly economic and technological. An increasingly mobile and professionalized labor force is an evident requirement for the coming modes of production. Professionalization will be defined by reference to generalized skills and attitudes and not, as in the older military establishments, by reference to overriding devotion to inherited social arrangements. In fact, for reasons of productive efficiency as well as ideological preference, we have defined our so-called free economy as one in which a given job of production may be done by any one of a number of different enterprises. Competition among and within the large corporations has become a matter of competing for professional competence as much as for raw materials and markets. Under these conditions the commitment of professional workers must be generalized. The company that bases its personnel policies on loyalties to a particular set of relations among people is anachronistic and probably short-lived in the contemporary world.

CIVIC PARTICIPATION

Exactly the same considerations hold true for commitment in civic, religious, and neighborhood patterns of human association. At the cost of ignoring many interesting variations among the different institutions, we shall consider the matter of education for civic commitment as illustrative of the entire complex. The Citizenship Education Project, with headquarters at Teachers College and financial backing from the Carnegie Corporation, devoted years of study and promotion to the idea of increasing the civic competence of the youth of the nation.[6] The specific practices encouraged by the project need not concern us here, but its basic assumptions are quite illuminating. It defined a symbolic system of the greatest possible generality, whose terms are those of the fundamental symbolic system of our political life, including democracy, freedom, equality, fair play, and institutional justice. The system of personal relations designated by these symbols was also of the most general character, being essentially one which requires that decisions be made in response both to popular demand and to the traditional ethical bases of the society. As with the teaching profession, the symbolic system for commitment has become universalized.

But commitment in civic affairs is not just the use of these universal symbols; it is also a matter of entering into particular relations with other people in response to common problems. The Citizenship Education Project recognized this. In fact its major emphasis has been upon teaching the skills of civic participation. But again, as is the case with the teaching profession, these are generalized skills that may be applied in whatever local polity one finds himself. Thus the Citizenship Education Project defines the person who is morally committed in civic affairs as one who interprets his civic world in the universalized symbols of American democrary and participates actively and intelligently in whatever local political situations he finds himself. *Thus commitment in civic affairs becomes no barrier to movement.* Consequently one is not required to live down or overcome personal conflicts, should they arise. The sense of a permanent condition of mobility reduces the pressure among persons. The Citizenship Education Project, then, can and does attack the problem of interpersonal conflict in civic participation by attention to skills of human relations, skills which are effective only among people whose lives touch tangentially.[7]

Now something very strange happens to political symbols when they are used in this universalized way. They have no unique referential quality; that is to say, they do not designate any particular, historically derived pattern of relations among people. Nor do they designate any concrete goal or aim of American society. For concrete goals we use such words as *security,* in various senses: *healthy economy, personal adjustment,* and the like. *Democracy, freedom,* and *justice* become the symbols of common consent; since they do not discriminate in any way, they serve to harmonize the association of people who have little in common other than these symbols themselves. They facilitate the surface cooperation of persons who lack a deeply sensed historical and structural unity in life experience.

This analysis, if correct, would in one sense support and in another sense deny the claim that people must agree on ultimates in order to cooperate effectively on proximate objectives. The overwhelming vitality of American society makes it abundantly evident that we can achieve efficient organization for the accomplishment of particular purposes. But those who would argue that this shows we are "one nation, under God" are probably missing the key to understanding the situation. We are, rather, one nation under a system of symbols so abstract that they effectively prevent differences in ultimate values from obtruding into the details of cooperation on particular objectives. The common acceptance of contentless symbols makes it unnecessary to concern ourselves with ultimates. Depending upon one's ideological or religious preferences, one can assert either that we are therefore agreed on ultimates or that ultimates simply do not matter one way or another. The structural relations in civic life are oblivious to this distinction.

Consider the interaction that occurs at a typical suburban cocktail party when semi-strangers are concerned to find out the important facts about each other. With whatever degree of intimacy the situation has stimulated, they will ask each other about occupation, number of children, methods of rearing them, political party affiliations and preferences, religious background and devotion, even attitudes toward literature, art, race, and sex. Knowing these things about another person enables one to classify him or her and to predict how the other will respond in varying situations. But notice: no one asks whether the other believes in democracy, nor what conception of freedom he holds, nor how he conceives of justice in the current scene. These questions would be embarrassing, not because they touch on what is regarded as inviolably private, but because the respondent would not know how to give information that the questioner would find in the least interesting. But in a group that is planning to present a petition to the local board of education, these same symbols appear frequently in such remarks as "All we ask is that justice be done," or "That action was high-handed and undemocratic." In fact it is an absence of any need to be specific about the meaning or content of these symbols that gives them their power.

The spirit of these remarks must be made clear. We have tried to show that the basic approach of the Citizenship Education Project corresponds rather exactly to the condition of commitment in civic affairs. This commitment has two aspects: first, a symbolic system for interpreting civic affairs that is universalized, and hence appropriate for a population that must maintain a condition of ready mobility; second, skills in participation, that is, actual modes of cooperation for common objectives, that are equally universal in the sense that they may be applied in any locality or social stratum. Both of these aspects of commitment are functionally relevant to the avoidance or resolution of any interpersonal conflict that might interfere with effective cooperation in solving civic problems. There is no reason to doubt that, consciously or unconsciously, the Citizenship Education Project has captured the spirit of the urban, industrial polity.

AGE AND SEX—THE FAMILY

So far we have discussed commitment only in connection with the kinds of relations that exist among ostensible peers, for in an adult's professional and political life, as well as in his religious participation and vocational pursuits, differences in sex and age are held to be of no social consequence. Yet people do differ in these respects, and somewhere in the total system these differences *must* be allowed to assume due importance, and when they do, the potentiality for interpersonal conflict is increased. Although the school is a situation in which differences in age are recognized as significant, sexual differences are treated *sub rosa*; that is to say, the symbolic formulations of commitment among teachers do not give explicit attention to the fact that teachers and students are of two sexes. Only in the nuclear family in contemporary America are persons ordered in relation to each other with overt acceptance of differences based on age and sex.[8] Thus we may discover rather more fundamental aspects of commitment in our culture as we turn to the nuclear family.

The first thing that strikes one as he compares the kind of human association found, say, in political life with that of the family is that the symbols of commitment, so abstract in other institutions, become here so immediately and personally compelling. The symbols themselves have changed remarkably within a few generations. Commitments are no longer mediated in terms of "fidelity," "chastity," "obedience," and the like. A casual reading of the editorial and advice columns in family magazines shows a preponderence of terms like "understanding," "mutuality," "sensitivity," "intuitiveness," and "love." One might be led at first glance to think that these refer to personal feeling states. They do not. And this is the second major qualitative distinction within familial commitments, that these symbols refer to the structural relations of persons of different ages and sexes, persons who relate to each other specifically in terms of these differences and who must resolve their interpersonal frictions within a system of commitments. Third and finally, these symbols do *not* relate the structure within the family to the world outside. Nowhere is the schism between the private world of the nuclear family and the public world of the great corporate superstructure revealed more clearly.

It is quite easy to see that the symbols of commitment in the family are more concrete, more immediately sensed, than those of professional, or political, or religious commitment. Some have interpreted this as a sign that the family is caught up in the materialism of contemporary culture. When *Life* magazine gives a spread on "What Every American Family Wants," it portrays an amazing variety of physical goods—washing machines, automobiles, grooming aids, bathrooms. But a closer examination of *Life* magazine also shows something else, that the sellers of these articles do not believe that their buyers desire these things simply for their possession. The tenor of advertising is quite clear: sellers assume that families will purchase these goods only when they are seen as contributing to the achievement of a particular form of interpersonal relations. This form has been characterized, and caricatured, as "togetherness," a slogan which emphasizes the minimization of interpersonal conflict. The term is not lacking in aptness when the relations within the family are considered; but if attention is given to the relation of the family to the larger community, a better term would be "apartheid."

Our point is that the symbols by which the person interprets the world of his nuclear family designate not just material goods but rather the kind of interpersonal relations these goods are supposed to help achieve. Commitment in the family becomes acceptance of a certain potentiality that can be actualized if one will give devotion to it. Thus, this substantive, actualizable quality of the symbols of commitment in family life make of it something quite different from commitment in other areas of life.

In our second generalization made above we asserted that the objectives designated by the contemporary symbols of commitment in family life were not intra-personal feeling states but structural relations. This is quite easily substantiated by purely linguistic analysis; the word *love* and the other words that have essentially the same meaning are relational terms, they imply an object as well as a subject. But more significant, perhaps, than linguistic analysis is an examination of the actual kinds of relations that these symbols mediate. Consider, for example, the relation of dependency between children and parents. There is, in sober fact, a mutuality in the dependency within contemporary suburbia that distinguishes it strongly from the relation of children to parents in agrarian America. The extension of the family into the rest of the community is largely accomplished by the presence of children. The phatic communication of neighborhood-type associations, wherever encountered, can be shared fully only by those who are in some kind of contact with children. More significant still, the symbols of commitment by which interpersonal conflict within the family is resolved are given their meaning in terms that invariably include relations to children. Thus, while the culture provides little or no economic function for children, their symbolic function has increased enormously. It is only stretching the point a little to make the contrast between the contemporary scene and the agrarian culture in this fashion: in agrarian culture the work of children was often indispensable to the achievement of the kind of life the culture defined as worth striving for; in contemporary suburban culture the good life itself is defined by structural relations that are almost inconceivable without the presence of children. Hence the term *mutuality* as part of the symbolic system of contemporary commitment in family life is descriptive of structural relations, not personal feeling states.

We now turn to our third generalization, in which we asserted that these symbols lack connection with the world outside the family. Again it is quite easy to point out the difference, say, between "mutuality" and "obedience," each considered as symbolizing something about the structural relation of dependency between children and parents. For "obedience" is a general sort of symbol; it applies not only to the relations within a family but also to the sorts of relations that people have to each other in a variety of different institutional settings. When dependency is considered in terms of obedience, the relations within the family partake of the more general structures within the society as a whole, such as those of employer-employee, teacher-student, or leader-led. "Mutuality," on the other hand, does not transfer; it pertains to a very peculiar kind of relation that is found only in the very limited system of interaction within the family. We would hypothesize that this absence of connection between the family as a system and the larger society should create grave problems for those who are moving from the so-called family of orientation to the family of procreation. And the sense of plight among suburban adolescents and parents would amply justify our hypothesis.

But there are rather more interesting ways to show the same phenomenon. Consider, for example, the currently tempestuous urge of parents to have their children go to college. The strain of interpersonal relations within the home, the frantic search for a school that will admit an average student, the difficulty faced by high schools that are trying to provide a rationally balanced curriculum for each student in the face of parental demand that Johnny be prepared for college—these are the manifest symptoms. But symptoms of what? Of social class aspirations? Not at all. For social class strivings are possible only when the individual family sees itself in quite determinate relations to a larger community, and, as we have been arguing all along, this does not hold for the family in the contemporary urban culture. This curiously frenetic form of behavior makes sense only when seen in connection with a culture that demands movement on the part of all its members. Entrance into college makes possible the smooth withdrawal of the children from the home; it prepares these children not for any particular spot in the social order but rather for indefinite mobility. The commitment of parents has an intensity that demands a finite duration, and children must be prepared to assume this commitment to persons other than parents at a rather early point in their career. In short it is entrance into college that connects the general pattern of commitment in the culture, a commitment that depends upon ease of withdrawal from any situation that threatens interpersonal conflict, with the pattern of commitment in the family that depends upon structural relations of the most intense kind. College entrance, we might say, is the rite of passage for suburban adolescents. The lack of connection between the family and the rest of the society makes college entrance a uniquely important event, a focal point for years of intra-family behavior. For only through this rite can parents honorably discharge their final obligation to enroll their children in the larger social order.

Thus moral commitment within the family is of an order different from other areas of life. Familial symbols possess a substantive and actualizable quality distinct from those found in professional or civic activity where symbols are abstract and hence possess generalized applicability. In contrast, within the family the symbols are personally compelling because of their immediate and deep expression of the structural relations of persons of different ages and sexes who must resolve their conflicts within a system of dependency which binds both child and parent. A child may leave a family without destroying it, but a parent cannot.

Perhaps some additional observations will help to emphasize our central point. The increasing professionalization of the world of work is diminishing the necessity for the involvement of self in the relations with others in the task to be performed. In fact the injection of personal commitments into organizational activity may disrupt its smooth operation. In addition, the structure of a professionalized organization resembles rather closely the mass-produced machine. Unlike the hand-fitted parts of a rifle produced by a skilled artisan, the separate pieces of the modern rifle are so machined that each part is replaceable by one which resembles it exactly, reducing the correction of malfunctioning to a minimum of time and effort.

In the same way, the positions which individuals occupy in the organization are standardized in their descriptions. The specific person is only a temporary occupant whose worth is measured in terms of his ability to fill a slot within a complex of positions. Replacements consist of those whose characteristics fit the properties called for in that position. There is no intention to denigrate the worth of the individual by this analogy, nor to deny that each person adds (or subtracts) a special quality to the job he performs. Our purpose is to draw attention to a basic difference in the structure of the relations among those in an organization and those of the family, and hence to the difference in the commitments demanded.

Even under these conditions, and with generalized rather than substantive symbols to express commitment, there is still the need for devices which minimize the inevitable friction between individuals in their pursuit of a common goal. In the military, diverse persons could be readily related to each other through an elaborated ritual of etiquette, but ceremonialized behavior can provide a basis on which those in conflict can relate to each other only where the generalized symbols are still subscribed to. When the social condition changes, as it has in the position of Negroes and whites in the south, the etiquette of race relations proves to be empty in the face of its violation. The ritual of family relations, once sharply evident in our agrarian past and still persistent in other countries of the world, has declined to a near minimum. Thus the nuclear family, by virtue of its composition by specific persons, cannot reduce its tensions by utilizing the principle of replaceable parts or by recourse to ritualized behavior.

As opposed to other institutional connections among the contemporary American people, the nuclear family is not one in which interpersonal conflict can be resolved by smooth and easy withdrawal from contact. Togetherness must be seen as a dynamic equilibrium in which powerful centrifugal forces are matched by an equally powerful centripetal pull. When the disruptive tendencies overpower, the only symbol by which separation is morally justified is that of the supreme cult of all in American life: self-fulfillment. One can divorce his mate and continue to maintain his posture as a human being of the highest commitment only if he is willing to acknowledge the inability of both parties to find fullest self-realization in the dissolved union. Thus the distinction between trespasser and trespassed against melts away. Rights, obligations, justice—the universal symbols by which transitory relations in the corporate world are kept smoothly ordered—have no ultimate sanction for commitment within the nuclear family.

And so once again, but perhaps more clearly now, we see the inescapable function of the school to bring the child from the world of the family and induct him into the corporate world, but to do this without destroying his willingness and ability to reëstablish his own nuclear family with all its potential for tragedy and for self-fulfillment. Only by dying can an American escape the drive for movement and change; this leaves only two alternatives for one who would live as a member of this new social system: either he can be carried along as a passive passenger, or he can be himself a moving force in determining his own destiny. The difference will be in the degree to which he *knows* what the system is.

12

THE ELEMENTS OF COMMITMENT AND SENSE OF SELF

THE SYMBOLS OF COMMITMENT RECONSIDERED

The fundamental symbols of commitment in American culture are derived from a peculiar historical development. The language of American political and moral ideals extends deeply into the Old Testament and classical Hellas as these were finally focused in the documents and thoughts of the liberal tradition in western Europe. But the meaning, the personally and socially compelling dynamism, of the language came from the American experience. Specifically it came from two centuries of agrarian experience in America. The Gettysburg Address, to choose only the most obvious example, is historically symbolic of the moral commitments of agrarian America. But in a non-historic sense, in a sense not related to specific events in time and space, it is also symbolic of the commitments of a separately identifiable urban culture. This fact of the non-historic character of our symbols as they function in the context of the urban culture is central to understanding certain problems in education for moral commitment.[1]

The overriding problem is that when symbols of moral commitment are divorced from a historical context, they become abstract in the pejorative sense of the term, for abstract symbols lack the power to unify personal and collective action. They serve poorly, if at all, to express a sense of self and the world. As the nature of the structural connections among people changes, so too must the meaning of the symbols by which these structures are understood and incorporated alter; else we have the vacuous quality of symbolic interaction so noticeable in the microcosm of suburban life.

Many observers of the contemporary scene have commented on the apparent irresponsibility that characterizes the higher levels of the power hierarchy in our industrial, military, and governmental systems.[2] In part this complaint stems from the excessively abstract nature of the symbols of commitment. Divorced from the historical process of their evolution, these symbols become tools of propaganda rather than expressions of personal and social commitment. The degradation of language, an apparently inescapable concomitant of the advertising age, finds its most blatant expression in the efforts of political and industrial leaders to excuse and justify antisocial conduct by appealing to abstract political and moral ideals. "Peace, Prosperity, and Progress" is an appealing phrase, not solely because of its alliteration, but more importantly because it captures words that are symbolic of the historic goals of American society. But as used in recent politics, these words degrade communication; they reflect a lack of responsiveness to actual conditions and problems.

Yet as always, when a total cultural movement is brought under analysis, there is a credit as well as a debit side to its ledger. By losing connection with a unique historical experience, the symbolic system of America becomes broader and more inclusive in intention as well as extension. The rights and obligations, the duties and privileges it expresses can now literally apply to all men, regardless of race, creed, or national origin. America's dramatic role as the Universal State of Western Civilization, if we may be excused a Toynbeean grandiloquence, makes it imperative that her language be truly universal and thus capable of incorporation by those whose historical experience has been different from that of agrarian America. It is not at all paradoxical that isolationism and McCarthyism were centered in the heartland of agrarian America where, more than elsewhere in the United States, the symbols of liberty and equality were expressive of actual commitment and behavior. For whereas these symbols in the Midwest were still historical in import, taking their meaning from, and giving deeper significance to, the actual experiences of a commercial agrarian society, on the eastern seaboard these same symbols had already been idealized and universalized.[3] Although Woodrow Wilson and Wendell Willkie spoke the language of the American agrarian experience, they spoke it in the universalized tongue of an urban industrial culture, and it is with the latter tongue that America today tries to capture the imagination and loyalty of the world.

But can a symbolic system be both socially compelling and abstractly universal? Does the absence of strong historical roots necessarily render a symbolic system vacuous and emotively neutral? There are scarcely any historical precedents by which we might sound out an answer to these questions. America has turned its back forever on the distinction between *jus cives* and *jus gentium* by which the Romans tried to resolve a similar problem. Nor can we utilize the stratagems of Stalin, who turned the universal symbols of Marxism outward to the world but appealed to the deeper historical sentiments of Russian destiny when the Nazis threatened to destroy him. For better or worse, America is committed to this experiment. The answers of future generations will reflect the effectiveness of education (and, as we shall try to demonstrate, not just education in general but deliberate education) in the coming years.

A SENSE OF SELF AND A SENSE OF THE WORLD

Here we must tread upon dangerous ground. We must face the question whether it is humanly possible to develop a viable sense of self and a sense of relatedness of self to a world within the contemporary urban-industrial culture. There is, of course, the quick affirmative answer of the modernist. Comparative anthropology leads us to believe that there are virtually no limits to the different kinds of adaptive behavior that people can work out and sustain within a cultural framework. Among the hundreds of identifiable cultures are to be found the different ways of doing almost all the things that people do, and what is according to nature at one time and place may be unnatural at another. *Prima vista,* no particular way of rearing children, making a living or making love, eating, drinking, or painting pictures is more natural or unnatural than another. We tend to smile at those whom David Riesman calls "old-fashioned moralists," who fulminate against particular kinds of behavior simply because the behavior is different from what it was at some other time. (In fact we tend to smile at Riesman when *he* sounds like an old-fashioned moralist.)[4] We are consuming more material goods at a faster rate than we used to do; we are more mobile and more highly educated than ever before; we have rid ourselves of a certain amount of superstition and a large amount of disease, poverty, and drudgery. And because of this, we are capable of directing our attention inward and outward in a more intelligent, more liberated fashion than our ancestors were able to do. Develop a sense of self and a sense of the world? Why, this is the unique privilege of each individual in America!

"The case for modern man," characteristically strongest when put in terms of counterattack upon those who would deny modernism, is weakest when it deals directly with the actual conditions of human life within the urban-industrial culture. The reason for this weakness should be evident. Modernism interprets a sense of self and sense of the world as a personal, an individual state of consciousness. But if we are to understand the problem of selfhood and relatedness, we must see it as an aspect of the actual ways people join with each other to do the things that people do. The argument for modernism says that there is no intrinsic reason why a mobile, productive, and materially comfortable style of life should prevent people from establishing a secure sense of self and a sense of stability and intelligibility in the world. But we have still to ask whether within the urban-industrial culture *as we know it* this sense is actually achieved. We rather doubt that any astute observer is likely to give an immediate and unqualified answer when the question is posed in this fashion.[5]

A clinical or therapeutic approach to the nature of self is obviously beyond the scope of this chapter, but one assumption common to our approach and to the clinical approach is worth stating. Selfhood is an achievement, not a biological datum. It can be achieved and maintained only within a social and physical setting, and the setting must provide somewhat stable expectations that answer to the self-concept of the individual. Any radical and prolonged disparity between the person's sense of himself and the responses he receives from his social and physical setting will either destroy the integrity of the self or—and this is more to our point—will so isolate the person from his world that the kind of connection we are calling commitment will be impossible to attain. The first eventuality—loss of an integral self-concept—produces the phenomena of clinically defined mental illness. The second—alienation—produces what may be called, in an admittedly metaphorical sense, social illness. The implications from this general assumption give us a clue to the problem of education for moral commitment in contemporary culture.

Building a sense of self is very much a matter of integrating and harmonizing certain general biological and social roles. No one can conceive of himself as just a person; his conceptions must be that of a man or a woman, someone who is young or old, producer of something and consumer of other things. A person is a *kind* of person, never just an undifferentiated blot. He is someone with a certain color of skin and a national tradition of one sort rather than another. He worships one god, or many, or none. He is a father or a mother, a son or a daughter, and perhaps he is a lover; he is never none of these things. Physical strength or physical weakness, intellectual competence or fatuity, openness or closedness to other people—every person stands somewhere on these and many, many other continua. From the standpoint of psychological therapy, it is important that a person's concept of himself correspond to reality. For our analysis that is less to the point than is the stark fact that selfhood is a finely differentiated rather than a gross unstructured affair.

A sense of the world is the reverse side of the same coin. One can conceive of himself as a Christian only when he conceives of the world as a place where being a Christian makes some difference. And he can establish a viable conception of the world as making some place for being a Christian, only when the world does, as a matter of fact, provide meaningfully for such differentiation. And this is why the currently frenetic search for autonomy, for selfhood-from-within, a search that is led by the many-striped existentialists and trailed by the bravado of *The Organization Man,* will be necessarily futile.[6] For selfhood, which is a personal achievement, depends upon the prior existence of a system of social relations that support and extend the elements on which a self is constructed. This analysis gives us a lever by which we can pry out the most important sense of our original question, i.e., whether the sense of self can be achieved in the contemporary urban-industrial culture.

If we look no further than Henry Adams' interesting juxtaposition of the Virgin and the Dynamo, we are likely to give immediate "no" to the question. For the Dynamo, the archetype of machine technology, recognizes nothing in persons beyond their capacity to do a particular job in a particular way.[7] Man or woman, Jew or Christian, young or old, the person who deals with the machine is responded to by the machine as simply another machine. The human being finds himself treated solely in relation to his mechanical function and his own self-concept becomes a stunted, mechanical view.

This has long been the distinguishing argument of the humanistic revolt against a machine culture. But only those unacquainted with the actual conditions of human association in production and oblivious to the dynamics inherent in contemporary technology itself could have seriously supported it. Looked at from the outside, the machine world is indeed inhuman and frightening to those who are concerned with seeing that human beings live as humans. But viewed from the inside, as has been revealed clearly in numerous studies, the machine world is still a human world.[8] When Lindbergh used the pronoun "we" in describing his solo flight across the North Atlantic, his listeners interpreted it as a mark of modesty. But it was perhaps also his unconscious affirmation that the inside of the world of flying was a world of people, as well as a world of inanimate machines. The machines did, indeed, impose a discipline on the group association, but as the subsequent history of aviation amply demonstrates, it was not a discipline that necessarily stifled selfhood. Since long before Lindbergh and on through the very recent studies of group association in the United States Air Force, the story of men and flying machines shows that the interpersonal but knowable properties of the machines establish a basis of stable expectations on which personally effective group association can be built.

Here is, indeed, the strongest argument for modernism. There is nothing in machine technology itself that prevents the effective development of self and a stable sense of the world. If it were otherwise, any further discussion of education for moral commitment would be fruitless. If we were forced to choose between the benefits of machine production on one hand and the achievement of a viable self-concept on the other, we would be in a hopeless dilemma. But fortunately, those are not our only options.

We did not choose the assembly line production process as our example because the flying machine more adequately represents the dynamic direction of machine technology. Although Marx's descriptions of mill workers in the nineteenth century does indeed present a picture of a form of association that stifles the development of selfhood, the gradual elimination of this form of industrial organization has been proceeding with ever greater acceleration. And measured either by hours or by number of persons, the demand for labor in the actual processes of technological production will continue to decrease. It has been predicted that the proportion included in the labor census figures under the heading "Mining and Manufacturing" will continue to decline from its high point reached in 1920. Moreover, that proportion will be composed almost entirely of highly trained technicians,[9] associated in very human ways as production teams. We sympathize with the disfranchised humanist who sees the world of technology as one vast nightmare stifling the human spirit, but the only way to overcome a nightmare is to awaken oneself into the world of reality.

The great threat to the achievement of selfhood and moral commitment is not, then, the world of production. On the contrary, the well-designed production team represents in microcosm precisely the kinds of relation that we would call one of commitment. First, each person has a determinate role in the team, a role he can perceive as an indispensable element in his own self-concept. Second, this role, which has been shown to be more than mere technical skill, is recognized in the group as performing a function. Third, the work of the team as a whole is disciplined and supported by objectively defined purposes. The stories that follow the launching of each new space vehicle are essentially descriptions of the "well-designed" production team. The long days and nights of work that go into these achievements do not, in any important sense, represent a sacrifice of self to group purposes. On the contrary, if we may judge from the published reports, Wernher von Braun and his associates, as well as their many successors, found within the objective purposes of their project a heightened sense of self and relatedness to the world. Whether a basically military purpose is a worthy purpose in the contemporary world is another question, but the presence of a moral commitment in this instance can scarcely be denied.[10]

The form of human association required by recent technology is probably the "saving remnant" in contemporary culture that enables us to speak meaningfully of what commitment might mean. We have emphasized the point that a sense of self must take account of the distinctiveness of the various elements that comprise personality. Studies of people-on-the-job show clearly that human beings are related to each other as people, not as isolated automatons. One worker is the old man of sage, if platitudinous, advice. Another is the young Lochinvar, expected to give signs of erotic passion whenever a desirable sex object comes into view. Still others have roles as clowns, as inhibitors or initiators of novel behavior, as rebels or reactionaries, as supporters or destroyers of the ostensible purposes of the team. The fact that no element of selfhood is automatically excluded from the role expectations of the production team contradicts the older sociological notion that urban culture segments the personality and makes one a punch operator on the job, a father in the home, a Grand Knight in Lodge meeting—all essentially different and mutually exclusive roles. It just doesn't happen that way. No one is merely a punch operator on the job; he is interrelated with a determinate group in many and quite subtle ways. These complex interrelations provide stabilizing expectations around which a matching complex of self-conceptions can be achieved.[11]

Still, the production team accounts for only a few of the many elements that a complete sense of self and relatedness must encompass. For commitment to a single task of production is not enough. Regardless of the amount of dedication that a person may give to his production job, unless that job itself is seen by the person as worthwhile for some larger social purpose, the member of the production team is still a social isolate. Just as commitment in the nuclear family is incomplete and self-defeating when taken out of relation to commitment to community so, too, is commitment in the production team incomplete when its work is not integrally related to larger social values.

There are really two different sides to the question that must be answered before this matter of sense of self and sense of the world can be understood. The first is the purely factual or empirical side: Is there commitment in the lives of men and women? If so, then commitment to what? And why commitment to those things rather than to other things? The second is the normative or ethical side: Is the given commitment justifiable?

Before we turn to a discussion of commitment as a facet of social structure, let us summarize the matter of commitment and sense of self. It is not inaccurate to say that a sense of self is primary to any discussion of commitment, for we can talk about commitment only in respect of persons who are, in some sense, aware of themselves as persons. But a sense of self is not a mere awareness that one is a person; it requires acceptance of being a particular person, possessing such distinguishing attributes as being of one sex rather than the other, as having a certain age and skin color, as coming from a particular national or religious tradition, as occupying one occupational status rather than others, as enjoying certain forms of art, and so on. Now this sense of self simply cannot be achieved and maintained apart from forms of human association that recognize and respond to these differences. There is much in contemporary human intercourse that militates against the achievement of a sense of self. But the most damning allegation against an industrial culture is that its basic technology requires that people be related to each other without any regard to those characteristics by which a sense of self is achieved and maintained. While this allegation might be sustained if directed against the nineteenth century factory mode of production, it is not true of the production team that is the basic form of association in truly contemporary technology. On the contrary, the production team, probably only less than the nuclear family, carries the burden of humanizing and personalizing all those complex relations that are beyond comprehension at the level of society as a whole. But to understand this last comment, we must now look to commitment in relation to social structure.

MORAL COMMITMENT AND STRUCTURAL CONNECTIONS

If we consider the specialist in a production team, the member of a neighborhood committee for the United Fund, and the teacher in a public school, we can quite readily detect four features common to all three. First, the individual must adapt and contribute to the task-orientation of the group with which he is associated. Second, he must know how to respond to a wide range of personality traits in his associates and at the same time express wide ranges of his own sense of selfhood. Third, he must maintain such capacity for movement that, at the appropriate moment, he can readily depart from that particular association and establish similar relations with new associates in a new situation. Finally, the goals or purposes of any particular form of face-to-face association are given their symbolic significance by the larger social system in which this association functions.

These features would be present whether or not the association is a pleasant one and whether or not it is effective in doing its job. Given the necessary competence among its members, "success" of a particular group depends upon the nuances of its relations, that is to say, upon the details of the interaction within the group and the relations sustained by the group to the larger social structure of which it is a part. The highly emotional tone that surrounds current discussion of groups springs from the fact that these groups *are* in microcosm the social agencies through which the work of the world gets done. Such expressions as the "other-directed personality" and the "organization man" appeal to something quite fundamental in American life today; they appeal to the day-to-day experience of most people in metropolitan culture who find themselves acting through group associations in performing their socially important functions.[12] Hence, the details of group operation become matters of great social consequence. Moralists, both the old-fashioned and ultra-modern varieties, have given attention to the legitimacy of the demands that a group can make on the individual. Psychologists have investigated the details of the influence of group association upon personality. Propagandists have pleaded for and against the deliberate use of refined group techniques in areas where they are at present not actively employed, for example in some aspects of church life and in teaching college classes.

For our purposes, the important point in respect to group association in contemporary culture is that it represents the medium through which commitment can be expressed. The great decisions that affect the total course of our nation are made, for good or ill, within the interrelated structures of group associations. (Who first said: "According to Christian theology, even the universe is ruled by a Committee of Three"?) But still more significant is the fact that even the ordinary citizen must exercise his commitments through various kinds of association. He performs his economic tasks through his production team, his civic tasks through his special committee, his religious observance through an age or sex group, and his esthetic participation through membership in an interest group. And whether he does his jobs well or poorly, that is to say, whether or not he makes a significant social contribution and reaps important psychical rewards for so doing, depends upon the details of his association with other people.

(Please do not interpose the trite objection that the social contributions of Bartok, Bergson, and Bohr cannot be explained by their group affiliations! This line of argument is an inevitable cul-de-sac; it diverts attention from the inquiry and turns it toward harangue. Agreed that the creative genius in music, philosophy, and science is God's noblest product. But even he must live in a social system. In an ultimate sense his creations are derivatives of that system; and, more in point, his achievements become social contributions only as they enter into the lives of other people who are associated in performing groups, study groups, and research teams.)

We would expect that the ability to function effectively in groups of this sort would become an important dimension of personality development. And if we look again at the nuclear family, in our society the basic determinant of personality structure, we find that the life of the child within that family is the basic model for all other forms of group association. Notice again the four features of group association we mentioned just above:

1. *Task-orientation.* What is the task to be performed by any particular nuclear family? Is it to amass wealth? To rise in the social scale? To meet the varied psychical needs of its members? To serve as a unit of consumption, if not production, in the economic system? It is, of course, all of these things. But the particular definition of any of these tasks is made within the interaction of the members of the family. As the child grows within the family, he must learn both to adapt to the already existing definitions of these tasks and to contribute to their re-definition. The amassing of wealth, for example, may be originally interpreted as accumulating enough money so that father may start a new business on his own, but the daughter who demonstrates academic aptitude must learn to contribute to the re-definition of that task so that it includes the getting together of enough money to enable her to pursue her education. Vocational counseling in schools recognizes that part of the job of preparing for an occupation is to learn how to educate one's family to accept the cost of training for that occupation as one of its obligations.

This is a terrifyingly subtle skill. Its development cannot wait until the last year of high school. But obviously it does not wait until then. It begins *in utero,* as it were, when the family's definition of itself and its goals responds delicately to the needs of the unborn child. Less fancifully, the child in a contemporary family throughout his life comes to perceive himself as having to adapt to the existing definitions of his family's tasks. But also, in a miniature mirror image of his later functions in other groups, he is also to contribute to the re-definitions of these tasks. A member of a United Fund Committee was speaking; he said, "I consider our job more than just raising a specified sum of money. We have an educational task to do. This community is pitifully ignorant of just what the United Fund does." This is what we mean by contributing to task-orientation. This is a skill; it is also a commitment built into personality by the interaction within the contemporary nuclear family.

2. *Responding to wide ranges of personality in others and expressing wide ranges of one's own personality in groups.* Where the task to be done is clearly and finally determined, one need only express those aspects of self that are immediately related to the task at hand. But where one must also contribute to the re-definition of those tasks, then another and rather more subtle form of interaction is required. One consequence of this form of interaction is that culturally defined sex roles lose their sharp edges. In the agrarian culture these sex roles were carefully differentiated, and those who did not repress their sensitivity to beauty and ugliness and their responsiveness to the feelings of other people, all defined as feminine traits, found themselves outcasts from their own tradition.[13] The nuclear family in contemporary America, however, not only permits, in effect it demands, that each member respond to every facet of the personality of the others and, in turn, express every facet of his own personality. The image of the G.I. father who dried the dishes and diapered the baby is probably fading from the contemporary scene, but this image was only the visual manifestation of something more fundamental. The child of either sex in the nuclear family must learn both "male" logic and "feminine" intuition. The virtues (from the Latin *vir,* i.e., "a real man") of temperance, courage, and justice are tempered in both sexes by Christian and feminine humility and forgiveness. A family system *can* train its young to respond to only those traits of other people that fit into a determined sex role. It *can* train its young to express only those features of self that are appropriate to one sex. But the mobile nuclear family of contemporary America must train for both response and expression in a different way. And in dominant forms of group association outside the family the same demand is made. The production team, for example, notes and respects the sex of each of its members; but it also demands that each, in the now trite but still appropriate words of George Herbert Mead, recurrently "take the role of the other."[14]

Imagine a suburban housewife describing herself and her life in the following way: "Who am I? I am a woman, but I must not be so entirely woman that I cannot feel what it is like to be a man. I am approaching middle age; this I must accept while rejecting neither my youth, thus losing my capacity to feel joy and sorrow as children feel them, nor my approaching old age and the capacity to share those colder and more dreadful feelings. I have my own economic and personal limitations. I know also that these are different from my friends' and neighbors', and I must feel as they feel their own strengths and weaknesses. My skin color and religion are parts of my being, and so are different colors and religions to those with whom I work and play. My vision of my own future has changed with changing associations, and so my own hopes and fears have been subtly influential in shaping the lives of others from the day of my birth. Who am I? It all depends."

This would be an odd way to talk but a normal way to behave. One can see, albeit dimly, a certain functional value in this form of human thought and feeling for an economic order that demands high levels of both production and consumption from its members. Where there are potentialities within the person, they must be given a chance for development. Hence the form of human association must provide opportunity for expressing and developing these potentialities in individuals. (This sounds terribly recondite for such a simple phenomenon. But after all, what symbols *do* we have to express in an everyday fashion the everyday reality of our lives?)

3. *Every group association is conditioned by the imminence of disruption.* Administrative procedure requires that a firm line be drawn between the *ad hoc* group, formed for the accomplishment of a limited task, and the organization of persons for the continuous operation of the enterprise. But as perceived by the individual, the distinction between the two is not sharp at all. In the neighborhood, in the church, in the company, in the political party every group is *ad hoc* in the sense that one's association with it is tempered by the deep, implicit awareness that one must be prepared to leave whenever the proper moment arrives.

The ability to relate one's self effectively to other people in the ways described above and yet be prepared to move at any time is without doubt the most difficult demand placed upon personality by the conditions of life in contemporary society. The fact that we can do it, and often in the absence of any clear rationale for our actions, means that we have been consciously or unconsciously trained in a very effective manner. It reflects the success of a most unusual system of personality development as found in the structural relations of the child in the contemporary nuclear family. In a continuously expanding fashion, the child participates in the definitions of his family's goals. He learns to respond to the subtlest nuances of interpersonal relations and to express all shades of his own personality in family association. Yet, from the very beginning, this association is shot through with impermanence. Parents know, with complete conscious awareness, that the child of today will be a mobile man or woman tomorrow, a person whose relation to the original "family of orientation" will be quite ephemeral once his independent course of movement is begun. (When do children learn this? There is some evidence that children become explicitly conscious of certain social class distinction around the fifth year in school, i.e., around the eleventh year of age. It may be that a full awareness of the fact that the relation to parents is of short-term duration is connected with the changing perceptions of other youngsters. But more evidence is needed before firm conclusions can be drawn.[15])

This condition of impermanence touches the deepest aspects of personality. It extends to the most fundamental human responses, those that are developed in the initial relations of the child to his parents. Guilt and anxiety are inevitable concomitants of the basic structure of the nuclear family itself. Yet, the system operates. And because it operates successfully, we may surmise that the family system provides for the release of guilt and the abatement of anxiety. Contemporary provisions for psychical freedom stand out most clearly if seen in contrast with an earlier system. The mobile young man in the family of the agrarian society could resolve his conflict with his father through the exercise of righteous anger. Father was a tyrant; Father did not respect his own children, worked them like mules in the field to aggrandize his own economic position. Father did not understand Mother's torn body, did not even know of the hidden tears she wept in the night. Goodbye, Father. We are well quit. Later when I am a man we may meet again as mutually respectful friends, but guilt and anxiety are at least temporarily alleviated. They will return, of course, to plague my relations to my own sons, to create the kind of conflict between me and my offspring that will enable *them* to say goodbye and well quit!

Traces of this pattern still remain, of course. The conflict between generations in the immigrant families was not greatly dissimilar. But in the nuclear family of the contemporary culture, this older pattern to train for mobility is gone. In that pattern, the child did not learn to participate in the definitions of his family's goals. Father interpreted the proper goals, and the child's only recourse was later rebellion. Aspects of self that did not fit directly into the family association were reserved, not expressed.

Within the nuclear family of the present day, however, a vastly different mechanism for overcoming guilt and anxiety exists. As young men and women leave home, they take with them all the burden of unpaid obligations for what their parents have done. Dad's diversion from economic success, Mom's emotional attachments to now departing children—these become debts that must be paid, not to Mom and Dad but to one's own children. When grandfather left his farm, his father's eyes were cold and his fist was clenched, his mother's tears bespoke resignation more than suffering. When grandson leaves for college, Dad gives a warm handshake and Mom's tears only add sparkle to a face full of love and hope. The pinched pocketbook and the silence of the deserted house enable Mom and Dad to feel that the sacrifice has been made, that the debt has been transferred with accumulated interest.

Thus, in contemporary industrial culture, one learns to leave the group. And perhaps it is because the important separations of people from each other come largely before death that death itself is largely ignored in America today. One's duties are to the living, to the persons directly in front of one at the moment. For those who are left behind, nothing can be added or taken away. To these persons immediately about, one can give consideration, tact, one's technical competence, and ultimately one's self. Guilt and anxiety are paid out day-by-day in direct association. It is the moral and psychological equivalent of the installment plan.

4. But no aspect of group association can be fully understood except as we see that *the meaning of any group association is conditioned by its relation to the total social system. Any* group association? Surely the string quartet that meets monthly has no purpose other than the enjoyment that comes from playing music. Or take the bowling team. The occasional morning coffee in the suburb. The street corner bull session of a summer night in the city. Can we say in any meaningful way that these group associations are conditioned by any relation to the vast, almost incomprehensible social system of metropolitan America?

Yes, we can say this, and it takes only a slight broadening of the focus of one's attention to see that the statement is true. The string quartet plays in the living room of a private house, not in the salon of a merchant prince. This change may or may not affect the quality of the music, but it clearly affects the quality of the interaction among the musicians. The bowling team meets on the premises of a very profitable business establishment, not on the village green. And suburb versus city makes sense only in the context of a particular kind of society. We are now accustomed to believe that one's life may be influenced by factors one is unaware of. Psychoanalysis and studies of radiation poisoning have taught us that. The difficulty at this point is in recognizing the reality behind such a term as "total social system" and to give a clear account of how the details of ordinary affairs are conditioned by that reality.

Let us look first at the extreme conditions. During World War II, production teams performed in quite distinctive ways depending on whether or not their production was related directly to the success of our arms in the global conflict. Studies of interaction among groups of soldiers in wartime show a clear differentiation between combat and noncombat troops. In both these instances, however, the participants were clearly aware that they were in (or not in) direct relation to larger social purposes.

But more often the relations are unusually subtle and hard to determine, and frequently precisely the wrong conclusions are drawn from the experience of extreme conditions. Principals of high schools advise their students to study hard because we are in a technological race with the Russians. More or less unconsciously, the student says to himself:

> If winning a technological race with the Russians is the only goal of our society, then I and my companions have no genuine role to play. The superintendent's words are pure cant, and probably everything else responsible adults say is also cant. If our lives here and now are to be meaningful to us, we must develop our own sets of symbols and values apart from the larger system represented by the superintendent's obvious nonsense.[16]

The student is correct, of course. The answer is not to be found in faking relations that are not there, but in teaching the student how to see the genuine relations that do exist. Associations of students, executives, bowlers, and chamber music enthusiasts are related to the larger social system. And awareness of the nature and scope of these relations is an achievement, not an immediate object of observation. It requires intellectual skills that can and should be the primary objectives of a school system in contemporary America.

SUMMARY

A sense of self becomes problematical for men and women whose relations to other people are tangential and fleeting, whose distinctive individual traits evoke no response in the social world, whose self-commitment must be expressed in symbols that have no organic, historical connection with day-to-day life. The anti-modernists build on these problematical features an attack against the entire social and economic bases of an urban industrial culture. The anti-modernist is fundamentally mad, no matter how cleverly he tries to conceal it.

A firm and healthy sense of self and its *sine qua non,* a firm, healthy relation to the people and things around one, are exemplified in the effective production team, a peculiarly modern phenomenon. Only when Americans will learn to see the corporate world of work and production not as set bureaucratic hierarchies but as complexly interwoven production teams shall we be able to understand what commitment ought to mean today and thus reduce somewhat the psychic costs we are now paying for our success as a nation. Notice we said *learn to see the corporate world.* This means new and better intellectual disciplines, a conception of formal education radically different from the one that served us in transition from our agrarian past. In the next chapter we outline the new disciplines we see as inherent in the life of contemporary man.

13

EDUCATION FOR COMMITMENT

We have indicated that commitment is not a state of personal feelings but rather a particular configuration of four structural elements including a person, an external world, the relations between these two, and the symbolic system by which the person can understand the world and his relations to it. We have been concerned to show that these elements are actually present within some of the dominant institutions of the society. And now our analysis must go somewhat deeper, so that we may determine just *what* configuration of these elements constitutes commitment. For whereas every fully socialized, that is to say every fully human, individual exists within some kind of configuration of these four elements, it is surely to miss the whole point of this book (and, more importantly, to misunderstand the society this book is designed to illuminate) to say that every individual exists within a system of commitment. Hence, we must distinguish what sort of configuration we are calling one of commitment.

Where does one begin as he tries to establish some stability in kaleidoscopic permutations among these elements? Many serious and dedicated scholars have taken the person to be the fixed point around which a viable configuration of the other elements could be established. The notion that there is a fixed entity which we call "human nature," that its healthy or right states can be distinguished from their opposites, and that all the other elements can and should be so ordered as to bring out the highest potentiality in human nature have long been encountered in the traditions of Western social philosophy.[1] There is more than a grain of truth in these notions, but there is a danger of madness in them too, for nothing so characterizes a philosopher as the tendency to conceive of his own unique traits as the highest form of human nature.

Others have taken human relations as the starting point.[2] This approach becomes particularly appealing to common sense in an age such as ours when smoothness in interpersonal relations figures so prominently as a conscious desideratum. For the contemporary American man or woman, the question: Are you happy? is taken to mean: Are your relations with other people smooth and harmonious? Yet common sense, on sober second thought, would not say that ease in interpersonal contacts, any more than happiness itself, is to be achieved by making it either a goal to be aimed at or a starting point for social analysis. On the contrary, interpersonal harmony is a quality occurring when other, more fundamental, matters are ordered properly.

In the political sphere, the most usual approach to commitment is to begin with varying symbol systems. "Africa for Africans," "free enterprise," "the coming victory of the proletariat," "The American way"—such slogans are taken not only as the proper way to arouse feelings of commitment but as the proper objects of commitment itself. But this cannot be taken seriously. In Japan, Western Europe, and America surely, in the Soviet Union most likely, and in other areas of the world within a short time, the age of ideology is ended.[3] Even propaganda such as Goebbels practiced is a rather quaint anachronism. Ours is an age of advertising, and the target of advertising soon learns to close his senses to its onslaught. As the onslaught increases in intensity or subtlety, the victim's senses become impervious to all symbolic appeals; a debasement of the currency of social communication has been effected. Thus, to take a symbol system for our starting point is to be avoided on purely practical grounds: an advertising approach to commitment would be inescapable, and an advertising approach is inevitably self-defeating.[4]

This leaves the world of people and things as a candidate for a starting point in the analysis of commitment. It is not accidental that the great theologians have always appealed to man from the standpoint of a description of the most fundamental features of the world as a whole.[5] For the Judaic-Christian tradition, man and the world are God's creations; that is the most fundamental thing one can say, that is the starting point for any approach to man's commitment.

Likewise the great atheists have begun with the world of men and things. Nietzsche and George Bernard Shaw have taken the evolution of the Life Force as that feature of the world which demands commitment simply by virtue of its primordial existence. For Marx that feature is called history and treated in the categories of dialectical materialism.

We mention these neither to endorse nor condemn them but rather to indicate that our approach—starting with the existing world of men and things—is not mere eccentricity. It is also to recognize the dangers inherent in trying to treat so profound a matter so briefly and yet to avoid superficiality, oversimplication, and conceit.

No one would want to claim that anyone could or should be committed to the world as a whole. If there is a God, there must be a Devil; the Life Force is opposed by Inertia, Eros by Thanatos, the Revolution by the Counterrevolution. Any analysis that begins with what the world really is must recognize that it contains a number of things, some worthy and some unworthy of commitment. Yet is dualism the proper scheme in which to intellectualize the complexity of life? Can we use the Hegelian dialectic without seriously distorting what we meant to describe?

Taking the world in a social, as opposed to a cosmological, sense, we see clearly that no dualism, no dialectic is quite adequate. We must grapple directly with the complexity and separateness of things as we encounter them in the social system of the metropolitan world. Yes, social system![6] Here is the world with which we must begin, and however great the temptation to slip into easy absolutes drawn from our hopes and dreams, the temptation must be resisted and the reality confronted.

The social system of contemporary America is a peculiar amalgam of vast, impersonal superstructures pursuing various and often conflicting goals; it is a slowly standardizing settlement pattern with differentiated neighborhood subcultures; it is the intensity of human interaction within the nuclear family; it is the confusing matrix out of which every boy and girl must develop a sense of selfhood and a capacity to relate that self to others; it is the fundamental, overriding fact which must be fully accepted before commitment can be discussed or education begin.

Only when the brute, ineluctable is-ness of our social system is accepted, can we see what sort of ordering of the elements we started with could properly be called commitment. We may begin with this principle: none of the symbols derived from our agrarian heritage adequately mediates the complexity and variety of the metropolitan world. So we may leave the matter of symbol systems to the last, to be considered after we have seen the ordering of the other elements.

COMMITMENT AND EXPERIENCE

A person is an individual man or woman, black or white, young or old, keener or duller of intellect, beautiful or ugly or in-between, highly sensitive or less so in response to beauty, love, and justice. What kind of relation can any person, each possessing many limitations and potentialities, have to so complex a reality as is our social system? One answer is mere inclusion. Any person can be in a society but not of it—the relation Aristotle defined as slavery.[7] This relation admits of no commitment, as we are using the term. The opportunity offered to immigrants to join the American social order as full members of it was, and still is, the most significant anti-slavery cause in the history of the human race.

Dismissing mere inclusion in the social system as an answer, is a genuinely meaningful relation possible between the specifically characterized individual and the vast social order of metropolitan culture? We believe that such a relation is possible, but it is different from that encountered in an agrarian world, different from the assumed relation that lies behind contemporary education. *For the contemporary American, the possibility of experiencing the range of basic forms within the social order in his own personal life is nonexistent.* Full recognition and acceptance of this feature of the world is again crucial to our whole analysis. Relating oneself to American society is not a matter merely of participating as a member of some segment of it and then extending that participation to the whole. The society does not admit of that sort of relation.

Did it ever? In a rather clear sense, it did. Consider any functional subsystem in the agrarian society—commerce, politics, military, etc. In each of these, the individual who was a full participant in the social order of his locality had a direct experience of the same basic form of social organization wherever found in the society. Relating oneself to another as buyer-and-seller was the same form of relation whether found in the backwoods of Illinois or in the large-scale mercantile marts of Boston and New York. Similarly in politics, the election, deliberations, and actions of a county court possessed the same form as its counterparts in the state capital or in Washington. Experience as a member of the local militia gave one a clear sense of the basic form of military organization wherever found in the society.[8]

This contrast with an agrarian past gives us a clearer meaning for the sort of relation we can begin with in defining commitment for our own times. It is distinctly not that of merely reproducing in one's personal experience the basic forms of social organization found everywhere in the society. It is, rather, the intellectualization of one's own experience, abstracting and re-ordering the data from personal observation so that different forms may be grasped and understood. In contrast with agrarian society, in which the direct and experienced relation between the individual and his social world defined commitment, the counterpart relation in metropolitan culture is *indirect* rather than direct, *cognitive* rather than emotive, *partially* rather than fully *participative, symbolically constructed* rather than historically experienced.

We have now seen two of the elements that go into the composition of commitment—a world that comes to us in the guise of metropolitan culture and a relation that must be built deliberately if it is to exist at all. Before we can continue the analysis and show how the other two elements—the person and the symbol system—must be ordered if commitment is to be achieved, we must turn to education. For the deliberate building of the relation necessary to commitment, as we have seen, involves a peculiarly intellectual conception of education, and it is from the educational requirements of this relation that conceptions of person and symbol systems must be derived.[9]

COMMITMENT THROUGH EDUCATION

Those who have followed our analysis to this point must have gained a quite pessimistic outlook. Commitment in contemporary culture would seem to involve knowledge and attitudes never before found on any sizeable scale in the history of mankind. Surely the conclusion must be drawn that commitment is an inappropriate term; we seem to be reduced to thinking of most people as slaves in Aristotle's sense.

There would be excellent reasons for holding this pessimistic view if one surveys only the actualities of the present political, economic, and educational scene. But if one also attends to the potentialities of the modern world, pessimism is tempered somewhat. The potentialities of society are, as always, educational in nature. Specifically: we now have some reason to believe that the mental and emotional habits necessary to relating oneself to a complex world can be institutionalized, can be taught in sufficient degree to a sufficiently large number to make commitment possible, slavery avoidable.

To explain what these potentialities are, we should prefer to look at education in a quasi-developmental fashion, i.e. to trace through the stages of a learner's life and show what education could, in principle do, at each stage. The treatment here is summary and schematic, an extension of the analysis given in previous chapters.

PRESCHOOL CHILDHOOD

We have already discussed the family in contemporary American culture from several perspectives. What does the child learn there that may contribute to the long-term goal of relating him to his total society? We suggest three kinds of learning of particular importance.

1. The child can learn that love is possible, even to modern man. Love can penetrate the peculiar alternation of solicitude and neglect that is structurally inescapable in the usual forms of child-rearing in our society. The trouble is, however, that in its search for love a family may take the route of escape from the larger society. The potentiality both for full participation in the love-bound family of modern culture and for escape from its atavistic and regressive pressures can be achieved for most people only in the early years of living in a family. Love, warmth, security—such terms are necessary for describing the proper educational environment of a home. We have demonstrated the structural significance of these interpersonal forces in a highly mobile society in which the nuclear family is the basic unit of mobility. We leave, to the large and growing body of specialists who make this their

field, practical suggestions for strengthening the positive and weakening the restrictive forces in modern family living.[10]

2. The child must learn a vague and permeating sense of dissatisfaction with himself and his environment. When this attitude concerns matters of the intellect, our language has a very positive word for it: curiosity. But in interpersonal relations and relations between a child and his material environment, we are more likely to conceive of dissatisfaction as a negative thing. We often fail to reward it when it appears; we teach it with methods that may, in fact, turn it into negative channels.

We do reward and thus reinforce the child's attempts to increase his limited powers to control certain things in the world around him, as his clothes when he tries to dress himself, his blocks when he builds, his speech when he tries to communicate his thoughts. One is reminded of Erik Erikson's moving anecdote of the young Sioux Indian child (three or four years old), who was told to close the door.[11] It was just within her power to do it, and her father waited patiently while she did the task slowly and with great exertion. Any feelings of dissatisfaction she may have had were ignored; she was learning, as Erikson would have us see the story, to trust her powers to do what had to be done in the world.

An American father is unlikely to behave in this way and, even less so, his daughter. She would evince frustration and aggression; he would reinforce her undesirable behavior either by doing her task for her or by expressing counter-aggression toward her, if, indeed, he didn't turn away from the whole enterprise once difficulty appeared. The American child would be learning, in any event, the same general and vague dissatisfaction that her mother must show toward the whole world, a feeling that has the most profound connections with the structure and processes of a dynamic, mobile society. The very bright and competent mother finds her powers ill-used in doing tasks that are mostly repetitive and monotonous. The less bright and incompetent mother finds herself unable to perform up to the level made mandatory by the mass media which express the goals of the most able and efficient women. In any case, a sense of dissatisfaction is inescapable in the role itself, and this is transmitted to and reinforced in the child.

3. The child must learn a clear sense of the distinction between the inside and outside of things; we might say a feeling for the partiality of perspective. This is easiest to describe by contrasts. An infant in some cultures is swaddled, in other cultures left naked and allowed to go about freely when not held by human arms. Among us the infant's clothes put little restrictions on his movements, but he is left for a considerable part of his time in enclosed spaces. These spaces—cribs, playpens, nurseries—are his alone, and nearly always they allow vision to the outside. We do not shut the door on him; we use specially designed gates that prevent his movement but offer no restrictions on his sight. On city streets we use strollers that serve the same purpose.

As the child leaves physically enclosed spaces, he learns to live in psychically restricted areas, recognizing always that there is an inside where freedom is not a problem but a given condition, and an outside to which one may look and from which others are watching without hindering or hurting those within.

The child moving in a stroller is the prototype of the mobile adult; he travels not nakedly in the world but inside a device which offers definite restrictions on his movement but also protection from the rough edges of things outside. He learns to complain effectively against its limitations, not with the object of seeking absolute freedom but of securing limited goals that are directly visible to him. Just so the nuclear family serves to limit and shield the mobile adult; it provides an inside of freedom for the expression of personal needs, and it remains distinguished from the outside to which it offers openings for vision. The picture window and the television screen, magazines, newspapers, neighborhood interaction, and jobs are all equally, but differently, ways in which the family admits access to the outside world without placing its own uniqueness in too great jeopardy. The nuclear family seeks a house in the suburbs in lieu of a city apartment, not to abolish but rather to expand and strengthen the walls which separate it from the outside. There is, as many observers have noted, a fine line to be drawn between madness and sanity in this behavior.[12]

Are these three—love, dissatisfaction, and the inside-outside feeling—all that need to be learned in the preschool years? Of course not. This is the period of most rapid learning of verbal, social, and motor skills. This is the period during which the bases are laid for all subsequent relations with peers and for all future self-insight. We have mentioned these three because they are not usually discussed when the relations of infancy and early childhood to social structure are under consideration.[13]

FIRST YEARS OF SCHOOL

The early years in school help the child to "build the bridge" between his home and the larger community, and a great deal of the literature on the early years of schooling shows a quite clear awareness that this relation between home and school is of utmost importance.[14] This relation is the key fact against which discussions of discipline, reading, social skills, and the like are most usually cast.

Occasionally one finds, however, a misleading image in these discussions. Sometimes the movement through school is described as a gradual widening by easy stages of the child's perspective from the home, out into the neighborhood, thence to his wider local community, area, region, and ultimately to the world as a whole. Yet this metaphor of gradual widening is entirely inappropriate. The kindergarten and first-grade teachers do not represent the life of the neighborhood to the child; rather do they present to him, as directly as he will ever experience it, the real and ideal world of adulthood. In this experience the child tests and proves the inside-outside distinction he learned earlier. The charming episodes of calling mother Miss So-and-So and vice versa, of bestowing and receiving love within the confines of the classroom, of finding pride in new powers and frustration in their slowness—all these are not relating the child to his neighborhood but to patterns of thought and action of the total society.

In school the child moves through one classroom after another, establishing and then breaking bonds with those who stand to him as representatives of the larger social order. Some relations last longer, some shorter, but even the first grader recognizes the transitory character of every contact. Here he learns, at first in a purely emotional way, that smoothness and harmony in interpersonal relations are essential to the whole system. His teachers have been trained (though with varying degrees of effectiveness) to avoid the wide oscillations between permissive and restrictive control of children that are found in most homes. They are taught to lower rather than raise their voices when seeking attention. They treat emotional outbursts, especially those accompanied by physical violence, as symptoms of some illness which is to be treated by keeping the patient quiet and isolated from his peers whom he might infect. For the main business of the classroom, the difference between boys and girls is of little or no consequence, though in play this difference may be the basis for separation.

The main business? It is to learn to learn, just as later we shall say that the main business of the whole social system is learning itself. Until the child enters school, the outside world comes to him as merely something to be sensed. He hears its noises coming from the radio and phonograph; he sees it on his television screen and through the windows of the family automobile. But it makes no demands; it merely exists to be sensed and ingested.

But the school says: you must *do* something with this world. You must classify your observations and speak of them intelligibly to others; you must read, and draw, and build, and calculate. You do these not only with the familiar materials of your inside world but with the varied and strange matters that come from the outside.

Very soon, just how soon is for specialists in childhood education to say, the disciplines of the adult culture come to be imposed on the child's ways of dealing with the observations and impressions he receives. These disciplines are absolutely essential to establishing the indirect, cognitive, and symbolic relation that lies at the basis of commitment in modern America. But how they are to begin in a child's life is hard to say. Let us look at one instance to see the degree of imposition involved. In *Tom Sawyer* and in Smith's *Where Did You Go?* . . . one reads and then remembers the peculiar discipline that boyhood peer culture exercises over beliefs. The discipline is that of ritual, incantation, and unquestioning acceptance. Yes, this is the way warts are cured. Yes, this is the way earthworms grow and the way marbles are played. It does not matter that experience fails to confirm the belief nor that the traditional rules introduce capricious elements in the game. A peer group is not concerned with such matters but with the exact transmission of its beliefs and practices.

In most societies of the world, it would appear, adult culture is of the same order. Its beliefs and practices differ from those of the childhood culture of the same society, but both are essentially static. Initiating the young man or woman into adult culture is merely a matter of changing his or her beliefs and practices; it is not, as with us, a matter of introducing entirely different forms of disciplining beliefs and practices.

The perishing of any culture creates a certain nostalgia, especially among those who experienced its values. The dissolution of peer cultures of prepubertal childhood is proceeding apace; its passing is mourned less in public than in the private conversations of men and women who regret that their children do not play the old games, who complain of the over-organization of childhood life in metropolitan society. But, regrets aside, it is clear that Little League Baseball has a more rational and just discipline than one-eyed cat. It is clear that nature study groups sponsored by the YMCA stand in closer accord to scientific observation than did the informal river gangs of agrarian boyhood.

The disciplines of experimentation, rational interpretation of observation, and impartiality of justice have penetrated the world of childhood. How this penetration may be brought under conscious control in schools and accomplished with a minimum loss of those values of spontaneity and mystery found in the childhood cultures of an earlier era are questions deserving study by educators and social scientists.

In the later years of childhood, that period Harry Stack Sullivan called the "quiet miracle of pre-adolescence," instruction comes to be the dominant mode of educational activity.[15] Very likely there is no aspect of our culture so little disciplined by scientific and ethical considerations as is instruction. Let us merely assert some of the fundamental principles at this point:

1. Instruction is not a matter of stuffing the head of a youngster. It is a relational affair, specifically a connection between what a learner does and the consequences of doing it. The closer and clearer this connection, the more effective the instruction.

2. Youngsters vary in the rate at which they can effectively participate in instruction. There is probably some correlation between rate and total capacity, but the degree of correlation is not known. It is unquestionably true that every learner could advance much further in any field of instruction if he were allowed to proceed at his own most effective rate.

3. It is clear that a classroom of the usual size and composition is more adequately adapted to the perpetuation of a traditional culture—one based on ritual, incantation, and unquestioning acceptance—than it is to giving instruction in the disciplines of science and rational ethics.

4. Instruction in the disciplines of our culture is not so much a matter of training in predetermined responses to predetermined stimuli as it is that of giving the learner reasons for the beliefs he accepts from others and constructs for himself.

In order to make the best use of this period, when youngsters are most capable of participating in the instructional process, we shall have to give up a great many of our traditionally based practices, with consequent implications for the structure of the teaching profession.[16] We may take it for granted that automated teaching can and will assume an increasingly significant part of the instructional task. The use of mechanical devices for individual instruction is inescapable if the principles listed above are to be acted on. Yet is there no way to use the power of social reinforcement inherent in childhood groups for educational purposes? It must be evident that the classroom teacher of the present time does not, given present demands cannot, take full advantage of the social force potential therein. The reason is equally evident: for purposes of instructing youngsters in the disciplines of thought and action that pertain to the adult society, social interaction among the youngsters themselves is a distracting and disruptive factor. This interaction must be carefully controlled in its times and places of occurrence if it is not to destroy the effectiveness of the teacher as he tries to carry on the main business of the school, instruction.

For understanding the possible role of interaction, let us rephrase our question in this fashion: is it possible that the basic forms of discipline in the adult culture could become the operative forms of discipline in a childhood peer culture so that the educative power of the childhood society could be used to instill these disciplines in every child? The argument one might give for a negative answer is a rather powerful one: there are no historical nor cross-cultural parallels for this form of discipline in childhood cultures. The sort of evidence gathered by Jean Piaget concerning the moral development of the child supports the view (but in ways that are not yet well understood), that a discipline based on ritual, incantation, and unquestioning acceptance is inherent in the very nature of any childhood culture.[17]

The argument for a positive answer is that we have not tried this approach on a large enough scale to show that it cannot be done. Furthermore, the historical and cross-cultural parallels for a scientific and ethical discipline of adult thought and action have appeared only recently, and these disciplines have yet to be completely triumphant even in our own culture.

Certainly the experiment would be worth trying. It would require rather extensive administrative changes, for example, the elimination of rigid age-graded groupings for children, the scheduling of rather long blocks of time in which supervision by adults is minimal, the provision of rich source materials for observation and experimentation, and opportunities for movement through various sorts of physical and social environments. It is evident that most students of later childhood education think these changes desirable, though usually for reasons different from those given here. This would indicate that the proper climate for change should not be too difficult to obtain.

ADOLESCENCE AND BEYOND

We are using the term adolescence to indicate a peculiar feature of American culture and not a biological event. There is, of course, a biological basis for this cultural phenomenon, but it does not pose its special educational problems merely because it is a period of rapid physical growth during which emerge the primary and secondary sexual characteristics of the adult man and woman. This period poses special educational problems for two reasons: i) It will see the termination of that period in which formal education is conducted apart from occupational interests and the beginning of the period in which formal education is closely integrated with occupational pursuits. ii) It will constitute the period in which the disciplines of thought and action of the adult society become conscious and foundational to all future learning.

Integration of Formal Education with Occupational Pursuits

There is no reason to hold that twelve or sixteen or any other number of years of schooling constitute either too little or too much education. Economically, years of full-time schooling for any individual must be subtracted from his production. Will increased capacity for production by that individual pay for these years in the long run? For how many years? For what proportion, what kind of people? We submit that while these questions may be asked in an economic sense, they cannot be answered by economic analysis. How many years of schooling does it take to produce a poet? How is his production to be measured? What is the productive value of a corporation executive's learning to understand himself better through the study of literature and philosophy? Or a lathe operator?

We tend to put questions like the proper number of years of schooling in economic terms because we recognize that there is, or rather ought to be, some demonstrable connection between secondary education and adult life. Merely to repeat an inherited curriculum generation after generation is no proper response to the demand for education in our own day. If we can find a common unit to measure both the activities in school and those in adult life, and economic productivity would appear to constitute such a unit, then we have a sound basis for judging among competing proposals for how much and what kind of schooling we should provide at the secondary level and beyond.

Perhaps we may salvage the basically correct insight here without having our gaze too restricted by a purely economic analysis. The common unit that best applies to adolescence and adult life in contemporary metropolitan culture is not productivity *per se* but rather productive learning. Let us attempt to define productive learning by noting some obvious instances of its absence. A worker whose skills have been rendered obsolete by technological change and who lacks the attitude and motivation (though not the intellectual capacity) for successful retraining somehow failed to learn productively in his school career. So also a housewife whose life becomes drab and meaningless when her children no longer need her constant attention. So also the citizen who casts his vote according to inherited prejudices rather than following a reasoned appraisal of the alternatives open to him. So also the young couple who commence to bear children merely because our society is rich enough to sustain them.

The formula for productive learning is simple enough: give instruction in the formal school system in such fashion that those who receive it will continue to discipline their thought and action in adult life as they were taught to do in school. The formula is a counsel of perfection; every educational reformer since the Sophists has urged it, largely without visible consequences. Two circumstances in the present state of our culture, however, transform this formula into a requirement for cultural survival. First, it is no longer the case that continued learning through adult life is a necessity only for the minority of professional scholars. It is now a necessity in the life of everyone who would not be a mere slave in the society he serves. Second, no longer can casual, informal processes of learning enable an adult to change his thought and action in response to the changes occurring around him. Not only is change too rapid for this gradual process; it is also too deep and penetrates too many aspects of life to permit an adequate adjustment by untutored trial and error.

Mention of the professional scholar brings to mind the caricature of the college lecturer who repeats to his classes the same notes he copied from his professor. This we rightly label clear dereliction of duty. Being a college professor requires not only the performance of a certain task, e.g. lecturing, but also requires continual increase in competence for the task through deliberate efforts to learn. And the same requirement holds for any teacher, any worker, housewife, citizen, parent, executive, in short for every adult.

But the scholar has one great advantage. He was *taught* that his job involves continuous self-education. He finds it not at all strange to believe that in doing his job he must study the findings of others and, more importantly, open his own eyes and discipline his observations. Into his formal education is built a method and attitude that carry quite naturally into a lifetime of productive learning. It does not weaken our case to point out that the teaching is often ineffective. The vehemence with which graduate schools are both attacked and defended shows clearly our main point: willingness and ability for continuous self-education are the measures of effectiveness of the formal education.

We must now face the really tough question: given the enormous complexity of modern life and the explosive rate at which new information is added to our culture, is it realistic to set the goal of productive learning for every graduate of every secondary school and college when even graduate schools have such difficulty in achieving it for a selected group and in restricted subject areas? This returns us to the attitude of tempered pessimism we mentioned just above. We do not believe the full educational potential of our culture has been realized, and until it has been tried more thoroughly than at present, we have no alternative but to set this goal for our education and to strive for its achievement.

Educational authorities in the Soviet Union have recognized this need for integrating continued learning with productive work and devised several plans by which youths from age sixteen upward could carry on an occupation and study at the same time.[18] These plans include alternate days of attendance at the shop and school, special academic classes given on the premises at larger factories, and a great expansion and reorganization of evening and home study courses given under the supervision of ministries of education in the various republics. These reforms are strongly influenced by a desire to eliminate the idea that secondary education terminates schooling for all save the small minority who enter a university or advanced technical school. Secondary education ought to be, Soviet educators believe, a period of transition to an adult life that includes continued schooling as a matter of course. And this goal is set not for the professional scholar alone but for all worker-citizens of the society.

Anyone who looks seriously at the educational demands of a technological society may find instructive lessons from the experience of the Soviet educators over the next several years. But quite apart from any political or ideological bias that would reject the Soviet solution to this problem as it now stands, theirs is, with only slight qualification, a purely mechanical solution; that is to say, it is merely a joining of work and study without any significant changes in either, just as two gears in a machine may alternately mesh and unmesh without changing in themselves. What we are proposing is much more radical. What we wish to see, on one hand, is a reconstruction of content and method in secondary and higher education, such that productive learning is a usual and consciously prized result of study. On the other hand, we wish to see changes in adult roles of worker, citizen, parent, and the like, such that the highest disciplines of thought and action in our culture can function more effectively in the lives of people and their institutions.

Disciplines of Thought and Action

We have used the expression "disciplines of thought and action" quite loosely in this chapter. Now we must be a bit more precise, even while recognizing that absolute precision is not possible when speaking, as we are, programmatically.

We have contrasted the ritual and incantation of a childhood culture with the disciplines of science and order that control thought and action in a technological culture. In childhood games a magic phrase, "King's X," brings special dispensations from the rules. For the major sports of our society, committees continually revise the rules so as to eliminate any special advantages that might possibly accrue to any player or team. In childhood, beliefs often are impervious to evidence; in modern science the very meaning of a belief is found in the evidence which supports it. We have shown how the progressives attempted to bring the disciplines of impartial justice and empirical science directly into the common-sense world of men, a world which changed more slowly than the technological world in which these disciplines had already triumphed so spectacularly. With nearly a half century of hindsight, we can see more clearly than they have what would be needed to make their efforts come to full fruition.

There is a strong case for identifying the disciplines of thought and action we are seeking with the academic disciplines, as organized for research and instruction in graduate schools. In the first place, these disciplines have showed extraordinary capacity for generating new knowledge at an ever increasing rate. In the second place, young men and women who become full participants in an academic discipline tend to show the temper and attitude we have characterized as the outcome of truly productive learning. Respectable physicists, of course, do make ordinarily stupid statements on public policy matters, but very likely the Committee for a Sane Nuclear Policy would have to cease functioning if it lacked the support of men and women whose minds have been formed under the aegis of academic disciplines.

(It is idle chatter to introduce the bogey of transfer of training into this discussion. Whatever results one may encounter in laboratory tests of memory power or the retention of information learned apart from any use of it, the fact remains that long and serious education in any of the academic disciplines has a permeating effect on the mind and character of those who receive it. To deny this would be a mild form of insanity.)

To equate the disciplines of thought and action that we must try to instill in our contemporary adolescents with the academic disciplines, however, is to turn the whole matter upside down. By their very nature the academic disciplines tend to proliferate and specialize, requiring of those who would learn them a restriction of interest and attention, whereas the disciplines of thought and action we are seeking have the world as their compass. It is all right to say that teaching in secondary schools is a simplification of the same disciplines that in more complicated form are taught in graduate schools. But it is not very helpful to say so. Let us rather say that the highest level of research and instruction in our society—whether found in graduate schools, industrial laboratories, or elsewhere—is but a refinement and specialized application of the more fundamental disciplines of thought and action inherent in the very structure of our social order. These more fundamental disciplines, we believe, can be analyzed and taught directly, allowing their specialized uses to come in due course in a citizen's life.

A detailed analysis of these disciplines is outside our present purposes. But we may suggest the following scheme for subsequent investigation.

i) The formal disciplines of logic and mathematics: These are called "formal" in a special sense, i.e., because the form of argument determines whether or not the argument is to be accepted. It is an inescapable fact about our culture that our knowledge of the physical world comes to us in arguments having mathematical or hypothetico-deductive *form*. The man or woman who cannot follow a mathematical argument is utterly precluded from understanding, as our culture interprets understanding, why the planets appear in their appointed plans, how a rheostat functions, what it means to say that a theory or a theorem has been proved. We need say little about the teaching of the formal disciplines; the need for them is recognized, and ingenious pedagogy to raise them to the level of explicit consciousness is rapidly proceeding.

ii) The discipline of experimentation: The formal disciplines, as it is customary to say, do not determine the truth of any statement about the world. They merely guarantee that the reasoning is cogent, while truth ultimately depends on observations made under the guidance of reasoning.

The customary way of speaking is correct, as far as it goes. But the actual story of experimentation in our society is of a different order altogether from what might be thought if one saw it merely as the testing of hypotheses derived from formal arguments. It is not too much to say that experiment has become a style of life, a way of looking at the world: in principle, every phenomenon that man encounters can be analyzed into a set of causal factors and the force of each factor measured. If the results of experiment can be organized into logico-mathematical theories, so much the better, but experiment does not wait on theory.[19] From the simplest home garden plot to vast state farms, from the tinkering of a shop mechanic to the organized industrial laboratory, from the schoolboy's chemistry set to Du Pont or Cape Canaveral—experiment never ceases. "What causes it to go?" is a question implying that there is *one* factor to be found, if only we are ingenious and persistent enough in our search for it.

Dirty hand, sweaty brows, tired muscles, and finally, a rapid pulse when the results are at hand—these are the dramatic concomitants of elections and other experiments. But even more significant to experimentation are the elements of design. It is in design that the heart of the discipline is to be found, whether the experiment concerns the physical, biological, social, or personal aspects of the world. It is scarcely necessary to point out how little this discipline has penetrated the ordinary secondary school program. It is a saddening sight to observe well-ordered high school laboratories where youngsters copy set procedures listed in workbooks and change their figures to get results matching what their textbook says ought to obtain. It is even sadder to observe no social and psychological laboratory at all in most high schools. To devise techniques of pedagogy to make the discipline of experiment, especially its design, a living force in the thought of young men and women is one of our crucial tasks in education.

iii) The discipline of natural history: It is far simpler to see a phenomenon, any sort of phenomenon, as a function of one causal factor which can be isolated by experiment than it is to see that same phenomenon as the outcome of a process in which many systemically intertwined factors are operating. Consider a simple thing, say, the regular occurrence of a certain pigmentation in a fruit fly. In principle, if not yet in fact, we can explain this phenomenon experimentally by isolating the particular gene, the molecule of DNA, which is causally effective in producing the pigmentation. Holding other factors constant, if a change in the molecular structure of the gene brings about a change in pigmentation, then we may say, with all the drama such a statement allows, that the *cause* has been isolated.

But suppose we approached the same phenomenon with different questions: What is the significance of this pigmentation in the relation between this little organism and its complex environment? Why, from all the colors of the rainbow, did the fruit fly come to have one, and only one, typical pattern of pigmentation? Answers to these questions are subject to the discipline of natural history. They would involve narrative of a very particular kind, one in which organism and environment are seen to maintain a viable relation despite the changes—gradual and cataclysmic—that occur in the latter. We lack the evidence on which to construct a narrative that will explain the pigmentation of a fruit fly, but for man and his plan in the natural world, the discipline of natural history is our only guide to a satisfactory explanation.

Much nonsense has been written (and likely will continue to be written) by those who choose to look at societies as organisms, being born, growing, and finally decaying. Natural history does not take the individual organism as its unit but rather the system of interrelationships exemplified in the organism. Natural history, like Nature itself, is unconcerned with the individual; its focus is on the complex, in which one system maintains its organization as a system by responding both to its own internal dynamics and to its changing relations to larger systems of which it is a part.

Single-factor interpretations of historical processes are always false. The demise of the saber-toothed tiger can be explained only when one sees what the tiger did to its environment as well as what the environment did to it. Technology becomes a dynamic force in social change only when it occurs within a certain system of relations to other natural and social factors. An urban slum is not caused in any simple sense at all; it is rather a subsystem sustaining many complex relations to the larger system of which it is a part. Corn is grown in Iowa and wheat in Kansas, but anyone who gives a simple climatological explanation of this phenomenon misses the point altogether.

The discipline of thought required to explain phenomena in this way is hard to achieve, harder still to teach. We have attempted to exemplify the discipline of natural history in this book, with what success we must allow our critics to decide. Our experience in trying to teach this discipline to others gives clear guidance on only one point: students who would achieve it must themselves open their eyes and see the world around them with quickened imagination and perception; they must attempt to construct the narrative for themselves and suffer defeat by the one stubborn fact which refuses to fit in its assigned place. This discipline, like all the others, cannot be poured into the heads of students.

iv) The discipline of esthetic form: Without logic and mathematics our culture would be unintelligible to itself. Without the constant search for causes and for systems the rest of world—

natural and historical—would be unintelligible chaos. Yet disciplined thought and action are not complete without discipline in the unique creation, the esthetic object which is sustained by its own internal relations, quite apart from its causes (and, of course, it *is* caused) and from the systemic relations it bears to other objects and events.

We may recognize three aspects to this discipline: There is, first, confrontation, the discipline of isolating the esthetic object for contemplation (or as Ziff would generalize it, for "aspection.")[20] One may confront a painting, a sonata, a ballet, or a sunset; but in any case one must *learn* to confront: to isolate and frame the object, to achieve detachment so as to see or hear or feel the object as it is in itself. There is, second, construction. If the esthetic object is anything that sustains the attitude of confrontation (as classical Chinese scholars are said to gaze for hours at a lump of amber), the art object is that which a human being constructs deliberately. The imagination to envisage new possibilities in familiar materials, the courage to abandon past success for a perilous unknown, the sheer technical skill and energy to carry through, and the moral integrity to abjure the phony pleasantry in solving the problems set by the matter at hand—these are marks of discipline in the artist.

There is, third, criticism. Disciplined criticism is at the opposite pole from the frequently heard: "I don't know anything about art, but I know what I like." How can one know what he likes until he knows what art is? Art consists of objects constructed from the possibilities and limited by the brute facts of certain materials, certain functions, and certain historical traditions. Until one can criticize in this temper, he has no idea what he likes or does not like.

The discipline of esthetic form poses certain unique educational problems. There are many art forms in our culture, and each of them requires long and assiduous study if one is to internalize the discipline of that form. Mathematics, experiment, and natural history can be generalized as disciplines of thought, but it is doubtful that the same is true of the arts. It seems rather more likely that the aspects of this discipline must be learned in very close relation to some one art form. We can see these aspects of the discipline applying to poetry and painting, symphonies and sculpture, drama, ballet, and architecture. We cannot see how an adolescent could learn them in this general fashion unless, or until, he had achieved a certain level of discipline in some one of them. The pedagogical problem here would, then, appear to be that of teaching the discipline of esthetic form in some one art, but teaching it in a way that encourages the individual student to seek this degree of discipline in his approach to other art forms in the culture.

These, in fine, are the disciplines of thought an adolescent must acquire if he is to have learned productively. Although we have presented them separately, it is easy to see that they overlap and interrelate all through. We have purposely not discussed these disciplines in behavioral, operational terms. Just how one would sample behavior at any age level to judge the degree to which these disciplines had been acquired is a neat problem for experimental design, but it is outside our purpose here. What one would *do* to teach these disciplines, what students would do to learn them are also questions outside our immediate purview. Nor are we even suggesting that these disciplines could serve as a basis for curriculum organization in secondary schools and colleges; other personal, social, and linguistic skills are necessary, and they could not be fitted easily into a curriculum organized on these lines.

For one who has learned these disciplines consciously and productively, commitment to American culture is at last possible. For these disciplines are not merely (if indeed they are at all) academic studies. Rather they are the primordial rules of thought that guide our most fundamental interpretations of the world. They are the substitutes in the contemporary world for the gossip and sorcery of primitive village life; that is to say, these disciplines are for us institutionally legitimate modes of social control.[21] A person who accepts these disciplines as integral to his own thinking and accepts the world as it is revealed through these disciplines has indeed established that relation to the world that deserves the title commitment.

We are convinced that the teaching of these disciplines is the prime obligation of our school system, for these are the disciplines of the public world.[22] They would never be learned simply by growing up in a nuclear family, a form of association disciplined mostly by the *ad hoc* adjustment of personalities. The mass media, serving the exploitative and predatory interests of business corporations, cannot be counted on to teach those disciplines which, in their internal affairs, they demand of their own employees. The dissolution of adult community means that there is no readily visible model of adult behavior that can be imitated by the young. Professionalized and specialized, the erstwhile community now looks to the school to do the educating it has lost the capacity for.

We are not, then, too concerned that the number four be taken as exactly the proper way to divide up the disciplines integral to our social order, but that these disciplines be recognized as having first claim on the limited time, intelligence, and money that we devote to education—on this point we are adamant.

14

MORAL COMMITMENT AND THE INDIVIDUAL

We have made our proposals. The final part of our task is to defend our analysis against the obvious charge that commitment is something other than the purely intellectual or cognitive activities we have described under the heading of "disciplines." Commitment is a matter of guts, of will and heart, the objection runs; commitment means a certain state of the emotions and not merely of the mind, as our argument would lead one to believe.

Let us meet this objection head on. It is an idea that is deep-rooted in our culture, and we shall have to make several detours to show why it is entirely misplaced. We shall have to show the radical difference between commitment in our culture and commitment as it exists in other cultures. We shall have to offer an interpretation of individuality and individual responsibility that is different from the one our culture inherited from its agrarian past. With these arguments we shall make our case proof against the objections that seem, at first glance, so destructive.

THE NEW MEANING TO "MORAL"

The world of contemporary metropolitan culture does not manifest itself to its new members as the great forces of the natural world manifested themselves to youths among the Plains Indians. Prayer, fasting, and solitary vigils now produce only giddiness and headaches; they vouchsafe not visions but vertigo. This is a pity, of course, but there it is.

The world today permits itself to be directly seen only in fragments. Its larger, more abiding features are abstract; they must be constructed in the mind, not perceived by the senses. Unlike the world of Irish familism, unlike the Navaho world of personal striving for adulthood, unlike any other world in which a whole society has been forced to live—the world of the contemporary American never permits its basic structure to be reproduced in the ordinary life and affairs of men and women.

Yet all too often we still speak and think of commitment as if it were the sort of dedication shown by the Irish peasant toward the preservation of his family's hold on the land. We see the steady disintegration of this sort of direct relation between a person and the demands of his world, and we complain that the contemporary world creates mass man, lacking in commitment, without roots in the realities of the world he inhabits. We decry conformity; we denounce anomie.[1] In short, we—we who would speak to and for education—fail to see the truth about our own world and the kind of commitment it permits and requires.

Cognitively, our world includes the disciplines by which it can be known. They differ from the disciplines of fasting, prayer, interpersonal loyalty, and self-sacrifice. They are, rather, the wholly impersonal disciplines of scientific experimentation, of natural history, esthetic form and mathematics. They are terrifying disciplines, for they permit no ultimate certainty, no relaxation into the "oceanic feeling" of being at one with the entire universe.[2] Their findings enlarge and change at a dizzying pace: today's most basic theories become uninteresting special cases tomorrow.

But this is no cause for despair. If even our extended lifetime gives us only a small glimpse into *all* the complexities of the world we now inhabit, these glimpses still surpass in richness of texture and order of pattern anything that might have been guessed by our ancestors. What does it matter that our vision of the natural world makes all mankind seem a rather irrelevant cosmic accident? A cognitive grasp of the natural and social world, unfettered by illusions of personal significance, can now be the normal, routine achievement of all men and women. In previous ages and cultures only the extraordinary mystic or scholar could accomplish this. If there is a good in universal education, surely this is part of it.

There are, of course, those who claim that scientific rationality, even in its broadest sense, gives only a partial, even a distorted view of the world. If they mean that there is an illuminative quality in the arts that is different from the light of scientific reason, their claim is true. But it is not damaging to our insistence that, in the purely cognitive sense, scientific rationality is the sovereign, supreme, jealously unique discipline for apprehending the physical and social world. If the truism that there is more to human life than mere cognition seems significant, it may be reiterated as often as one likes. Still our point is this: one aspect of commitment in the contemporary world *is* cognition. It is, moreover, the prerequisite without which all the other relations between a person and his world could not add up to commitment. A man or woman might have the most positive feelings toward this society, might work with assiduous self-sacrifice for its welfare, might pray for it each day, and yet all these would not constitute commitment to our culture in the absence of a rationally disciplined, objective grasp of the fundamentally impersonal structures and processes that constitute our physical and social world.

The world in which we live can be known only by rationally

ordered disciplines for which science in its broad sense is the prototype. One could say, then, that the touchstone of our analysis is the relation between the individual and his world, i.e. that scientific, rational knowledge of the world is the basic relation from which conceptions of the world, personality, and symbol systems are derived. One could say this, but we choose to put it the other way for this reason: the objectivity of rational thought means that it *is* a part of the world external to any individual. To learn how the world is organized, what forms, patterns, and regularities are to be apprehended in the environment, means to accept an external discipline for one's cognitions. It isn't necessary that a world be of this sort; the world of Irish familism and Navaho self-proving were different. We believe the difference is better described by saying that these are different social and material worlds, each of which makes its distinctive demands for a particular kind of person and a particular kind of symbolic expression.

What relation, then, between an individual person and his world *is* demanded by the world of contemporary metropolitan culture? Clarity, vigor, and breadth of thought as discussed under the disciplines of education? These, of course, are essential; without them the world is not, and chaos obtains. But is nothing beyond knowledge necessary? Other social and material worlds have demanded obedience, reverence, devotion, self-abnegation, love, sacrifice, prayer. . . . Does our world demand only disciplined thought?

Not quite. But it doesn't demand any of these other forms of worship. In fact it makes worship very difficult. Awe and respect are almost inevitable concomitants of the disciplined study of anything, but worship is a quite personal relation between worshiper and object worshiped. The world as it reveals itself through the disciplines of science, history, and criticism is not personal. For a person who simply *will* worship, the human imagination can find attributes of personality in virtually anything—a stone, a statue, or constellations of stars. Our world is supremely indifferent in this regard. Its richness and order may be worshiped or not; it neither demands nor prohibits this relation. Freedom of worship is thus to be seen as a structural feature of the world of metropolitan culture.

But are there no demands of a distinctly moral character in the very structure of our culture? Yes and no. Let us state the negative side of the answer first. The recognition of a social system in which social functions are performed irrespective of the personal motives of those who have specific roles in the system was one of Marx's keenest and most enduring insights. (This insight need not be associated with the naive determinism and linear causation found elsewhere in Marx.[3]) A school, a corporation, or political unit simply could not operate if its operation depended on a unanimity of motives in those who perform its functions. It operates on its own internal logic and structure. When it fails to operate well, we seek to improve it by changing its structure: by reorganizing it. We got rid of hereditary kingship and hereditary control of business enterprises because those systems do tend to elevate the personal motives of leaders to greater structural significance than mobile, technological systems can tolerate.

Let us be quite clear about what we are asserting and denying. In one of the usual senses of "moral," when we talk about the moral quality of a man or his actions, we refer to his motives. Now some motives are higher and better than other motives; some motives are narrow and purely self-regarding; others are wider and have regard for other people. But the social functions that are essential to our way of life do not hinge on any person's having one sort of motivation rather than another. Care and diligence in the maintenance of aircraft are essential to our transport system; the motivations of aircraft mechanics are not. Notice that it makes perfect sense to ask a mechanic why he chooses to work for United Airlines. He may answer by reference to the pay, the security, the absence of unwelcome supervision, and so on. But it doesn't make much sense to ask him, "What are your motives for working here?"

We may ask him, quite meaningfully, if the occasion should arise, "What was the motive behind your act of deliberate sabotage?" The difference between these two questions is, in part, that working for United Airlines is a functional activity within a social system. One's motives are largely irrelevant. Only when one acts contrary to the accepted function of a position in a social system does the question of motives become relevant.[4] The point is just this—the system as such does not demand any special motives in those who operate it. Insofar as "moral" has reference to motives, our world, in its larger features, makes no moral demands on individuals. This is the negative answer to the question: Are there no demands of a distinctly moral character in the very structure of our culture?

The positive answer has two parts:

1) All cultures have rules that regulate the behavior of individuals; in our culture these rules must be universal and irrespective of persons as such. This is a distinctly moral demand that arises from the nature of our world.

2) There are very high costs, including the cost of living under impersonal rules, that are inherent in the very structure of our world. There is a distinctly moral demand that every individual accept his share of the cost, however he may feel about having to pay it.

The first point is one we have made many times over. An individual person has a distinct size, shape, color, sex, age, intelligence, ability, religious affiliation, ethnic background, pattern of hates, loves, visions and dreams. Some of the rules under which he must live recognize some of these properties as relevant to the demands made of him. But these rules do not treat him as a unique individual; their demand is not to him as John Smith but to anyone of a certain kind: he must register for military training because he is a member of the class of males over eighteen years in age.

Furthermore, an increasingly narrow range of properties is relevant to the more important demands put on an individual. Beyond a certain minimum point, years of age have relevance to fewer and fewer of the rules to which one is subject. The same is true of sex: at the moment the chief administrative position in

Western governments is barred to women, but this rule is in only a few countries a matter of law, and in no country morally justifiable. The same is true of race, religion, social status of parents, etc. Those rules which still operate as vestiges from earlier cultural patterns have no moral significance in our world. But is it not *moral* that such distinctions have no relevance?

It is a bit odd, however, to speak of a *moral* demand when looking at an individual person. Because of the rapid change inherent in our dynamic culture, individuals frequently find themselves in situations in which conflicting rules put conflicting demands on their actions. We say that such a person faces a moral problem. Yet the decision as to which rule ought to be followed is quite frequently made purely by reference to the disciplines of thought discussed earlier. *Which of these rules actually fits with the nature of the world in which we live?* So put, the question is purely intellectual; it is most usually answered by tracing the natural history of the rules and examining their place in the system in which the actor finds himself.

There are, of course, ultimate moral dilemmas that cannot be solved by intellect, which is to say they cannot be solved at all. These arise most frequently in philosophy classes, not in the context of practical life. If life were for most people most of the time merely a series of moral dilemmas, a viable social system would be impossible. For the most part, what we call moral problems are situations in which the rules that we appeal to give conflicting answers, but the decision as to which has more weight is determined by appeal to the disciplines of intellect. It is for this reason that it is a bit odd to speak of a situation like this as posing a moral demand on the individual; the demand is simply for clear thinking.

But how is one to follow the rules when they conflict with his immediate desires? More generally, how is one to act in the way demanded by the world? Is not this kind of action really central to the kind of ordering that we speak of as commitment?

Surely yes. And when we shall have understood this answer, we shall find it contains all that can be said about the other two questions. To explain how and why this is so, we must refer to the final element in commitment: the symbol system by which the individual and his relation to the external world may be understood and interpreted.

Symbols drawn from traditional religions are no longer adequate for the contemporary world. Their origin is in a cultural system based on interpersonal and familial loyalty. Extended to include the impersonal structures of our social and physical world, the symbolic message of Christianity or Judaism becomes attenuated, if not actually unintelligible. This judgment implies no disrespect to the great achievements of twentieth-century theologians, particularly Reinhold Niebuhr, Paul Tillich, and Jacques Maritain. The depth of social sensitivity shown by these men and the enormous ingenuity demonstrated in their efforts to express contemporary social insights in the traditional language of Christianity are worthy of universal admiration. But those achievements in themselves actually help to establish our case: as they stand, that is to say, as they are known and utilized in the common sense world of metropolitan culture, the symbols of the traditional religions are not adequate for understanding and interpreting commitment in a context of impersonal structures. It is no accident that church membership is conceived as an affair of family and locality, that the executives of the electrical companies convicted of corporate collusion were regarded as excellent church members. The symbols of Christianity and Judaism make sense, give adequate expression to the demands for interpersonal commitment within the family and local neighborhood. Within the larger structures of society and nature, no.

In an almost diametrically opposite way, the symbols used to explain and justify politico-economic systems fail to account for commitment within the family and neighborhood. One is not a member of the proletariat or the bourgeoisie in the context of his own home. This was not always so. Self-consciousness about social class or other ideologically expressed relation to the larger structures of the society could be, in some historical moments has been, the central symbolic expression of family and community interaction. But this isn't true now. The symbols for interpreting human behavior in families and neighborhoods are not translatable into the political and economic terms by which we ordinarily describe and justify the large-scale, impersonal, corporate structures of contemporary culture. We have argued this point before; we recall it here only to emphasize that the traditional religious, political, and economic symbol systems are inadequate to express commitment in contemporary culture.

And so we must ask again: What kind of action *is* demanded by the kind of world we live in? How is one to know what the world demands? How is he to learn to act in accordance with his knowledge?

The committed person *knows* what his world demands of him and acts accordingly, because of his knowledge. We have already shown that one can know these demands through the disciplines of thought. Of these disciplines of thought, only the discipline of natural history provides a symbolic medium through which an individual can interpret the complex relations he sustains with his world. And knowing oneself as a part of a social system *is* accepting the moral demands inherent in that system.

Knowing oneself as worker, mother, voter, taxpayer, consumer, and wife is to accept the moral demands arising from each of these roles. Seeing the interconnections among the varied corporate structures in which one's personal life is embedded and knowing how all these are both connected with and also separated from the interpersonal life of family and neighborhood are ways of accepting the world and its demands on conduct.

To ask anything more from commitment is to erect symbol systems into absolutes. Particularly, we should reinterpret what it means to teach young citizens of this nation to love their country. No barrier is imposed to prevent love of family, friends, locality, religion, or even institution, nor does anything prevent our projection of love from the minute part we can see to the whole which we know only through symbols. To know it well is to recognize that America is no longer the kind of place that easily admits of the sort of personal identification we could call "love of country." It is not only too large, too complex, too impersonal an entity for anyone to love; it is also too implacable in its demands. Our nation, beyond any that has ever existed, offers freedom, order, and opportunity. And beyond any other, our nation exacts a price for its goods. Our freedom from material want, from poverty, drudgery, disease, and ignorance will endure only so long as we pay the high price for these great goods, the price of submission to the discipline of a technological culture—not to technology *per se* but to the forms of rational thought and action and to the ordered relations with others in the superstructures which channel and direct our energies. This discipline exhibits itself not only in the time clocks at the production end but also in the need to surround oneself with innumerable physical objects, each of which demands care and attention.

So also is there a cost we must pay for our freedom from arbitrary acts by persons in power. God, we are told, is no respecter of persons, which leads us to believe that God is a bureaucrat. Only in a society which places power in impersonal rules is there a guarantee of freedom from arbitrary personal acts of injustice. This does not deny that there is favoritism, inefficiency, and gross neglect of duty, but these are corruptions of the ideal, and we must be continually alert to eradicate the offenders, otherwise the entire system will come crashing down around us. The price is high, and we have been admonished quite enough by men who would wish to exercise power over other men without rational, impersonal control. Commitment, we would suggest, is the recognition and acceptance of the price we have to pay for freedom from the whimsical, capricious, or malicious acts of persons in power. But let us not be misunderstood on this point either. We argued earlier that the size, complexity, and interdependence of the great superstructures of the public world do not preclude the presence of a great deal more freedom and creativity than these organizations at present allow. Commitment in this particular instance means that one seeks to expand the areas of freedom and exhibit more personal initiative within a system that remains fundamentally *corporate* in form. That a certain price in external regulation and control has to be paid does not mean that all freedom is lost. In fact the values that can accrue from rationalized organization of our public life—not only the material values of mass production but also the ethical values of restraining the power of man over man—will not accrue unless individuals constantly strive to extend the limits of freedom at all levels within the organization.

In short, part of the price of being an American is *being* an organization man. Autonomy is not, as Whyte would have us believe, a viable alternative. On the contrary, the very attempt to discover an alternative is a form of mental and social illness, a denial of reality. The important question is not whether, but what kind of organization man? One who simply occupies a niche on an organization chart? Or one who strives to extend the bounds of his own freedom to act with initiative and resourcefulness at whatever level he finds himself? Truly to understand the reality of the dynamic world we live in is to see that the second sort of individual is not only preferable ethically but that without him our emerging social structure will not stand. Note again that the cognitive grasp of what our world demands furnishes the ground for commitment.

We could continue through the list of social goods and their costs; for example, the omnipresence of the goal of self-fulfillment does indeed broaden and extend the lives of millions of individuals, but it makes any naive contentment in life impossible. But we leave it to the reader to trace this duality in all our values. We turn instead to the final question: Is there any ultimate purpose in this social system?

Order and stability in the social and physical world are essential to personal integrity for the individual. From the simplest expectation that one's footfall will find solidity to the most complex predictive hypothesis in the physical sciences, one stakes his whole integrity as a person on orderliness in the physical world. One or two or even several misjudgments can be tolerated when, as is usually the case, reasons for the misjudgments can be found. But if life presented a preponderance of wholly inexplicable failures of the physical world to accord with expectations, personality would disintegrate.

This need for orderliness in the physical world has exact parallels in the social world. In our day-by-day encounters with other human beings, our expectations are fulfilled: a smile from us elicits a smile from others; a frown, a frown. Approaching a stranger on the street we incline to the right, he does likewise, and our bodies pass without grating contact. Children learn to speak the language of their parents; time and money spent in acquiring the skills necessary for practicing a highly technical vocation are returned with suitable interest during a lifetime of productive work.

Although both nature and society violate our expectations occasionally—the unanticipated earthquake destroys the solidity of the ground; a technological revolution renders hard-won skills economically useless—the more we know, the more our expectations include divergencies from simple uniformity. A sense of self, then, becomes a more differentiated, complex phenomenon as one's image of the natural and social world becomes more complex. "I'm just a farmer" means a different concept of self in an age when agricultural technology has reached the level it has with us as contrasted with what that statement meant in an age when only the grossest expectations of natural processes were part of the conceptual apparatus of the farmer. Just so, "I am a teacher." "I am a mother." One's concept of self is not divorceable from the expectations one has of the world he inhabits.

But the increasing accuracy of our knowledge and the consequent complexity of the natural and social worlds do not assure the integrated relation of a man and his world, the relation we are calling commitment. On the contrary, this very complexity creates a deep fissure in the modern soul; a break between intellect and esthetic sensitivity on one hand and the moral conscience on the other. Intellectually and esthetically modern man delights in diversity and change, in the unusual, the unique. The discipline of experiment has taught us to appreciate the obdurate fact which disproves the neat generalization; we like our order complex and richly textured, not monotonously simple. Modern cosmological theories, the slowly emerging picture of the nucleus of the atom, the story of evolution, the new history—wherever the light of research is allowed to shine, we see not chaos but subtle and diverse patterns that replace the simple mechanical notions that satisfied our ancestors.

A world like this, so delightful to the mind's eye, creates a peculiar problem for the kind of moral conscience we have inherited. It is not that we have created insoluble moral dilemmas for ordinary citizens. For most of us, fortunately, in most of our actions, the right thing to do is not only very obvious, it is also the most natural, the easiest thing to do. As we pointed out earlier, organized civil life would be impossible if truly difficult moral problems were the common experience of ordinary men. A decent society, such as ours is, separates right conduct from wrong in such measure that it is far more likely that right conduct will happen than wrong. This relates also to our point about motives: they are irrelevant except when a person deliberately, willfully violates codes of right conduct.

But our conception of morality has it not only that we should act rightly but that we should do so for some higher reason, to serve some higher purpose, to fulfill some final meaning in the world. *Ad maiorem gloriam Dei*, for the sake of Duty itself, for my Country, my Race, my Class, my Way of Life . . . throughout the history of Western civilization different claimants to be the supreme object of commitment have been heard. But now, as Nietzsche saw, those who are self-consciously literate and attentive to the world can no longer take any such claims seriously.[5] We have created a world in which an individual can find it easy and natural to behave decently toward his neighbors, to practice the classical virtues of temperance, magnanimity, and justice, even the Christian virtue of humility. The price we pay for such a world is that we give up the belief that there is a final reason, an ultimate meaning to justify human existence.

Two questions immediately arise: Is it not true that life is terribly flat, stale, ultimately unsupportable when deprived of final meaning? And what about the unremitting conflict with world communism and our social need, not merely for decent and humane behavior, but for courage, dedication, and sacrifice that go beyond what can be called conventional morality?

Neither of these questions is easily answered. Socrates' noble dictum, "The unexamined life is not worth living," is obviously an intellectualist's conceit (when said by anyone save that person who chose to die rather than stop examining life aloud). But modern men and women have no choice. The very conditions of life—the mobility, the highly symbolic quality of all human action, the widespread literacy—all increase the complexity of the world and the corresponding sense of self in the individual. Thus our life itself leads inevitably to its own examination. The discouraging feature of the present situation is the lack of education to engage in any fundamental examination of life. The historical accident that kept religion out of the public schools is only partly responsible for this. Neither is there evidence that parochial school training in this country or teaching by the "agreed syllabus" in English state schools does a measurably better job than American secular, public schools in giving students the capacity to examine their own existence in the drama of human history.[6]

Perhaps the final step in the democratic experiment is that the society no longer poses an ultimate meaning to life. Instead it builds within each individual such a complex sense of self that the person is forced to create meaning, order, and purpose for himself.

It may be that human beings are incapable of making this experiment a success. Still, having embarked on it, we must not falter simply because there is no guarantee of a favorable outcome. We cannot remake the genetic constitution of the human race, but we can attempt to build the theory and practice of a new kind of education that, if achieved, would make ultimate freedom possible.

But what sort of education would that be? Our answer is in the four intellectual disciplines that we outlined earlier. We are quite aware that there are aspects of personality that can be reached only with great struggle, if at all, through purely cognitive procedures. We know the frantic efforts that men make to escape from freedom. We are not oblivious to the authoritarian personality and the deeply destructive urges that go with it.[7] Original sin is no quibbling point in theology.

Still we must hold to the principle, even as Mr. Bestor formulated it, that a democratic society is morally required to give its finest, its fundamentally intellectual education to all its citizens. Any citizen so educated may indeed find life flat, stale, ultimately unbearable. The culture has few or no compelling myths, superstitions, or illusions to comfort him. But he may, on the other hand, find the *quest* for meaning, the freedom to *create* his own purposes, the most rewarding life of all. The disciplines of thought and action that we described ever so briefly above we regard as the best education for men and women who will undertake to live a life of ultimate freedom.

But what about the survival of a democratic society? Now that we are faced with the challenge of communism, a system that asserts a monolithic purpose for all its members, a system that is now pressing us with its full power throughout the world, can we afford to set individuals loose to find their own meaning in life? Does not the preservation of freedom require its limitation at least during the critical years of the present world conflict?

Answers to these questions are not to be found by statistical measures used according to the theory of games.[8] It is not a matter of comparing the freedom we sacrifice for present security against the freedom we might lose if the spread of communism is not halted. This way of looking at the matter assumes what we may call the "rat-race-and-withdrawal" theory of public life. The answer to the demand for commitment and dedication is to replace this obnoxious theory of public life with something more adequate.

The rat-race-and-withdrawal theory of public life is so much a part of the climate of opinion among contemporary intellectuals that its public expression cannot seem other than trite.[9] They proclaim that the public world, the world of great corporate superstructures, is nothing but a rat race. The business corporations exist only to exist: mass advertising creates mass demand to consume the products of mass production, and so around and around forever, all to no purpose other than that the wheels increase in number and speed. Governmental structure is necessary to keep these business corporations from destroying one another domestically and to help spread their influence throughout the world before the (really quite similar) Russian corporate structures spread *their* influence throughout the world. The meaninglessness of the whole competition is nowhere better revealed than in the growth of gigantic military systems which, to justify their existence, will eventually blow the rat race to utter cosmic oblivion.

"Official" education, as received in school, through the mass media, from pulpit and White House makes the rat race sound terribly important; it makes responsibility and authority in the corporate, public world seem exciting and worthy of attainment. But the "informal" education among the *cognoscenti* teaches that the only sensible style of life for man is to exploit that easily exploitable system as efficiently as he can and to use his already acquired leisure and comfort to build a private world in which to pursue self-cultivation until the system blows itself to pieces.

It does not really matter on this theory that television fare is generally inane, vulgar drivel, that urban redevelopment is creating habitation more fit for poultry than human beings, that the natural beauty of our continent is being destroyed with all deliberate speed, that the basic decisions affecting us as a nation are ever further removed from popular inspection and control, that compulsory education for a large proportion of our urban youth is nothing more than custodial supervision, that some public agencies, such as those responsible for transportation and mental health, function at the lowest imaginable level of efficiency—none of these things matter very much since the whole corporate system is a rat race, and anyway there's nothing an individual can do about it. The system, moreover, does provide excellent opportunities for the individual to withdraw and seek his own self-fulfillment through music, literature, arts and crafts that may be pursued in the private world of the home and family. Here indeed, is the way of wisdom, the cultivation of one's own garden, as Voltaire so sagely advised.

And in the present world crisis, on the rat-race-and-withdrawal theory, the society must make certain demands on the individual in order that the system may be preserved. By a combination of force and fraud, it exacts as large a proportion of the individual's time and personality as it can; the individual resisting as hard as he can. By a kind of balance of tensions, depending on internal and external pressures on the system, a compromise is achieved between individual freedom and social survival.

The rat-race-and-withdrawal theory does account for many facts of public life—the graft and corruption revealed daily in the press and the cynicism with which these revelations are greeted, the senselessly huge salaries paid to corporate presidents, signifying the absence of any genuine social reward for socially useful service, and so on. An individual can order his life on the premises of this theory, but he does so at the cost of violating the very realism and disillusionment he cherishes. For this concept of isolated individualism is pure romanticism; self-fulfillment is not to be found in withdrawal into a private world but in productive work in the public world. It does not matter that the public world is imperfect, that its hugeness swallows up the small efforts of individual men and women, that the rapidity of change means that every achievement is soon superseded. For this public, corporate world, despite everything, is *real.* Here there is reality to success and failure; whether the human race survives or not depends on how we learn to work the institutional forms demanded by the density and consumption requirements of *homo sapiens* on this planet.

We hold, therefore, that the key to eliciting excellence in the manifold actions of Americans is not in some phony emotionalism, the use of fraud to persuade individuals to give up their self-enhancing actions in order to perform socially useful services. Rather it is to be found in the intellectual discipline which finally enables the individual to see both his private and public worlds as his own. Distance, change, complexity, mobility—these ineluctable features of modern public life do make it look like a gigantic rat race. The appeals we make to youth, trying to enlist them in causes they do not understand, are transparent to all but the hopelessly stupid. Psychic withdrawal often appears to be the only alternative to madness.

But a firm intellectual grasp of the real nature of this system—with all its complexity, impermanence, dynamism, and freedom—gives the individual a sense of being of, as well as in, his society. That is commitment. Courage, creativity, and leadership spring out of this ordering of an individual, his world, and the symbols by which he understands both. The symbols are those of the appropriate intellectual disciplines.[10]

The obvious alternative is sure to fail. The only way in which we could create a national purpose to match that of communism is by destroying the very freedom we are supposed to serve. We should have to institute strenuous controls over the flow of information. We should have to devise all sorts of rewards and punishments to support an orthodoxy. We should have to substitute myth and superstition for the truth about our natural and social worlds. There are those groups who, out of fear and hostility, would be willing to do just that.

But aside from the moral abhorrence which the suggestion arouses, the appeal to an ultimate meaning served by our national existence would not, in all likelihood, bring our youth to any great pitch of enthusiasm. The young men and women who volunteered to serve as teachers in East Africa and in the Peace Corps made it quite clear that their motives were not those of furthering a particular economic and political system, but overwhelmingly in promoting their own self-growth through the experience of serving other people. They believed, rightly we hope, that what they had to offer was superior to the Russians' contribution because the Americans would be willing to teach, build roads, and improve sanitation without insisting on any particularly American purpose these improvements were to serve. Africans, Asians and South Americans should decide for themselves the ultimate values, if any, to be served by prolonging human life, reducing drudgery, ignorance, and disease.

Perhaps in the long run, the society that agrees to tolerate the tension between public and private worlds, that gives the individual a chance to create his own meaning in both these worlds, that provides him with the tools and symbols to understand the richness and complexity of the world around him without shallow myths and legends—perhaps *that* is the society that can evoke man's highest loyalties and deepest commitments. American education, we believe, ought to be dedicated to that possibility.

Notes and References

Chapter One

INTRODUCTION. EDUCATION AND THE PROBLEM OF COMMITMENT IN CONTEMPORARY AMERICAN LIFE

1. Max Lerner, *America as a Civilization* (New York: Simon and Schuster, 1957).
2. For further discussion and references, see chap. vii.
3. Raymond Williams, *The Long Revolution* (New York: Columbia University Press, 1961), p. xiii.
4. Richard Pares, *The Historian's Business and Other Essays* (Oxford: Clarendon Press, 1961), p. ix.
5. David Riesman, "The Uncommitted Generation, 'Junior Organization Men' in America," *Encounter*, (November, 1960), pp. 25-30.

Chapter Two

EDUCATION AND THE TRANSFORMATION OF AMERICA

1. The *Great Debate* is the title of a collection of some of the more garish of recent comments on education to appear in the popular press. The editors have made no effort to help the reader separate truth from willful lie, of which there is more than a little present. The collection is edited by C. Winfield Scott, Clyde M. Hill, and Hobert W. Burns (Englewood Cliffs, N.J.: Prentice-Hall Spectrum Books, 1959).
2. Arthur Bestor, *Educational Wastelands* (Urbana: University of Illinois Press, 1953). The finger of accusation is pointed in chap. vii, entitled "Interlocking Directorate of Professional Educationists." For the moral imperatives, compare chap. ii of *Educational Wastelands*, "The Ideal of Disciplined Intelligence," with Bestor's "Education and

Its Proper Relationship to the Forces of American Society," *Daedalus* (Winter, 1959), pp. 75-90. In the latter, he no longer asserts that the ideal of disciplined intelligence is inherent in American democracy, as he had held earlier. By an application of what Riesman calls the countercyclical policy, Bestor now maintains that the ideal of disciplined intelligence is of particular concern to the school just because of its absence in the vaguely anti-intellectual American culture. See David Riesman, *Constraint and Variety in American Education* (Garden City: Doubleday Anchor Books, 1958), p. 110.

3. Arthur Bestor, *The Restoration of Learning* (New York: Alfred A. Knopf, 1956), esp. chaps. xv, xxv. (Since this was written, Professor Bestor has moved to the University of Washington.)

4. Compare Jacques Barzun, *Of Human Freedom* (Boston: Little Brown, 1939), with the same author's *House of Intellect* (New York: Harper & Brothers, 1959). In the first book, Barzun sees that there have been excesses in the habit of mind labeled "Progressive," but he senses a self-corrective tendency already in operation. Twenty years later he seems to regard the whole enterprise as hopeless.

5. Barzun, *House of Intellect*, p. 100.

6. Compare Aristotle's *Politics*, Book VIII, 13-17, and Plato's *Republic, passim*, especially 441c–445b, 535a–541b, with John W. Gardner, *Excellence* (New York: Harper & Brothers, 1961), chap. i.

7. Mr. Gardner is by no means unaware that there are fundamental contradictions in American life; indeed the subtitle of *Excellence* points directly to one of them: "Can We Be Equal and Excellent Too?" His arguments on this question deserve far more extensive criticism than we can give them here. But may we suggest some questions which his book raises. Aristotle not only *classified* virtues or excellencies, he also *ordered* them hierarchically with pure contemplation as the highest good of man. Does Dr. Gardner seriously believe that he has successfully reconciled the Aristotelian basis of his approach with the American tradition of egalitarianism and exaltation of the dignity of productive labor? Curiously the only explicit reference to Aristotle in *Excellence* (p. 12) has the Philosopher sounding like a radical egalitarian, while Plato is not mentioned at all. This is very strange. Is it not also appropriate to ask whether Dr. Gardner really thought through his conception of leadership and authority as being appropriate to the new technological era into which we are moving? "Who is going to manage the society?" (*Excellence*, p. 81) is merely a sugar-coated version of Plato's fatal question, "Who shall rule the state?" (Cf. Karl Popper, *The Open Society and Its Enemies* [London: Routledge and Kegan Paul, 1952], I, 120.) Has Dr. Gardner fully satisfied himself on Popper's charge: "I do not hesitate to say that Plato utterly corrupted and confused the theory and practice of education by linking it up with his theory of leadership. . . . Plato's assumption that it should be the task of education (or more precisely, of the educational institutions) to select the future leaders

and to train them for leadership, is still largely taken for granted. By broadening these institutions with a task that must go beyond the scope of any institution, Plato is partly responsible for their deplorable state." (*Open Society*, I, 127.) Popper's argument in defense of this view should be compared with Dr. Gardner's chap. vii, entitled, "Education as a Sorting-Out Process."

8. Martin Mayer, *The Schools* (New York: Harper & Brothers, 1961).

9. Mr. Conant has expressed a certain "distasteful weariness" with attempts to "decide what we mean by the word 'education.'" (James Bryant Conant, *The Child, the Parent, and the State* [Cambridge: Harvard University Press, 1960], p. 1.) This is not surprising, really, for no one can listen to those debates very long without becoming similarly fatigued. Furthermore, in all his educational writings, even those going back into the middle of the 1930's, Mr. Conant has showed the same preference for attention to immediate problems with the objective, readily available facts at hand. It is interesting also that before becoming president of Harvard in 1933, Mr. Conant's branch of science was organic chemistry, which was at that time, of all the physical sciences, the least theoretical and most closely tied to laboratory facts. This same antitheoretical bias is seen in his interpretation of the nature of science: see J. B. Conant, *Science and Common Sense* (New Haven: Yale University Press, 1951), p. 24: "The dynamic view . . . regards science as an activity," as opposed to the static view of science as an "interconnected set of principles, laws, and theories, together with a vast array of systematized information." Needless to say, Mr. Conant prefers the dynamic view.

10. Perhaps stemming from his experiences as High Commissioner and later Ambassador to the Federal German Republic, Mr. Conant has come to view the Cold War as the determining factor in setting educational policies in this country, even in regard to such matters as local administration: "If we really wish to improve secondary education in the United States to meet the national needs in this period of a global struggle, surely district reorganization is a matter of urgency in almost every state in the Union." (*The Child, the Parent, and the State*, p. 39.) It is clear throughout his *American High School Today* (New York: McGraw-Hill, 1959), unquestionably the most influential publication in American education since World War II, that if he were pressed to justify his proposals, his ultimate appeal would be to the security of the nation in its global struggle. He has an almost mystical devotion to "this mixed-up, confused society of ours." (The quotation is from his *Citadel of Learning* [New Haven: Yale University Press, 1956], p. 27.) He prefers, it would seem, that it remain that way.

11. Raymond P. Harris, *American Education: Facts, Fancies, and* Folklore (New York: Random House, 1961). Harris is not at all hesitant when it comes to answering big questions, p. 272: "The greatest

need of the American public schools at the present time is financial support." Page 273: "The real crisis in American education is the meagerness of resources that forces the professionals in most public schools to operate at levels of efficiency below those of which they are capable." Page 281: "The real tasks of American education . . . are those of matching learning experiences to the individual needs and abilities of all pupils." Page 296: "Further improvement in public education requires only public confidence and public support." The absence of qualification in these statements leads one to wonder whether Mr. Harris may not be whistling in the dark to conceal a nagging suspicion that things may not be so clear after all.

12. Myron Lieberman's arguments are thus directly relevant to the thesis of this book. See his *The Future of Public Education* (Chicago: University of Chicago Press, 1960), p. 75: "Centralization and professionalization are inevitable, not in spite of what people think but because enough people will eventually think long enough and hard enough about public education to realize that no other policy makes sense." Given the human capacity for prolonged delusion, it is difficult to see just what "inevitable" means in that context. But the prediction is undoubtedly correct. The schools will have to be brought into the mainstream of American corporate organization, though as we argue in chap. ix, they must also maintain a crucial distinctiveness. Sections of *The Future of Public Education* were published in *The Nation* early in 1959, culminating with the very provocative "Let Educators Plan Our Schools," March 7, 1959. Reaction to this series spread far outside the pages of *The Nation*.

13. See *Decade of Experiment. The Fund for the Advancement of Education, 1951–61* (New York: The Fund, 1961). Compare Lieberman, *op. cit.*, chap. xii.

14. A brochure, published by the Institute, explains the process:

> The American Institute of Biological Sciences, representing 84,000 biologists, established the Biological Sciences Curriculum Study (BSCS) in January 1959 to seek the improvement of biology education. A steering committee composed of outstanding college biologists, high school teachers and other educators, all interested in improving the quality of the teaching of biology in the schools of America, was established under the chairmanship of Dr. Bentley Glass of the Johns Hopkins University. The BSCS, with headquarters on the campus of the University of Colorado, has been financially supported primarily by grants of over $2 million from the National Science Foundation.
>
> In seeking to improve high school biology, the BSCS has designed new materials for high school students. Preliminary experimental editions of these materials were prepared by teams of specially selected high school biology teachers and university research biologists at a Summer Writing Conference in 1960. During the 1960-61 school year, this preliminary experimental

edition of BSCS High School Biology was used by 14,000 students in selected schools throughout the United States. In the summer of 1961, a Second Summer Writing Conference—again made up of selected high school teachers and university research biologists—revised the materials based on the experience in the schools and on reviews of the books by scientific and educational societies and by individual biologists, educators, psychologists, child development specialists, and other interested persons.

15. C. Wright Mills, *The Power Elite* (New York: Oxford University Press, 1956). The utter condemnation with which he holds the "power elite" is given full vent in his last chapter: "The men of the higher circles are not representative men; their high position is not a result of moral virtue; their fabulous success is not firmly connected with meritorious ability. Those who sit in the seats of the high and mighty are selected and formed by the means of power, the sources of wealth, the mechanics of celebrity, which prevail in their society. They are not men selected and formed by a civil service that is linked with the world of knowledge and sensibility. They are not men shaped by nationally responsible parties that debate openly and clearly the issues this nation now so unintelligently confronts. They are not men held in responsible check by a plurality of voluntary associations which connect debating publics with the pinnacles of decision. Commanders of power unequaled in human history, they have succeeded within the American system of organized irresponsibility" (p. 361). (Mills' unexpected death on March 20, 1962 was a great loss. It is hard to name another critic of American life who has his depth and intensity.)

16. See John Kenneth Galbraith, *American Capitalism: The Concept of Countervailing Power* (Boston: Houghton Mifflin, 1952).

17. John Kenneth Galbraith, *The Affluent Society* (Boston: Houghton Mifflin, 1958). Galbraith contends that we can eliminate poverty by correcting the social imbalance between investment in human resources and investment in material resources (p. 317). He says that an increased allocation of funds to education will provide the essential personnel for an increase in wealth (p. 272). In fact, the effect of education "is to increase the range of wants to be satisfied and to lessen the dependence on those which must be contrived" (p. 280).

18. A. A. Berle, Jr., *Power without Property* (New York: Harcourt, Brace, 1959), p. 20: "So I hope these essays will be taken for what they are: studies of one of the major forces (but not the only major force) which is steadily and almost unintentionally transforming American life—and doing this with less agony, less noise, less waste (yes, less waste in spite of a plethora of that) than seems to be the case in the other twentieth-century revolutions currently proceeding in most of the world."

19. *Ibid.*, p. 22: "So, it seems, the ultimate protection of indi-

viduals lies not in the play of economic forces in free markets, but in a set of value judgments so widely accepted and deeply held in the United States that public opinion can energize political action when needed to prevent power from violating these values." Page 135: "In a democracy, this core of ideas, conceptions and desires is a consensus of choices made by individuals who seek illumination, guidance, perhaps leadership from men they trust, as to the life values they hope to realize. But leadership toward and development of a consensus of opinion on life values are not the product of the centers of power and responsibility directing the economic machinery. They come out of the universities and institutions of learning, the daily and periodical press, the authors who write more formally in books. Occasionally, the men who lead may take office in public life, or even directorships in corporations; but their dedication is to humanity and truth. They are our spiritual elite. Over the years an Albert Schweitzer or a William James, a Eugene O'Neill, or a John Dewey has more causative power than all the Lords Temporal of economic institutions."

20. David Riesman, Nathan Glazer, and Reuel Denney, *The Lonely Crowd* (New York: Doubleday, 1953). One of Riesman's critics claims his work is a denigration of the middle class and that his view is basically pessimistic. He argues that the "autonomous" type which Riesman proposes as a solution from the impasse of personal conformity is by Riesman's own reasoning nearly impossible of realization. See Robert Wheeler, "Mr. Riesman's Consumers," *The American Scholar*, XXVI (Winter 1956-57), 39-50.

21. William H. Whyte, Jr., *The Organization Man* (New York: Doubleday, 1957). The protest against conformity is in some measure a condemnation of the restrictions placed upon the individual by corporate organization. The ideology of the organization man is analyzed by William M. Evan in "Organization Man and Due Process of Law," *American Sociological Review*, XXVI (August, 1961), 540-547, who proposed two countervailing forces to overcome the deleterious effects of the structure of management in industrial organizations. He speculates that these effects extend to community and family. "As a result of the premium put on cautious behavior calculated not to offend the preferences and expectations of a superior, the organization man may tend to transfer this behavior pattern and principle of behavior to community life and engage in only 'conformist' activity. . . . A related effect of the ideology may be observable in family values and child rearing patterns of the organization man. The values of seeking approval from superiors, of 'teamwork' and of 'togetherness' may be transplanted from the corporation to the family" (p. 544). Whyte had made much of the same point in his analysis of suburbia. On p. 330 he wrote: "As far as social values are concerned, suburbia is the ultimate expression of the interchangeability so sought by organization. It is classless, or, at least, its people want

it to be. As in the organization, so in the dormitories there has been a great broadening of the middle, and a sort of 'declassification' of people from the older criteria of family background."

22. Recently Riesman has been assuming much more of an activist position. With others, he has initiated a twentieth-century "Committee of Correspondence" which had the great good fortune to draw unfavorable criticism in the editorial pages of *Life*. A recent sympathetic treatment by Eric Larrabee, "Riesman and His Readers," says his objective was not to delimit but to free individuals (*Harper's Magazine* [June, 1961], pp. 59-65).

23. See Riesman, *Constraint and Variety in American Education* (Garden City: Doubleday Anchor Books, 1958).

24. This distinction between public and private is as profound as any that may be proposed in the social sciences. Following quite logically from her preoccupation with the growth of modern totalitarianism, Hannah Arendt has investigated historical roots of the distinction (*The Human Condition* [Chicago: University of Chicago Press, 1958], Part II). John Dewey made his new interpretation of that distinction a central point in his social philosophy (*The Public and Its Problems* [New York: Henry Holt, 1927], chap. i).

Richard Pipes argues that the attempt in the U.S.S.R. to eliminate the distinction—an attempt deeply rooted in Marxism itself—leads to the impossibility of genuine personal commitment ("The Public Mood," *Harper's Magazine* [May, 1961], pp. 107-113).

An interesting thesis on the polarity of these two realms is given by Sir Ernest Barker in his *Principles of Social and Political Theory* (Oxford: Clarendon Press, 1951), Book VI.

25. The once prevalent "nature versus nurture" controversy now appears as a false question in the argument over their relative importance in learning and personality. It is now generally accepted that both genetic and environmental factors operate in intricate linkages. Anthropologists hold that if we accept the organic factors as given, then personality and learning are both reflections of the sociocultural environment. If this is so, then the study of the environment is a necessary procedure for understanding the individual. See John J. Honigmann, *Culture and Personality* (New York: Harper & Brothers, 1954). See also Solon T. Kimball, "An Anthropological View of Learning," *The National Elementary Principal*, XL (1961), 23-27. What promises to be a significant advance in joining learning theory and educational method is found in Jerome S. Bruner, *The Process of Education* (Cambridge: Harvard University Press, 1960).

The several reports by Jean Piaget of his studies of the psychic development of children provide us with the single most encompassing set of data we have to answer regarding questions of how children learn to categorize. See *The Child's Conception of the World* (New York: Humanities Press, 1951); *The Origins of Intelligence in Children* (New York: International Universities Press, 1952); *The Lan-*

guage and Thought of the Child, 3d rev. ed. (New York: Humanities Press, 1959).

26. The doctrine in education that you "teach the child, not subjects" represents a type of slogan which supports the implicit assumption of an individually atomistic world. Powerful influences from psychology, psychoanalysis, and common-sense experience lend credence to the belief. Within an ideological climate of this type, it is not difficult to ignore the importance of the social environment or to consider it an evil without actually ever understanding what was being condemned. See Evan, *op. cit.* This point of view is expressed by the great anthropologist, Edward Sapir, whose cultural orientation and bias for the individual caused him to write, "The major activities of the individual must directly satisfy his own creative and emotional impulses, must always be something more than means to an end. The great cultural fallacy of industrialism, as developed up to the present time, is that in harnessing machines to our uses, it has not known how to avoid the harnessing of the majority of mankind to its machines. The telephone girl who lends her capacities, during the greater part of the living day, to the manipulation of a technical routine that has an eventually high efficiency value, but that answers to no spiritual needs of her own, is an appalling sacrifice to civilization. As a solution of the problem of culture, she is a failure—the more dismal, the greater her natural endowment. As with the telephone girl, so it is to be feared, with the great majority of us, slave-stokers of fires that burn for demons we would destroy, were it not that they appear in the guise of our benefactors" ("Culture, Genuine and Spurious," in *Culture, Language and Personality* [Berkeley, Calif.: University of California, 1956]). (This first appeared in the *American Journal of Sociology,* Vol. XXIX [1924].) Our rejoinder: "Once the demons are destroyed, what then?" Actually, Sapir lets his rhetoric run away with him, for he later proposes to build a new culture for the individual. We have no disagreement with the objective, we only say it cannot be done by focusing on the individual alone, as so many believe.

27. We were tempted to include here a complete history of the idea of social system or social structure and to show how the idea might be formulated so as to be defensible against the charges, some of which are quite perceptive, that are frequently brought forward. But this turns out to be quite another study altogether. In this book we use both terms, "social system" and "social structure," in an undefined way, allowing the illustrations from agrarian, Irish, Navaho, suburban, and other cultural units to carry the intent. We do not allow biological or mechanical metaphors that might inhere in these terms to creep into our analysis unobserved. We do not conceal political biases, revolutionary or reactionary, in our use of the terms. We are aware, that is to say, of the pitfalls on the trail we take. We hope to have avoided them. For those who want to follow the notions

of social system and social structure, the following citations are recommended as starting points: (1) George P. Murdock, *Social Structure* (New York: Macmillan, 1949). An empirical approach utilizing the cross-cultural survey materials of the Institute of Human Relations, Yale University; (2) S. F. Nadel, *The Theory of Social Structure* (Glencoe, Ill.: Free Press, 1957). An extraordinary combination of sophistication in contemporary logic and theory, and extensive experience in anthropological field work gives Nadel a most illuminating perspective on the theoretical developments he treats.

The two names one would think of first have most conveniently provided their own interpretation for the background of their work. See Claude Levi Strauss, "Social Structure," in A. L. Kroeber (ed.), *Anthropology Today* (Chicago: University of Chicago Press, 1953), pp. 524-553. His is the most rigorous formal model attack. See also Talcott Parsons, "Culture and Social System," in Parsons, Shils, Naegele, and Pitts (eds.), *Theories of Society* (Glencoe, Ill.: Free Press, 1961), II, 963-996.

28. In 1929, Alfred North Whitehead published *The Aims of Education and Other Essays* (New York: Macmillan). In its preface he wrote, "The students are alive, and the purpose of education is to stimulate and guide their self-development. It follows as a corollary from this premise that the teachers also should be alive with living thoughts. The whole book is a protest against dead knowledge, that is to say, against inert ideas." Mayer's description (*op. cit.*) of what happens in the classroom provides little evidence that Whitehead's ideas have been put to practice, although most educators would heartily endorse his objectives and we feel certain that thousands training for teaching have had his essays as assigned reading. How does one explain this failure? We believe that not until an organizational structure which favors the educative process has been developed will it be possible to introduce the kind of curriculum and methods Whitehead advocates. We shall analyze this problem at length in chap. ix.

Chapter Three

AMERICA: THE PROMISED LAND

1. It is our intention in this chapter to present an overview of the development and characteristics of American civilization. Obviously, it is possible to touch upon only a few of the manifold aspects of such a broad subject in this limited space. Those which we have chosen to give emphasis to have been included either because they are especially relevant to later analysis or because they add illumination to our particular orientation, or both. For those who through interest or need desire to examine some full-scale interpretative studies of the American scene there are several worthy of serious attention. In scope,

originality, and scholarly competence we would rank Vernon L. Parrington, *Main Currents of American Thought* (New York: Harcourt, Brace, 1927-30), among the best. Others include Ralph H. Gabriel, *The Course of American Democratic Thought*, rev. ed. (New York: Ronald Press, 1956); Henry Parkes, *The American Experience* (New York: Vintage Books, 1959); and Charles and Mary Beard, *The Rise of American Civilization* (New York: Macmillan, 1936). A comprehensive analysis of the contemporary scene is found in Max Lerner's *America as a Civilization* (New York: Simon and Schuster, 1957). For a popular treatment of the subject, see James Truslow Adams, *The American: The Making of a New Man* (New York: Scribner's, 1944). A great classic, of course, is Alexis de Tocqueville, *Democracy in America* (New York: Knopf, 1945).

Many writers express or report upon the belief and feeling, once currently held, that America occupied a preëminent position in the divine plan. Gabriel (*op. cit.*, p. 22) says: "Liberty, according to a widely accepted version of American mythology of the early nineteenth century, had been established by Deity in an empty western continent so that, freed from the burden of European tradition, it might flourish and become an inspiration to the world." It is Gabriel's contention that one of the three doctrines of the democratic faith was that of the mission of America. Lerner (*op. cit.*, p. 719) suggests that preoccupation with God's design on the American continent "had its origin in Puritan theocracy, and although watered down in subsequent years, was never lost." He also writes (p. 28): "Some of the early historians believed they saw the hand of God operating exclusively in American history and did not trouble to inquire why He should have shown so special a solicitude for this particular breed of children. Not counting the inevitable drivel about the superior virtues of Anglo-Saxonism, there were also a few accepted historians (Bancroft, Fiske, Mahan, come to mind) who wrote of Americans as A Chosen People in the Biblical sense of one through whose history some Higher Power works out an inscrutable design for the whole human race." The linkage of one's tribe or people with the supernatural, or belief in the possession of special superior qualities, is a common ethnocentric phenomenon. The Jews believe themselves to be the Chosen People. Brazilians say, "God is a Brazilian." The Chinese categorized people into either barbarians or Chinese. However, widespread belief that America occupies a special place in a divine plan has now been lost. On those occasions when we ask our students if they had been taught of a divine mission for this country, only rarely does one admit that he believes in such a plan.

2. Parrington (*op. cit.*, I, iv-v) attributes the origin of these views to French romantic theory as interpreted by Jefferson and others—views which found a congenial environment outside New England: "Exploring the equalitarian premises of the doctrine of natural rights, it amplified the emerging democratic theory by substituting for the Puritan conception of human nature as vicious, the conception of

human nature as potentially excellent and capable of indefinite development. It asserted that the present evils of society are the consequence of vicious institutions rather than of depraved human nature; and that as free men and equals *it is the right and duty of citizens to recreate social and political institutions* to the end that they shall further social justice, encouraging the good in men rather than perverting them to evil. Romantic theory went further and provided a new economics and a new sociology. . . . The political state, rightly conceived, must be reckoned no other than a great public-service corporation, with government as its responsible agent." (Italics ours.)

3. "So we stand on the brink of a new age: the age of an open world and of a self capable of playing its part in that larger sphere. An age of renewal when work and leisure and learning and love will unite to produce a fresh form for every stage of life, and a higher trajectory for life as a whole." Thus wrote Lewis Mumford in a poetic and optimistic way about the future. The thesis in his *The Transformation of Man* (London, Allen and Unwin, 1957) (p. 191 quoted), is that we are entering upon a new stage in the history of humanity.

4. See V. Gordon Childe, *What Happened in History* (New York: Penguin Books, 1946). Childe's systematic interpretation of the successive stages in man's development has received near universal acceptance. The deliberate utilization of nature's laws in the domestication of plants and animals he describes as an economic and scientific revolution. New interpretation, however, is beginning to challenge the validity of his obvious reliance upon assumptions drawn from economic determinism. Carleton S. Coon, *The Story of Man* (New York: Knopf, 1955), is an authoritative and more comprehensive account of man from an anthropologist's perspective.

5. See Parkes, *op. cit.*, chaps. xi, xii, for a description of industrial growth and its accompanying ideology. In Sigfried Giedion, *Mechanization Takes Command* (New York: Oxford University Press, 1948), technological change on a world basis is carefully traced.

6. Some measure of the skyrocketing sums spent by industry on research and development is given by figures provided by the National Science Foundation which show a jump from $3.6 billion in 1953 to an estimated $11 billion for 1961 (National Science Foundation, *Reviews of Data on Research and Development,* No. 30 [September, 1961]). By contrast, in 1940 the sums spent on research by all agencies were less than one billion dollars.

7. The scope and development of contemporary social science may be grasped by examining two volumes which range comprehensively over the field: A. L. Kroeber (ed.), *Anthropology Today* (Chicago: University of Chicago Press, 1953), and Robert K. Merton, Leonard Broom, and Leonard S. Cottrell, Jr. (eds.), *Sociology Today* (New York: Basic Books, 1959).

8. H. G. Wells, *The Outline of History* (Garden City: Garden City, 1925).

9. Sinclair Lewis, *Arrowsmith* (New York: Harcourt, Brace, 1925).

10. We have discovered no single satisfactory critique of the agrarian world-view. Parrington's second volume (*op. cit.*), *The Romantic Revolution in America,* utilizes the literature of a recorded view of the antagonists, but these do not reach to the basic levels of agrarian inspiration. Parkes' analysis (*op. cit.*) in his chapter entitled "The Agrarian Mind" draws almost entirely upon literature from New England and is not acceptable. In *Virgin Land* by Henry Nash Smith, he turns to literature of the Midwest for his analysis, but the resulting picture is incomplete. Unfortunately, there is nothing for America's heartland which approaches the depth of perceptive understanding displayed by William Faulkner in his descriptions of northern Mississippi life in *Light in August* or *As I Lay Dying.*

11. For a brief comment on the meaning of death in urban society, see Lerner, *op. cit.,* pp. 618-620. Contrast his analysis with the account of a funeral in a small Alabama town in Renwick C. Kennedy, "Alas, Poor Yorick," *The Alabama Historical Quarterly,* II (1940), 405-415. See also James Agee, *A Death in the Family* (New York: McDowell Obolensky, 1957).

12. See the following for analyses of age and sex functions: Melville J. Herskovits, *The Economic Life of Primitive Peoples* (New York: Knopf, 1940), pp. 110-119; Ralph Linton, "Age and Sex Categories," *American Sociological Review,* VII (1942), 589-603; James West, *Plainville, U.S.A.* (New York: Columbia University Press, 1945), pp. 107-111; Margaret Mead, *Sex and Temperament in Three Primitive Societies* (New York: Morrow, 1935); and Margaret Mead, *Male and Female: A Study of the Sexes in a Changing World* (New York: Morrow, 1949).

13. It is a curious commentary on the orientation in our culture which sees the sexual problem almost entirely as one which revolves around the sufferings of the female sex. For example, Lerner devotes thirteen pages to a section entitled "The Ordeal of the American Woman" (*op. cit.,* pp. 599-611). The ordeal of men, if any, is ignored. The critical problems which men face are made quite explicit in our chapter x.

14. See Solon T. Kimball, "Cultural Influences Shaping the Role of the Child," *Those First School Years* (published by the Department of Elementary School Principals), XL, (1960), 18-32.

15. For a concise anthropological analysis of the American nuclear family, see Conrad M. Arensberg, "The Family and Other Cultures," in *The Nation's Children* (New York: Columbia University Press, 1960). Also see Ruth Anshen, *The Family: Its Function and Destiny* (New York: Harper and Brothers, 1959).

16. Stephen Vincent Benét's unfinished epic poem, *Western Star* (New York: Farrar and Rinehart, 1943), begins with these lines:

Americans are always moving on.
It's an old Spanish custom gone astray,

A sort of English fever, I believe,
Or just a mere desire to take French leave,
I couldn't say. I couldn't really say.
But, when the whistle blows, they go away.
Sometimes there never was a whistle blown,
But they don't care, for they can blow their own
Whistles of willow-stick and rabbit-bone,
Quail-calling through the rain
A dozen tunes but only one refrain,
We don't know where we're going, but we're on our way!
[From *Western Star* by Stephen Vincent Benét; Holt, Rinehart and Winston, Inc.; Copyright, 1943, by Rosemary Carr Benét.]

17. See W. Lloyd Warner, *American Life: Dream or Reality* (Chicago: University of Chicago Press, 1953).
18. George Herbert Mead, *Mind, Self, and Society* (Chicago, University of Chicago Press), 1934.
19. Emile Durkheim, *Suicide* (Glencoe, Ill.: Free Press, 1951).
20. See Bertram Shaffner, "Animal Studies and Human Behavior," *Human Organization,* XV (1956), 11-14.

Chapter Four

THE IMMEDIATE PAST: MIDWEST AGRARIANISM AND MAIN STREET TOWNS

1. Although the emancipation of slaves and the preservation of the Union are frequently cited as primary contributors to the Civil War, we believe that this struggle was primarily a contest between two antithetical agrarian systems. Consider, for example, that hostilities had begun on the Kansas frontier several years previous to secession, and that the first draft of a constitution for that state by Free Soil adherents prohibited the residence of Negroes, free or slave (Alice Nichols, *Bleeding Kansas* [New York: Oxford University Press, 1954], p. 47). Other evidence is also available. In chap. xiv of *Virgin Land: The American West as Symbol and Myth* (New York: Vintage Books, 1957; first published by Harvard University Press, 1950), Henry Nash Smith describes the new agrarianism arising west of the Appalachians after 1830 as based on a new technology, surpluses, the need for free access to markets, geography, and the myth of a Promised Land in the Garden of the World. He writes (p. 179): ". . . But by the 1830's a new calculus and new symbols were required to interpret the new West that was being created by forces wholly foreign to the agrarian assumptions. . . . These changes spelled the end of the

simple economy which in the first stages of settlement had corresponded at least approximately to the agrarian ideal. In the long run the virtuous yeoman could no more stand his ground against the developing capitalism of merchant, banker, and manufacturer in the Northwest than he could against the plantation system in the Southwest."

Additional interpretative support for this thesis can be found in Henry Bamford Parkes, *The American Experience* (New York: Vintage Books, 1959), chap. x, "The Civil War." One relevant comment on the consequences of the War follows (p. 233): "Meanwhile Northern industrial and financial interests had taken advantage of the Secession of the South to establish a firm hold over the Federal Congress. Although Northern businessmen *had not caused the war*, their aggrandizement was certainly the most conspicuous of its results. . . . By attempting to leave the Union in order to maintain Negro slavery, the South had brought about the final and irreparable defeat of agrarianism." (Italics ours.)

2. Frederick J. Turner, *The Frontier in American History* (New York: Henry Holt, 1920). Turner first advanced his theory in a paper first presented in Chicago in 1893. (Vernon L. Parrington [Main Currents in American Thought (New York: Harcourt, Brace, 1927-30), p. 159] notes that Edwin Laurence Godkin, in "Aristocratic Opinions of Democracy," *North American Review* [January, 1865], presented substantially the same theory.) Currently, there is a reëxamination of the validity of Turner's thesis. Future evaluation will probably assign greater importance to the democratic forces in urban centers than has been customary. In Carl Bridenbaugh, *Cities in Revolt* (New York: Knopf, 1955), he assembles data which show the rich and varied intellectual and cultural life of the colonial cities and their undoubted influence upon the back country.

3. See James Truslow Adams, *The American* (New York: Scribner's, 1944).

4. H. Richard Niebuhr, *The Social Sources of Denominationalism* (New York: Henry Holt, 1929); and *The Kingdom of God in America* (Chicago: Willett, Clark, 1937).

5. See Parrington, *op. cit.*, III (*The Beginnings of Critical Realism in America*), 259-282 ("The Plight of the Farmer"). ". . . While capitalism had been perfecting its machinery of exploitation, he [the farmer] had remained indifferent to the fact that he himself was the fattest goose that capitalism was to pluck. He had helped indeed to provide the rope for his own hanging. He had voted away the public domain to railways that were now fleecing him; he took pride in the county-seat towns that lived off his earnings; he sent city lawyers to represent him in legislatures and in Congress; he read middle-class newspapers and listened to bankers and politicians, and cast his votes for the policy of Whiggery that could have no other outcome than his own despoiling. . . . Clearly, it was high time for the deflated farmer

to get into politics on his own account if he were to save himself from beggary, and so during the Gilded Age began a great agrarian revolt against capitalism that was to turmoil the next quarter of a century —a revolt that was to mark the last effective organization of the farmers to combat the new order, the last flare-up of an old fashioned agrarian America before it was submerged by the Middle Class" (p. 262).

6. Smith, *op. cit.*, p. 138.

7. Hamlin Garland, *A Son of the Middle Border* (New York: Macmillan, 1923). The numerous writings of Hamlin Garland provide a rich source for those who seek to understand pioneer life on the Middle Border. He ruthlessly stripped away the romantic illusions to reveal the stark reality which settlers on the prairies faced. Parrington calls Garland's *Main-Travelled Roads* and *Prairie Folks* a landmark, "for they were the first authentic expression and protest of an agrarian America then being submerged by an industrial revolution" (*op. cit.*, III, 294). "The figures of bitter men and despondent women fill his pages and darken the colors of his realism. It is the cost of it all that depresses him—the toll exacted of human happiness" (III, 392).

8. One of the infrequently reported aspects of rural life was the traveling milliner or "cat-wagon" with her caravan of girls who made hats for the women and gave sexual comfort to the men.

9. Harriet Connor Brown, *Grandmother Brown's Hundred Years, 1827-1927*, (Boston: Little, Brown, 1929). This original account of pioneer life was recorded through the interest of one of Grandmother Brown's daughters-in-law. It is rich in the detail of daily living and of aspirations of those times.

10. Garland, *A Son of the Middle Border*, p. 20.

11. *Ibid.*, p. 50.

12. Brown, *op. cit.*, p. 167.

13. The ultimate resignation to divine Providence was far from universal. Each locality possessed a goodly proportion of those who did not attend religious services, although they might read the Bible regularly. A few were outright hostile and there was always a scattering of atheists. Even the godly were sorely put to retain their faith under conditions of stress. One illuminating example of this Job-like attitude is given by Ise in his description of a conversation between his mother and the visiting preacher. She protests the lack of rain which causes humans and animals to suffer and denies that trust in God is a solution because He obviously hasn't done His share. Nor does she accept divine punishment as an explanation, for she doesn't believe that the Lord would want children without shoes or cattle without feed (John Ise, *Sod and Stubble: The Story of a Kansas Homestead* [New York: Wilson-Erickson, 1936], pp. 246-251).

14. Garland, *A Son of the Middle Border*, chap. xxxv.

15. Adams, *op. cit.*, pp. 329-330.

16. Southern womanhood has been extolled and damned but few

have stated a part of the reality more movingly than Stephen Vincent Benét in his epic poem, *John Brown's Body* (New York: Farrar and Rinehart, 1941), pp. 155-156:

> *The velvet sheathing the steel demurely*
> *In the trained, light grip that holds so surely.*
>
> * * *
>
> *She was often mistaken, not often blind,*
> *And she knew the whole duty of womankind,*
> *To take the burden and have the power*
> *And seem like the well-protected flower.*
> *To manage a dozen industries*
> *With a casual gesture in scraps of ease,*
> *To hate the sin and to love the sinner*
> *And to see that the gentlemen got their dinner*
> *Ready and plenty and piping-hot*
> *Whether you wanted to eat or not.*
>
> * * *
>
> *This was the creed that her mother taught her*
> *And the creed that she taught to every daughter.*
>
> [From *John Brown's Body;* Holt, Rinehart And Winston, Inc.; Copyright 1927, 1928 by Stephen Vincent Benét; Copyright renewed 1955, 1956 by Rosemary Carr Benét.]

In considerable contrast is the description given us of a Yankee school teacher who came to teach in a north Alabama town of the antebellum South (Joseph G. Baldwin, *The Flush Times of Alabama and Mississippi* [New York: Sagamore Press, 1957; first published 1853]). An extract from Baldwin's uncomplimentary description follows (p. 213): "Miss Charity was one of those 'strong-minded women of New England' who exchange all the tenderness of the feminine for an impotent attempt to attain the efficiency of the masculine nature; one of that fussy, obtrusive, meddling class, who, in trying to *double-sex* themselves, *unsex* themselves, losing all that is lovable in woman, and getting most of what is odious in man."

Neither New England nor the South gave us the image of an idealized woman for the agrarian period. It arose on the Middle Border.

17. Hamlin Garland varies the theme in "A Branch Road," published in his collection of stories, *Main-Travelled Roads* (New York: Harper and Brothers, 1909). A young farm youth, feeling the guilt of having deserted his love, returns to find her married and a worn-out drudge at thirty. He urges her to flee with him and promises to give her the tender love that will restore her health and beauty.

18. Every person who has an interest in education should read Jesse

Stuart, *The Thread That Runs So True* (New York: Scribners, 1949). It is an account which describes one man's attempt to improve education in a remote Kentucky county and the adversities of parental indifference or hostility, poverty, and politics which he had to meet.

19. Brown, *op. cit.*, p. 214: "One morning—it was the fifth of May, 1888—he went away. He was just a little past eighteen years old—my last baby. I stood at the door to watch him go down the street. I cannot *tell* you how I felt. It was a lovely spring morning, but I felt as if the end of the world had come. No children in my home any more! The last one going from me. Oh, oh, oh! And yet I would not have held him back!"

20. Garland, *A Son of the Middle Border*, p. 239.

21. The assumption of residential stability among families of countryside and small town is hardly supported by the facts. When the country was being settled there was a constant flux due to the arrival of new families and departure of those who failed or sought greener pastures. Lewis E. Atherton, in *Main Street on the Middle Border* (Bloomington, Ind.: Indiana University Press, 1954), described families similar to the Garlands as follows (p. 17): "They were literally wanderers in the Middle Border, a part of it only in the same ephemeral sense that multitudes of others belonged to the new states being created." He continues (p. 17): "Even those who remained in one locality felt the pressure of the constant stream of transients that flowed around them. Small towns acquired their old families rapidly—people who had lived there for a whole generation! And even they were affected by the technological revolution which constantly battered and reshaped their community. Like the Garlands, they saw their children choose careers differing from their own, thus lessening the sense of stability and continuity which all societies crave."

22. Although Robert Ingersoll is barely remembered today, in the last quarter of the nineteenth century he was a controversial figure who advocated atheism and preached a religion of humanity. For a brief sketch of his career, see Ralph H. Gabriel, *The Course of American Democratic Thought*, rev. ed. (New York: Ronald Press, 1956), pp. 189-194.

23. E. W. Howe, *The Story of a Country Town* (New York: Boni, 1926); Sinclair Lewis, *Main Street* (New York: Harcourt, Brace, 1920); Edgar Lee Masters, *Spoon River Anthology* (New York: Macmillan, 1928); Sherwood Anderson, *Winesburg, Ohio* (New York: Huebsch, 1919).

24. For an excellent anthropological description of a midwestern village and rural life, see James West, *Plainville, U.S.A.* (New York: Columbia University Press, 1945). Although this report is based upon materials gathered just previous to the Second World War, the style of life described has changed little in three-quarters of a century or more.

25. Ise, *op. cit.*, p. 305. In *Sod and Stubble,* the affairs of the town constantly intrude into Ise's account of farm life. The local creamery or lumber yard is viewed as a profiteering monopoly. Townspeople introduce new leisure-time pursuits such as croquet and crokinole. Bicycles appear. Squabbles over politics and booze attract attention. The young people meet and make new friends.

26. Atherton, *op. cit.* See chap. ix, "The City Comes to Main Street."

27. *Ibid.*, p. 75: "Lastly, every community had a group of inhabitants who simply ignored the middle-class code of respectability and religious observance. They drank and fought and caroused and 'cussed,' or they hunted on Sunday, shunned the churches, and pursued their simple pleasures without yielding to community pressure to lead a 'better' life. Here, then, was the cultural pattern—a dominant middle-class Protestant group given to religion and stern morality; an upper-class group of 'respectable' people who failed to see any necessary connection between pleasure and sin; Catholics; foreigners; and a 'lower' class, which ignored the dominant code except perhaps for temporary allegiance following revival meetings. In spite of latent antagonisms, villagers lived close together and could not avoid influencing one another. It was a rare boy indeed who grew to manhood solely as the product of one cultural layer."

28. Solon T. Kimball and Marion Pearsall, *The Talladega Story,* (University, Ala.: University of Alabama Press, 1954), pp. xxiii-xxxii.

29. Joseph Stanley Pennell, in *The History of Rome Hanks and Kindred Matters* (New York: Scribner's, 1944), attempts to interconnect the traumatic experience of Civil War days with the flat civilian life of veterans in a Kansas town. Although the past lies heavy on the lives of these men it has little meaning in the ongoing minutiae of daily living. For the third-generation descendant, living in metropolis, the past has become utterly senseless. The vignettes of small-town life are accurate.

30. Booth Tarkington, *Alice Adams* (New York: Grosset and Dunlap, 1921), and *The Magnificent Ambersons* (New York: Grossett and Dunlap, 1918).

31. Sinclair Lewis, *op. cit.; Babbitt* (New York: Grosset, 1922).

32. John Marquand, *The Point of No Return* (Boston: Little, Brown, 1949); Thomas Wolfe, *You Can't Go Home Again* (New York: Harper and Brothers, 1940).

33. This section, "Social Class and the Town-Community," was originally published by Solon T. Kimball in *Sociologia* (São Paulo, Brazil), XXI (May, 1959), 186-202, under the title "Classe Social e Comunidáde nos Estados Unidos." Minor editorial changes have been made from the original text.

Chapter Five

PROGRESSIVE EDUCATION: THE TRANSITION FROM AGRARIAN TO INDUSTRIAL AMERICA

1. Certainly no note of impending reversal is to be found in the *Essays for John Dewey's Birthday* edited by K. D. Benne and William O. Stanley (Urbana: University of Illinois, Bureau of Research, 1950). The essays by Horace S. Fries and Foster McMurray are basically critical in tone, but both assume that criticism means reformulating and extending the Deweyan tradition; they also assume that the problems Dewey worked on—i.e., problems concerned with the nature of scientific method and social planning—are the problems that ought to be attacked. Ten years later, these assumptions would not have been made.

2. Lawrence A. Cremin, *The Transformation of the School* (New York; Knopf, 1961), p. 89: "Finally, and perhaps most important, the progressives were fundamentally moderates, and for all their sense of outrage, moderates take time. . . . The real radicals of the nineties —men like Eugene Victor Debs and Daniel DeLeon—had little patience for reform through education: they directed their energy to the drive for political power which they saw as the only real source for genuine social alleviation. But for the much larger group, impelled by conscience yet restrained by conservatism, education provided a field par excellence for reform activities untainted by radicalism." This book is the first and will likely be long regarded as the definitive history of progressive education. But notice in this instance Cremin tends to look for revolutionary tendencies in the ideological and political sphere, while our emphasis is on the dynamic forces found in technology and changing social relations. A full understanding, of course, would have to combine both these emphases.

3. Bertrand Russell, "Dewey's New Logic," in P. A. Schilpp (ed.), *The Philosophy of John Dewey* (Evanston, Ill.: Library of Living Philosophers, 1939), p. 137: "Dr. Dewey has an outlook which, where it is distinctive, is in harmony with the age of industrialism and collective enterprise." This is Russell at his worst; at his best, of course, he stands with the immortals.

4. There is, admittedly, no historical justification for thus narrowing the meaning of the term "progressive." Cremin (*op. cit*) has demonstrated the range of ideas and the heterogeneity of persons caught up, centrally or peripherally, in the overall movement known by that name. Indeed, John Dewey and his fellow pragmatists in education were not the first to voice and act on many of the ideas that have come to be associated with their names. (See Herbert W. Schneider, *A History of American Philosophy* [New York: Columbia University Press, 1946].) But they did provide three key elements without which the public and professional discussions of education

would have been far different from what they in fact were during the period we are considering. First, they provided for the in-group, the fellow believers, a fundamental set of doctrines around which controversy could and did flourish. (See John L. Childs, *American Pragmatism and Education* [New York: Holt, Rinehart, and Winston, 1956].) Second, they set the problems and issues on which debate could be joined between pragmatists and their manifold enemies. (See John S. Brubacher, *Modern Philosophies of Education,* 2d ed. [New York: McGraw-Hill, 1950].) Third, the pragmatists, particularly John Dewey, had an almost clairvoyant insight into the social relevance of educational issues, and with this insight they kept educational discussions tied to major debates of public policy. As early as 1899, Dewey formulated the problem of schools in an urban, industrial society wherein "concentration of industry and division of labor have practically eliminated household and neighborhood occupations—at least for educational purposes. But [he continues,] it is useless to bemoan the departure of the good old days. . . . It is radical conditions which have changed, and only an equally radical change in education suffices. We must recognize our compensations—the increase in tolerance, in breadth of social judgment . . . [etc.]. Yet there is a real problem: how shall we retain these advantages, and yet introduce into school something representing the other side of life . . . ?" (*The School and Society* [Chicago: University of Chicago Press, 1900], pp. 25-26). The evolution of Dewey's educational thought should be interpreted as a deepening sense of what was good about the good old days, how radical was the change in conditions, why the compensations have their own unique value, and where one might seek theoretical bases for an education that would suffice. Seen in this way, Dewey's last major statement on education (*Experience and Education* [New York: Macmillan, 1955; copyright 1938]) has an easily intelligible continuity with his earlier writings. See also Martin S. Dworkin, "Editor's Introduction" to *Dewey on Education* (New York: Columbia University, Teachers College, 1960).

5. Marie Sandoz: *Old Jules* (Boston: Little, Brown, 1935). This is an effective social and political allegory as well as an engrossing novel.

6. The discussion in this section is focused on the midwestern agrarian system, especially as it came to dominate all American agriculture after 1861. (See discussion and reference in Chap. iv.)

7. Alexis de Tocqueville, *Democracy in America,* ed. Phillips Bradley (New York: Vintage Books, 1954), Vol. I, Chap. xvii.

8. Gunnar Myrdal, *An American Dilemma* (New York: Harper and Brothers, 1944), pp. 887-893.

9. R. Freeman Butts and Lawrence A. Cremin, *A History of Education in American Culture* (New York: Henry Holt, 1953), pp. 379-384.

10. For examples of the exceptions, see Elsie R. Clapp, *Community Schools in Action* (New York: Viking Press, 1939). For the ideology

of the community school expressed as program, see Edward G. Olsen, *School and Community* (New York: Prentice-Hall, 1945); also Lloyd Allen Cook and Elaine Forsyth Cook, *A Sociological Approach to Education* (New York: McGraw-Hill, 1950), especially Part IV.

11. This is said without prejudice to Cremin's study (*op. cit.*) which is notably chary of evaluations. But we simply cannot say what was the meaning of certain events and ideas until we see their outcome, and that is still in doubt. The emergence, for example, of a distinct profession (with specialized training and all the appurtenances) of educational administration and the bureaucratization of the schools was not unrelated to the growth of progressive thought. But we cannot tell exactly what that relation meant until we see what happens to the concentration of power that has accumulated around administrative positions. Compare V. T. Thayer, "The School: Its Task and Its Administration," in William H. Kilpatrick (ed.), *The Educational Frontier* (New York: D. Appleton-Century, 1933), chap. vii, with the same author's discussion of administration in *The Role of the School in American Society* (New York: Dodd, Mead, 1960), especially pp. 270-273, 309-311. In the former work, Thayer seemed to recognize the reality of a power struggle in which both the *form* of administration and the *concept* of schooling were at issue. In the latter, he has lost that idea altogether and talks about issues in administration in terms of public relations and theories of learning. For samples of the passions that this matter arouses and the spadework in research that will have to be done before our understanding can be clarified on this topic, see Charles Robert Kelly, *Toward an Interpretation of the New Movement of 1915 in Educational Administration* (unpublished Ed.D. project, Teachers College, Columbia University, 1961).

12. A national, as opposed to a regional, vision was certainly characteristic of Horace Mann. Even as Mann speaks as secretary to the Board of Education of Massachusetts, he uses the term "Commonwealth" more as synonymous with "Republic" than as referring solely to Massachusetts. See *The Republic and the School*, ed. Lawrence A. Cremin (New York: Columbia University, Teachers College, 1957).

13. William F. Ogburn, *Social Change* (New York: Viking Press, 1932) pp. 201-202: ". . . industry and education are correlated parts of culture, hence a change in industry makes adjustments necessary through changes in the educational system. Industry and education are two variables, and if the change in industry occurs first and the adjustment through education follows, industry may be referred to as the independent variable, and education as the dependent variable." It is easy to see that the progressives accepted at least a variation of Ogburn's thesis of cultural lag. But the variation is itself significant. Because education changes less immediately and automatically in response to changes in the material culture (in Ogburn's terms it is less adaptive than industry taken as a social organization), it also

follows that in educational change there is a chance for intelligent planning to operate. While the progressives often complained of the slowness of educational change, they would not have preferred a purely mechanical connection such that every change in technology produced an immediate and corresponding change in the schools.

14. This point is argued technically in James E. McClellan, "Dewey and the Concept of Method," *The School Review* (Summer, 1959), pp. 213-228.

15. The first essay in John Dewey, *The Influence of Darwin and Other Essays in Contemporary Thought* (New York: Henry Holt, 1910).

16. William H. Kilpatrick, "A Reconstructed Theory of the Educative Process," *Teachers College Record,* XXXII (March, 1931); revised and published as a separate pamphlet (January, 1935). "In the history of civilization there emerge from time to time epoch-making reconstructions of world outlook. . . . When these shifts of fundamental conception arise, the effects reach far both in scope and depth. No region of thought or endeavor can escape. . . . Education, which properly represents both the growing and the conserving aspects of the individual and social process, becomes then involved in the very essence of the reconstruction. If intelligence is to play its proper part in this process, education must itself be remade so that it can respond adequately to the new demands thus laid upon it." Whatever may have been the actual effect of the progressives in changing behavior in schools, in theory they were willing to see unlimited change there in order that certain values would survive in the larger social order.

17. Here, as throughout this chapter, we are presenting our own interpretation, which is certainly not the only one available. While *we* see the absence of final, ultimate, and eternal values as related to a background of radically Protestant theology, others have seen it differently, perhaps as deriving from the new cosmology of Peirce and Whitehead in which not even physical laws were seen as permanent but merely as transient phases of a changing universe. (See Max Fisch, *Classic American Philosophers* [New York: Appleton-Century-Crofts, 1951], p. 23.) And it is certainly true that the progressives read and referred to scientific literature more than they did to theology. (See Kilpatrick, *op. cit.*) But if one follows Dewey's convoluted arguments against the existence of final values (in the usual sense), in his *Theory of Valuation* (Chicago: University of Chicago Press, 1939), pp. 40–50, one must surely see that it is not a mere corollary to a cosmological view. Dewey's argument, in fact, has much in common with James Luther Adams' summary of Paul Tillich's attack on idolatry: "If language is to express vividly our sense of being grasped by something unconditional, it must use symbols drawn from the actual world of subject-object correlation. Yet the use of 'objective' symbols brings with it the danger of objectifying God. It

also gives rise to the 'half-blasphemous and mythological concept of the existence of God.' To draw the divine down into the world of objects is to commit idolatry. This idolatry before an objectively 'existing' God is the ever present danger of all religion" ("Tillich's Concept of the Protestant Era," in Paul Tillich, *The Protestant Era* [Chicago: University of Chicago Press, 1948], p. 301). Tillich is trying to have that which is not limited by context clearly marked off from that which is so limited. Dewey is concerned that symbols properly referring to a context not be treated as if they were super-contextual in meaning. The convergence is striking.

18. John Dewey, *A Common Faith* (New Haven: Yale University Press, 1934). The statement must be understood correctly. Dewey did not fall into the idolatrous doctrine that the most cooperative and egalitarian community is worthy of worship. According to Dewey, nothing is worthy of worship. See Edward L. Schaub, "Dewey's Interpretation of Religion," in Schilpp (ed.), *op. cit.*

19. Wilbur J. Cash, *The Mind of the South* (New York: Knopf, 1941), pp. 80-85.

20. See R. Freeman Butts, *The American Tradition in Religion and Education* (Boston: Beacon Press, 1950), especially "Summary of Historical Considerations," pp. 209-212.

21. See Cremin, *op. cit.*, pp. 58-75, 363-65.

22. Hannah Arendt, *Between Past and Future* (New York: Viking Press, 1961), p. 178: ". . . that complex of educational theories . . . under the banner of progressive education . . . in America about twenty-five years ago completely overthrew, as though from one day to the next, all traditions and all the established methods of teaching and learning." Miss Arendt, a few pages before, had claimed ignorance of matters educational. We believe her.

23. See: Kelly, *op. cit., passim;* Cremin, *op. cit.*, chap. iv. It is instructive to notice how little the pedagogical changes in rather consciously experimental schools were directly related to progressivist beliefs. See W. M. Aikin, *The Story of the Eight-Year Study* (New York, Harper & Brothers, 1942). Another source is the series of community studies in which schools were investigated along with churches, families, local governments, and class structure. These studies, some made during the height of the popularity of progressive ideology, fail to show any significant effect on the schools themselves. The classic is Robert S. Lynd and Helen M. Lynd, *Middletown, A Study in Contemporary American Culture* (New York: Harcourt, Brace, 1929). Other studies of a somewhat similar nature are summarized and evaluated in Maurice R. Stein, *The Eclipse of Community* (Princeton: Princeton University Press, 1960).

24. The deep moral sense of the progressives must never be forgotten. A non-pragmatist, Philip H. Phenix, writes: "But pragmatists tend to swallow up values in process: they are . . . determined to banish fixed traditional codes of value and . . . absorbed with the

methods of reconstructing them" (*Education and the Common Good* [New York: Harper & Brothers, 1961], p. 12). A pragmatist, George S. Counts, writes: ". . . democracy rests on basic morality. It can thrive only if elementary standards of decency and humanity in all public relations and in the conduct of all public affairs are observed . . . men must be guided by the canons of simple honesty, truthfulness, and intellectual integrity; in the exercise of power they must be just, humane, and merciful [etc.]" (*Education and American Civilization* [New York: Columbia University, Teachers College, 1952], p. 283). Just how much more traditional would Mr. Phenix prefer that a code of values should become? What moral values does he see banished in John L. Childs, *Education and Morals* (New York: Appleton-Century-Crofts, 1950)? Mr. Phenix is undoubtedly correct when he says (*ibid.*) that for the progressives, "the transcendent ground and goal of the moral enterprise are obscured, if not explicitly denied." But this does not mean that traditional moral codes are being banished or even reconstructed in any fundamental sense; what it does mean is that the moral enterprise assumes that we know elemental right and wrong without having to be told, and without any particular "ground and goal" having to be supplied. Inquiry and intelligence, i.e., the process and methods of which the progressives made so much, are required when we have to move from elemental right and wrong to the complex rights and wrongs of a social order in radical change. It is difficult to see how this claim could be denied.

25. The case is here somewhat overstated, perhaps, but in essentials, we believe it is true. Note the word *fundamental* and its recurrence. It would be easy to document that the overwhelming proportion of literature on educational method is in no sense "fundamental." Let us consider only philosophies of education that at least pretend to some status other than that of a cookbook. Check carefully through Theodore Brameld, *Toward a Reconstructed Philosophy of Education* (New York: Dryden Press, 1956), and you will find a quite systematic (and wrongheaded) social diagnosis as well as carefully elaborated proposals for curriculum organization. But one will not find the slightest indication that Professor Brameld knows or cares what is being done in the "reconstruction" of various teaching fields or how in practice these disciplines relate to the Utopian goals he thinks should be set for our society. Possibly in reaction against this way of doing philosophy of education, examples of which are quite numerous, Philip H. Phenix, in his *Philosophy of Education* (New York: Henry Holt, 1958), treats extensively and wisely of the various fields of study to be found in the school. But professor Phenix, self-consciously outside of the pragmatic-progressive stream, does not even attempt to show how these fields of knowledge relate to the social setting in which schooling occurs. Practically any well-known book in philosophy of education will show one or the other of these obvious lacunae. For a list of other references, see Frederick C. Gruber,

Foundations for a Philosophy of Education (New York: Thomas Y. Crowell, 1961) pp. 37-38. Because of their lack of concern with educational technology, among other reasons, philosophers of education have been virtually by-passed in the extraordinary reconstruction of schools currently underway. (See chap. ii.) The influence of the progressives cannot be entirely negligible in this.

26. See B. Paul Komisar and James E. McClellan, "The Logic of Slogans," in R. S. Ennis and B. O. Smith (eds.), *Language and Concepts in Education* (Chicago: Rand McNally, 1961), pp. 195-214.

27. Washington: The Commission, 1961.

28. John Dewey, *Philosophy and Civilization* (New York: Minton Balch, 1931); *Liberalism and Social Action* (New York: G. Putnam, 1935). Both of these (despite the brevity of the latter) belong in the canon of Dewey's serious writing. They show not only what political doctrines he espouses, but also his firm belief that a philosopher is inextricably involved in politics, whether he will or no.

29. Theodore Brameld, *Philosophies of Education in Cultural Perspective* (New York: Dryden Press, 1955), especially Part II, entitled "Progressivism, Education as Cultural Transition."

30. As we mentioned earlier in connection with Dewey's conservatism and his *Common Faith* there is for him a supremacy in the shared. But nowhere is this made clearer than in his powerful, often acidly critical, essays delivered as the Larwil Lectures and published as *The Public and Its Problems* (New York: Henry Holt, 1927). After expressing his hostility toward much of industrial capitalism, he concludes by saying (p. 219), "We lie, as Emerson said, in the lap of an immense intelligence. But that intelligence is dormant and its communications are broken, inarticulate, and faint until it possesses the local community as its medium."

31. *Ibid.*, pp. 107-109.

Chapter Six

METROPOLIS IN TIME AND SPACE

1. The classic study demonstrating the correspondence between community and culture is contained in Lewis Mumford's *The Culture of Cities* (New York: Harcourt Brace, 1938). Chapter IV, "Rise and Fall of Megalopolis" and Chapter VII, "Social Basis of the New Urban Order," are particularly relevant for our purposes. Two of his more recent works are, *The Transformation of Man* (New York: Harper and Brothers, 1956) and *The City in History: Its Origins, Its Transformations, and Its Prospects* (New York: Harcourt Brace, 1961).

See also Conrad M. Arensberg, "American Communities," *Ameri-*

can Anthropologist, Vol. 57, No. 6 [1955], pp. 1143-1162. Arensberg examines a number of variant types of American communities and their associated cultural forms. He writes of metropolis (p. 1159): "Within the huge metropolitan space, the new super-city is struggling to take the form of a great wheel of internal traffic arteries and peripheral belts. This is the great decentralized city of the automotive age, and no planning can reverse its evolution, just as no plans which belie its form, from traffic roads to slum clearance, can do more than delay or impede its taking its characteristic shape."

2. The Census Bureau has established a Standard Metropolitan Statistical Area consisting of any area containing a city exceeding 50,000 persons including inhabitants of adjacent areas.

3. The sources for population statistics include, "The Census of 1960," *Scientific American,* Vol. 205 [1961], pp. 39-45, by Philip M. Hauser; *The New York Times,* August 16, 1961; and "U. S. Census of Population, 1960—Final Report," PC (1) 1B, Washington, D.C.

4. "The City as a Way of Life," and "The City Beautiful," two chapters describing city transformation between 1880-1910 in *American Skyline* (New York: Mentor Books, 1956), by Christopher Tunnard and Henry H. Reed, Jr., are very helpful for recapturing the effects of economic forces and life style during this period.

5. Max Lerner, *America as a Civilization* (New York: Simon and Schuster, 1957), says a new type of American character has developed within the frame of the city. In writing of the conditions which were responsible, he said (p. 168): "What this means is that city living has carried men and women ever further away from their instinctual endowment. The city is not the root of the planlessness, the tensions, and the conformism of American life, but it is the envelope that encloses them. Or, to change the figure, the city is the battleground of the values of the culture." His section, "City Lights and Shadows," (pp. 155-172) graphically depicts the sense and smell of the city. See also *The Exploding Metropolis* (Garden City: Doubleday, 1958), by The Editors of *Fortune.*

6. See "The Growth of a City: An Introduction to a Research Project," in *The City* (Chicago: University of Chicago Press, 1925), pp. 47-62, by Robert E. Park, Ernest W. Burgess, and Roderick D. McKenzie. Ecological studies of other cities have demonstrated that the "hub" pattern is not universally applicable in all its details, but for its day the conceptualizing of the variations in urban patterning was a great advance. An interesting variant is described by Harlan W. Gilmore in "The Old New Orleans and The New: A Case for Ecology," *American Sociological Review,* Vol. 9, No. 4 [1944], pp. 385-394.

7. See Russell Lynes, *A Surfeit of Honey* (New York: Harper and Brothers, 1957). In an original and entertaining essay on the new cultural alignments of metropolitan culture, Lynes claims (p. 15) that the social divisions of America should be viewed as a series of vertical pyramids. "Instead of broad upper, middle, and lower classes that cut

across the society of the nation like the clear, but uneven slices on a geological model, we now have a series of almost free-standing pyramids, each with its several levels and each one topped by an aristocracy of its own." For example, those engaged in business, entertainment, matters of intellect, the underworld, labor, politics, and sports are grouped in such pyramids. These are joined at the top by a class of Upper Bohemians, free spirits recruited from the separate pyramids, who communicate with each other and set the style for the whole. See also *The Tastemakers.* (New York: Harpers, 1954).

8. A comprehensive demographic analysis of metropolis is contained within *Metropolis and Region* (Baltimore: Johns Hopkins, 1960), by Otis D. Duncan, *et al.*

9. See Eshref Shevky and Marilyn Williams, *The Social Areas of Los Angeles: Analysis and Typology* (Berkeley: University of California, 1949). This is a technical study of factors of social standing, degree of urbanization and segregation (actually homogeneity) based upon the 1940 U. S. Census.

10. The analysis of suburbia has been reserved for those chapters in which we describe and dissect the nuclear family. The literature about suburban life, sociological, descriptive, and fictional, is accumulating with some rapidity. One of the best and first studies was *Crestwood Heights* (*op. cit.*). A more recent study by Robert C. Wood, *Suburbia: Its People and Their Politics* (Boston: Houghton-Mifflin, 1959), is far more sympathetic than some others. He does grant, however, that irrationalities exist. For example (p. 19): "There is no economic reason for its existence and there is no technological basis for its support. There is only the stubborn conviction of the majority of suburbanites that it ought to exist, even though it plays havoc with both the life and government of our urban age." Our rejoinder would be that sometimes people know better than theorists what is best. In fact, the salvation of the city may well lie in a radical decentralization of its services which are now controlled through huge bureaucracies. In this sense, the central city represents the anachronism.

11. Cameron Hawley, *Executive Suite* (Boston: Houghton Mifflin, 1952).

12. Nelson Algren will be best remembered for his *The Man with the Golden Arm*, but *The Neon Wilderness* portrays the brutal and hopeless lives of the urban flotsam.

13. Paddy Chayefsky, *Television Plays* (New York: Simon and Schuster, 1955). Chayefsky explains that in "Marty" and "The Mother" he had presented literal reality with a psychological orientation. Without intending it he has also described the social reality which fashions the psychic characteristics of his characters.

14. William F. Whyte, *Street Corner Society* (Chicago: University of Chicago Press, 1955). A sociological analysis of corner-boys in an Italian neighborhood in Boston.

15. Arensberg, "American Communities" (*op. cit.*), p. 1159: "The

old graduated concentric zones of the industrial city are fast disappearing. The mosaic that takes their place is a crazy-quilt of discontinuities, where the fault-line between toney garden suburb and Levittown or rich Sutton Place and squalid Dead End is abrupt, sudden, and hostile, sometimes even policed with a guard or marked by a ten-foot fence. It is no wonder that the persons who grow up in such juxtapositions see nothing of the community pattern as a whole, no longer have intimate connection with and reference toward ordered groups a little 'better' or a little 'worse' than themselves, but turn inward instead to the welter of their peer-group segregation."

16. The question may legitimately be asked whether metropolis actually represents a type of community as Conrad M. Arensberg has defined the term. He writes (p. 248): "Communities seem to be basic units of organization and transmission within a society and its culture. The definition is suggested both by their repetitive character and by their characteristics of personnel, form, and function." Subsequently he adds (p. 249): "Now what distinguishes communities from other human associations based upon territoriality and land use is precisely their repetitive character and their wholeness and inclusiveness. They are like units not so much only as collections of culture traits or social institutions repeated again and again, but first of all as population aggregates." Arensberg would say that metropolis fits the definition. See "The Community as Object and as Sample," *American Anthropologist,* Vol. 63, No. 2 [1961], pp. 241-64, by Conrad M. Arensberg.

17. This section, "Social Differentiation and Metropolitan Culture" and the introductory paragraphs at the beginning of the chapter were originally published in *Sociologia, op. cit.* Minor editorial changes have been made in the original text.

Chapter Seven

VALUING IN CONTEMPORARY AMERICA: A FAMILY CENTERED PERSPECTIVE

1. This chapter, then, and the one which follows may be read somewhat in the fashion that one looks at an optical illusion in which figure and ground can, at will, be interchanged. To the economic determinist who insists that the modern nuclear family is a product of the growth of corporate organization, one can always reply that the same evidence may be read in the other way, that the modern corporate system is the outcome of the extension of the nuclear family. Both are equally half-truths.

2. For a treatment of "values" as expressing fixed and irrevocable moral judgments, see Philip H. Phenix, *Education and the Common Good* (New York: Harper & Brothers, 1961). Professor Phenix as-

serts, for example, that "if marriages are to be permanent and productive of humane values, marriage partners need to select one another not on the basis of romantic attraction and immediate sexual satisfaction, but out of regard for the long-term potentialities in the relationship for the creation of a worth-full shared life." This is not what we mean by "values."

3. John Dewey, "Theory of Valuation," *International Encyclopedia of Unified Science* (Chicago: University of Chicago Press, 1939), Vol. II, No. 4, p. 6: "As far, then, as the terminology of the present discussion is concerned, the word 'valuation' will be used, both verbally and as a noun, as the most neutral in its theoretical implications, leaving it to further discussion to determine its connection with prizing, appraising, enjoying, etc."

4. Aristotle, *Nichomachean Ethics:* "Let us resume our inquiry and state . . . what is the highest of all goods achievable by action. Verbally there is very general agreement; for both the general run of men and people of superior refinement say that it is happiness."

5. Ruth Benedict, *The Chrysanthemum and the Sword* (Boston: Houghton Mifflin, 1946), pp. 290-296. There would seem to be no way to translate "happiness" into Japanese so that the word could stand for the highest of all goods achievable by action. It would take a major cultural change to make that idea have any meaning in Japan.

6. William I. Thomas, "The Four Wishes and the Definition of the Situation," reprinted in Talcott Parsons, Edward Shils, Kaspar D. Naegele, and Jesse R. Pitts (eds.), *Theories of Society* (Glencoe, Ill.: Free Press, 1961), II, 741-744. (Taken from *The Unadjusted Girl,* in *Contributions of W. I. Thomas to Theory and Social Research* [New York: Social Science Research Council, 1951].) It should be noted that Thomas himself did not hold a naive view of "four wishes" somehow acting like a beefed-up company of fates, pushing people this way and that. "The significant point about the wishes . . . is that they are the motor element, the starting point of activity" (p. 743). More recent theorists would rather work with a generalized concept of *drive* or *need* than with the specified wishes given by Thomas. Cf. Edward C. Tolman, "A Psychological Model," in Talcott Parsons and Edward Shils (eds.), *Toward a General Theory of Action* (Cambridge: Harvard University Press, 1952), pp. 279-360.

7. The allusion is to Ralph Linton's classic and pioneering study showing the relation between changes in technology and in customs among the Tanala of western Madagascar: *The Study of Man* (New York: D. Appleton Century, 1936), chap. xx.

8. Dewey gave the image explicit statement in *How We Think* (Boston: D. C. Heath, 1933), pp. 13-14. In William James the image is rather diffuse, as much a characteristic of the man as a parable in his writing. See his *Psychology* (New York: Henry Holt, 1890), I, 23; also his *Pragmatism* (London: Longmans Green, 1908), p. 203. If one is to apprehend the full force of the change from the model of

choosing proposed by Dewey and James, one should contrast their paradigms with those being given by contemporary economists. For example, Kenneth Boulding describes the contrast this way (*The Image* [Ann Arbor, Mich.: Ann Arbor Paperbacks, 1961], pp. 84-85): "We suppose his [economic man's] mind to be like a department store, full of images of commodities, each with a convenient price tag attached. . . . As the searchlight of his consciousness contemplates five pounds of cheese and a dozen grapefruit it must also reveal whether this conbination is better or worse than four pounds of cheese and a dozen and a half grapefruit. [With this information, together with all the other utilities and probabilities of all other possible combinations of goods,] economic man, clever fellow that he is, now maximizes the expected values of his choices, a feat of mathematical agility which it would take centuries of experience and enormous electronic calculators to perfect." It is clear that economic man is no longer even a plausible fiction; it is equally clear that Dewey and James implicitly held a vision of economic man in their picture of the pedestrian at the fork in the road. For a more detailed analysis of the consequences of the breakdown of this pragmatic model, see Herbert A. Simon, "A Behavioral Model of Rational Choice," *Quarterly Review of Economics,* LXIX (February, 1955), 99-118.

9. Stories are taken from William H. Whyte, Jr., *The Organization Man* (Garden City: Doubleday Anchor Books, 1957), chap. xxii. It is probably the human poignancy in Whyte's description of Park Forest that makes the rest of his thesis carry a conviction that it does not merit.

10. Ernest W. Burgess and Harvey J. Locke, *The Family—From Institution to Companionship* (New York: American Book, 1945). The subtitle is misleading; the thesis of the book is actually the more sensible idea that *as an institution* the family is founded today more on interpersonal and less on contractual bases than it used to be.

11. The high divorce rate of America might lead some to conclude that marriage among us is merely another temporary attachment in a life of movement. While there may be very limited subcultures, e.g., Hollywood, where this is true, it is not generally true of even the most urban marriage. See William J. Goode, *After Divorce* (Glencoe, Ill.: Free Press, 1956), p. 18: "In most cases of divorce, the two spouses do undergo a rather powerful experience. Whether it is the legal action of divorce which has the greatest emotional effect, or the prior experience of long conflict, misunderstandings, bitterness, boredom, embarrassment, or guilt, the total experience is a difficult one for most individuals. . . . It is indeed a rare case in which both parties, with no guilt or bitterness, separate and divorce in a cool fashion, with no regrets." Goode's study further supports our analysis as he shows that the more a family lives the typical metropolitan-suburban life that we describe, the less frequently divorce occurs (*op. cit.,* chap. v). There is another point on which Goode's analysis corresponds to ours; namely, that the American dating pattern, with its emphasis on inter-

personal attraction, is functionally related to the whole social system, including the family. For Goode's very suggestive hypotheses for further research, see his article "The Sociology of the Family," in R. K. Merton, Leonard Broom, and L. S. Cottrell, Jr. (eds.), *Sociology Today* (Glencoe, Ill.: Free Press, 1959), pp. 178-196.

12. John R. Seeley, R. Alexander Sim, and E. W. Loosley, *Crestwood Heights* (New York: Basic Books, 1956), p. 57.

13. Burgess and Locke, *op. cit.*, chap. ii.

14. This is a profound social change. In a brilliantly penetrating article written in 1942, Talcott Parsons said many of the things that still need to be said about the American family pattern and its relation to the world of occupations ("Age and Sex in the Social Structure of the United States," reprinted in Clyde Kluckhohn, Henry A. Murray, and David M. Schneider (eds.), *Personality in Nature, Society, and Culture* [New York: Knopf, 1956], pp. 363-375). But even Parsons did not anticipate the functional significance of adolescent love attachments, dismissing them (p. 373) as "unrealistic romanticisms." In light of his perspicacity elsewhere, it seems most plausible to conclude not that Parsons was wrong, but that a genuine change has occurred since 1942.

15. Will Herberg, *Protestant-Catholic-Jew: An Essay in American Religious Sociology* (Garden City: Anchor Books, 1960), pp. 57-64.

16. See Max Lerner, *America as a Civilization* (New York: Simon and Schuster, 1957), chap. xi and an exhaustive bibliography, pp. 991-996. Curiously, Lerner does not mention the very important essay that provides fundamental concepts for understanding the arts as elements of a culture: Meyer Schapiro, "Style," in A. L. Kroeber (ed.), *Anthropology Today* (Chicago: University of Chicago Press, 1952), pp. 287-312. See also the wise and humorous treatment of the popular arts by Reuel Denney, *The Astonished Muse* (Chicago: University of Chicago Press), 1957.

17. This was just the point, of course, that divided the world into two camps during the bitter Pasternak controversy. The Soviet side, insisting that a judgment on a work of art is ultimately a social and political judgment, is given very intelligently in the letter to Boris Pasternak from the Editorial Board of *Novi Mir*, reprinted in Edward Crankshaw's *Khrushchev's Russia* (Baltimore: Penguin Books, 1959), pp. 153-174.

18. Some interesting details and a cross-section of opinions about this phenomenon are contained in *Mass Culture: The Popular Arts in America*, ed. David Manning White and Bernard Rosenberg (Glencoe, Ill.: Free Press, 1957). The essays in Parts II and VIII are particularly relevant.

19. Sinclair Lewis, *Main Street: The Story of Carol Kennicott* (New York: Grosset and Dunlap, 1921).

20. Russell Lynes, "Upper Bohemians." *Harper's*, (February, 1953), pp. 46-52.

21. Leo Rosten ["Leonard Q. Ross"], *The Education of Hyman*

Kaplan (New York: Harcourt, Brace, 1937). The importance of continuity and cumulativeness in American symbols has been noted by many commentators; it is a central point in Henry Bramford Parkes, *The American Experiences* (New York: Knopf, 1947).

22. A typically "high morals" kind of language is found throughout Robert E. Mason, *Educational Ideals in American Society* (Boston: Allyn and Bacon, 1960).

23. A powerful expression of the private world of metropolitan culture is to be found in the brilliant collection called *Stories from the New Yorker: 1950-1960* (New York: Simon and Schuster, 1960). These stories, almost without exception, deal in a realm of human relationships entirely divorced from the public, corporate world—the world of work, production, and politics. "Divorced from" means just this: one could not imagine anything that happened in these stories as having any recognizable consequences in the public world, nor could one imagine that any problem arising in these stories could be affected significantly by anything that occurs in the public world. There is a constantly sensed exception, of course: nuclear warfare could destroy the whole setting. This is no indictment; this is how things are. The other side of the coin is less beautiful; there is an irritating vacuity in the literature of the public world since it so seldom seems to have anything to do with the way people actually live. This point is made with typically condescending tolerance by Max Lerner, *op. cit.*, pp. 356-360. Whatever evaluation one puts on the actualities of American public life, no one is likely to claim that "political philosophy" is a major art among Americans today, as it so obviously was before 1800. See Harold Laski, *The American Democracy* (New York: Viking Press, 1948), p. 396.

Chapter Eight

SCIENCE AND SELF-FULFILLMENT

1. The idea of national character and national consciousness cannot be kept out of the discussion. See Margaret Mead, "National Character," in A. L. Kroeber, (ed.), *Anthropology Today* (Chicago: University of Chicago Press, 1953).

2. Archibald MacLeish, *J.B.* (Boston: Houghton Mifflin, 1957). A play in verse.

3. The charge that Americans are materialistic in some distinctive sense is one that has been made and scotched time and time again ever since there was a person who could be called American. See Harold J. Laski, *The American Democracy* (New York: Viking Press, 1948), p. 725: "The view that America is more materialistic than other peoples is a myth that is not even edifying." The matter keeps coming up for two reasons: the troublesome imprecision of the term "material-

ist," and the extraordinary material success of Americans. The word, "materialist" may mean, just to mention the most obvious difference, either a philosophical doctrine concerning the nature of ultimate reality, or an attitude toward life and values. There need be no correlation between the two. The ancient philosophical materialists, including the Stoics and Atomists, held that the world was ultimately made of material stuff, but they utterly despised the pursuit of material goods beyond those necessary for the maintenance of life. Likewise, some men who have been most successful in gaining material goods and power have, like Cecil Rhodes, espoused the most idealistic metaphysics. Now, in a technical-philosophical sense of the term, America has never been a land of materialism; the two philosophical doctrines that can be called distinctly American—transcendentalism and pragmatism—are both varieties of idealism, i.e., the belief that mental processes are partly, if not wholly, constitutive of the ultimately Real.

If we rid ourselves of the superstition that Americans are the most gifted race of men in the field of material ingenuity, and if we recognize the obvious truth that greed has no national boundaries, then little is left of the notion that Americans are materialists in attitude. The little truth that is left is this: Americans have put a very heavy (and successful) emphasis on gaining control over the physical world in order that later on they or their progeny could be occupied with something else. And, of course, this emphasis can become a more permanent preoccupation. But Robin Williams (*American Society* [New York: Knopf, 1951], p. 409) may have overstated the case for attitudinal materialism: "Once a high standard of living has been enjoyed . . . it is extremely difficult to reduce the level of sensation. As new wants emerge and are satisfied over a period of time, they become expected, accepted, 'normal,' and in this process they, at the same time, come to be felt as rights to which one has a moral claim." Williams' point is that this tendency is universal in human beings, that Americans, merely because their standard of living has risen so high, appear inordinately concerned with material sensation. But in the ten years since Williams wrote, there is some reason to believe that simplicity in objects, refinement in sensation, dignity and elegance in taste are gaining ground—even in Detroit. Articles in *Harper's Magazine* and advertisements in the *New Yorker* are accurate, even perversely sensitive, barometers of the changing climate. See also David Potter, *People of Plenty—Economic Abundance and the American Character* (Chicago: University of Chicago Press, 1959).

4. See Vernon Louis Parrington, *Main Currents in American Thought* (New York: Harcourt, Brace, 1927–30), III (*1860-1920, The Beginnings of Critical Realism in America*), 74-75: ". . . With its Calvinistic antecedents—Scotch-Irish and Huguenot as well as New England Puritan—America had always been unfriendly to a pagan evaluation of man's duties and destiny, and the revolutionary

movement of the forties had been kept within sober ethical bounds. John Humphrey Noyes was probably the most radical American of the times, yet the Perfectionism of his earlier years, with its ascetic religiosity, bore little resemblance to the later communism of the Oneida Community. But the liberalism of the fifties was casting off all Hebraic restraints and running wild, proclaiming a new heaven about to appear on the free continent of America, and bidding the youth of the land live joyously as children of the earth. Paganism for the first time lifted up its head and surveyed the American scene—a youthful paganism, lusty and vigorous, that suggested amazing applications of the respectable doctrines of freedom and individuality, to the scandal of older fashioned folk. Too long had a God of wrath dispossessed a God of love. Life is good in the measure that it is lived fully, and to live fully is to live in the flesh as well as the spirit. . . . As the current of emotionalism gathered force, a frank *joie de vivre* submerged the old reticences; candor, frankness, a very lust of self-expression, was the new law for free men and women—a glorification of the physical that put to rout the traditional Hebraisms."

5. Silas Lapham's career shows this clearly (William Dean Howells, *The Rise of Silas Lapham* [Boston: Tichnor, 1885]). See the perceptive comments by H. S. Commager, *The American Mind* (New Haven: Yale University Press, 1950), pp. 57-60.

6. A. J. Ayer, *Language, Truth, and Logic* (New York: Dover Books, 1949), chap. i.

7. See R. Duncan Luce and Howard Raiffa, *Games and Decisions* (New York: John Wiley, 1957), chap. i.

8. There is a large literature dealing with this momentous decision, but none of it contradicts Truman's statement on the actual persons composing the two or three committees which insisted on the direct, military use of the bomb. See Harry S. Truman, *Memoirs* (Garden City: Doubleday, 1955), Vol. I, chap. xxvi. The list of persons concerned, excluding the Joint Chiefs of Staff, is given on p. 419. Cf. C. P. Snow, *The New Men* (New York: Scribner's, 1955).

9. Ludwig Wittgenstein, *Tractatus Logico-Philosophicus* (London: Routledge and Kegan Paul, 1922), #7: "Whereof one cannot speak, thereof one must be silent." The *Tractatus* is the outstanding statement of scientific positivism.

10. See M. J. Aschner, "The Language of Teaching," in B. O. Smith and R. H. Ennis (eds.), *Language and Concepts in Education* (Chicago: Rand McNally, 1961), pp. 112-126.

11. John Kenneth Galbraith, *The Affluent Society* (Boston: Houghton Mifflin, 1958).

12. On the general topic of social organization for work, see chap. ix. On the specific points in this paragraph: (1) The ideology of work as an aspect of self-fulfillment: see William H. Whyte, Jr., *The Organization Man* (Garden City: Doubleday Anchor Books, 1957), Parts II and III. (2) Relation of productivity and satisfaction on

job: the literature on this is immense and still growing. A good starting place is Mason Haire, "Industrial Social Psychology," in Gardner Lindzey (ed.) *Handbook of Social Psychology* (Cambridge: Addison-Wesley Press, 1954). (3) On the problem of exploitation of individuals by large-scale organizations (and, inevitably, vice versa): see Daniel Bell, *Work and Its Discontents* (Boston: Beacon Press, 1956), and Seymour Lipset, M. Trow, and J. S. Coleman, *Union Democracy* (Glencoe, Ill.: Free Press, 1956).

13. An entertaining collection of essays and articles describing play in America is found in Eric Larrabee and Rolf Meyersohn (eds.), *Mass Leisure* (Glencoe, Ill.: Free Press, 1958).

14. Karl Marx and Friedrich Engels, *The Communist Manifesto*, Sec. II.

15. The allusions are two recently fashionable sermons by psychologists: Gardner Murphy, *Human Potentialities* (New York: Basic Books, 1958), and Gordon Allport, *Becoming* (New Haven: Yale University Press, 1955). More powerful in its impact however, than either of these is a collection of essays toward the same theme, Clark E. Monstakas, *The Self, Explorations in Personal Growth* (New York: Harper & Brothers, 1956).

16. C. Northcote Parkinson. *Parkinson's Law and Other Studies in Administration* (Boston: Houghton Mifflin, 1957).

17. Natalie Rogoff, "Social Stratification in France and the United States," in Reinhard Bendix and Seymour Lipset (eds.), *Class, Status, and Power* (Glencoe, Ill.: Free Press, 1953).

18. C. Wright Mills, *The Power Elite* (New York: Oxford University Press, 1956); N. S. Khrushchev, *Speeches in America* (New York: Crosscurrents Press, 1960), pp. 125-140, meeting with United States trade union leaders, San Francisco, September 20, 1959. The agreement on this point, however, does not imply any overall similarity. Mills was not a Communist; he wasn't even a Marxist, for he lacked (unfortunately) the Marxist's sensitivity to social system.

19. One could multiply documentation *ad nauseam* on this point. It would be difficult however, to find a stronger statement than that made by John W. Gardner, (*Excellence* [New York: Harper & Brothers, 1961], p. 141): "If we believe what we profess concerning the worth of the individual, then the idea of self-fulfillment within a framework of moral purpose must become our deepest concern, our national preoccupation, our passion, our obsession." Gardner is quite right, self-fulfillment must become our symbol for the supreme value, not because of what we profess but because of how we live. It is fitting, perhaps, that what was once seen as a possibility has now become a necessity. Compare Gardner's statement with Laski's (*op. cit.*, p. 403): "America is different. It is opportunity, it is promise, it is experiment . . . there is no reason to put up the barriers against that ache for self-fulfillment which the Old World dare not satisfy lest, in so doing, it disturb the pattern of social relations upon which the sta-

bility of its constituent societies depend. . . . America can offer fulfillment. It has the means of renovation." Gardner is correct. It is not just that we can afford to make self-fulfillment a supreme value; the point is that the "pattern of social relations" known as American society would fall apart completely if we did not arouse in all of our citizens that "ache for self-fulfillment." But see it said officially: "Text of the Report Submitted by the President's Commission on National Goals," *New York Times,* November 28, 1960:

Introduction. "The paramount goal of the United States was set long ago. It is to guard the rights of the individual, to ensure his development and, to enlarge his opportunity. . . ."

Part I. *Goals at Home.* (1) "The Individual." "The status of the individual must remain our primary concern. All our institutions—political, social, and economic—must further enhance the dignity of the citizen, promote the maximum development of his capabilities, stimulate their responsible exercise, and widen the range and effectiveness of opportunities for individual choice.

"From this concern springs our purpose to achieve equal treatment of men and women, to enlarge their incentives and to expand their opportunities for self-development and self-expression. From it comes our insistence on widely distributed political and economic power, on the greatest range of free choice in our economy, and on the fair and democratic exercise of public and private power. It underlies the value we put on education. It guides the pursuit of science. It is the source of our interest in the health and welfare of every citizen [etc.]." Without this value, we are collectively nothing.

20. C. I. Lewis, *An Analysis of Knowledge and Valuation* (La Salle, Ill.: Open Court, 1946), p. 486: "The final and ruling assessment of value in experience must answer to the continuing rational purpose directed to the comprehensive and consummatory end of a life found good on the whole." It should be said that there is nothing passive nor accommodating about Lewis' interpretation of this statement. Yet he is unconcerned also with the social milieu of experience, a milieu which insists that each experience must be less than its ultimate, and continued growth in depth and intensity of *each* experience is a moral requirement transcending merely finding experience good on the whole.

21. See Karen Horney, *Neurosis and Human Growth—The Struggle Toward Self-Realization* (New York: Norton, 1950). Her analysis of the "ideal self" and case studies of its tyranny over possible self-growth are revelatory of exactly the point we are making. For a particularly poignant study of how the creed of self-fulfillment makes its impact on the teaching profession, see Arthur T. Jersild, *When Teachers Face Themselves* (New York: Columbia University, Teachers College, 1955).

22. See Larrabee and Meyersohn, *op. cit.,* for some instances.

Chapter Nine

THE CORPORATE SOCIETY AND EDUCATION

1. Henry Adams, *The Education of Henry Adams: An Autobiography* (Boston: Houghton Mifflin, 1946; first issued 1907), p. 456. Adams' *Autobiography* is a valuable source for some of the changes affecting America during the last half of the nineteenth and early years of the twentieth centuries. His pithy comments on the formal education he received are a salutary antidote for some of the romantic nostalgia for education in the good old days. Recently there has been a revival of interest in his writings, as evidenced by the issuance of Elizabeth Stevenson (ed.), *A Henry Adams Reader* (New York: Doubleday, 1958). "The New York Gold Conspiracy" in this collection contains some observations on the uses of corporations. W. H. Jordy, *Henry Adams: Scientific Historian* (New Haven: Yale University Press, 1952), is a recent authoritative analysis.

2. Adams, *Autobiography*, p. 500.

3. The Center for the Study of Democratic Institutions (Santa Barbara, Calif.), an offshoot of the Fund for the Republic, has sponsored a number of discussions on problems affecting the relations between corporations, government and law, public welfare, the individual, and related topics, under the general title of "The Free Society." The advice and participation of several prominent Americans have been elicited in this endeavor, and pamphlets authored by several of these have been issued. Two of these, *The Corporation and the Economy* (1959) and *The Economy Under Law* (1960), containing text by W. H. Ferry and edited notes of the participants' discussions, are particularly relevant. The published remarks reflect a common deep concern, but also widely divergent views about what should be done. See also Chester I. Barnard, *Elementary Conditions of Business Morals* (Berkeley: University of California Press), 1958.

4. See Richard Hofstadter, *The Age of Reform: from Bryan to F.D.R.* (New York: Knopf, 1955), as a recent evaluation of this era. Lawrence A. Cremin, in his *Transformation of the Schools* (New York: Knopf, 1961), shows the relation between the progressive movement and education.

5. See chap. xxi, "The Gospel of Wealth and Constitutional Law," in Ralph Henry Gabriel, *The Course of American Democratic Thought* (New York: Ronald Press, 1956). In this chapter Gabriel creates an extraordinarily insightful synthesis of the philosophical and social currents in American life which led the Supreme Court, in the 1880's and subsequently, to transform "the old due-process clause into an instrument with which it built the individualism of the gospel of wealth into a constitutional law of the nation" (p. 298). In the process, he notes, the Supreme Court developed the antithetical "doctrine of the police power of the states" (p. 298), a concept drawn from

Jacksonian democracy that the people rule, and the regulation of private property is an exercise of the people's powers in the states.

6. The Sherman Act was invoked more often (between its passage and the passage of the Clayton Act) against unions than against corporations, "and it is significant that while working men have been sent to prison under the Act, no case appears . . . in which an officer of one of the great corporations has ever been imprisoned" (Harold Laski, *The American Democracy* [New York: Viking Press, 1948], p. 209).

7. See Alexander Flick (ed.), *History of the State of New York* (New York: Columbia University Press, 1934), Vol. VI.

8. Louis M. Hacker, *The Triumph of American Capitalism* (New York: Simon & Schuster, 1940), p. 435.

9. U.S. Department of Commerce, Bureau of the Census, "The Magnitude and Distribution of Civilian Employment in the U.S.S.R. 1928-1959," Series P-95, No. 58 of International Population Reports (April, 1961), p. 57.

10. Carey McWilliams in his *Factories in the Field* (Boston: Little Brown, 1939) gave us one of the first descriptions of corporately organized big business in agriculture. A subsequent study by Walter Goldschmidt, *As You Sow* (New York: Harcourt, Brace, 1947), contrasts the effects of different types of agricultural organization upon the form of community. He found that big organization was not a necessary complement to the efficient use of technology and science, but that where corporation farming flourished, communities did not. John Steinbeck has given us two novels of the plight of migratory agricultural workers (there are two million of these in the United States): *Grapes of Wrath* (New York: Viking Press, 1939), and *In Dubious Battle* (New York: Viking Press, 1939).

11. The corporately organized grocery chains now account for 39 percent of all sales. I.G.A. affiliates do 47 percent and unaffiliated independents only 14 percent (*New York Times,* July 2, 1961).

12. See Robert and Helen Lynd, *Middletown* (New York: Harcourt, Brace, 1929), and Lloyd Warner and Josiah Low, *The Social System of the Modern Factory* (New Haven: Yale University Press, 1947). Both of these studies describe the internal social changes in community life stemming from the introduction of the factory system.

13. John Kenneth Galbraith demonstrates in the first several chapters of his *American Capitalism: The Concept of Countervailing Power* (Boston: Houghton Mifflin, 1952) that the concept of the "competitive model," based upon theories of classical economics, does not fit the power concentrated oligopoly or crypto-monopoly of modern industrial organization. He contends that insecurity about the present system arises from the ideas which interpret the world, not its reality.

14. Warner discovered over eight hundred voluntary associations in Newburyport, Mass. a town of 15,000 persons. For a detailed de-

scription of the types and activities of these groups, see Lloyd Warner and Paul Lunt, *The Social Life of a Modern Community* (New Haven: Yale University Press, 1941), chap xvi.

15. See William Lloyd Warner, *American Life: Dream and Reality* (Chicago: University of Chicago Press, 1953), chap. ix.

16. The common interests which bring suburbanites into associations are focalized around school and children, locality, and church. These activities are almost entirely female dominated. Male participation occurs spasmodically and grudgingly. See John R. Seeley, R. Alexander Sim, and E. W. Loosely, *Crestwood Heights* (New York: Basic Books, 1956), and the account of Park Forest in William H. Whyte, Jr., *The Organization Man* (New York: Simon & Schuster, 1956). In contrast, Elisabeth Day's study of an established German and Irish neighborhood in New York City's West Side, containing 39,000 persons in 1956, of which about one-third were recent Puerto Rican immigrants, contained ninety-five organized groups. Of these, *only nineteen* could be counted as voluntary associations. The remainder were public or private agencies, including schools, churches, welfare agencies, and the like. Voluntary associations were absent among the Puerto Ricans. (*Methods of Community Organization in Urban Renewal* [unpublished doctoral thesis, Columbia University, Teachers College, 1958].)

17. A new national association for the overweights is called TOPS (Take Off Pounds Sensibly) and has enrolled 14,000 members with great future expectations for growth.

18. William McDonald (ed.), *Documentary Source Book of American History, 1606-1926* (New York: Macmillan, 1928), p. 20. Quoted by Earl Latham in Edward S. Mason (ed.), *The Corporation in Modern Society* (Cambridge: Harvard University Press, 1959), p. 320.

19. The concept of "countervailing power" developed by Galbraith in his *American Capitalism* is advanced as a regulatory mechanism to restrain economic power where competition has disappeared. The restraint becomes vested in strong buyers. He believes that "the provision of state assistance to the development of countervailing power has become a major function of government—perhaps *the* major domestic function of government" (p. 133). The legislative assistance given to labor unions in their struggle to establish bargaining power with the corporations is cited as one example of the indirect control exerted by government upon corporate power. One significant consequence arising from the growth of countervailing power has been the strengthening of "the capacity of the economy for autonomous self-regulation" which lessens "the amount of overall governmental control or planning that is required or sought" (p. 155).

20. One does not have to search far for authoritative conclusions to support the view. For example, Abram Chayes ("The Modern Corporation and the Rule of Law," in Mason (ed.), *op. cit.*) has declared that the great corporation is the dominant nongovernmental

institution of modern American life: "The university, the labor union, the church, the charitable foundation, the professional association—other potential institutional centers—are all in comparison both peripheral and derivative." He quotes William T. Gossett, vice president and general counsel of the Ford Motor Company, as saying, "During the past 50 years, industry in corporate form has moved from the periphery to the very center of our social and economic system. Indeed, it is not inaccurate to say that we live in a corporate society" (p. 27). Peter F. Drucker, in *Concept of the Corporation* (New York: John Day, 1946), calls the large business unit "the very center of modern industrial society," and the corporations "our representative social institutions" (p. 5). A. A. Berle, Jr., in *The 20th Century Capitalist Revolution* (New York: Harcourt, Brace, 1954), feels the need to justify his treatment of the corporation, "not as a business device, but as a social institution in the context of a revolutionary century" (p. 24). Future historians of social thought may marvel at this insistence on the right to consider the corporation as a social institution, but the fact is that in 1950 this orientation was novel.

21. The concentration of wealth and productive power in the hands of a few industrial giants has been the subject of a number of studies. Those frequently cited include reports of the Temporary National Economic Committee (TNEC), especially Clair Wilcox, *Competition and Monopoly in American Industry* (Washington, D.C.: TNEC, 1940), Monograph No. 21; Robert A. Brady, *Business as a System of Power* (New York: Columbia University Press, 1943); M. A. Adelman, "The Measurement of Industrial Concentration," *Review of Economics and Statistics*, Vol. xxxii, No. 4 (November, 1951); A. A. Berle and Gardner C. Means, *The Modern Corporation and Private Property* (New York: Macmillan, 1932); National Resources Planning Board, *The Structure of the American Economy* (Washington, D.C.: Government Printing Office, 1939), Part I; Federal Trade Commission, *The Concentration of Productive Facilities*, 1947 (Washington, D.C.: Government Printing Office, 1949). See also other writings by Berle and Galbraith. The *Wall Street Journal* regularly reports the continuing concentration of economic control.

22. John Marquand, *Sincerely, Willis Wayde* (Boston: Little Brown, 1955).

23. Booth Tarkington, *The Magnificent Ambersons* (New York: Grossett and Dunlap, 1918).

24. See Norton Long, "The Corporation, Its Satellites, and the Local Community," in Mason (ed.), *op. cit.*, pp. 202-217. He writes (pp. 214-215): "While their economic position has made the managers seem to be the appropriate and duty-bound incumbents of top-level civic statuses, their lack of family legitimacy and enduring local residence identification in the community makes them more the representatives of a foreign power than the rightful chiefs of the local tribe." Long's lively treatment of his subject leaves little doubt of the

deleterious effects of corporations upon the local community.

25. Cameron Hawley, *Executive Suite* (Boston: Houghton Mifflin, 1952).

26. Long, *op. cit.*, pp. 209, 211.

27. Chester I. Barnard, *The Functions of the Executive* (Cambridge: Harvard University Press, 1938). This study is a classic in its field and has had wide influence. Barnard's insistence that ultimate authority rests with the one who executes an order and not the superordinate is a novel idea, and recalls Jeremy Bentham's dictum that coercion can never win allegiance.

28. See Galbraith, *op. cit.*, pp. 121-123, 142.

29. F. W. Taylor, *Principles of Scientific Management* (New York: Harper & Brothers, 1911).

30. Two significant findings which are of particular relevance to us should be mentioned. In the Philadelphia textile mills study the extension to the employees of even a modicum of control over their working situation, and a reduction in the volume of supervisory direction, increased output, but also led to marked beneficial changes in their personal lives (Elton Mayo, *The Social Problems of an Industrial Civilization* [Cambridge: Harvard University Press, 1945], chap. iii). In the Western Electric Study, the results obtained from the Relay Assembly Test Room demonstrated the powerful effect of an experimental setting when combined with an approach which dignifies an activity (F. J. Roethlisberger and William J. Dickson, *Management and the Worker* [Cambridge: Harvard University Press, 1940]. See also Elton Mayo, *The Human Problems of an Industrial Civilization* [New York: Macmillan, 1933], and F. J. Roethlisberger, *Management and Morale* [Cambridge: Harvard University Press, 1941].) For reasons which are only partly understandable, the Mayo "approach" has been bitterly attacked. The major complaint seems to be that an elite management will apply the results to freeze workers in a happy and docile state. There is no evidence as yet that such is the case. For an example of the anti-Mayo position see Clark Kerr and Lloyd Fisher, "Plant Sociology: The Elite and the Aborigines," in Mirra Komarovsky, (ed.), *Common Frontiers of the Social Sciences* (Glencoe, Ill.: Free Press, 1957), pp. 281-309. Conrad M. Arensberg and Geoffrey Tootell present an able counterview in the same volume, entitled "Plant Sociology: Real Discoveries and New Problems" (pp. 310-337).

31. Chris Argyris, *Personality and Organization* (New York: Harper & Brothers, 1957). Argyris summarizes a massive body of evidence to demonstrate the debilitating effects of industrial organization upon the worker. It is his contention that the needs of organizations and those of individuals are incompatible.

32. *Ibid.*

33. See Solon T. Kimball and Marion Pearsall, *The Talladega Story: A Study in Community Process* (University, Ala.: University

of Alabama Press, 1954), chaps. vi, vii. This is a description of the isolation of workers within the community, their cultural characteristics, and the implicit conflict between them and industrial managers.

34. Ellwood P. Cubberly, *Public School Administration* (Boston: Houghton Mifflin, 1916), p. 338: "Our schools are, in a sense, factories in which the raw products (children) are to be shaped and fashioned into products to meet the various demands of life. The specifications for manufacturing come from the demands of twentieth-century civilization, and it is the business of the school to build its pupils according to specifications laid down. This demands good tools, specialized machinery, continuous measurement of production to see if it is according to specifications, the elimination of waste in manufacture, and a large variety in the output."

35. *Ibid.*, p. 435: "In a rapidly increasing number of our cities the best principles of corporation control have been worked out and are being put into practice in the educational organization. In such the board of education for the city acts much as the board of directors for a business corporation, listening to reports as to the progress of the business, approving proposals as to extensions or changes in the nature of the business, deciding lines of policy to be followed, approving the budget for annual maintenance, and serving as a means of communication between the stockholders and the executive officers."

36. Mark Atwood, *An Anthropological Approach to Administrative Change: The Introduction of a Guidance Program in a High School* (unpublished doctoral dissertation, Columbia University, 1960). This study describes the adversely disturbing effects among staff resulting from the introduction of a guidance program in a New York City high school. See also Howard S. Becker, "The Teacher in the Authority System of the Public School," *Journal of Educational Psychology* xxvii (1953), 128-141.

37. The theory of educational administration as taught in teachers colleges has been a major contribution to the "chain of command" plan of organization. V. T. Thayer, in an analysis published in 1933 ("The School: Its Task and Its Administration—III," in William H. Kilpatrick [ed.], *The Educational Frontier* [New York: Appleton-Century], chap. vii), demonstrates the direct influence of business organization by quoting from the authors of standard texts on school administration. He quotes (p. 220) from a study by George Counts of a superintendent in Chicago who upon assuming office announced that the schools "must adopt the motto of other big business: 'organize, deputize, supervise.' " The effect was to sanction centralized control in the superintendent's office and downward delegation of authority "until it reaches the individual child in his relation with the teacher." Thayer condemned this system, showed its ill effects, and proposed an alternative approach. See also note 11 in chap. v of this book.

Thorstein Veblen, in *The Higher Learning in America* (New York: Huebsch, 1918), asserted that American universities are directly or indirectly dominated by business. For him, college presidents were blurred carbon copies of captains of industry. It must be admitted that universities, like other institutions, sometimes suffer from authoritarian leadership; however, the organizational pattern of a university is considerably different from industry because of its great emphasis upon the educative process. Simon Marcson's distinction between *executive authority* and *colleague authority* is particularly helpful in distinguishing the organizational emphasis. The latter is characteristic of a university, but Marcson also found that professional employees in an industrial research laboratory sought to work as colleagues and, as a consequence, found themselves in conflict with the *executive authority* system. His analysis (*The Scientist in American Industry* [Princeton, N.J.: Princeton University, Industrial Relations Section, 1960]) is directly relevant to school organization.

Chapter Ten

THE NATURE OF COMMITMENT: A COMPARATIVE APPROACH

1. The reader will probably note that in comparison with other chapters, this one contains relatively few references to the standard literature. There is a reason for this which deserves a word of explanation. In our initial discussions which eventually led to the decision to join together to write a book about American education, we posed a number of questions, one of which was the meaning of "commitment." We concluded that until we had some agreement and some understanding of what we meant when we used this term that we would not be able to proceed in any profitable or orderly fashion in our endeavor. We also believed that unless we were able to find some rationale that would enable us to identify the major commitment or commitments of American society, it would be impossible to evaluate the past performance or project the future requirements of education and the educative process for our type of society. Our first step was to seek enlightenment from the existing literature. This effort proved relatively fruitless. Undoubtedly, someone, somewhere has concerned himself with the nature of commitment. We have been unable to find any such reference, and such references as we did uncover treat commitment in such a superficial manner that they could not serve our purposes. We decided that before we could proceed further, we would be forced to develop a theory of commitment within which we could organize our substantive material. Accordingly, working independently and with a minimum of consultation, we set to the task. It should be remembered that each of us, from necessity, utilized those assumptions, method of logic, reasoning, and concrete data that were distinctive to our respective disciplines of anthropology or philosophy.

Because of this, our first analyses were widely different except in one crucial respect: both of us were forced to conclude that the concept "commitment" belongs in the category of objective, public phenomena such as "citizenship" rather than in the category of personal, internal states of individuals such as we mean by terms like "pain" or "joy." For us, this was a discovery of great import since it denied the currently accepted doctrine which explains commitment as a purely personal matter and, in addition, challenges the assumptions and validity upon which a great deal of teaching is based. Further exploration has strengthened our belief in the correctness of our original position.

To correct a misinterpretation that might arise from a casual reading of the introduction to this chapter, we are *not* advocating corporatism over individualism, whatever that might mean. On the contrary, as we have explained at various points, our analysis is directed toward an education that will heighten individuality within this corporate age. What we *are* trying to overcome in this chapter is the verbal and conceptual confusion that arises when one tries to describe commitment as if it were a property possessed by individuals.

An acknowledgment and a further word of explanation seem necessary. Most of the material describing Irish familism and Navaho tribalism was gathered by direct field research by one of the authors. The original analysis utilizing these materials was first presented at the 1957-58 Faculty Seminar of the Institute for Religious and Social Studies at the Jewish Theological Seminary in New York City. Subsequently, the paper was read and commented upon by Dr. C. M. Arensberg, a colleague in the Irish research.

2. For a description of Irish familism, see Conrad M. Arensberg and Solon T. Kimball, *Family and Community in Ireland* (Cambridge: Harvard University Press, 1940).

3. Many anthropologists and popular writers have cultivated the Navaho field and a complete bibliography would run to several hundred titles. For a description of tribal life from which much of this section was taken, see Solon T. Kimball and John H. Provinse, "Navajo Social Organization in Land Use Planning," *Applied Anthropology,* I (1942), 18-25. The best-rounded account of Navaho life is found in Clyde Kluckhohn and Dorothea Leighton, *The Navaho* (Cambridge: Harvard University Press, 1946). A recent excellent monograph is Tom T. Sasaki, *Fruitland, New Mexico: A Navaho Community in Transition* (Ithaca, Cornell University Press, 1960).

4. A good discussion of initiation ceremonies may be found in the recently published translation of Arnold van Gennep's classic, *The Rites of Passage* (Chicago, Chicago University Press, 1960).

5. Ruth Benedict, *Patterns of Culture* (New York: New American Library, 1948), pp. 63-64.

6. Katherine Spencer, *Mythology and Values: An Analysis of Navaho Chantway Myths* (Philadelphia: American Folklore Society,

1957). This monograph did not become known to the authors until after the original analysis and conclusions about the nature of commitment among the Navaho had been written. Naturally, we were pleased and excited to discover the startling correspondences between the realities of social behavior and the symbolic representation of these in supernatural mythology as analyzed by Miss Spencer. The material presented here represents a severe condensation of her elaborate analysis.

Chapter Eleven

THE SYMBOLS OF COMMITMENT AND INSTITUTIONAL LIFE

1. John L. Childs, *Education and Morals* (New York: Appleton-Century-Crofts, 1950), p. 7.

2. Compare this to the discussion in chap. viii on the prescribed rituals that center around science, particularly medical science. In those cases there is complete congruence between the acts and the subjective beliefs. In the case of Christmas shopping the connections are attenuated at best. It is not right to say that the ritual is meaningless; it is correct to say that its social meaning may have no relation to the thought and feelings of those who do it.

3. Scientific studies of the pre–World War II United States military establishment are simply unavailable. There have been many studies since, particularly the massive "Studies in Social Psychology in World War II." See especially Samuel A. Stouffer *et al.*, *The American Soldier, Adjustment During Army Life* (Princeton: Princeton University Press, 1949), chap. ii, "The Old Army and the New."

In thinking of the days before World War II, one must remember that the United States had the vast international commitment of a major world power, yet even as late as 1940 had a Regular Army of only 165,000 men. See Robin N. Williams, Jr., *American Society* (New York: Knopf, 1951), pp. 235-237. See also Morris Janowitz, *Sociology and the Military Establishment* (New York: Russell Sage Foundation, 1958), pp. 15-24, 28-36.

4. See Jesse Stuart, *The Thread That Runs So True* (New York: Scribner's, 1949).

5. See Jerome Maurice Page, *A Survey and Analysis of Teacher Recruitment Policies and Practices, Including an Analysis of Teacher Supply and Demand* (unpublished Ed.D. project, Columbia University, Teachers College, 1958), Part II. Page's study makes it clear that high mobility *within* the profession is a continuing feature of educational life and that recruitment practices, pension and welfare schemes, etc., should be adjusted to this fact.

6. Different aspects of the work of the Citizenship Education Pro-

ject are reported in many documents, including among others: *Resources for Citizenship; Laboratory Practices in Citizenship Education for College Students;* and *Building Better Programs in Citizenship.* The last, written by William S. Vincent, Hall Bartlett, Lora Tibbetts, and James Russell, is the most instructive on the nature and purpose of the project, and chap. xvii is a very informative historical review of citizenship education in American schools. These are publications of the project, and are available from Teachers College, Columbia University.

7. See Vincent *et al., op. cit.,* p. 13.

8. This is an overstatement, of course. It assumes that the corporate structure on one hand (chap. ix) and the nuclear family on the other (chap. vii) are the only structurally significant institutional forms. This is coming more and more to be the case, but there are vestigial organizations, such as the fraternal lodge and its female auxiliary, in which age and sex are the predominant bases for interpersonal relations. But in the corporate world, including the voluntary associations and the small group production teams by which work gets done, age and sex have little structural significance.

Chapter Twelve

THE ELEMENTS OF COMMITMENT AND SENSE OF SELF

1. It would be very difficult to overestimate the importance of this fact: our political symbols have taken on a radically different cast as they have lost their involvement with the unique history of America. In the days of the Revolution, America stood for universal rights of man; her fortunate location across the Atlantic merely allowed her to realize what was actually inherent in the universal, liberalizing traditions of the Enlightenment. This is the meaning the "shot heard 'round the world." But by the time of the Gettysburg Address, there were two reasons for Americans to believe in Tom Paine's view of the uniqueness of the American experience more than in Thomas Jefferson's (earlier) views that America represented the first instance of what would or could become the lot of all mankind: the general success of reaction in Europe and the devotion to America engendered by the war itself. Then followed the dizzy days of European colonialism and the gradual dominance in America of a Manifest Destiny to export not merely American ideals but the American experience itself, particularly the experience of absorbing enormous numbers of immigrants into the main body of American Life. The highpoint of this wave was Wilson's tragic mission to Europe in 1918-19.

Two sobering facts have since emerged: (1) our political ideals have no concrete meaning apart from the rich complexity of American life itself, and (2) this complexity has its origin in a historical experience that cannot be exported. What can be exported is the set of symbols, the language of politics as it were, which has served us well in solving some of our political problems. Because these symbols have been abstracted from widely divergent histories, their meaning is often not altogether understood alike by all who use them. But even so, if it had not been for Wilson's success in forcing Europe to talk in the typical American language of "self-determination," "democracy," "freedom for all men," and the like, the United Nations would never have been possible. (It is conceivable that it would not have been necessary, for undoubtedly those political symbols were more than minimal factors in loosing the revolutionary forces that brought on World War II.) On the general topic of American political thought and language, see R. H. Gabriel, *The Course of American Democratic Thought,* rev. ed. (New York: Ronald, 1956). On the immigrants' relation to the symbols, see Oscar Handlin, *The Uprooted* (Boston: Little Brown, 1953).

As we now see irony everywhere in history, we may see it here also. The same political symbols that no longer have direct, organic connection with the American scene, that are for us abstract rather than historically mediating, may come alive again in those nations that are now in the early stages of transition from agrarianism to industrialism. But as they come alive in Africa or Asia or South America, they will belong then to the Africans, etc. We have proprietary rights on our history, but not on any particular way of describing it. See Russell Davenport *et al., The Permanent Revolution* (New York: Prentice-Hall, 1951).

2. C. Wright Mills, *The Power Elite* (New York: Oxford University Press, 1956); Floyd Hunter, *Community Power Structure* (Chapel Hill: University of North Carolina Press, 1953); Karl Popper, *The Open Society and Its Enemies* (London: Routledge and Kegan Paul, 1952); Charles Frankel, *The Case for Modern Man* (New York: Harper & Brothers, 1955), and on and on. The diagnosis differs in each case, but the symptom of irresponsibility (or, less loaded, "unresponsiveness") of power is agreed on by practically all who study it.

3. There may be a clue here for criticizing and refining the well-known thesis of Gunnar Myrdal concerning the levels of American values and the depth of "the American Creed" (*An American Dilemma* [New York: Harper & Brothers, 1944], Appendix i, pp. 1027-1035). On the connection between the *political* symbols and the emerging creed of self-fulfillment that grew out of them, see James Truslow Adams, *The Epic of America* (New York: Blue Ribbon Books, 1931) especially the concluding chapter.

4. David Riesman *et al., The Lonely Crowd* (Garden City: Doubleday Anchor Books, 1954), pp. 200-202. Cf. Riesman, "Private People and Public Policy," reprinted in *Best Articles and Stories* (April, 1959), pp. 46-56.

5. The strongest case against modernism, of course, is not merely

that it creates an age of anxiety, but that it fails to produce the stable character and personality that can live with anxiety. Erich Fromm has made this the main thesis of all his works since 1937. When he comes to talk of a new communal life as an answer to this deficiency, he talks nonsense. Compare the telling social criticism in chaps. 1-5 of *The Sane Society* (New York: Rinehart, 1955) with the weak romanticism of chap. 8.

6. This must exclude, in the final analysis, the Christian existentialists, for their conception of selfhood must always include one relation—to God. But for some of the other existentialists see Rollo May *et al., Existence, A New Dimension in Psychiatry and Psychology* (New York: Basic Books, 1958). For the bravado in William H. Whyte, Jr., *The Organization Man* (New York: Doubleday, 1957), see chap. xxv.

7. Henry Adams, *Mont-St. Michel and Chartres* (Boston: Houghton Mifflin, 1922).

8. See Chapter IX above.

9. J. Frederic Dewhurst and associates, *America's Needs and Resources* (New York: Twentieth Century Fund, 1955), chap. xx. The production of that magnificent volume itself represents precisely the sense of the team within corporate structure that we have been describing.

10. The team enterprise shown in the remarkable television program produced by Edward R. Murrow on the first launching of the Atlas missile reminded one very much of the old silent films showing Lindbergh's precarious takeoff from Mitchell Field.

11. Excellent bibliography in Max Lerner, *America as a Civilization* (New York: Simon & Schuster, 1957), for chap. iv, "The Culture of Science and the Machine."

12. See George C. Homans, *The Human Group* (New York: Harcourt, Brace, 1950); also Wilbert Moore, *Industrial Relations and the Social Order* (New York: Macmillan, 1951).

13. Lewis E. Atherton, *Main Street on the Middle Border* (Bloomington, Ind.: Indiana University Press, 1954).

14. G. H. Mead, Charles Morris (ed.), *Mind, Self, and Society* (Chicago: University of Chicago Press, 1934), p. 152.

15. Cf. Harry Stack Sullivan's discussion of how the pre-adolescent of this age chooses a chum (*The Interpersonal Theory of Psychiatry* [New York: W. W. Norton, 1953], chap. xvi). Sullivan virtually ignores the effect of social stratification as a factor, but he makes it quite clear that *choosing* is occurring where hitherto there had been random acceptance or rejection of playmates. Sociometric studies make it plain that social distinctions do play a significant role in the dynamics of choice. Compare Bernice L. Neugarten, "Social Class and Friendship Among School Children," *American Journal of Sociology,* LI (1942), 305-313.

16. This is as convenient a point as any to make reference to James

S. Coleman's factually irrelevant and conceptually inadequate study of adolescent life (*The Adolescent Society: The Social Life of the Teenager and Its Impact on Education* [Glencoe, Ill.: Free Press, 1961]). Its irrelevance comes from treating the status system among adolescents (yes, there actually *is* a recognizable status system in each of the ten schools studied by Coleman!) quite out of relation either to the life history of the youngsters themselves or to the surrounding systems of family, class, corporation, and community. To say that this study is conceptually inadequate is to judge the main proposals, namely that the fundamentally hostile and aggressive status drives among adolescents (perfectly understandable phenomena when seen either developmentally or systematically) be manipulated—"channeled" is Coleman's word—by administrators and teachers so as to increase attention to academic studies. If one can overcome his initial rejection, there is a great deal of information here that with a different conceptual treatment could be quite interesting, particularly the sometimes rather subtle differences between the symbols and objects around which the main status systems develop in different schools, ranging from the farm community to the upper income metropolitan suburb; also manner and degree of integration between the girls' hierarchies and the boys' has latent significance, but Coleman has not showed it. As an unrelated afterthought he remarks that "a boy or girl has no experience, either in his daily life or school classes, with the impersonal world of large institutions" (p. 328). He proposes to remedy this basic gap in their education by having them play Monopoly on computers, status points going to the otherwise socially deprived academic grinds. Extraordinary!

Chapter Thirteen

EDUCATION FOR COMMITMENT

1. "That human nature and society can have conflicting demands, and hence that a whole society can be sick, is an assumption which was made very explicitly by Freud. . . . He starts out with the premise of a human nature common to the human race, throughout all cultures and ages, and of certain ascertainable needs and strivings inherent in that nature." Thus writes Erich Fromm in *The Sane Society* (New York: Rinehart & Co., 1955), p. 19. Though Fromm makes essentially the same assumption, he has a slightly different conception of what human nature is. The pragmatic conception is set forth in John Dewey's *Human Nature and Conduct* (New York: Henry Holt & Co., 1922). An interesting but now anachronistic statement of the behaviorist position on human nature is given in E. L. Thorndike's *Human Nature and the Social Order* (New York: Macmillan, 1940). Perhaps

we have too quickly forgotten the gist of Thorndike's thesis (p. 957): "Man has the possibility of almost complete control of his fate, and if he fails, it will be by the ignorance or folly of men."

2. The interpersonal relations approach tends to blend with the human nature approach; for in much of modern thought *human* nature, as opposed to man's biological nature, is a product of social experience. But then to hold with a doctrine of universality in human nature, one would have to show or see universals in social experience. Some do just this. (See Gardner Murphy, *Human Potentialities,* New York: Basic Books, 1958.) Others who begin with interpersonal relations move away altogether from any dependence on a theory of human nature. Some outstanding work has resulted from this approach; e.g., Kurt Lewin, *Field Theory in Social Science* (New York: Harper and Brothers, 1951); also Harry Stack Sullivan, *The Interpersonal Theory of Psychiatry* (New York, W. W. Norton & Co. 1953), especially Part I and Chapter 22. The most thoroughly consistent statement of this view as it relates to education and morals is put forth by R. Bruce Raup, especially in his essay, "The Community Criterion in Judgmental Practice." *Studies in Philosophy and Education,* September, 1960.

3. Daniel Bell, *The End of Ideology* (Glencoe: The Free Press, 1960). Especially relevant is his essay on the plight of ideology in the USSR, "Ten Theories in Search of Reality," pp. 300-334.

4. This point has appeared frequently in the many books dealing with "Madison Avenue." But it is made especially clear in a curiously neglected volume called *The Pacifiers,* by Mack Hanan (Boston: Little, Brown and Co., 1960), especially its Conclusion, p. 285 *et seq.*

5. Paul Tillich, *Systematic Theology* (Chicago: University of Chicago Press, 1951), Vol. I, pp. 18-28, 163-168. "Man occupies a preeminent position in ontology not as an outstanding object among other objects, but as that being who asks the ontological question and in whose self-awareness the ontological answer can be found." This is Tillich, but it could as easily be St. Thomas Aquinas or Immanuel Kant.

6. We do not argue that a social system, by virtue of its primordial influence on the mind and personality, is the ultimate reality in human experience, i.e., that reality which cannot be transcended by human concepts. That argument *can* be made very effectively. See David Bidney, *Theoretical Anthropology* (New York: Columbia University Press, 1953); and Theodore Brameld, *Cultural Foundations of Education* (New York: Harper's, 1957), especially Part II. But it is unnecessary, from our point of view, to argue that social system is primary in a metaphysical sense. It *is* primary in a political-psychological sense. The fundamental problem of men today, especially intellectuals, is that of learning to accept, not the perfection or even goodness of our social system, but its simple existence.

7. Politics, 1254a, 1255b.

8. There are many amusing tales of the pre-Civil War militia and its "Annual Muster," but probably none surpasses that of Lincoln's service in the Illinois militia during the Black Hawk War. See Ida Tarbell, *The Life of Abraham Lincoln,* (New York: The Macmillan Co., 1924) Chapter VI.

9. Just as Plato could not describe the good society and *then* say what kind of education it required. To raise the question of the nature of justice forced him almost immediately into a discussion of education for the good life.

10. See Percival M. Symonds, *The Dynamics of Parent-Child Relationships* (New York: Columbia University Press, 1949).

11. Erik Erikson, *Childhood and Society* (New York: W. W. Norton and Co., 1950), pp. 106-107.

12. This is a favorite thesis of novelists and sociologists alike; compare Richard Yates, *Revolutionary Road,* (Boston: Little, Brown & Co., 1961), with John R. Seeley, R. Alexander Sim, E. W. Loosley, *Crestwood Heights,* (New York: Basic Books, Inc, 1956), p. 57.

13. The dominant theme is usually this: different social classes have different ways of dealing with the various tasks—weaning, toilet training, etc.—involved in child rearing. These differences have consequences in personality that relate, again, to the differences in social class. There is obvious sense in this, but as we view the current scene, social class is coming to be less significant as a mode of social stratification than it was earlier. The more significant mode will likely be position in the corporate system, a mode that, unlike social class, does not need a stable geographical base. See Allison Davis, *Social Class Influences Upon Learning,* (Cambridge: Harvard University Press, 1948). For cross-cultural comparisons, see J. W. M. Whiting and I. L. Child, *Child Training and Personality* (New Haven: Yale University Press, 1953). In most cultures, including the class structure analyzed by Davis, child-rearing in its most crucial early months and years could be regarded as setting the basis for the particular personality type required for a certain range of positions in a stable social system. *All* of that assumption is now doubtful if not patently false.

14. Somewhat dated, but very human is Dorothy Baruch, *Parents and Children Go to School,* (Chicago: Scott, Foresman & Co., 1939).

15. Harry Stack Sullivan, *The Interpersonal Theory of Psychiatry,* (New York: W. W. Norton Co., 1953).

16. See Chapter XI.

17. Jean Piaget, *The Moral Judgment of the Child,* (London: Kegan Paul, 1932). But see also, Barbel Inhelder and Jean Piaget, *The Growth of Logical Thinking from Childhood to Adolescence,* (New York: Basic Books, 1958). The latter *seems* to show that by age seven or eight, the simpler operations of the propositional calculus are already part of the thinking process in children, provided, of course, that the content of the propositions is sufficiently concrete and meaningful to the children. The whole question of *possibility* in childhood,

as opposed to usual *performance* of children, is one for which we have yet to formulate a feasible experimental design.

18. William K. Medlin, *et al., Soviet Education Programs,* (Washington: U.S. Department of Health, Education, and Welfare, 1960).

19. Ernest Nagel, *The Structure of Science,* (New York: Harcourt, Brace and World, Inc., 1961), Chapter V, "Experimental Laws and Theories."

20. Paul Ziff: "Reasons in Art Criticism" in I. Scheffler, (ed.) *Philosophy and Education,* (Boston: Allyn & Bacon, 1957), p. 230. In the analysis of the discipline of esthetic form we are indebted to a series of discussions on the topic with Prof. Arno Bellack of Teachers College, Columbia.

21. Cf. A. Irving Hallowell: "Aggression in Saulteaux Society" in Clyde Kluckhohn, Henry A. Murray, and D.N. Schneider, (editors) *Personality in Nature, Society, and Culture* (New York: Alfred A. Knopf, 2nd Edition 1956), pp. 246-260.

22. We are well aware that it takes neither special courage nor exceptional insight to stand up in favor of intellectual discipline at a time when aggressive militarism depends on academic prowess. We honor those who urged the same principles when there were better reasons and fewer causes for doing so. See Harry S. Broudy, *Building a Philosophy of Education,* (New York: Prentice-Hall Inc., 1954). Chapters 6, 7, 8, and 9 as well as references therein. Also Philip H. Phenix, "Key Concepts and the Crisis in Learning," *Teachers College Record.* 58: 137-143 [December 1956]. The theses (1) that there is a discipline (or set of disciplines) of thought and action right within the life of the culture, (2) that the young can learn these in such a way that they are not merely controlled by external forces but by personally-accepted knowledge, and (3) that such knowledge frees the individual from the pain of feeling robbed when paying the psychic costs attendant on living in our civilization—these theses curiously are presaged throughout the very fine work by K. B. Berkson, *The Ideal and the Community,* (New York: Harper and Brothers, 1958).

Very careful and detailed analyses are needed before the nature of intellectual discipline itself can be determined. Bruner and his associates have tried two ends of the chain, as it were: the phenomenon of concept formation at its most primitive on one hand and the phenomenon of scientific *behavior* on the other. See Jerome S. Bruner, Jacqueline Goodnow, and George A. Austin, *A Study of Teaching* (New York: John Wiley & Sons, 1956) and Jerome S. Bruner, *The Process of Education* (Cambridge: Harvard University Press, 1960). A vigorous and quite readable defense of what we may call the unitarian view of intellectual discipline is found in H. Gordon Hullfish and Philip G. Smith, *Reflective Thinking: The Method of Education* (New York: Dodd, Mead & Company, 1961). Hullfish and Smith are seeking a single method or process of thinking that encompasses the disciplines we have described. For a treatment of the more specific discipline we have called natural history, see Solon T. Kimball, "Darwin and the Future of Education," *The Educational Forum,* November 1960, pp. 59-72.

Chapter Fourteen

MORAL COMMITMENT AND THE INDIVIDUAL

1. For a very clear-headed critique of this talk about mass nonconformity, etc., see Daniel Bell, *The End of Ideology* (Glencoe: The Free Press, 1960), chap. 1.

2. The phrase, "oceanic feeling," was used by Sigmund Freud to mean, "a feeling of indissoluble connection, of belonging inseparably to the external world as a whole." Needless to add, Freud could find no evidence for such a feeling in himself. *Civilization and Its Discontents* (London: The Hogarth Press, 1930), p. 9 *et seq.*

3. The problem of reconciling a Marxian theory of social system with the allocation of personal responsibility for concrete actions has not been an easy one for Soviet social philosophy. See Herbert Marcuse, *Soviet Marxism: A Critical Analysis* (New York: Columbia University Press, 1958), chap. 10, "Soviet Ethics—The Externalization of Values."

4. For a fuller treatment of the distinction between reasons and motives and the place of this distinction in various theories of human nature, see R. S. Peters, *The Concept of Motivation* (London: Routledge and Kegan Paul, 1958).

5. Friedrich Nietzsche, *Beyond Good and Evil,* translated by Marianne Cowan, (Chicago: Henry Regnery Co., 1955), p. 114. "We have no other choice; we must seek new philosophers, spirits strong or original enough to give an impulse to opposing valuations, to transvalue and turn upside down the 'eternal values'." (Written in 1885). Poor Nietzsche. Those who really did away with the idea of deducing values from the nature of God (or the God of nature), who put man's *will* back to its central place in ethics, were not at all terrifying supermen, but a group of very mild-mannered, innocuous English and Viennese philosophers like G. E. Moore and Moritz Schlick. In a decent orderly society, most human beings eventually, though not without travail, grow up to have decent, orderly *wills.*

6. Some suggestions for a suitable education in this regard are found in James E. McClellan's "Why Should the Humanities Be Taught?" *Journal of Philosophy,* Vol. LV, No. 23 [Nov. 6, 1958], pp. 997-1108.

7. Erich Fromm, *Escape from Freedom* (New York: Farrar and Rinehart, 1941). T. W. Adorno, E. Frenkel-Brunswik, D. J. Levinson,

and R. N. Sanford, *The Authoritarian Personality* (New York: Harper & Brothers, 1950).

8. Which is not to say, of course, that statistics and theory of games are *never* useful tools in solving social problems. See James E. McClellan's "Theory in Educational Administration," *School Review*, Vol. 68 [Summer, 1960], pp. 210-227.

9. Paul Goodman: "The Calling of American Youth," *Commentary*, March, 1960, pp. 217-229. The way Mr. Goodman describes the rat-race is frighteningly familiar; however the world may actually run, surely this is our usual way of talking and thinking about it.

10. We are aware that others before us have held stark and uncompromising views that bear some resemblance to what we are asserting here. We are aware that in the 1920's, a period that in its apparent affluence superficially resembled our own times, views similar to ours were asserted by men who later recanted in the face of events—depression, Fascism, etc.—they took to be signs of social disintegration. We do not discount the strength of the super-rationalists on one hand and the irrationalists on the other who would attack our theses. See the "Epilogue for 1957" to Morton G. White, *Social Thought in America* (Boston: Beacon Press, 1957), pp. 247-281, and William Barrett, *Irrational Man: A Study in Existential Philosophy* (Garden City: Doubleday and Company, 1958). But we should like to make this much clear: whatever may be the case with others whose views are in some ways like ours, we are not propounding a doctrine of dark despair, we are not praising a soul-less wasteland. We are describing a world with limitations and restrictions, but withal the locus (if there is one) of man's encounter with love and self-fulfillment. In short, the world may be different from our description of it. If so, we welcome new facts that show us where our perceptions were wrong. But we despise, in advance, the critic who objects to our conception of education on the grounds that it lacks a sufficient basis in morality.

Bibliography

ADAMS, HENRY, *The Education of Henry Adams: An Autobiography.* Boston: Houghton Mifflin, 1946.

———, *Mont-St. Michel and Chartres.* Boston: Houghton Mifflin, 1922.

ADAMS, JAMES TRUSLOW, *The American: The Making of a New Man.* New York: Scribner's, 1944.

———, *The Epic of America.* New York: Blue Ribbon Books, 1931.

ADELMAN, M. A., "The Measurement of Industrial Concentration," *Review of Economic Statistics,* Vol. XXXII, No. 4 (November, 1951).

ADORNO, T. W., E. FRENKEL-BRUNSWIK, D. J. LEVINSON, and R. N. SANFORD, *The Authoritarian Personality.* New York: Harper and Brothers, 1950.

AGEE, JAMES, *A Death in the Family.* New York: McDowell-Obolensky, 1957.

AITKIN, W. M., *The Story of the Eight-Year Study.* New York: Harper and Brothers, 1942.

ALGREN, NELSON, *The Man with the Golden Arm.* New York: Doubleday, 1949.

———, *The Neon Wilderness.* Gloucester, Mass: Peter Smith, 1960.

ALLPORT, GORDON, *Becoming.* New Haven: Yale University Press, 1955.

ANDERSON, SHERWOOD, *Winesburg, Ohio.* New York: Huebsch, 1919.

ANSHEN, RUTH, *The Family: Its Function and Destiny.* New York: Harper and Brothers, 1959.

ARENDT, HANNAH, *The Human Condition.* Chicago: University of Chicago Press, 1958.

———, *Between Past and Future.* New York: Viking Press, 1961.

ARENSBERG, CONRAD M., "American Communities," *American Anthropologist,* Vol. 57, No. 6 (1955), pp. 1143-1162.

———, "The Community as Object and as Sample," *American Anthropologist,* Vol. 63, No. 2 (1961), pp. 241-64.

———, "The Family and other Cultures," *The Nation's Children*. New York: Columbia University Press, 1960, pp. 50-75.

——— and SOLON T. KIMBALL, *Family and Community in Ireland*. Cambridge: Harvard University Press, 1940.

ARGYRIS, CHRIS, *Personality and Organization*. New York: Harper and Brothers, 1957.

——— and GEOFFREY TOOTELL, "Plant Sociology: Real Discoveries and New Problems," in Mirra Komarovsky (ed.), *Common Frontiers of the Social Sciences*. Glencoe, Ill.: Free Press, 1957, pp. 310-337.

ATHERTON, LEWIS E., *Main Street on the Middle Border*. Bloomington, Ind.: Indiana University Press, 1954.

ATWOOD, MARK, *An Anthropological Approach to Administrative Change: The Introduction of a Guidance Program in a High School*. Unpublished doctoral dissertation, Columbia University, 1960.

AYER, A. J., *Language, Truth, and Logic*. New York: Dover Books, 1949.

BALDWIN, JOSEPH G., *The Flush Times of Alabama and Mississippi*. New York: Sagamore Press, 1957.

BARKER, SIR ERNEST, *Principles of Social and Political Theory*. Oxford: Clarendon Press, 1951.

BARNARD, CHESTER I., *Elementary Condition of Business Morals*. Berkeley: University of California Press, 1958.

———, *The Functions of the Executive*. Cambridge: Harvard University Press, 1938.

BARRETT, WILLIAM, *Irrational Man: A Study in Existential Philosophy*. Garden City: Doubleday, 1958.

BARUCH, DOROTHY, *Parents and Children Go to School*. Chicago: Scott, Foresman, 1939.

BARZUN, JACQUES, *House of Intellect*. New York: Harper and Brothers, 1959.

———, *Of Human Freedom*. Boston: Little, Brown, 1939.

BEARD, CHARLES, and MARY BEARD, *The Rise of American Civilization*. New York: Macmillan, 1936.

BECKER, HOWARD S., "The Teacher in the Authority System of the Public School," *Journal of Educational Psychology* XXVII (1953), 128-141.

BELL, DANIEL, *The End of Ideology*. Glencoe, Ill.: Free Press, 1960.

———, *Work and Its Discontents*. Boston: Beacon Press, 1956.

BENDIX, REINHARD and SEYMOUR LIPSET (eds.), *Class, Status, and Power*. Glencoe, Ill.: Free Press, 1953.

BENEDICT, RUTH, *The Chrysanthemum and the Sword*. Boston: Houghton Mifflin, 1956.

———, *Patterns of Culture*. New York: New American Library, 1948.

BENÉT, STEPHEN VINCENT, *John Brown's Body*. New York: Farrar and Rinehart, 1941.

———, *Western Star*. New York: Farrar and Rinehart, 1943.

BENNE, K. D., and WILLIAM O. STANLEY (eds.), *Essays for John Dewey's Birthday*. Urbana: University of Illinois, Bureau of Research, 1950.

BERKSON, K. B., *The Ideal and the Community*. New York: Harper and Brothers, 1958.

BERLE, A. A., JR., *Power Without Property*. New York: Harcourt Brace, 1959.

———, *The 20th Century Capitalist Revolution*. New York: Harcourt, Brace, 1954.

———, and GARDNER C. MEANS, *The Modern Corporation and Private Property*. New York: Macmillan, 1932.

BESTOR, ARTHUR, "Education and Its Proper Relationship to the Forces of American Society," *Daedalus* (Winter, 1959), pp. 75-90.

———, *Educational Wastelands*. Urbana: University of Illinois Press, 1953.

———, *The Restoration of Learning*. New York: Knopf, 1956.

BIDNEY, DAVID, *Theoretical Anthropology*. New York: Columbia University Press, 1953.

BOULDING, KENNETH, *The Image*. Ann Arbor, Mich.: Ann Arbor Paperbacks, 1961.

BRADY, ROBERT A., *Business as a System of Power*. New York: Columbia University Press, 1943.

BRAMELD, THEODORE, *Cultural Foundations of Education*. New York: Harper and Brothers, 1957.

———, *Philosophies of Education in Cultural Perspective*. New York: Dryden Press, 1955.

———, *Toward a Reconstructed Philosophy of Education*. New York: Dryden Press, 1956.

BRIDENBAUGH, CARL, *Cities in Revolt*. New York: Knopf, 1955.

BROUDY, HARRY S., *Building a Philosophy of Education*. New York: Prentice-Hall, 1954.

BROWN, HARRIET CONNOR, *Grandmother Brown's Hundred Years, 1827-1927*. Boston: Little, Brown, 1929.

BRUBACHER, JOHN S., *Modern Philosophies of Education*, 2nd ed. New York: McGraw-Hill, 1950.

BRUNER, JEROME S., *The Process of Education*. Cambridge: Harvard University Press, 1960.

———, JACQUELINE GOODNOW, and GEORGE A. AUSTIN, *A Study of Thinking*. New York: John Wiley and Sons, 1956.

BURGESS, ERNEST W. and HARVEY J. LOCKE, *The Family—From Institution to Companionship*. New York: American Books, 1945.

BUTTS, R. FREEMAN, *The American Tradition in Religion and Education*. Boston: Beacon Press, 1950.

———, and LAWRENCE A. CREMIN, *A History of Education in American Culture*. New York: Henry Holt, 1953.

CASH, WILBUR J., *The Mind of the South.* New York: Knopf, 1941.

CHAYEFSKY, PADDY, *Television Plays.* New York: Simon and Schuster, 1955.

CHAYES, ABRAM, "The Modern Corporation and the Rule of Law," in Edward S. Mason (ed.), *The Corporation in Modern Society.* Cambridge: Harvard University Press, 1959.

CHILDE, V. GORDON, *What Happened in History.* New York: Penguin Books, 1946.

CHILDS, JOHN L., *American Pragmatism and Education.* New York: Holt, 1956.

———, *Education and Morals.* New York: Appleton-Century Crofts, 1950.

CLAPP, ELSIE R., *Community Schools in Action.* New York: Viking Press, 1939.

COLEMAN, JAMES S., *The Adolescent Society: The Social Life of the Teenager and Its Impact on Education.* Glencoe, Ill.: Free Press, 1961.

COMMAGER, H. S., *The American Mind.* New Haven: Yale University Press, 1950.

CONANT, JAMES BRYANT, *American High School Today.* New York: McGraw-Hill, 1959.

———, *The Child, the Parent, and the State.* Cambridge: Harvard University Press, 1960.

———, *Citadel of Learning.* New Haven: Yale University Press, 1956.

———, *Science and Common Sense.* New Haven: Yale University Press, 1951.

COOK, LLOYD ALLEN and ELAINE FORSYTH COOK, *A Sociological Approach to Education.* New York: McGraw-Hill, 1950.

COON, CARLETON S., *The Story of Man.* New York: Knopf, 1955.

COUNTS, GEORGE S., *Education and American Civilization.* New York: Columbia University, Teachers College, 1952.

CRANKSHAW, EDWARD, *Khrushchev's Russia.* Baltimore: Penguin Books, 1959.

CREMIN, LAWRENCE A., *The Transformation of the School.* New York: Knopf, 1961.

CUBBERLY, ELLWOOD P., *Public School Administration.* Boston: Houghton Mifflin, 1916.

DAVENPORT, RUSSELL et al., *The Permanent Revolution.* New York: Prentice-Hall, 1951.

DAVIS, ALLISON, *Social Class Influences Upon Learning.* Cambridge: Harvard University Press, 1948.

DAY, ELIZABETH, *Methods of Community Organization in Urban Renewal.* Unpublished doctoral thesis, Columbia University, Teachers College, 1958.

Decade of Experiment. The Fund for the Advancement of Education, 1951-61. New York: The Fund, 1961.

DENNEY, REUEL, *The Astonished Muse.* Chicago: University of Chicago Press, 1957.

DE TOCQUEVILLE, ALEXIS, *Democracy in America.* New York: Knopf, 1945.

DEWEY, JOHN, *A Common Faith.* New Haven: Yale University, 1934.

———, *Experience and Education.* New York: Macmillan, 1955; copyright, 1938.

———, *How We Think.* Boston: D. C. Heath, 1933.

———, *Human Nature and Conduct.* New York: Henry Holt and Co., 1922.

———, *The Influence of Darwin and Other Essays in Contemporary Thought.* New York: Henry Holt, 1910.

———, *Liberalism and Social Action.* New York: G. Putnam, 1935.

———, *Philosophy and Civilization.* New York: Minton Balch, 1931.

———, *The Public and Its Problems.* New York: Henry Holt, 1927.

———, *The School and Society.* Chicago: University of Chicago Press, 1900.

———, "Theory of Valuation," *International Encyclopedia of Unified Science.* Chicago: University of Chicago Press, Vol. II, No. 4 (1939), p. 6.

DEWHURST, J. FREDERIC and Associates, *America's Needs and Resources.* New York: Twentieth Century Fund, 1955.

DRUCKER, PETER F., *Concept of the Corporation.* New York: John Day, 1946.

DUNCAN, OTIS D., et al., *Metropolis and Region.* Baltimore: Johns Hopkins, 1960.

DURKHEIM, EMILE, *Suicide.* Glencoe, Ill.: Free Press, 1951.

DWORKIN, MARTIN S., *Dewey on Education.* New York: Columbia University, Teachers College, 1960.

ENNIS, R. S., and B. O. SMITH (eds.), *Language and Concepts in Education.* Chicago: Rand McNally, 1961.

ERIKSON, ERIK, *Childhood and Society.* New York: W. W. Norton and Co., 1950.

EVAN, WILLIAM M., "Organization Man and Due Process of Law," *American Sociological Review,* XXVI (August, 1961), pp. 540-547.

FAULKNER, WILLIAM, *As I Lay Dying.* New York: Modern Library, 1946.

———, *Light in August.* New York: Modern Library, 1950.

FEDERAL TRADE COMMISSION, *The Concentration of Productive Facilities, 1947.* Washington, D. C.: Government Printing Office, 1949.

FISCH, MAX, *Classic American Philosophers.* New York: Appleton-Century-Crofts, 1951.

FLICK, ALEXANDER (ed.), *History of the State of New York.* New York: Columbia University Press, 1934.

Fortune, Editors of, *The Exploding Metropolis*. Garden City: Doubleday, 1958.

FRANKEL, CHARLES, *The Case for Modern Man*. New York: Harper and Brothers, 1955.

FREUD, SIGMUND, *Civilization and Its Discontent*. London: Hogarth Press, 1930.

FROMM, ERICH, *Escape from Freedom*. New York: Farrar and Rinehart, 1941.

———, *The Sane Society*. New York: Rinehart, 1955.

GABRIEL, RALPH H., *The Course of American Democratic Thought*, rev. ed. New York: Ronald Press, 1956.

GALBRAITH, JOHN KENNETH, *The Affluent Society*. Boston: Houghton Mifflin, 1958.

———, *American Capitalism: The Concept of Countervailing Power*. Boston: Houghton Mifflin, 1952.

GARDNER, JOHN W., *Excellence*. New York: Harper and Brothers, 1961.

GARLAND, HAMLIN, *Main-Travelled Roads*. New York: Harper and Brothers, 1909.

———, *A Son of the Middle Border*. New York: Macmillan, 1923.

GIEDION, SIGFRIED, *Mechanization Takes Command*. New York: Oxford University Press, 1948.

GILMORE, HARLAN W., "The Old New Orleans and the New: A Case for Ecology," *American Sociological Review*, Vol. 9, No. 4 (1944), pp. 385-394.

GOLDSCHMIDT, WALTER, *As You Sow*. New York: Harcourt Brace, 1947.

GOODE, WILLIAM J., *After Divorce*. Glencoe, Ill.: Free Press, 1956.

———, "The Sociology of the Family," in R. K. Merton, Leonard Broom, and L. S. Cottrell, Jr. (eds.), *Sociology Today*. Glencoe, Ill.: Free Press, 1959, pp. 178-196.

GOODMAN, PAUL, "The Calling of American Youth," *Commentary*, March, 1960, pp. 217-229.

GRUBER, FREDERICK G., *Foundations for a Philosophy of Education*. New York: Thomas Y. Crowell, 1961.

HACKER, LOUIS M., *The Triumph of American Capitalism*. New York: Simon and Schuster, 1940.

HALLOWELL, A. IRVING, "Aggression in Saulteaux Society," in Clyde Kluckhohn, Henry A. Murray, and D. N. Schneider (eds.), *Personality in Nature, Society, and Culture*, 2nd ed. New York: Knopf, 1956, pp. 246-260.

HANAN, MACK, *The Pacifiers*. Boston: Little, Brown, 1960.

HANDLIN, OSCAR, *The Uprooted*. Boston: Little, Brown, 1953.

HARRIS, RAYMOND P., *American Education: Facts, Fancies, and Folklore*. New York: Random House, 1961.

HAUSER, PHILIP M., "The Census of 1960," *Scientific American*, 205 (1961), pp. 39-45.

HAWLEY, CAMERON, *Executive Suite*. Boston: Houghton Mifflin, 1952.

HERBERG, WILL, *Protestant-Catholic-Jew: An Essay in American Religious Sociology*. Garden City: Anchor Books, 1960.

HERSKOVITS, MELVILLE J., *The Economic Life of Primitive Peoples*. New York: Knopf, 1940.

HOFSTADTER, RICHARD, *The Age of Reform: from Bryan to F.D.R.* New York: Knopf, 1955.

HOMANS, GEORGE C., *The Human Group*. New York: Harcourt, Brace, 1950.

HONIGMANN, JOHN J., *Culture and Personality*. New York: Harper and Brothers, 1954.

HORNEY, KAREN, *Neurosis and Human Growth—The Struggle Toward Self-Realization*. New York: Norton, 1950.

HOWE, E. W., *The Story of a Country Town*. New York: Boni, 1926.

HOWELLS, WILLIAM DEAN, *The Rise of Silas Lapham*. Boston: Tichnor, 1885.

HULLFISH, H. GORDON, and PHILIP G. SMITH, *Reflective Thinking: The Method of Education*. New York: Dodd, Mead and Company, 1961.

HUNTER, FLOYD, *Community Power Structure*. Chapel Hill: University of North Carolina Press, 1953.

INHELDER, BARBEL, and JEAN PIAGET, *The Growth of Logical Thinking from Childhood to Adolescence*. New York: Basic Books, 1958.

ISE, JOHN, *Sod and Stubble: The Story of a Kansas Homestead*. New York: Wilson-Erickson, 1936.

JAMES, WILLIAM, *Pragmatism*. London: Longmans Green, 1908.

———, *Psychology*. New York: Henry Holt, 1890.

JANOWITZ, MORRIS, *Sociology and the Military Establishment*. New York: Russell Sage Foundation, 1958.

JERSILD, ARTHUR T., *When Teachers Face Themselves*. New York: Columbia University, Teachers College, 1955.

JORDY, W. H., *Henry Adams: Scientific Historian*. New Haven: Yale University Press, 1952.

KELLY, CHARLES ROBERT, *Toward an Interpretation of the New Movement of 1915 in Educational Administration*. Unpublished Ed.D. project, Teachers College, Columbia University, 1961.

KERR, CLARK, and LLOYD FISHER, "Plant Sociology: The Elite and the Aborigines," in Mirra Komarovsky (ed.), *Common Frontiers of the Social Sciences*. Glencoe, Ill.: Free Press, 1957, pp. 281-309.

KILPATRICK, WILLIAM H., "A Reconstructed Theory of the Educative Process," *Teachers College Record*, XXXII (March, 1931).

——— (ed.), *The Educational Frontier*. New York: Appleton-Century, 1933.

KIMBALL, SOLON T., "An Anthropological View of Learning," *The National Elementary Principal*, XL (1961), pp. 23-27.

———, "Classe Social e Comunidade nos Estados Unidos," *Sociologia,* Vol. XXI, No. 2 (1959), pp. 186-202.
———, "Cultural Influences Shaping the Role of the Child," *Those First School Years* (Department of Elementary School Principals) XL (1960), pp. 18-32.
———, "Darwin and the Future of Education," *The Educational Forum,* November, 1960, pp. 59-72.
———, and MARION PEARSALL, *The Talladega Story: A Study in Community Process.* University, Ala.: University of Alabama Press, 1954.
———, and JOHN H. PROVINSE, "Navajo Social Organization in Land Use Planning," *Applied Anthropology,* I (1942), pp. 18-25.
KLUCKHOHN, CLYDE, and DOROTHEA LEIGHTON, *The Navaho.* Cambridge: Harvard University Press, 1946.
———, HENRY A. MURRAY, and DAVID M. SCHNEIDER (eds.), *Personality in Nature, Society and Culture.* New York: Knopf, 1956.
KOMAROVSKY, MIRRA (ed.), *Common Frontiers of the Social Sciences.* Glencoe, Ill.: Free Press, 1957.
KOMISAR, B. PAUL, and JAMES E. MCCLELLAN, "The Logic of Slogans," in R. S. Ennis and B. O. Smith (eds.), *Language and Concepts in Education.* Chicago: Rand McNally, 1961, pp. 195-214.
KROEBER, A. L. (ed.), *Anthropology Today.* Chicago: University of Chicago Press, 1953.
KHRUSHCHEV, N. S., *Speeches in America.* New York: Crosscurrents Press, 1956.
LARRABEE, ERIC, "Riesman and His Readers," *Harper's Magazine* (June, 1961), pp. 59-65.
———, and ROLF MEYERSOHN (eds.), *Mass Leisure.* Glencoe, Ill.: Free Press, 1958.
LASKI, HAROLD, *The American Democracy.* New York: Viking Press, 1948.
LERNER, MAX, *America As a Civilization.* New York: Simon and Schuster, 1957.
LEWIN, KURT, *Field Theory in Social Science.* New York: Harper and Brothers, 1951.
LEWIS, C. I., *An Analysis of Knowledge and Valuation.* La Salle, Ill.: Open Court, 1946.
LEWIS, SINCLAIR, *Arrowsmith.* New York: Harcourt, Brace, 1925.
———, *Babbitt.* New York: Grosset and Dunlap, 1922.
———, *Main Street: The Story of Carol Kennicott.* New York: Grosset and Dunlap, 1921.
LIEBERMAN, MYRON, *The Future of Public Education.* Chicago: University of Chicago Press, 1960.
LINTON, RALPH, "Age and Sex Categories," *American Sociological Review,* VII (1942), pp. 589-603.
———, *The Study of Man.* New York: D. Appleton Century, 1936.

LINDZEY, GARDNER (ed.), *Handbook of Social Psychology*. Cambridge: Addison-Wesley Press, 1954.

LIPSET, SEYMOUR, M. TROW, and J. S. COLEMAN, *Union Democracy*. Glencoe, Ill.: Free Press, 1956.

LONG, NORTON, "The Corporation, Its Satellites, and the Local Community," in Edward S. Mason (ed.), *The Corporation in Modern Society*. Cambridge: Harvard University Press, 1959, pp. 202-217.

LUCE, R. DUNCAN, and HOWARD RAIFFA, *Games and Decisions*. New York: John Wiley, 1957.

LYND, ROBERT S., and HELEN M. LYND, *Middletown, A Study in Contemporary American Culture*. New York: Harcourt, Brace, 1929.

LYNES, RUSSELL, *A Surfeit of Honey*. New York: Harper and Brothers, 1957.

———, *The Tastemakers*. New York: Harper and Brothers, 1954.

———, "Upper Bohemians," *Harper's* (February, 1953), pp. 46-52.

MACLEISH, ARCHIBALD, *J. B.* Boston: Houghton Mifflin, 1957.

MARCSON, SIMON, *The Scientist in American Industry*. Princeton, N. J.: Princeton University, Industrial Relations Section, 1960.

MARCUSE, HERBERT, *Soviet Marxism: A Critical Analysis*. New York: Columbia University Press, 1958.

MARQUAND, JOHN, *The Point of No Return*. Boston: Little, Brown, 1949.

———, *Sincerely, Willis Wayde*. Boston: Little, Brown, 1955.

MARX, KARL, and FRIEDRICH ENGELS, *The Communist Manifesto*.

MASON, EDWARD S. (ed.), *The Corporation in Modern Society*. Cambridge: Harvard University Press, 1959.

MASON, ROBERT E., *Educational Ideals in American Society*. Boston: Allyn and Bacon, 1960.

MASTERS, EDGAR LEE, *Spoon River Anthology*. New York: Macmillan, 1928.

MAY, ROLLO, et. al., *Existence, A New Dimension in Psychiatry and Psychology*. New York: Basic Books, 1958.

MAYER, MARTIN, *The Schools*. New York: Harper and Brothers, 1961.

MAYO, ELTON, *The Human Problems of an Industrial Civilization*. New York: Macmillan, 1933.

———, *The Social Problems of an Industrial Civilization*. Cambridge: Harvard University Press, 1945.

MCCLELLAN, JAMES E., "Dewey and the Concept of Method," *The School Review* (Summer, 1959), pp. 213-228.

———, "Theory in Educational Administration," *School Review*, Vol. 68 (Summer, 1960), pp. 210-227.

———, "Why Should the Humanities Be Taught?" *Journal of Philosophy*, Vol. LV, No. 23 (November 6, 1958), pp. 997-1108.

MCDONALD, WILLIAM (ed.), *Documentary Source Book of American History, 1606-1926*. New York: Macmillan, 1928.

McWilliams, Carey, *Factories in the Field.* Boston: Little, Brown, 1939.

Mead, George Herbert, *Mind, Self, and Society.* Chicago: University of Chicago Press, 1934.

Mead, Margaret, *Male and Female: A Study of the Sexes in a Changing World.* New York: Morrow, 1949.

———, "National Character" in A. L. Kroeber (ed.), *Anthropology Today.* Chicago: University of Chicago Press, 1952.

———, *Sex and Temperament in Three Primitive Societies.* New York: Morrow, 1935.

Medlin, William K, et al., *Soviet Education Programs.* Washington: U. S. Department of Health, Education, and Welfare, 1960.

Merton, Robert K., Leonard Broom, and Leonard S. Cottrell, Jr. (eds.), *Sociology Today.* New York: Basic Books, 1959.

Mills, C. Wright, *The Power Elite.* New York: Oxford University Press, 1956.

Moore, Wilbert, *Industrial Relations and the Social Order.* New York: Macmillan, 1951.

Morris, Charles (ed.), *Mind, Self, and Society.* Chicago: University of Chicago Press, 1934.

Moustakas, Clark E., *The Self-Exploration in Personal Growth.* New York: Harper and Brothers, 1956.

Mumford, Lewis, *The City in History: Its Origins, Its Transformations, and Its Prospects.* New York: Harcourt, Brace, 1961.

———, *The Culture of Cities.* New York: Harcourt, Brace, 1938.

———, *The Transformation of Man.* New York: Harper and Brothers, 1956.

Murdock, George P., *Social Structure.* New York: Macmillan, 1949.

Murphy, Gardner, *Human Potentialities.* New York: Basic Books, 1958.

Myrdal, Gunnar, *An American Dilemma.* New York: Harper and Brothers, 1944.

Nadel, S. F., *The Theory of Social Structure.* Glencoe, Ill.: Free Press, 1957.

Nagel, Ernest, *The Structure of Science.* New York: Harcourt, Brace, and World, 1961.

National Resources Planning Board, *The Structure of the American Economy,* Washington, D.C.: Government Printing Office, 1939.

National Science Foundation, *Reviews of Data on Research and Development,* No. 30 (September, 1961).

Neugarten, Bernice L., "Social Class and Friendship Among School Children," *American Journal of Sociology,* LI (1942), pp. 305-313.

Nichols, Alice, *Bleeding Kansas.* New York: Oxford University Press, 1954.

Niebuhr, Reinhold, *The Kingdom of God in America.* Chicago: Willett, Clark, 1937.

———, *The Social Sources of Denominationalism.* New York: Henry Holt, 1929.

Nietzsche, Friedrich, *Beyond Good and Evil.* Chicago: Henry Regnery Co., 1955.

Ogburn, William F., *Social Change.* New York: Viking Press, 1932.

Olsen, Edward G., *School and Community.* New York: Prentice-Hall, 1945.

Page, Jerome Maurice, *A Survey and Analysis of Teacher Recruitment Policies and Practices, Including an Analysis of Teacher Supply and Demand.* Unpublished Ed.D. project, Columbia University, Teachers College, 1958.

Pares, Richard, *The Historian's Business and Other Essays.* Oxford: Clarendon Press, 1961.

Park, Robert E., Ernest W. Burgess, and Roderick D. McKenzie, *The City.* Chicago: University of Chicago Press, 1925.

Parkes, Henry Bamford, *The American Experience.* New York: Knopf, 1947.

Parkinson, C. Northcote, *Parkinson's Law and Other Studies in Administration.* Boston: Houghton Mifflin, 1957.

Parrington, Vernon L., *Main Currents of American Thought.* (3 vols.) New York: Harcourt Brace, 1927-30.

Parsons, Talcott, "Age and Sex in the Social Structure of the United States," in Clyde Kluckhohn, Henry A. Murray, and David M. Schneider (eds.), *Personality in Nature, Society, and Culture.* New York: Knopf, 1956, pp. 363-375.

———, and Edward Shils (eds.), *Toward a General Theory of Action.* Cambridge: Harvard University Press, 1952.

———, Edward Shils, Kasper D. Naegele, and Jesse R. Pitts (eds.), *Theories of Society.* Glencoe, Ill.: Free Press, 1961.

Pennell, Joseph Stanley, *The History of Rome Hanks and Kindred Matters.* New York: Scribner's, 1944.

Peters, R. S., *The Concept of Motivation.* London: Routledge and Kegan Paul, 1958.

Phenix, Philip H., *Education and the Common Good.* New York: Harper and Brothers, 1961.

———, "Key Concepts and the Crisis in Learning," *Teachers College Record, 58:* (December, 1956), pp. 137-143.

———, *Philosophy of Education.* New York: Henry Holt, 1958.

Piaget, Jean, *The Child's Conception of the World.* New York: Humanities Press, 1951.

———, *The Language and Thought of the Child.* New York: Humanities Press, 1959.

———, *The Moral Judgment of the Child.* London: Routledge and Kegan Paul, 1932.

———, *The Origins of Intelligence in Children.* New York: International Universities Press, 1952.

Pipes, Richard, "The Public Mood," *Harper's Magazine* (May, 1961), pp. 107-113.

POPPER, KARL, *The Open Society and Its Enemies*. London: Routledge and Kegan Paul, 1952.

POTTER, DAVID, *People of Plenty—Economic Abundance and the American Character*. Chicago: University of Chicago Press, 1959.

RAUP, R. BRUCE, "The Community Criterion in Judgmental Practice," *Studies in Philosophy and Education*, September, 1960.

RIESMAN, DAVID, *Constraint and Variety in American Education*. Garden City: Doubleday Anchor Books, 1958.

———, "The Uncommitted Generation, 'Junior Organization Men' in America," *Encounter* (November, 1960), pp. 25-30.

———, NATHAN GLAZER, and REUEL DENNEY, *The Lonely Crowd*. New York: Doubleday, 1953.

ROETHLISBERGER, F. J., *Management and Morale*. Cambridge: Harvard University Press, 1941.

———, and WILLIAM J. DICKSON, *Management and the Worker*. Cambridge: Harvard University Press, 1940.

SANDOZ, MARIE, *Old Jules*. Boston: Little, Brown, 1935.

SAPIR, EDWARD, *Culture, Language, and Personality*. Berkeley, Calif.: University of California, 1956.

SASAKI, TOM T., *Fruitland, New Mexico: A Navaho Community in Transition*. Ithaca: Cornell University Press, 1960.

SCHAPIRO, MEYER, "Style," in A. L. Kroeber (ed.), *Anthropology Today*. Chicago: University of Chicago Press, 1952, pp. 287-312.

SCHEFFLER, I. (ed.), *Philosophy and Education*. Boston: Allyn and Bacon, 1957.

SCHILPP, P. A. (ed.), *The Philosophy of John Dewey*. Evanston, Ill.: Library of Living Philosophers, 1939.

SCHNEIDER, HERBERT W., *A History of American Philosophy*. New York: Columbia University Press, 1946.

SCOTT, WINFIELD, CLYDE M. HILL, and HOBERT W. BURNS (eds.), *The Great Debate*. Englewood Cliffs, N. J.: Prentice-Hall Spectrum Books, 1959.

SEELEY, JOHN R., R. ALEXANDER SIM, and E. W. LOOSLEY, *Crestwood Heights*. New York: Basic Books, 1956.

SHAFFNER, BERTRAM, "Animal Studies and Human Behavior," *Human Organization*, XV (1956), pp. 11-14.

SIMON, HERBERT A., "A Behavioral Model of Rational Choice," *Quarterly Review of Economics*, LXIX (February, 1955), pp. 99-118.

SKEVKY, ESHREF, and MARILYN WILLIAMS, *The Social Areas of Los Angeles: Analysis and Typology*. Berkeley: University of California, 1949.

SMITH, B. O., and R. H. ENNIS (eds.), *Language and Concepts in Education*. Chicago: Rand McNally, 1961.

SMITH, HENRY NASH, *Virgin Land: The American West as Symbol and Myth*. New York: Vintage Books, 1957.

SNOW, C. P., *The New Men*. New York: Scribner's, 1955.

SPENCER, KATHERINE, *Mythology and Values: An Analysis of Navaho Chantway Myths.* Philadelphia: American Folklore Society, 1957.

STEIN, MAURICE R., *The Eclipse of Community.* Princeton: Princeton University Press, 1960.

STEINBECK, JOHN, *In Dubious Battle.* New York: Viking Press, 1939.

———, *Grapes of Wrath.* New York: Viking Press, 1939.

STEVENSON, ELIZABETH (ed.), *A Henry Adams Reader.* New York: Doubleday, 1958.

Stories from the New Yorker: 1950-1960. New York: Simon and Schuster, 1960.

STOUFFER, SAMUEL A., et al., *The American Soldier, Adjustment During Army Life.* Princeton: Princeton University Press, 1949.

STRAUSS, CLAUDE LEVI, "Social Structure," in A. L. Kroeber (ed.), *Anthropology Today.* Chicago: University of Chicago Press, 1953, pp. 524-553.

STUART, JESSE, *The Thread That Runs So True.* New York: Scribner's, 1949.

SULLIVAN, HARRY STACK, *The Interpersonal Theory of Psychiatry.* New York: W. W. Norton, 1953.

SYMONDS, PERCIVAL M., *The Dynamics of Parent-Child Relationships.* New York: Columbia University Press, 1949.

TARBELL, IDA, *The Life of Abraham Lincoln.* New York: Macmillan, 1924.

TARKINGTON, BOOTH, *Alice Adams.* New York: Grosset and Dunlap, 1921.

———, *The Magnificent Ambersons.* New York: Grossett and Dunlap, 1918.

TAYLOR, F. W., *Principles of Scientific Management.* New York: Harper and Brothers, 1911.

THAYER, V. T., *The Role of the School in American Education.* New York: Dodd, Mead, 1960.

———, "The School: Its Task and Its Administration," in William H. Kilpatrick (ed.), *The Educational Frontier.* New York: D. Appleton-Century, 1933, chap. vii.

THOMAS, WILLIAM I., "The Four Wishes and the Definition of the Situation," in Talcott Parsons, Edward Shils, and Jesse R. Pitts (eds.), *Theories of Society.* Glencoe, Ill.: Free Press, 1961, II, pp. 741-744.

THORNDIKE, E. L., *Human Nature and the Social Order.* New York: Macmillan, 1940.

TILLICH, PAUL, *The Protestant Era.* Chicago: University of Chicago Press, 1948.

———, *Systematic Theology.* Vol. I. Chicago: University of Chicago Press, 1951.

TOLMAN, EDWARD C., "A Psychological Model," in Talcott Parsons

and Edward Shils (eds.), *Toward A General Theory of Action.* Cambridge: Harvard University Press, 1952, pp. 279-360.
TRUMAN, HARRY S., *Memoirs.* Garden City: Doubleday, 1955.
TUNNARD, CHRISTOPHER, and HENRY H. REED, JR., *American Skyline.* New York: Mentor Books, 1956.
TURNER, FREDERICK J., *The Frontier in American History.* New York: Henry Holt, 1920.
"U. S. Census of Population, 1960—Final Report," PC (1) 1B, Washington, D. C.
U.S. DEPARTMENT OF COMMERCE, BUREAU OF CENSUS, "The Magnitude and Distribution of Civilian Employment in the U.S.S.R. 1928-1959," Series P-95, No. 58 of International Population Reports (April, 1961), p. 57.
VAN GENNEP, ARNOLD, *The Rites of Passage.* Chicago: Chicago University Press, 1960.
VEBLEN, THORSTEIN, *The Higher Learning in America.* New York: Huebsch, 1918.
VINCENT, WILLIAM S., HALL BARTLETT, LORA TIBBETTS, and JAMES RUSSELL, *Building Better Programs in Citizenship.* New York: Citizenship Education Project, Columbia University, Teachers College.
WARNER, WILLIAM LLOYD, *American Life: Dream and Reality.* Chicago: University of Chicago Press, 1953.
———, and JOSIAH LOW, *The Social System of the Modern Factory.* New Haven: Yale University Press, 1947.
———, and PAUL LUNT, *The Social Life of a Modern Community.* New Haven: Yale University Press, 1941.
WELLS, H. G., *The Outline of History.* Garden City: Garden City, 1925.
WEST, JAMES, *Plainville, U.S.A.* New York: Columbia University Press, 1945.
WHEELER, ROBERT, "Mr. Riesman's Consumers," *The American Scholar,* XXVI (Winter 1956-57), pp. 39-50.
WHITE, DAVID MANNING, and BERNARD ROSENBERG (eds.), *Mass Culture: The Popular Arts in America.* Glencoe, Ill.: Free Press, 1957.
WHITE, MORTON G., *Social Thought in America.* Boston: Beacon Press, 1957.
WHITEHEAD, ALFRED NORTH, *The Aims of Education and Other Essays.* New York: Macmillan, 1929.
WHITING, J. W. M., and I. L. CHILD, *Child Training and Personality.* New Haven: Yale University Press, 1953.
WHYTE, WILLIAM F., *Street Corner Society.* Chicago: University of Chicago Press, 1955.
WHYTE, WILLIAM H., JR., *The Organization Man.* Garden City: Doubleday Anchor Books, 1957.

WILCOX, CLAIR, *Competition and Monopoly in American Industry.* Washington, D.C.: TNEC, 1940, Monograph No. 21.

WILLIAMS, RAYMOND, *The Long Revolution.* New York: Columbia University Press, 1961.

WILLIAMS, ROBIN, *American Society.* New York: Knopf, 1951.

WITTGENSTEIN, LUDWIG, *Tractatus Logico-Philosophicus.* London: Routledge and Kegan Paul, 1922.

WOLFE, THOMAS, *You Can't Go Home Again.* New York: Harper and Brothers, 1940.

WOOD, ROBERT C., *Suburbia: Its People and Their Politics.* Boston: Houghton-Mifflin, 1959.

YATES, RICHARD, *Revolutionary Road.* Boston: Little, Brown, 1961.

INDEX